CCNA Self-Study:
CCNA Basics (CCNAB)

Cisco Press

Cisco Press
201 West 103rd Street
Indianapolis, IN 46290 USA

CCNA Self-Study: CCNA Basics (CCNAB)

Cisco Systems, Inc.

Copyright© 2003 Cisco Systems, Inc.

Cisco Press logo is a trademark of Cisco Systems, Inc.

Published by:
Cisco Press
201 West 103rd Street
Indianapolis, IN 46290 USA

Printed in the United States of America 1 2 3 4 5 6 7 8 9 0

First Printing December 2002

Library of Congress Cataloging-in-Publication Number:

ISBN: 1-58705-107-9

Warning and Disclaimer

This book is designed to provide information about selected topics for the CCNA exam. Every effort has been made to make this book as complete and as accurate as possible, but no warranty or fitness is implied.

The information is provided on an "as is" basis. The authors, Cisco Press, and Cisco Systems, Inc., shall have neither liability nor responsibility to any person or entity with respect to any loss or damages arising from the information contained in this book or from the use of the discs or programs that may accompany it.

The opinions expressed in this book belong to the author and are not necessarily those of Cisco Systems, Inc.

The Cisco Press self-study book series is as described, intended for self-study. It has not been designed for use in a classroom environment. Only Cisco Learning Partners displaying the following logos are authorized providers of Cisco curriculum. If you are using this book within the classroom of a training company that does not carry one of these logos, then you are not preparing with a Cisco trained and authorized provider.

For information on Cisco Learning Partners please visit: www.cisco.com/go/authorizedtraining. To provide Cisco with any information about what you may believe is unauthorized use of Cisco trademarks or copyrighted training material, please visit: http://www.cisco/logo/infringement.html.

Trademark Acknowledgments

All terms mentioned in this book that are known to be trademarks or service marks have been appropriately capitalized. Cisco Press and Cisco Systems, Inc., cannot attest to the accuracy of this information. Use of a term in this book should not be regarded as affecting the validity of any trademark or service mark.

Feedback Information

At Cisco Press, our goal is to create in-depth technical books of the highest quality and value. Each book is crafted with care and precision, undergoing rigorous development that involves the unique expertise of members from the professional technical community.

Readers' feedback is a natural continuation of this process. If you have any comments regarding how we could improve the quality of this book or otherwise alter it to better suit your needs, you can contact us through e-mail at feedback@ciscopress.com. Please make sure to include the book title and ISBN in your message.

We greatly appreciate your assistance.

Publisher	John Wait
Editor-In-Chief	John Kane
Cisco Representative	Anthony Wolfenden
Cisco Press Program Manager	Sonia Torres Chavez
Cisco Marketing Communications Manager	Tom Geitner
Cisco Marketing Program Manager	Edie Quiroz
Executive Editor	Brett Bartow
Managing Editor	Patrick Kanouse
Development Editor	Dayna Isley
Project Editor	Marc Fowler
Copy Editor	Krista Hansing
Technical Editors	Agoussi Amon, CCNA
	Craig Dorry, CCIE 9072
	Matt Talbert, CCIE 1854
Team Coordinator	Tammi Ross
Book Designer	Gina Rexrode
Cover Designer	Louisa Klucznik
Production Team	Mark Shirar
Indexer	Larry Sweazy

CISCO SYSTEMS

Corporate Headquarters
Cisco Systems, Inc.
170 West Tasman Drive
San Jose, CA 95134-1706
USA
http://www.cisco.com
Tel: 408 526-4000
    800 553-NETS (6387)
Fax: 408 526-4100

European Headquarters
Cisco Systems Europe
11 Rue Camille Desmoulins
92782 Issy-les-Moulineaux
Cedex 9
France
http://www-europe.cisco.com
Tel: 33 1 58 04 60 00
Fax: 33 1 58 04 61 00

Americas Headquarters
Cisco Systems, Inc.
170 West Tasman Drive
San Jose, CA 95134-1706
USA
http://www.cisco.com
Tel: 408 526-7660
Fax: 408 527-0883

Asia Pacific Headquarters
Cisco Systems Australia,
Pty., Ltd
Level 17, 99 Walker Street
North Sydney
NSW 2059 Australia
http://www.cisco.com
Tel: +61 2 8448 7100
Fax: +61 2 9957 4350

Cisco Systems has more than 200 offices in the following countries. Addresses, phone numbers, and fax numbers are listed on the Cisco Web site at www.cisco.com/go/offices

Argentina • Australia • Austria • Belgium • Brazil • Bulgaria • Canada • Chile • China • Colombia • Costa Rica • Croatia • Czech Republic • Denmark • Dubai, UAE • Finland • France • Germany • Greece • Hong Kong Hungary • India • Indonesia • Ireland • Israel • Italy • Japan • Korea • Luxembourg • Malaysia • Mexico The Netherlands • New Zealand • Norway • Peru • Philippines • Poland • Portugal • Puerto Rico • Romania Russia • Saudi Arabia • Scotland • Singapore • Slovakia • Slovenia • South Africa • Spain • Sweden Switzerland • Taiwan • Thailand • Turkey • Ukraine • United Kingdom • United States • Venezuela • Vietnam Zimbabwe

iv

About the Technical Reviewers

Agoussi Amon is currently a lead network engineer and experienced data security consultant at Magnificat Integrated Systems, in London. Agoussi has 10 years of technical experience in demanding commercial IT environments, including "blue chip" and ISP companies. Agoussi earned a Master's degree (computer science) from Université Catholique de Louvain in Louvain, Belgium.

Agoussi has extensive in-depth network security knowledge and experience, and he excels in applying analytical and strategic thinking to network design, implementation, and security. Agoussi is currently a CCNA and is working toward his CCIE Security certification.

Craig Dorry, CCIE No. 9072, is a network design/support engineer for AT&T for a Fortune 50 Financial Services Client.

Matt Talbert is a systems engineering manager for Cisco Systems and has been a CCIE for more than six years (CCIE No. 1854). Matt has been with Cisco Systems, Inc., since 1996 and has held positions as a systems engineer, consulting systems engineer, and systems engineering manager in both the Service Provider and Enterprise lines of business. Matt also holds a Bachelor of Science degree in electrical engineering from the University of Texas at Austin and a Master of Science degree in Engineering Management from Southern Methodist University. He has more than 16 years of industry experience in telecommunications, and he specializes in routing protocols and large-scale network design.

Acknowledgments

Cisco would like to acknowledge Charles Newby, Partrick Lao, Cheryl Josephs, Dayna Isley, and Ching-hsiu Wu for their invaluable contributions to this book. Their dedication and hard work made this book possible.

Contents at a Glance

Contents

Foreword

CCNA Self-Study: CCNA Basics (CCNAB) is a Cisco authorized, self-paced learning tool that helps you understand fundamental concepts covered on the Cisco CCNA exam. This book was developed in cooperation with the Cisco Internet Learning Solutions group, the team within Cisco responsible for the development of the CCNA exam. As an early-stage exam preparation product, this book presents important networking fundamentals using the Open Systems Interconnect (OSI) seven-layer model. Whether you are studying to become CCNA certified, or you are simply seeking to gain a better understanding of basic internetworking terminology and technologies, you will benefit from the information presented in this book.

Cisco and Cisco Press present this material in text-based format to provide another learning vehicle for our customers and the broader user community in general. Although a publication does not duplicate the instructor-led or e-learning environment, we acknowledge that not everyone responds in the same way to the same delivery mechanism. It is our intent that presenting this material via a Cisco Press publication will enhance the transfer of knowledge to a broad audience of networking professionals.

Cisco Press will present other books in the Certification Self-Study Series on existing and future exams to help achieve Cisco Internet Learning Solutions Group's principal objectives: to educate the Cisco community of networking professionals and to enable that community to build and maintain reliable, scalable networks. The Cisco Career Certifications and classes that support these certifications are directed at meeting these objectives through a disciplined approach to progressive learning.

In order to succeed with Cisco Career Certifications and in your daily job as a Cisco certified professional, we recommend a blended learning solution that combines instructor-led training with hands-on experience, e-learning, and self-study training. Cisco Systems has authorized Cisco Learning Partners worldwide, which can provide you with the most highly qualified instruction and invaluable hands-on experience in lab and simulation environments. To learn more about Cisco Learning Partner programs available in your area, please go to: http://www.cisco.com/go/authorizedtraining.

The books Cisco Press creates in partnership with Cisco Systems will meet the same standards for content quality demanded of our courses and certifications. It is our intent that you will find this and subsequent Cisco Press certification self-study publications of value as you build your networking knowledge base.

Thomas M. Kelly
Vice-President, Internet Learning Solutions Group
Cisco Systems, Inc.
November 2002

Introduction

Professional certifications are an important part of the computing industry and will continue to become more important. Many reasons exist for these certifications, but the most popularly cited reason is that of credibility. All other considerations held equal, the certified employee/consultant/job candidate is considered more valuable than the one who is not.

Goals and Methods

CCNA Self-Study: CCNA Basics (CCNAB) focuses on introducing networking techniques, terminology, and technology. *CCNA Self-Study: CCNA Basics (CCNAB)* is the prerequisite for the Interconnecting Cisco Network Devices (ICND) course, which is the recommended training path for individuals seeking certification as a Cisco Certified Network Associate (CCNA). ICND presents the concepts, commands, and practice required to configure Cisco switches and routers.

As the first step toward preparing for the CCNA certification exam, the methods used in this book are designed to make you much more knowledgeable about CCNA-related topics. To that end, the book helps you prepare for the ICND course and CCNA certification exam by using the following methods:

- Providing a firm foundational knowledge of networking concepts

- Helping you discover which networking topics you have not mastered

Who Should Read This Book?

This book is intended to increase your chances of passing the CCNA exam by introducing you to the concepts that the exam covers. This book is not designed to be a general networking topics book, although it can be used for that purpose.

To fully benefit from *CCNA Self-Study: CCNA Basics (CCNAB)*, you must have the following prerequisite skills and knowledge:

- Basic computer literacy

- Basic understanding of PC hardware

- Basic understanding of PC software

- Basic understanding of networking business drivers

The strategy you use to prepare for the CCNA exam might be slightly different than strategies used by other readers, based on the skills, knowledge, and experience you already have obtained. For instance, if you have taken the CCNA Basics course, you might take a different approach than someone who is learning routing and switching via on-the-job training. Regardless of the strategy you use or the background you have, this book is designed to help you prepare for the ICND course.

How This Book Is Organized

Although this book could be read cover to cover, it is designed to be flexible and to enable you to move easily between chapters and sections of chapters to cover just the material that you need more work with.

Book Objectives

Upon completing this book, you will be able to perform the following overall tasks:

- Describe computer hardware basics, binary and hexadecimal number systems, basic networking terminology, and internetworking concepts
- Identify the major components of a network system, including clients and servers, network interface cards (NICs), internetworking devices, media, and topologies
- Describe the functions, operations, and primary components of local-area networks (LANs), metropolitan-area networks (MANs), wide-area networks (WANs), virtual private networks (VPNs), intranets, extranets, storage-area networks (SANs), and content networks (CNs)
- Define the major network access methods and outline the key features of each
- Describe the functions and operations of switching technologies
- Explain the purposes of networking addresses, routing protocols, and routed protocols
- Explain the format and significance of each of the following components of a network system: IP addressing, classes, reserved address space, and subnetting
- Calculate valid subnetwork addresses and mask values so that user/network requirements are met when given an IP address scheme
- Describe the functions, operations, and primary components of WAN technologies
- Describe the functions, operations, and primary components required to provide remote access services
- Describe the functions, operations, and primary components of wireless technologies
- Describe the functions, operations, and primary components of optical networking
- Explain the purposes and techniques for voice, data, and video convergence

Icons and Symbols

This section shows some of the Cisco icons and symbols used in this book.

Book Organization

This book is organized into 31 chapters, 2 appendixes, and 1 glossary. Chapters 1 through 31 are divided into nine parts: Part I to Part IV. Part X of this book consists of two appendixes.

The chapters and appendixes cover the following topics:

- **Part I: Introduction to Networking**—This introductory section addresses the components of a computer and the role of computers in a networking system. Using a basic approach to learning networking, it starts with the most fundamental component of a network—the computer—and moves to more complex systems. The more you know about computers, the easier it is to understand networks and how they are designed and built.

  — **Chapter 1: Computing Basics**—This chapter presents the basics of computer hardware. It also introduces different number systems and the processes used to convert a number from one number system to another.

— **Chapter 2: Networking Fundamentals**—This chapter covers common networking terminology. It also describes the OSI reference model, the functions of each OSI layer, and the TCP/IP model.

— **Chapter 3: Network Devices**—This chapter discusses the devices used in Layers 1 through 3 of the OSI reference model, as well as network devices such as firewall and AAA servers, voice gateway, digital subscriber line access multiplexer (DSLAM), and optical platforms.

— **Chapter 4: Network Topologies**—This chapter describes physical and logical topologies and discusses various topologies used in networking.

• **Part II: Network Types**—This part introduces some of the common network types, including local-area networks (LANs), wide-area networks (WANs), metropolitan-area networks (MANs), storage-area networks (SANs), content networks (CNs), and virtual private networks (VPNs).

— **Chapter 5: Understanding Ethernet Technologies**—This chapter discusses different types of Ethernet technologies, including Fast Ethernet, Gigabit Ethernet, and 10-Gigabit Ethernet. It also explains how these technologies work.

— **Chapter 6: WANs**—This chapter provides an overview of WAN technology and discusses WAN devices, service providers, and WAN physical and data link layer standards.

— **Chapter 7: Other Types of Networks**—This chapter introduces the basic features of metropolitan-area networks (MANs), storage-area networks (SANs), content networks (CNs), and virtual private networks (VPNs). This chapter also describes VPN benefits and technologies.

• **Part III: Network Media**—This part of the book discusses several types of network media, including twisted-pair cable, coaxial cable, fiber-optic cable, and wireless communication. The information, concepts, and procedures for assembling and cabling Cisco routers and switches are presented as well.

— **Chapter 8: Network Media Types**—This chapter describes the common types of network media. including twisted-pair cable, coaxial cable, fiber-optic cable, and wireless.

— **Chapter 9: Cabling the LAN**—This chapter discusses cabling concepts and implementation as they apply to a campus network using Ethernet.

— **Chapter 10: Cabling the WAN**—This chapter discusses how to distinguish between the connectors and interface types used in connecting dedicated and dialup lines.

• **Part IV: Switching Fundamentals**—This part discusses some possible problems in a LAN, and some solutions that can improve LAN performance. It presents information about LAN congestion and its effect on network performance, and the advantages of LAN segmentation in a network. In addition, it explains the advantages and disadvantages of using bridges, switches, and routers for LAN segmentation, and the effects of switching, bridging, and routing on network throughput. Finally, this part discusses virtual LANs (VLANs) and their benefits.

— **Chapter 11: Shared LAN Technology**—This chapter discusses the basic concepts of traditional LAN technology and the roles that hubs, bridges, and switches play in a LAN environment.

— **Chapter 12: LAN Switching Basics**—This chapter discusses LAN switching technology, such as full-duplex transmission and switching methods. This chapter also introduces the Spanning-Tree Protocol.

— **Chapter 13: Multilayer Switching Devices**—This chapter describes OSI Layers 2, 3, and 4 switching devices and technologies.

— **Chapter 14: Virtual LANs**—This chapter provides an introduction to virtual LANs (VLANs), compares traditional shared LANs and VLANs, and discusses the benefits of VLANs.

• **Part V: TCP/IP**—In this part, you learn about the TCP/IP protocol stack components, such as protocols to support file transfer, e-mail, remote login, and other applications. You also learn about reliable and unreliable transport layer protocols and about connectionless datagram (packet) delivery at the network layer (TCP/IP Internet layer). Finally, you learn how the Internet Control Message Protocol (ICMP) provides control and message functions at the network layer and how Address Resolution Protocol (ARP) and Reverse ARP (RARP) work.

— **Chapter 15: TCP/IP Overview**—This chapter defines protocols—specifically, communication protocols. It discusses the Transmission Control Protocol/Internet Protocol (TCP/IP) protocol stack and introduces TCP/IP applications.

— **Chapter 16: Transport Layer**—This chapter describes the functions and services of the TCP/IP transport layer.

— **Chapter 17: TCP/IP Internet Layer Overview**—This chapter describes the protocols that operate at the TCP/IP Internet layer and covers their functions.

• **Part VI: IP Addressing and Routing**—This part examines IP addressing and the five classes of IP addresses, along with subnetworks and subnet masks and their roles in IP addressing schemes. In addition, this part discusses the difference between routing and routed protocols and tells how routers track distance between locations. Finally, this part introduces the distance-vector, link-state, and hybrid routing approaches and tells how each resolves common routing problems.

— **Chapter 18: Networking Addressing**—This chapter describes network-addressing schemes.

— **Chapter 19: IP Subnetting and Calculation**—This chapter discusses how to plan and create subnets for Class B and Class C IP addresses.

— **Chapter 20: Routing Basics**—This chapter describes the process and subsequent components involved in routing.

— **Chapter 21: Routing Protocols**—This chapter describes various routing protocols.

• **Part VII: WAN Technologies**—This part of the book introduces the various protocols and technologies used in wide-area network (WAN) environments. You learn about the basics of WANs, including common WAN technologies, types of wide-area services, encapsulation formats, and link options. You also learn about point-to-point links, circuit switching, packet switching, virtual circuits, dialup services, and WAN devices.

— **Chapter 22: Traditional WAN Services**—This chapter introduces various WAN connection options and technologies, including leased line, Frame Relay, ATM, and SONET.

— **Chapter 23: Dialup Access Technologies**—This chapter describes the functions and operation of dialup access technologies, including ISDN, Point-to-Point Protocol (PPP), Password Authentication Protocol (PAP), Challenge Handshake Authentication Protocol (CHAP), and High-Level Data Link Control (HDLC).

— **Chapter 24: Analog Modems**—This chapter describes different types of analog modems and the analog modem standards.

— **Chapter 25: Digital Subscriber Line**—This chapter describes two main different types of digital subscriber line (DSL), DSL standards, and DSL encapsulation and protocols. This chapter also discusses the advantages and disadvantages of the DSL technology.

— **Chapter 26: Cable Modems**—This chapter describes cable modem, cable modem transmission, and the benefits of cable modem.

- **Part VIII: Wireless Technology**—This part examines wireless-enabling technologies, including radio frequency (RF) modulation, unlicensed frequencies, spread spectrum, and wireless LAN (WLAN). It highlights the differences between licensed and unlicensed frequencies, the differences between direct-sequence and frequency-hopping spread-spectrum technologies, and the differences between the various WLAN topologies. This part also covers security in the wireless environment.

— **Chapter 27: Wireless Concepts**—This chapter explains various types of wireless technology and related terminology.

— **Chapter 28: Wireless LANs**—This chapter explains wireless LAN (WLAN) technology and wireless bridging, and defines in-building and building-to-building wireless LANs.

- **Part IX: Optical Networking Fundamentals**—This part teaches you how optical networks provide speed, data transportation, capacity, and scalability. You learn about the optical network function, the enhanced scalability provided by dense wavelength-division multiplexing (DWDM), and the solutions that optical networks provide.

— **Chapter 29: Basics of Optical Networks**—This chapter describes the key drivers of the optical networks and the features of fiber-optic systems. This chapter also discusses the components of optical transmission and their features.

— **Chapter 30: Optical Fibers**—This chapter describes types of fiber, the loss factors, and fiber filter technology.

— **Chapter 31: Optical Transmission and Multiplexing**—This chapter introduces SONET/SDH technology and describes how DWDM systems work. This chapter also discusses the benefits of DWDM systems.

- **Part X: Appendix**—This part includes two appendixes.

— **Appendix A: Introduction to Converged Networking**— This appendix describes how traditional voice, video, and data networks are implemented and explains various types of voice-over-data technologies. This appendix describes the need for converged voice, video, and data networks. In addition, this appendix introduces the Cisco Architecture for Voice, Video and Integrated Data (AVVID) and new applications for converged networks.

— **Appendix B: Answers to Review Questions**—This appendix provides the answers to the review exercises at the end of each chapter.

- **Glossary**—The glossary defines the terms and abbreviations related to networking utilized in this book.

Introduction to Networking

Upon completing this chapter, you will be able to:

- Identify the major components of a personal computer
- Name the Ethernet adapter used for a laptop computer
- State the functions of network interface cards (NICs)
- List the components needed for NIC installation
- Describe the units used to measure the size of digital data
- Convert a decimal number to a binary number
- Convert a binary number to a decimal number
- Convert a hexadecimal number to a binary number
- Convert a binary number to a hexadecimal number

CHAPTER 1

Computing Basics

This chapter presents the basics of computer hardware. It also introduces different number systems and the processes used to convert a number from one number system to another.

PC Components

Because computers are important building blocks in a network, it is important to be able to recognize and name the major components of a personal computer (PC). Many networking devices, such as routers and switches, are special-purpose computers and have many of the same parts as normal PCs. For a computer to be a reliable means of obtaining information, it must be in good working order. If the need arises to troubleshoot a simple hardware or software problem, you should be able to recognize, name, and state the purpose of the following PC components (this information pertains to laptops as well):

- **Bus**—A bus is a collection of wires through which data is transmitted from one part of a computer to another. The bus connects all the internal computer components to the CPU. The Industry-Standard Architecture (ISA) and the peripheral component interconnect (PCI) are two types of buses.

- **CD-ROM drive**—The CD-ROM drive is a compact disk read-only memory drive that can read information from a CD-ROM.

- **Central processing unit (CPU)**—The CPU is the "brain" of the computer, where most of the calculations take place (see Figure 1-1).

Figure 1-1   *CPU*

- **Expansion card**—The expansion card is a printed circuit board that can be inserted into a computer to give the computer added capabilities.

- **Expansion slot**—The expansion slot is an opening in a computer where an expansion card can be inserted to add new capabilities to the computer (see Figure 1-2).

Figure 1-2 *Expansion Slots*

- **Floppy disk drive**—This disk drive can read and write to floppy disks (see Figure 1-3).

Figure 1-3 *Floppy Disk Drive*

- **Hard disk drive**—This device reads and writes data on a hard disk.

- **Microprocessor**—A microprocessor is a silicon chip that contains a CPU.

- **Motherboard**—The motherboard is the main circuit board of a computer (see Figure 1-4). The motherboard is crucial because it is the nerve center of the computer system. Everything else in the system plugs into it, is controlled by it, and depends on it to communicate with other devices on the system.

Figure 1-4   *Motherboard*

- **Power supply**—This component supplies power to a computer.

- **Printed circuit board (PCB)**—The PCB is a thin plate on which chips (integrated circuits) and other electronic components are placed.

- **Memory**—Memory is the internal storage area in a computer.

- **Random-access memory (RAM)**—Also known as *read-write memory*, RAM can have new data written into it as well as stored data read from it. A drawback of RAM is that it requires electrical power to maintain data storage. If the computer is turned off or loses power, all data stored in RAM is lost unless the data was previously saved to disk.

- **Read-only memory (ROM)**—ROM is computer memory on which data has been prerecorded.

- **Erasable programmable read-only memory (EPROM)**—EPROM is a special type of memory that can be read only by the computer and can be erased by exposure to ultraviolet light.

- **System unit**—The system unit is the main part of a PC. It includes the chassis, microprocessor, main memory, bus, expansion cards, and ports. The system unit does not include the keyboard, the monitor, or any other external devices connected to the computer.

- **Backplane**—The backplane is a large circuit board that contains sockets for expansion cards.

- **Socket**—A socket is a receptacle into which a connector or an expansion card can be plugged.

- **Interface**—The interface is a piece of hardware, such as a modem connector, that enables otherwise incompatible devices to be connected.

- **Mouse port**—This port is designed for connecting a mouse to a PC.

- **Network card**—The network card is a printed circuit board that provides network communication capabilities to and from a personal computer.

- **Parallel port**—The parallel port is an interface capable of transferring more than 1 bit simultaneously. It is used to connect external devices, such as printers.

- **Power cord**—The power cord is used to connect an electrical device to an electrical outlet to provide power to the device.

- **Serial port**—This interface can be used for serial communication in which only 1 bit is transmitted at a time.

- **Sound card**—A sound card is an expansion board that handles all sound functions.

- **Video card**—The video card is a board that plugs into a PC to give it display capabilities.

- **Universal Serial Bus (USB) port**—This interface enables peripheral devices, such as mouse devices, modems, and keyboards, to be plugged in and unplugged without resetting the system. USB ports eventually might replace serial and parallel ports.

NOTE   Note that some computers have a network card, a sound card, a video card, and other cards integrated into the motherboard.

PC Versus Laptop

Laptop computers and notebook computers are becoming increasingly popular. The main difference between PCs and laptops is that laptop components are smaller than those found in a PC. The expansion slots are known as PC card slots, Personal Computer Memory Card International Association (PCMCIA) card slots, or PC slots in laptop computers. The PC card slots are place where devices such as network interface cards (NICs), modems, hard drives, and other useful devices (usually the size of a thick credit card) are connected (see Figure 1-5).

Figure 1-5   *PCMCIA Card*

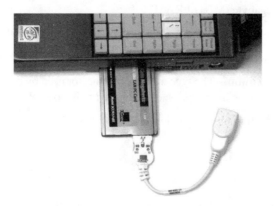

NIC

As shown in Figure 1-6, a NIC is a printed circuit board that provides network communication capabilities to and from a personal computer. Also called a *LAN adapter*, a NIC plugs into a motherboard and provides a port for connecting to the network. The NIC constitutes the computer interface with the LAN.

Figure 1-6   *Network Interface Card*

The NIC communicates with the network straight through a cable and with the computer through an expansion slot. When a NIC is installed in a computer, it requires an interrupt request line (IRQ), an input/output (I/O) address, a memory space for the operating system (such as DOS or Windows), and drivers to perform its function. An IRQ is a signal that informs a CPU that an event needing its attention has occurred. An IRQ is sent over a hardware line to the microprocessor. An example of an interrupt being issued is a key being pressed on a keyboard. The CPU must move the character from the keyboard to RAM. An I/O address is a location in memory used to enter or retrieve data from a computer by an auxiliary device. In DOS-based systems, upper memory refers to the memory area between the first 640 kilobytes (KB) and 1 megabyte (MB) of RAM.

When selecting a NIC for a network, you should consider the following:

- **Type of network**—Ethernet NICs are designed for Ethernet LANs.

- **Type of medium**—The type of port or connector used by the NIC for network connection is specific to medium type, such as twisted-pair, coaxial, fiber-optic, or wireless.

- **Type of system bus**—PCI slots are faster than ISA slots. As a result, the latter are being phased out.

NIC Installation

The NIC enables hosts to connect to the network. The NIC is considered a key component. To install a NIC as shown in Figure 1-7, you need the following resources:

- Knowledge of how the network card is configured, including jumpers, "plug-and-play" software, and erasable programmable read-only memory.

- Use of network card diagnostics, including the vendor-supplied diagnostics and loopback test (see the documentation for the card).

- Capability to resolve hardware resource conflicts, including IRQ, I/O base address, and direct memory address (DMA), which is used to transfer data from RAM to a device without going through the CPU.

Figure 1-7   *Installing a NIC*

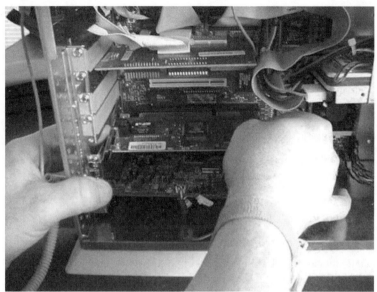

Bit, Bytes, and Measurement Terms

Computers are electronic devices made up of electronic switches. At the lowest levels of computation, they depend on these electronic switches to make decisions. As such, computers react only to electrical impulses. These impulses are understood by the computer as either "on" or "off" states (1s or 0s).

Computers can understand and process only data that is in a binary format, which is represented by 0s and 1s. These 0s and 1s represent the two possible states of an electronic component and are referred to as *binary digits (bits)*.

Most computer coding schemes use 8 bits to represent each number, letter, or symbol. A series of 8 bits is referred to as a *byte*; 1 byte represents a single addressable storage location (see Table 1-1).

Table 1-1   *Units of Information*

Unit	Bytes*	Bits*
bit (b)	1/8 byte	1 bit
byte (B)	1 byte	8 bits
kilobyte (KB)	1000 bytes	8000 bits
megabyte (MB)	1 million bytes	8 million bits
gigabyte (GB)	1 billion bytes	8 billion bits

*Common or approximate bytes or bits

As shown in Table 1-1, the following are commonly used computer measurement terms:

- **bit**—The smallest unit of data in a computer. A bit equals 1 or 0, and it is the binary format in which data is processed by computers.

- **byte**—A byte is a unit of measure used to describe the size of a data file, the amount of space on a disk or other storage medium, or the amount of data being sent over a network. 1 byte equals 8 bits of data.

- **kb (kilobit)**—A kilobit is approximately 1000 bits.

- **kB (kilobyte)**—A kilobyte is approximately 1000 bytes (1024 bytes, exactly).

- **kbps (kilobits per second)**—This is a standard measurement of the amount of data transferred over a network connection.

- **kBps (kilobytes per second)**—This is a standard measurement of the amount of data transferred over a network connection.

- **Mb (megabit)**—A megabit is approximately 1 million bits.

- **MB (megabyte)**—A megabyte is approximately 1 million bytes (1,048,576 bytes, exactly). A megabyte is sometimes referred to as a *meg*.

- **Mbps (megabits per second)**—This is a standard measurement of the amount of data transferred over a network connection.

- **MBps (megabytes per second)**—This is a standard measurement of the amount of data transferred over a network connection.

NOTE   It is a common error to confuse kB with kb and MB with Mb. Remember to do the proper calculations when comparing transmission speeds that are measured in kB with those measured in kb. For example, modem software usually shows the connection speed in kilo*bits* per second (for example, 45 kbps). However, popular browsers display file-download speeds in kilo*bytes* per second, meaning that with a 45-kbps connection, the download speed would be a maximum of 5.76 kBps. In practice, this download speed cannot be reached because of other factors consuming bandwidth at the same time.

- **Hz (hertz)**—A hertz is a unit of frequency. It is the rate of change in the state or cycle in a sound wave, alternating current, or other cyclical waveform. It represents one cycle per second and is used to describe the speed of a computer microprocessor.

- **MHz (megahertz)**—A megahertz is one million cycles per second. This is a common measurement of the speed of a processing chip, such as a computer microprocessor.

- **GHz (gigahertz)**—A gigahertz is one thousand million, or 1 billion (1,000,000,000), cycles per second. This is a common measurement of the speed of a processing chip, such as a computer microprocessor.

NOTE   PC processors are getting faster all the time. The microprocessors used on PCs in the 1980s typically ran at less than 10 MHz (the original IBM PC was 4.77 MHz). Processor speeds are getting faster all the time. Currently, there are processors with speeds of up to 2.3 GHz.

Decimal-to-Binary Conversion

Computers recognize and process data using the binary, or base 2, numbering system. The binary number system uses only two symbols (0 and 1) instead of the ten symbols used in the decimal numbering system, or base 10 number system. The position, or place, of each digit represents the number 2 (the base number) raised to a power (exponent), based on its position ($2^0, 2^1, 2^2, 2^3, 2^4$, and so on). See Table 1-2 for examples.

Table 1-2   *Base 2 Number System*

Number of Symbols	2							
Symbols	0, 1							
Base Exponent	2^7	2^6	2^5	2^4	2^3	2^2	2^1	2^0
Place Value	128	64	32	16	8	4	2	1
Example: Convert decimal 35 to binary.	0	0	1	0	0	0	1	1

Converting a decimal number to a binary number is one of the most common procedures performed while working with IP addresses. IP addresses identify a device on a network and the network to which it is attached. An IP address is 32 bits long. To make them easy to remember, IP addresses are usually written in dotted-decimal notation. Therefore, IP addresses are four decimal numbers separated by dots. An example is the address 166.122.23.130. Keep in mind that a decimal number is a base 10 number.

To convert a decimal number to binary, you must first find the biggest power of 2 that will "fit" into the decimal number. Consider the decimal number 35. Looking at Table 1-2, what is the greatest power of 2 that is less than or equal to 35? Starting with the largest number, 2^5 (32) is smaller than 35. Place a 1 in that column and calculate how much is left over by subtracting 32 from 35. The result is 3.

Next, check to see if 16 (the next lower power of 2) fits into 3. Because it does not, a 0 is placed in that column. The value of the next number is 8, which is larger than 3, so a 0 is placed in that column, too.

The next value is 4, which is still larger than 3, so it, too, receives a 0. The next value is 2, which is smaller than 3. Because 2 fits into 3, place a 1 in that column. Next, subtract 2 from 3; the result is 1.

The value of the last number is 1, which fits in the remaining number. Thus, place a 1 in the last column. Therefore, the binary equivalent of the decimal number 35 is 100011.

Binary-to-Decimal Conversion

As with binary-to-decimal conversion, there is usually more than one way to solve the conversion. Use the method that is easiest.

Consider the following example:

Convert the binary number 10111001 to a decimal number. As shown in Table 1-3, the number in the 2^7 (128) column is 1, so the decimal total is 128. Next, there is a 0 in the 2^6 (64) column.

The decimal total is 128 + 0 = 128. Now, there is a 1 in the 2^5 (32) column. The decimal total becomes 128 + 32 = 160. Next, there is a 1 in the 2^4 (16) column. Adding the value to the decimal total gives 160 + 16 = 176. The next column, 2^3, has a 1, so the value 8 needs to be added to the decimal total 176 + 8 = 184. Next, there are 0s in the 2^2 and 2^1 columns. Add 0s to the decimal total: 184 + 0 + 0 = 184. Finally, there is a 1 in the 2^0 (1) column. Now add 1 to 184. The result is 185. The decimal equivalent of the binary number 10111001 is 185.

Table 1-3   *Base 2 Number System*

Number of Symbols	2							
Symbols	0, 1							
Base Exponent	2^7	2^6	2^5	2^4	2^3	2^2	2^1	2^0
Place Value	128	64	32	16	8	4	2	1
Example: Binary Number	1	0	1	1	1	0	0	1
Decimal Number Total: 185	128	0	32	16	8	0	0	1

Binary-to-Hex Conversion

The base 16, or hexadecimal (hex), number system is used frequently when working with computers because it can be used to represent binary numbers in a more readable form. The computer performs computations in binary, but there are several instances in which the binary output of a computer is expressed in hexadecimal form to make it easier to read.

Converting a hexadecimal number to binary form, and vice versa, is a common task when dealing with the configuration register in Cisco routers. Cisco routers have a configuration register that is 16 bits long. That 16-bit binary number can be represented as a four-digit hexadecimal number. For example, 0010000100000010 in binary equals 2102 in hex.

Layer 2 Media Access Control (MAC) addresses are typically written in hex. For Ethernet and Token Ring, these addresses are 48 bits, or six octets (one octet is 1 byte). Because these addresses consist of 6 distinct octets, they can be expressed as 12 hex numbers instead.

Instead of writing 10101010.11110000.11000001.11100010.01110111.01010001, the much shorter hex equivalent can be written: AA.F0.C1.E2.77.51. To make handling hex versions of MAC addresses even easier, the dots are placed only after each four hex digits, as in AAF0.C1E2.7751.

The most common way for computers and software to express hexadecimal output is using "0x" in front of the hexadecimal number. Thus, whenever you see "0x," you know that the number that follows is a hexadecimal number. For example, 0x1234 means 1234 in base 16. It is referred to as base 16 because it uses 16 symbols. Combinations of these symbols can represent all possible numbers. Because there are only ten symbols that represent digits (0, 1, 2, 3, 4, 5, 6, 7, 8, and 9) and because base 16 requires six more symbols, the extra symbols are the letters $A, B, C, D, E,$ and F. The A represents the decimal number 10, B represents 11, C represents 12, D represents 13, E represents 14, and F represents 15.

The position of each symbol (digit) in a hex number represents the base number 16 raised to a power (exponent) based on its position. Moving from right to left, the first position represents 16^0 (or 1), the second position represents 16^1 (or 16), the third position represents 16^2 (or 256), and so on.

Converting binary to hex is easy because base 16 (hexadecimal) is a power of base 2 (binary). See Table 1-4.

Table 1-4   *Binary and Hexadecimal Number Systems*

Decimal	Binary	Hexadecimal
0	00000000	00
1	00000001	01
2	00000010	02
3	00000011	03
4	00000100	04
5	00000101	05
6	00000110	06
7	00000111	07

continues

Table 1-4   *Binary and Hexadecimal Number Systems (Continued)*

Decimal	Binary	Hexadecimal
8	00001000	08
9	00001001	09
10	00001010	0A
11	00001011	0B
12	00001100	0C
13	00001101	0D
14	00001110	0E
15	00001111	0F
16	00010000	10
32	00100000	20
64	01000000	40
128	10000000	80
255	11111111	FF

Every four binary digits (bits) are equal to one hexadecimal digit. Table 1-5 shows binary conversions.

Table 1-5   *Binary-to-Hexadecimal Conversions*

Binary	Hexadecimal
0000	0
0001	1
0010	2
0011	3
0100	4
0101	5
0110	6
0111	7
1000	8
1001	9
1010	A
1011	B
1100	C
1101	D

Table 1-5   *Binary-to-Hexadecimal Conversions*

Binary	Hexadecimal
1110	E
1111	F

So, if there is a binary number that looks like 01011011, it can be broken into two groups of 4 bits. These groups look like the following: 0101 and 1011. When converting these two groups to hex, they look like 5 and B, so the hexadecimal equivalent of the binary 01011011 is 5B.

No matter how large the binary number is, always apply the same conversion. Start from the right of the binary number and break the number into groups of four. If the number of numbers is not divisible by four, add 0s to the left end until there are four digits (bits) in every group. Then convert each group of four to its hex equivalent.

Hex-to-Binary Conversion

To convert from hexadecimal to binary, convert every hex digit into four binary digits (bits). For example, convert hex AC (0xAC) to binary. First convert hex A, which is 1010 binary, and then convert hex C, which is 1100 binary. So, the conversion of hex AC is 10101100 binary.

Summary

In this chapter, you learned the following key points:

- Computers are vital components of every network. The more you know about computers, the easier it is to understand networks.

- It is important to be familiar with the components of a computer and to understand the functions of a NIC. It is also important to be able to install a NIC.

- Computers can recognize and process data only by using the binary numbering system. The binary number system is made up of 0s and 1s.

- The hexadecimal number system is used frequently at higher levels of computation. The hexadecimal number system uses 16 symbols: 0, 1, 2, 3, 4, 5, 6, 7, 8, 9, A, B, C, D, E, and F.

Review Exercises

1 What is the main circuit board of a computer?

   a. PC subsystem

   b. Motherboard

   c. Backplane

   d. Computer memory

2 What are PCMCIA slots?

   a. Slots used in laptops

   b. Slots used as expansion slots in all computers

   c. Expansion slots for a NIC card

   d. Slots for certain specialized devices

3 How does a network card communicate with the network?

   a. Serial connection

   b. Parallel connection

   c. Backplane

   d. None of the above

4 Which of the following correctly describes the resources needed before you install a NIC?

   a. Knowledge of how the network card is configured

   b. Knowledge of how to use the network card diagnostics

   c. Capability to resolve hardware resource conflicts

   d. All of the above

5 Match the following terms with their definitions:

   1. bit

   2. byte

   3. kbps

   4. MHz

   a. The smallest unit of data in a computer

   b. A standard measurement of the rate of data being transferred over a network connection

   c. A unit of frequency; the rate of change in the state or cycle in a sound wave, alternating current, or other cyclical waveform

   d. A unit of measure used to describe the size of a data file, the amount of space on a disk or other storage medium, or the amount of data being transferred over a network

6 What is the decimal number 151 in binary?

    a. 10100111

    b. 10010111

    c. 10101011

    d. 10010011

7 What is the binary number 11011010 in decimal?

    a. 186

    b. 202

    c. 218

    d. 222

8 Convert the binary number 0010000100000000 to a hexadecimal number.

    a. 0x2100

    b. 0x2142

    c. 0x0082

    d. 0x0012

9 Convert the hexadecimal number 0x2101 to a binary number.

    a. 0010 0001 0000 0001

    b. 0001 0000 0001 0010

    c. 0100 1000 0000 1000

    d. 1000 0000 1000 0100

Upon completing this chapter, you will be able to:

- Define basic networking terminology

- Describe some commonly used network applications

- Describe the main purposes of networking

- Describe the benefits of the OSI reference model

- Discuss the functions of each of the seven layers of the OSI reference model and provide examples of each

- Describe the basic process of communication among the layers of the OSI reference model

- Describe the functions of the TCP/IP protocol model and provide examples of each

- Compare and contrast the OSI model and the TCP/IP model

CHAPTER 2

Networking Fundamentals

This chapter covers common networking terminology. It explains how standards ensure greater compatibility and interoperability among various types of network technologies. It also describes how the OSI reference model networking scheme supports networking standards. In addition, this chapter describes the basic functions that occur at each layer of the OSI model and the TCP/IP model. As you work through this chapter, you will learn about the basic functions that take place at each layer of the OSI model, which will serve as a foundation as you begin to design, build, and troubleshoot networks.

Basic Networking Terminology

Computer networking, like most professions, has its own jargon. This includes technical terms, abbreviations, and acronyms.

Without a good grasp of the terminology, it is difficult to understand the concepts and processes in this book. This chapter covers some of the terminology used in this book. Note that this is not intended to be a comprehensive glossary of networking terms. It is intended to be a quick reference that defines and briefly discusses some of the most important and most basic words, phrases, and acronyms that will enable you to navigate the next few modules. Each definition is expanded in the chapters that follow. Refer to the glossary for a more comprehensive list of definitions.

Network Interface Card (NIC)

NIC (pronounced "nick") refers to the network interface card, also called the *LAN adapter* or just the *network interface*. This card typically goes into an Industry-Standard Architecture (ISA), peripheral component interconnect (PCI), or Personal Computer Memory Card International Association (PCMCIA, or PC card) slot in a computer and connects to the network medium that, in turn, is connected to other computers on the network.

Media

Media refers to the various physical environments through which transmission signals pass. Common network media include twisted-pair, coaxial, and fiber-optic cable, as well as the atmosphere through which wireless transmission occurs.

Protocol

A network *protocol* is a set of rules by which computers communicate. Protocols are like the syntax of a language, which is the order in which processes occur. Many different types of computer protocols exist. The term *protocol suite* describes a set of several protocols that perform different functions related to different aspects of the communication process.

Cisco IOS Software

The *Cisco Internetworking Operating Software (IOS) Software* is the industry-leading and most widely deployed network system software. Cisco IOS Software delivers intelligent network services on a flexible networking infrastructure, enabling the rapid deployment of Internet applications.

Cisco IOS Software provides a wide range of functionality, from basic connectivity, security, and network management to technically advanced services. The functionality of Cisco IOS Software is the result of an evolution. First-generation networking devices could only store and forward data packets. Today, Cisco IOS Software can recognize, classify, and prioritize network traffic; optimize routing; support voice and video applications; and much more. Cisco IOS Software runs on most Cisco routers and Cisco switches. These network devices carry most of the Internet traffic today.

Client

A *client* is a computer or software program that requests services from a server. For example, an e-mail client is software that enables a user to send and receive e-mail to others using the services of an e-mail server.

Server

A *server* is a computer or software program in a network that provides services to clients. Servers are often dedicated, meaning that the servers perform no other tasks than their server tasks. Several different types of servers exist, such as a file server, a print server, a database server, a network server, and so on.

Network Operating System (NOS)

NOS, which stands for network operating system, usually refers to server software such as Windows NT, Windows 2000 Server, Novell NetWare, and UNIX. The term sometimes refers to the networking components of a client operating system, such as Windows 95 or the Macintosh OS.

Connectivity Devices

The term *connectivity devices* refers to several different device types, all of which are used to connect cable segments, connect two or more smaller networks (or subnets) into a larger network, or divide a large network into smaller ones. The term encompasses repeaters, hubs, switches, bridges, and routers. The connectivity devices are discussed in more detail in Chapter 3, "Network Devices."

LAN

A *local-area network (LAN)* is a network that is confined to a limited geographic area. This can be a room, a floor, a building, or even an entire campus.

MAN

A *metropolitan-area network (MAN)* is a network that is larger in size than a LAN and smaller in size than a WAN. This is a network that covers approximately the area of a large city or metropolitan area.

WAN

A *wide-area network (WAN)* is made up of interconnected LANs. It spans wide geographic areas by using WAN links such as leased carrier lines or satellite technology to connect computers in different cities, countries, or even different continents.

Physical Topology

The *physical topology* refers to the layout or physical shape of the network. Computers arranged so that cabling goes from one to another in a linear fashion have a *linear bus* topology. When the last connection connects back to the first to form a ring, that is referred to as a *ring* topology. If the systems "meet in the middle" by connecting to a central hub, that is referred to as a *star* topology. When multiple redundant connections make pathways, that is referred to as a *mesh* topology.

Logical Topology

The *logical topology* is the path that the signals take from one computer to another. The logical topology might or might not correspond to the physical topology. For instance, as shown in Figure 2-1, a network can be a physical star topology, in which each computer connects to a central hub; inside the hub, however, the data can travel in a circle, making it a logical ring topology.

Figure 2-1   *Physical Star Topology and Logical Ring Topology*

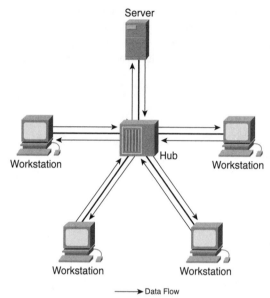

Physical: Star Topology
Logical: Ring Topology

Network Applications

Network applications are software programs that run between different computers connected over a network connection. Some of the most common uses of network applications include using a web browser program to find content from the World Wide Web (WWW) or using an e-mail program for sending e-mail to friends and family over the WWW.

Network applications are selected based on the type of work that needs to be done. A complete set of application layer programs is available to interface with the Internet. Each application program type is associated with its own application protocol. Following are some examples:

- The WWW uses the *Hypertext Transfer Protocol (HTTP)*. HTTP is the communications protocol used to establish a connection with a World Wide Web server and transmit Hypertext Markup Language (HTML) pages to the client browser (see Figure 2-2).

Figure 2-2   *WWW Request-Response*

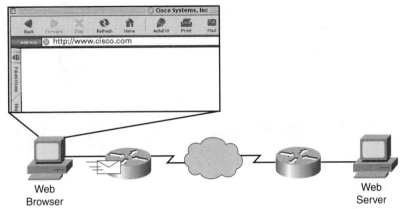

- Many electronic mail (e-mail) programs support the *Post Office Protocol version 3 (POP3)* and *Internet Message Access Protocol (IMAP)* application layer protocol for e-mail. POP3 is a standard e-mail server commonly used on the Internet. It provides a message storage container that holds incoming e-mail until users log on and download it. IMAP permits client e-mail applications to access remote message stores as if they were local without actually transferring the message.

- File utility programs use the *File Transfer Protocol (FTP)* for transferring files between remote computers.

- Remote access programs use the *Telnet protocol* for connecting to remote computers.

- Network-management programs use the *Simple Network Management Protocol (SNMP)* for monitoring the network device status and activities.

It is important to emphasize that the application layer is just another protocol layer in the OSI or TCP/IP models. The programs interface with application layer protocols.

E-mail client applications (such as Eudora, Microsoft Outlook, Pegasus, and Netscape Messenger) work with the POP3 protocol. The same is true with web browsers. The two most popular WWW browsers are Microsoft Internet Explorer and Netscape Communicator. The appearance of these two browser programs is similar, and they both work with the application layer HTTP protocol.

E-mail enables you to send messages between connected computers. The procedure for sending an e-mail document involves two separate processes. The first is to send the e-mail to the user's post office, and the second is to deliver the e-mail from that post office to the user's e-mail client, which is the recipient (see Figure 2-3).

Figure 2-3   *Sending E-mail*

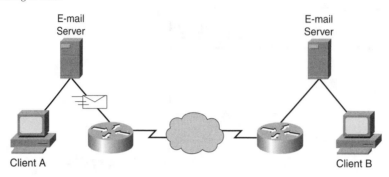

Understanding Network Computers

One of the primary purposes of a network is to increase productivity by linking computers and computer networks so that people have easy access to information regardless of differences in time, place, or type of computer system.

Because companies have adopted their networks as part of their business strategy, it is typical to subdivide and map corporate networks to the corporate business structure. In Figure 2-4, the network is defined based on the grouping of employees (users).

Figure 2-4   *Defining Components of the Network*

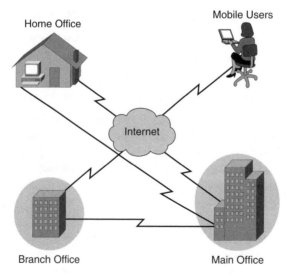

In Figure 2-4, the main office is where internal and remote offices are connected via a LAN and where the bulk of corporate information is located. A main office can have hundreds or even thousands of people who depend on network access to do their jobs. The main office might have several LANs, or it might be a campus that contains several buildings. Because all employees need access to central resources and information, it is common to see a high-speed backbone LAN as well as a legacy data center with mainframe computers and applications.

A variety of remote access locations connect to the main office or each other using WAN services, including the following:

- Branch offices
- Home offices
- Mobile users

The following sections describe these remote access locations in more detail.

Branch Offices

In branch offices, smaller groups of people work and connect to each other via a LAN. To connect to the main office, these users have to use WAN services. Although some corporate information might be stored at a branch office, branch offices more likely have local network resources, such as printers, but have to access information directly from the main office. The frequency of accessing the main office determines whether the WAN is based on permanent or dialup connections.

Home Offices

When individuals work out of their homes, this setup is called a home office. Home-office workers most likely require on-demand connections, such as digital subscriber line (DSL) or cable modem, to the main office or the branch office to access information or use network resources such as file servers.

Mobile Users

Mobile users connect to the main office LAN when they are at the main office, at the branch office, or on the road. Their network access needs are based on where they are located at a given point in time.

To understand what types of equipment and services to deploy in a network and when to deploy them, it is important to understand the business and user needs. Figure 2-5 shows one example of how to map an organization's business or user requirements to a network. In this example, the business needs might require LAN connectivity within the campus to interconnect the servers and end users' PCs, and WAN connectivity might be required to connect the campus to the remote branch office and telecommuters. The WAN connection to the remote branch office requires a permanent connection (such as a leased line), and the connection for the telecommuters requires dialup connections such asDSL or cable modem.

Figure 2-5   *Mapping an Organization's Requirements to the Network*

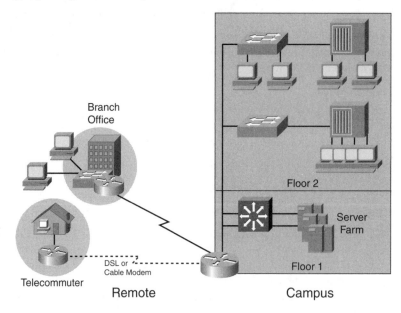

The Open System Interconnection (OSI) Model

The early development of LANs, MANs, and WANs was chaotic in many ways. The early 1980s saw tremendous increases in the number and size of networks. As companies realized the money they could save and the productivity they could gain by using networking technology, they added networks and expanded existing networks almost as rapidly as new network technologies and products were introduced.

By the mid-1980s, these companies began to experience difficulties from all the expansions they had made. It became more difficult for networks that used different specifications and implementations to communicate with each other. The companies realized that they needed to move away from proprietary networking systems. Proprietary systems are privately developed, owned, and controlled. In the computer industry, proprietary is the opposite of open. *Proprietary* means that one company or a small group of companies controls all usage of the technology. *Open* means that free usage of the technology is available to the public.

To address the problem of networks being incompatible and incapable of communicating with each other, the International Organization for Standardization (ISO) researched different network schemes. As a result of this research, the ISO created a network model that would help vendors create networks that would be compatible with and operate with other networks.

The OSI reference model, released in 1984, was the descriptive scheme that the ISO created. This reference model provided vendors with a set of standards that ensured greater compatibility and interoperability among the various types of network technologies that were produced by the many companies around the world.

The OSI reference model is the primary model used as a guideline for network communications. Although other models exist, most network vendors today relate their products to the OSI reference model, especially when they want to educate users on the use of their products. The OSI reference model is considered the best tool available for teaching people about sending and receiving data on a network.

The OSI reference model defines the network functions that occur at each layer. More important, the OSI reference model is a framework that facilitates an understanding of how information travels throughout a network. In addition, the OSI reference model describes how information, or data packets, travels from application programs (for example, spreadsheets, documents, and so on) through a network medium (for example, wires, and so on) to another application program that is located in another computer on a network, even if the sender and receiver have different types of network media.

The OSI reference model has seven numbered layers, each of which illustrates a particular network function. The seven layers of the OSI reference model are as follows:

- **Layer 7**—Application layer
- **Layer 6**—Presentation layer
- **Layer 5**—Session layer
- **Layer 4**—Transport layer
- **Layer 3**—Network layer
- **Layer 2**—Data link layer
- **Layer 1**—Physical layer

This separation of networking functions is called *layering*. Dividing the network into seven layers provides the following advantages:

- Breaks network communication into smaller, simpler parts.
- Standardizes network components to allow multiple-vendor development and support.
- Allows different types of network hardware and software to communicate.

- Prevents changes in one layer from affecting the other layers so that they can be developed more quickly.

- Breaks network communication into smaller components to make learning easier.

Each individual OSI layer has a set of functions that it must perform for data packets to travel from a source to a destination on a network. The following sections briefly describe each layer in the OSI reference model, as shown in Figure 2-6.

Figure 2-6   *The Seven Layers of the OSI Model*

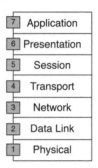

Layer 7: The Application Layer

The application layer is the OSI layer that is closest to the user. It provides network services to the user's applications. It differs from the other layers in that it does not provide services to any other OSI layer; instead, it provides services only to applications outside the OSI model. Examples of such applications are spreadsheet programs and word-processing programs. The application layer establishes the availability of intended communication partners and also synchronizes and establishes agreement on procedures for error recovery and control of data integrity.

Layer 6: The Presentation Layer

The presentation layer ensures the information that the application layer of one system sends out is readable by the application layer of another system. If necessary, the presentation layer translates among multiple data formats by using a common format. The common Layer 6 graphic standards are PICT, TIFF, and JPEG. Examples of Layer 6 standards that guide the presentation of sound and movies are MIDI, MPEG, and so on.

Layer 5: The Session Layer

As its name implies, the session layer establishes, manages, and terminates sessions between two communicating hosts. The session layer provides its services to the presentation layer. It also synchronizes dialogue between the two hosts' presentation layers and manages their data exchange. In addition to handling session regulation, the session layer offers provisions for efficient data transfer, class of service, and exception reporting of session layer, presentation layer, and application layer problems. Examples of Layer 5 protocols are the Network File System (NFS), Structured Query Language (SQL), X-Window System, and AppleTalk Session Protocol (ASP).

Layer 4: The Transport Layer

The transport layer segments data from the sending host's system and reassembles the data into a data stream on the receiving host's system. The boundary between the transport layer and the session layer can be thought of as the boundary between application protocols and data-flow protocols. Whereas the application, presentation, and session layers are concerned with application issues, the lowest four layers are concerned with data-transport issues.

The transport layer attempts to provide a data-transport service that shields the upper layers from transport-implementation details. Specifically, issues such as reliability of transport between two hosts are the concern of the transport layer. In providing communication service, the transport layer establishes, maintains, and properly terminates virtual circuits. Transport error detection and recovery and information flow control are used to provide reliable service. Examples of Layer 4 protocols are the Transmission Control Protocol (TCP), User Datagram Protocol (UDP), and Sequenced Packet Exchange (SPX).

Layer 3: The Network Layer

The network layer is a complex layer that provides connectivity and path selection between two host systems that might be located on geographically separated networks. Additionally, the network layer is concerned with logical addressing. Examples of Layer 3 protocols are the Internet Protocol (IP), Internetwork Packet Exchange (IPX), and AppleTalk.

Layer 2: The Data Link Layer

The data link layer provides reliable transit of data across a physical link. In so doing, the data link layer is concerned with physical (as opposed to logical) addressing, network topology, network access, error notification, ordered delivery of frames, and flow control.

Layer 1: The Physical Layer

The physical layer defines the electrical, mechanical, procedural, and functional specifications for activating, maintaining, and deactivating the physical link between end systems. Such characteristics as voltage levels, timing of voltage changes, physical data rates, maximum transmission distances, physical connectors, and other similar attributes are defined by physical layer specifications.

Data Communication

All communications on a network originate at a source and are sent to a destination. The information that is sent on a network is referred to as data or data packets. If one computer (Host A) wants to send data to another computer (Host B), the data must first be packaged by a process called *encapsulation*. The package is then de-encapsulated. The following two sections discuss encapsulation and de-encapsulation in more detail.

Encapsulation

Encapsulation wraps data with the necessary protocol information before network transit. Therefore, as the data moves down through the layers of the OSI model, each OSI layer adds a header (and maybe also a trailer) to the data before passing it down to a lower layer. The headers and trailers contain control information for the network devices and receiver, to ensure proper delivery of the data and to ensure that the receiver can properly interpret the data. For example, think of a header as an address on an envelope. An address is required on the envelope so that the letter inside the envelope can be delivered to the desired recipient.

Figure 2-7 illustrates how encapsulation occurs by showing the manner in which data travels through the layers. The following conversion steps occur to encapsulate data:

1 The user data is sent from an application to the application layer.

2 The application layer adds the application layer header (Layer 7 header) to the user data. The Layer 7 header and the original user data become the data that is passed down to the presentation layer.

3 The presentation layer adds the presentation layer header (Layer 6 header) to the data. This then becomes the data that is passed down to the session layer.

4 The session layer adds the session layer header (Layer 5 header) to the data. This then becomes the data that is passed down to the transport layer.

5 The transport layer adds the transport layer header (Layer 4 header) to the data. This then becomes the data that is passed down to the network layer.

6 The network layer adds the network layer header (Layer 3 header) to the data. This then becomes the data that is passed down to the data link layer.

7 The data link layer adds the data link layer header and trailer (Layer 2 header and trailer) to the data. A Layer 2 trailer is usually the frame check sequence (FCS), which is used by the receiver to detect whether the data is in error. This then becomes the data that is passed down to the physical layer.

8 The physical layer then transmits the bits onto the network medium.

Figure 2-7   *Data Encapsulation*

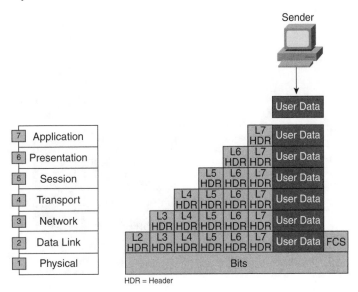

De-encapsulation

De-encapsulation

When the remote device receives a sequence of bits, the physical layer at the remote device passes the bits to the data link layer for manipulation (see Figure 2-8). The data link layer performs the following:

1 It checks the data link trailer (the FCS) to see if the data is in error.

2 If the data is in error, it may be discarded and the data link layer may ask for the data to be retransmitted.

3 If the data is not in error, the data link layer reads and interprets the control information in the data link header.

4 The data link layer strips the data link header and trailer and then passes the remaining data up to the network layer based on the control information in the data link header.

Figure 2-8   *Data De-encapsulation*

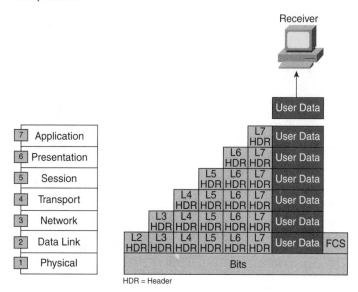

This process is referred to as *de-encapsulation*. Each subsequent layer performs a similar de-encapsulation process. Think of the de-encapsulation process as the process of reading the address on a letter to see if it is for you, and then removing the letter from the envelope if the letter is addressed to you.

Peer-to-Peer Communication

For data packets to travel from the source to the destination, each layer of the OSI model at the source must communicate with its peer layer at the destination. This form of communication is referred to as *peer-to-peer communication*. During this process, the protocols at each layer exchange information, called *protocol data units (PDUs)*, between peer layers. Each layer of communication on the source computer communicates with a layer-specific PDU and with its peer layer on the destination computer, as illustrated in Figure 2-9.

Data packets on a network originate at a source and then travel to a destination. Each layer depends on the service function of the OSI layer below it. To provide this service, the lower layer uses encapsulation to put the PDU from the upper layer into its data field. Each layer then adds whatever headers the layer needs to perform its function. As the data moves through Layers 7 through 5 of the OSI model, additional headers are added. The grouping of data at the Layer 4 PDU is called a *segment*.

Figure 2-9   *Peer-to-Peer Communication*

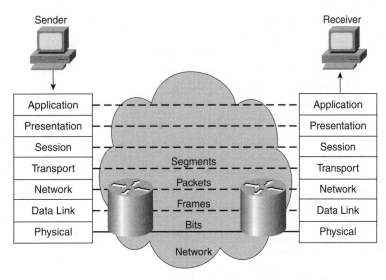

The network layer provides a service to the transport layer, and the transport layer presents data to the internetwork subsystem. The network layer moves the data through the internetwork by encapsulating the data and attaching a header to create a *packet* (the Layer 3 PDU). The header contains information required to complete the transfer, such as source and destination logical addresses.

The data link layer provides a service to the network layer. It encapsulates the network layer information in a *frame* (the Layer 2 PDU). The frame header contains the physical addresses required to complete the data link functions, and the frame trailer contains the FCS. The data link layer provides a service to the network layer by encapsulating the network layer information in a frame.

The physical layer provides a service to the data link layer. The physical layer encodes the data link frame into a pattern of 1s and 0s *(bits)* for transmission on the medium (usually a wire) at Layer 1.

Network devices such as hubs, switches, and routers work at the lowest three layers. The first layer that deals with the end-to-end transport between end users is the transport layer.

The TCP/IP Model

Although the OSI reference model is universally recognized, the historical and technical open standard of the Internet is Transmission Control Protocol/Internet Protocol (TCP/IP). The TCP/IP reference model and the TCP/IP protocol stack make data communication possible between any two computers anywhere in the world at nearly the speed of light. The TCP/IP model has historical importance, just like the standards that allowed the telephone, electrical power, railroad, television, and videotape industries to flourish.

The U.S. Department of Defense (DoD) created the TCP/IP reference model because it wanted a network that could survive any conditions, even a nuclear war. To illustrate further, imagine a world at war, crisscrossed by different kinds of connections, including wires, microwaves, optical fibers, and satellite links. Then imagine that information/data (in the form of packets) must flow, regardless of the condition of any particular node or network on the internetwork (which, in this case, might have been destroyed by the war). The DoD wants its packets to get through every time, under any conditions, from any one point to any other point. This very difficult design problem brought about the creation of the TCP/IP model, which has since become the standard on which the Internet has grown.

The TCP/IP model has four layers, as follows:

- Application layer
- Transport layer
- Internet layer
- Network access layer

The following sections describe each TCP/IP model layer in more detail.

NOTE   It is important to note that some of the layers in the TCP/IP model have the same names as layers in the OSI model. However, do not confuse the layers of the two models. Even with the same name, the layers have different functions in each model.

Application Layer

The designers of TCP/IP felt that the higher-level protocols should include the session and presentation layer details. They simply created an application layer that handles high-level protocols, issues of representation, encoding, and dialogue control. TCP/IP combines all application-related issues into one layer and ensures that this data is properly packaged for the next layer.

Transport Layer

The transport layer deals with the quality-of-service issues of reliability, flow control, and error correction. One of its protocols, the Transmission Control Protocol (TCP), provides excellent and flexible ways to create reliable and low-error network communications.

Internet Layer

The purpose of the Internet layer is to send source packets from any network on the internetwork and have them arrive at the destination.

Network Access Layer

The name of the network access layer is very broad and somewhat confusing. This layer is also called the *host-to-network layer*. It includes the LAN and WAN protocols and all the details in the OSI physical and data link layers.

OSI Model Versus TCP/IP Model

Figure 2-10 shows a comparison between the OSI model and the TCP/IP model. The two models have similarities and differences.

Figure 2-10   *OSI Model Versus TCP/IP Model*

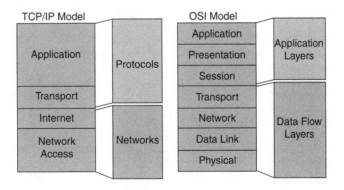

Similarities between the two models include the following:

* Both models have layers.
* Both models have application layers, although they provide very different services.

- Both models have comparable transport and network layers.

- Both models assume packet-switched (not circuit-switched) technology.

- Networking professionals need to know both models.

Differences between the two models include the following:

- TCP/IP combines the presentation and session layer issues into its application layer.

- TCP/IP combines the OSI data link and physical layers into one layer: the network access layer.

- TCP/IP appears simpler because it has fewer layers.

- TCP/IP protocols are the standards around which the Internet developed, so the TCP/IP model gains credibility just because of its protocols. In contrast, networks are not typically built on the OSI protocol, even though the OSI model is used as a guide.

NOTE   Remember that the OSI reference model is used as a guideline. Vendors try to match that model as much as possible; therefore, you should use the OSI reference model as the focal point for network design and implementation.

Summary

In this chapter, you learned the following key points:

- The ISO created and released the OSI model in 1984 to provide vendors with a set of standards to ensure greater compatibility and interoperability among various types of network technologies.

- The OSI reference model reduces complexity, standardizes interfaces, facilitates modular engineering, ensures interoperable technology, accelerates evolution, and simplifies teaching and learning.

- Each layer of the OSI model has a set of unique functions. The seven layers of the OSI model are the application, presentation, session, transport, network, data link, and physical layers.

- Encapsulation is the process by which data is wrapped in a particular protocol header before network transit.

- The TCP/IP model has four layers: application, transport, Internet, and network access.

Review Exercises

1 Match each of the following terms with the correct definition:

1. LAN

2. WAN

3. Protocol

4. Physical topology

e. The layout or physical shape of the network

f. A network that is confined to a limited geographic area

g. A network that spans wide geographic areas by using serial links to connect computers in different cities, in different countries, or even on different continents

h. A set of rules by which computers communicate

2 Which of the following is an example of a network application?

a. E-mail

b. Word processor

c. Spreadsheet

d. Database

3 Which of the following does not describe a main-office network?

a. A main office is where everyone is connected via a local-area network (LAN) and where the bulk of corporate information is located.

b. A main office can have only up to 500 people who depend on network access to do their jobs.

c. A main office might have several LANs, or it might be a campus that contains several buildings.

d. In a main office, it is common to see a high-speed backbone LAN as well as a legacy data center with mainframe computers and applications.

4 What is the OSI model?

a. A conceptual framework that specifies how information travels through networks

b. A model that describes how data makes its way from one application program to another throughout a network

c. A conceptual framework that specifies which network functions occur at each layer

d. All of the above

5 Which of the following is the correct order for the OSI reference model layers?

1: Physical	2: Data link	3: Transport
4: Network	5: Presentation	6: Session
7: Application		

1: Physical	2: Data link	3: Network
4: Transport	5: Session	6: Presentation
7: Application		

1: Physical	2: Data link	3: Network
4: Session	5: Transport	6: Application
7: Presentation		

1: Physical	2: Network	3: Session
4: Data link	5: Transport	6: Application
7: Presentation		

6 Which layer of the OSI model handles physical addressing, network topology, network access, error notification, ordered delivery of frames, and flow control?

a. The physical layer

b. The data link layer

c. The transport layer

d. The network layer

7 Which of the following best defines encapsulation?

a. Segmenting data so that it flows uninterrupted through the network

b. Compressing data so that it moves faster

c. Moving data in groups so that it stays together

d. Wrapping data in a particular protocol header

8 An e-mail message is sent from Host A to Host B on a LAN. Before this message can be sent, the data must be encapsulated. Which of the following best describes what happens after a packet is constructed?

a. The packet is transmitted along the medium.

b. The packet is put into a frame.

c. The packet is segmented into frames.

d. The packet is converted to binary format.

9 In the TCP/IP model, which layer deals with reliability, flow control, and error correction?

a. Application

b. Transport

c. Internet

d. Network access

10 Which of the following regarding TCP/IP is true?

a. TCP/IP combines the OSI data link and session layer issues into its application layer.

b. TCP/IP combines the OSI data link and physical layers into one layer.

c. TCP/IP combines OSI network and application layers into one network layer.

d. TCP/IP combines the bottom four layers of the OSI model into one Internet layer.

Upon completing this chapter, you will be able to:

- Describe the functions, features, and operation of network devices used at Layer 1 of the OSI model

- Describe the functions, features, and operation of network devices used at Layer 2 of the OSI model

- Describe the functions, features, and operation of network devices used at Layer 3 of the OSI model

- Describe the functions, features, and operation of voice gateways, digital subscriber line access multiplexers (DSLAMs), and optical platforms

- Describe the functions, features, and operation of firewalls and AAA servers

CHAPTER 3

Network Devices

This chapter discusses the devices used in Layers 1 through 3 of the OSI reference model, as well as network devices such as firewalls, AAA servers, voice gateways, digital subscriber line access multiplexers, and optical platforms.

Layer 1 Devices

Layer 1, the physical layer, of the OSI reference model, provides the fundamentals to troubleshooting networks; therefore, it is important to know and understand how Layer 1 devices work. The protocol data unit (PDU) at Layer 1 is a bit. Thus, all the Layer 1 devices must deal with bits.

The function of Layer 1 devices is simply to facilitate the transmission of a signal. This section introduces the following two common Layer 1 devices:

- Repeaters
- Hubs

Repeaters

Repeaters are networking devices that exist at Layer 1, the physical layer, of the OSI reference model. To begin understanding how a repeater works, it is important to understand that as data leaves a source and goes out over the network, it is transformed into either electrical or light pulses that pass along the networking media. These pulses are referred to as *signals*. When signals leave a transmitting station, they are clean and easily recognizable. However, the longer the cable length is, the weaker and more deteriorated the signals become as they pass along the networking media. The purpose of a repeater is to regenerate and retime network signals at the bit level, allowing them to travel a longer distance on the media (see Figure 3-1).

Figure 3-1   *Repeater*

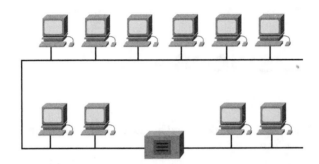

The term *repeater* originally meant a single port "in" and a single port "out" device. Today multiple-port repeaters also exist. Repeaters are classified as Layer 1 devices in the OSI model because they act only on the bit level and look at no other information.

Hubs

The purpose of a hub is to regenerate and retime network signals. The characteristics of a hub are similar to those of a repeater. Because they share similar characteristics, a hub is also known as a multiport repeater. The difference between a repeater and a hub is the number of cables that connect to the device. Whereas a repeater typically has only 2 ports, a hub generally has from 4 to 20 or more ports, as shown in Figure 3-2. Whereas a repeater receives on one port and repeats on the other, a hub receives on one port and transmits on all other ports.

Figure 3-2   *Hub*

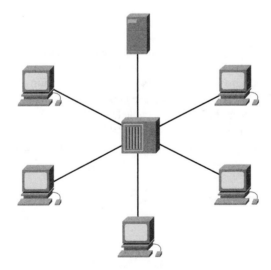

The following are the most important properties of hubs:

- Amplify signals
- Propagate signals through the network
- Do not require filtering
- Do not require path determination or switching
- Are used as network-concentration points

Hubs are commonly used in Ethernet 10BASE-T or 100BASE-T networks. Hubs are used to create a central connection point for the wiring media and to increase the reliability of the network. By allowing any single cable to fail without disrupting the entire network, hubs increase the reliability of the network. This feature differs from the bus topology, in which failure of one cable disrupts the entire network. (Network topology is discussed more in Chapter 4, "Network Topologies.") Hubs are considered Layer 1 devices because they only regenerate the signal and repeat it out all of their ports (network connections).

In Ethernet networks, all the hosts are connected to the same physical medium. Signals that are sent out across the common medium are received by all devices. A *collision* is a situation that can occur when 2 bits propagate at the same time on the same network. The area within the network from where the data packets originated and collided is called a *collision domain*. All shared-media environments are collision domains, or *bandwidth domains*.

As mentioned earlier in this section, the function of Layer 1 devices is simply to facilitate the transmission of signals. The devices recognize no information patterns in the signals, no addresses, and no data. When two wires are connected using hubs or repeaters, all the interconnections are part of a collision domain.

Layer 2 Devices

In this section, you learn more about Layer 2, which is the data link layer of the OSI model. The purpose of Layer 2 devices, such as bridges and switches, is to reduce collisions, which waste bandwidth and prevent packets from reaching their destination. Bridges and switches use the Media Access Control (MAC) address on network interface cards (NIC) to switch data frames. This section discusses the following three common Layer 2 devices:

- Network interface cards (NICs)
- Bridges
- Layer 2 switches

NICs

NICs are considered Layer 2 devices because each individual NIC throughout the world carries a unique code, called a *Media Access Control (MAC) address*. This address is used to control data communication for the host on the LAN. The NIC controls the access of the host to the medium. Figure 3-3 shows an example of a NIC.

Figure 3-3   *NIC*

Bridges

A *bridge* is a Layer 2 device designed to create two or more LAN segments, each of which is a separate collision domain. In other words, bridges were designed to create more usable bandwidth. The purpose of a bridge is to filter traffic on a LAN to keep local traffic local yet allow connectivity to other parts (segments) of the LAN for traffic that is directed there. Every networking device has a unique MAC address on the NIC. The bridge keeps track of which MAC addresses are on each side of the bridge and makes forwarding decisions based on this MAC address list.

Bridges filter network traffic by looking only at the MAC address. Therefore, they can rapidly forward traffic representing any network layer protocol. Because bridges look only at MAC addresses, they are not concerned with network layer protocols. Consequently, bridges are concerned only with passing or not passing frames, based on their destination MAC addresses. The following are the important properties of bridges:

- Are more "intelligent" than hubs. That is, they can analyze incoming frames and forward (or drop) them based on MAC address information.

- Collect and pass packets between two or more LAN segments.

- Create more collision domains, allowing more than one device to transmit simultaneously without causing a collision.

- Maintain MAC address tables.

Figure 3-4 shows an example of how a bridge is used. The appearances of bridges vary greatly, depending on the type.

Figure 3-4   *Bridge*

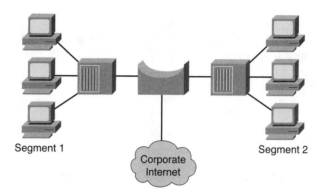

Segment 1   Segment 2

Corporate
Internet

What defines a bridge is its Layer 2 filtering of frames and how this is actually accomplished. To filter or selectively deliver network traffic, bridges build tables of all MAC addresses located on a network segment and other networks, and map them to associated ports. The process is as follows:

1   If data comes along the network medium, a bridge compares the destination MAC address carried by the data to MAC addresses contained in its tables.

2   If the bridge determines that the destination MAC address of the data is from the same network segment as the source, it does not forward the data to other segments of the network. This process is known as *filtering*. By performing this process, bridges can significantly reduce the amount of traffic between network segments by eliminating unnecessary traffic.

3   If the bridge determines that the destination MAC address of the data is not from the same network segment as the source, it forwards the data to the appropriate segment.

4   If the destination MAC address in unknown to the bridge, the bridge broadcasts the data to all devices on a network except the one on which it was received. The process is known as *flooding*.

A *broadcast* is a data packet that is sent to all nodes on a network. A *broadcast domain* consists of all the devices connected to a network that receive the data packet broadcast by a node to all other nodes on the same network. Because every device on the network must pay attention to broadcasts, bridges always forward them. Therefore, all segments in a bridged environment are considered to be in the same broadcast domain.

As was the case in the repeater/hub combination, another device, called a *switch*, is used for multiple bridge connections. The next section discusses switches in greater detail.

Layer 2 Switches

Layer 2 switches, also referred to as LAN switches (see Figure 3-5), often replace shared hubs and work with existing cable infrastructures to ensure that the switches are installed with minimal disruption of existing networks.

Figure 3-5   *LAN Switch*

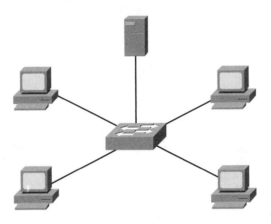

Like bridges, switches connect LAN segments, use a table of MAC addresses to determine the segment on which a frame needs to be transmitted, and reduce traffic. Switches operate at much higher speeds than bridges, however, and can support new functionality, such as virtual LANs (VLANs). VLANs are discussed more in Chapter 14, "Virtual LANs."

Switches are data link layer devices that, like bridges, enable multiple physical LAN segments to be interconnected into single larger networks. Similar to bridges, switches forward and flood traffic based on MAC addresses. Because switching is performed in hardware, it is significantly faster than the switching function performed by a bridge using software. Think of each switch port as a microbridge. Each switch port acts as a separate bridge and gives the full bandwidth of the medium to each host. This process is called *microsegmentation*. Microsegmentation allows the creation of private or dedicated segments—that is, one host per segment. Each host receives instant access to the full bandwidth and does not have to compete for available bandwidth with other hosts. Because only one device is connected to each switch port, collisions are minimized.

However, as with a bridge, a switch forwards a broadcast message to all the segments on the switch. All segments in a switched environment are therefore considered to be in the same broadcast domain.

Layer 3 Devices

In networking, there are two addressing schemes: One uses the MAC address, a data link (Layer 2) address; the other uses an address located at the network layer (Layer 3) of the OSI model. An example of a Layer 3 address is an IP address. Layer 3 devices interconnect network segments or entire networks and pass data packets between networks based on Layer 3 information. This section covers the following topics:

- Routers
- Multilayer switches

Routers

A *router* is a type of internetworking device that passes data packets between networks based on Layer 3 addresses. A router can make decisions regarding the best path for delivery of data on the network.

Working at Layer 3 allows the router to make decisions based on network addresses instead of individual Layer 2 MAC addresses. Routers also can connect different Layer 2 technologies, such as Ethernet, Token Ring, and Fiber Distributed Data Interface (FDDI). Routers also commonly connect Asynchronous Transfer Mode (ATM) and serial connections. However, because of their capability to route packets based on Layer 3 information, routers have become the backbone of the Internet and run the IP protocol (see Figure 3-6).

Figure 3-6   *Router*

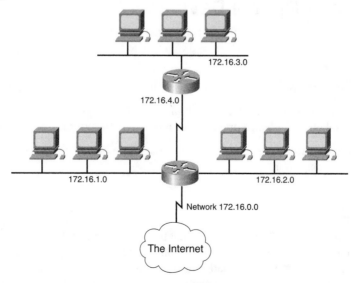

The purpose of a router is to examine incoming packets (Layer 3 data), choose the best path for them through the network, and then switch them to the proper outgoing port. Routers are the most important traffic-regulating devices on large networks. Routers enable virtually any type of computer to communicate with any other computer anywhere in the world.

Multilayer Switches

A multilayer switch works much like a Layer 2 switch. In addition to switching using Layer 2 MAC addresses, a multilayer switch uses Layer 3 network addresses (IP).

Traditionally, Layer 3 functions have occurred only within routers, which depend on software to perform routing functions. However, over the past few years, improved hardware has allowed many Layer 3 routing functions to occur in hardware. Layer 3 routing has traditionally been a software-bound process that creates network bottlenecks. With the advent of high-speed, hardware-based multilayer switches, Layer 3 functions can be performed as quickly as Layer 2 functions. Layer 3 no longer is a bottleneck.

Layer 3 functions include added capability for quality of service (QoS) and for security. Packets can be prioritized based on the network (IP) that they are coming from or the network to which they are being sent. Traffic from specific networks can be barred from entering the network.

A multilayer switch also can examine Layer 4 information, including TCP headers that can help identify the type of application from which the packet came or to which the packet is directed.

Voice, DSL, and Optical Devices

Recent networking demands of voice and data network integration and fast data transmission for end users and network backbones have resulted in the development of the following new networking devices:

- Voice gateways for handling converged packetized voice and data traffic

- Digital subscriber line access multiplexers (DSLAMs) used at the service provider's central office for concentrating DSL modem connections from hundreds of homes

- Optical platforms for sending and receiving data over fiber-optic cable, providing high-speed connection

Voice Gateway

A *gateway* is a special-purpose device that performs an application layer conversion of information from one protocol stack to another. The Cisco AS5400 Series Universal Access Server provides cost-effective platforms that combine routing, remote access, voice gateway, firewall, and digital modem functionality. Figure 3-7 shows a Cisco AS5400 Series Universal Gateway, which offers universal port data, voice, wireless, and fax services on any port at any time.

Figure 3-7   *Cisco AS5400 Series Universal Gateway*

DSLAM

A *digital subscriber line access multiplexer (DSLAM)* is a device used in a variety of digital subscriber line (DSL) technologies. A DSLAM serves as the point of interface between a number of subscriber premises and the carrier network. Figure 3-8 shows a Cisco 6100 Series Advanced DSL Access Multiplexer.

Figure 3-8   *Cisco DSLAM 6100*

Optical Platforms

Several optical platforms are available on the market for the optical networking, which is primarily a backbone, wide-area technology. Figure 3-9 shows a Cisco ONS 15454 Dense Wavelength-Division Multiplexing (DWDM) Optical Network System. The Cisco ONS 15454 provides the functions of multiple network elements in a single platform.

Figure 3-9   *Optical Platform—Cisco ONS 15454 DWDM Optical Network System*

Firewalls and Authentication, Authorization, and Accounting Servers

Other common network devices that do not work at the lower three layers include firewalls and Authentication, Authorization, and Accounting (AAA) servers. Both firewalls and AAA servers are components or devices related to network security. Because of increased Internet and extranet connections, as well as more telecommuters and mobile users accessing enterprise networks from remote site, the importance of network security increases.

Firewalls

The term *firewall* refers to either a firewall program(s) running on a router or server or a special standalone hardware component of a network. A firewall protects the resources of a private network from users in other networks.

Working closely with a router program, a firewall examines each network packet to determine whether to forward it to its destination (see Figure 3-10). Using a firewall is like using a traffic cop to ensure that only valid traffic can enter or leave certain networks.

Figure 3-10   *Firewalls*

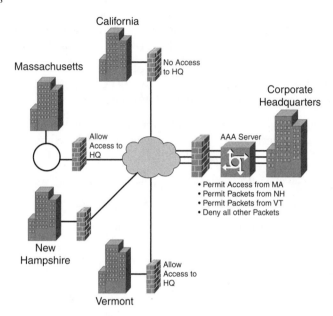

AAA Servers

An *AAA server* is a server program that handles user requests for access to computer and network resources. An AAA server provides authentication, authorization, and accounting services for an enterprise. The AAA server ensures that only authentic users can get into the network (authentication), that the users are allowed access only to the resources they need (authorization), and that records are kept of everything the users do after they are allowed entry (accounting).

An AAA server is like the credit card system. To put charges on a credit card, the merchant must verify that the credit card actually belongs to the person using it (authentication). The merchant must also check that the credit card has enough credit left for the requested charge amount (authorization), and then the merchant must record the charge to the user's account (accounting).

Summary

In this chapter, you learned the following key points:

- Networking devices are products used to connect networks. Hubs, switches, and routers interconnect devices within LANs, MANs, and WANs. Networking devices function at different layers of the OSI model.

- Repeaters regenerate, amplify, and retime signals before sending them along the network.

- The term *hub* (also called a *multiport repeater*) is used instead of *repeater* when referring to the device that serves as the center of a network. Hubs work at Layer 1 only and make no decisions. A hubs-only environment is a shared-access environment within which collisions occur. As devices are added to the network, more collisions occur and performance declines dramatically.

- LAN switches work at Layer 2 and make limited MAC hardware address decisions. Ethernet switches provide dedicated LAN connections.

- Working at Layers 2, 3, and 4, multilayer switches enable implementation of Layer 3 QoS and security functionality. Multilayer switches perform many of the same functions as routers do, but they do so in hardware.

- Routers can make decisions regarding the best path for delivery of data on the network.

- Various types of servers provide services to computers and users accessing the network.

- Firewalls and AAA servers provide security to the network.

Review Exercises

1 Repeaters can provide a simple solution for which of the following problems?

   a. Too many types of incompatible equipment on the network

   b. Too much traffic on a network

   c. Too-slow data-transmission rates

   d. Too many nodes or not enough cable

2 What is one disadvantage of using a hub?

   a. A hub cannot extend the network operating distance.

   b. A hub cannot filter network traffic.

   c. A hub cannot send weakened signals over a network.

   d. A hub cannot amplify weakened signals.

3 Which of the following is true concerning a bridge and its forwarding decisions?

   a. Bridges operate at OSI Layer 2 and use IP addresses to make decisions.

   b. Bridges operate at OSI Layer 3 and use IP addresses to make decisions.

   c. Bridges operate at OSI Layer 2 and use MAC addresses to make decisions.

   d. Bridges operate at OSI Layer 3 and use MAC addresses to make decisions.

4 Which of the following is true concerning the function of a switch?

   a. Switches increase the sizes of collision domains.

   b. Switches combine the connectivity of a hub with the traffic regulation of a bridge.

   c. Switches combine the connectivity of a hub with the traffic direction of a router.

   d. Switches perform Layer 4 path selection.

5 What does a router route?

   a. Layer 1 bits

   b. Layer 2 frames

   c. Layer 3 packets

   d. Layer 4 segments

6 Which of the following statements is true?

   a. A gateway is a special-purpose device that performs an application layer conversion of information from one protocol stack to another.

   b. The Cisco AS5400 Series Universal Gateway offers unparalleled capacity in only two rack units, with universal port data, voice, wireless, and fax services on any port at any time.

   c. A DSLAM serves as the point of interface between a number of subscriber premises and the carrier network.

   d. All of the above.

7 What are the functions of AAA servers?

   a. To ensure that only authenticated users can get into the network.

   b. To ensure that the users are allowed access only to the resources they need.

   c. To ensure that records are kept of everything the authentic users do after the users are allowed entry.

   d. All of the above.

8 Which of the following is a function of firewalls? (Select all that apply.)

   a. Software-based

   b. Hardware-based

   c. Filter traffic

   d. Layer 2 devices

   e. None of the above

Upon completing this chapter, you will be able to:

- Define physical and logical topologies

- Define and discuss the bus topology

- Define and discuss star and extended-star topologies

- Define and discuss the ring topology

- Define and discuss mesh and partial-mesh topologies

CHAPTER **4**

Network Topologies

The network topology defines the way in which the computers, printers, network devices, and other devices are connected. In other words, the topology of a network describes the layout of the wire and devices as well as the paths used by data transmissions. The topology greatly influences the way the network works.

Physical Topology Versus Logical Topology

Networks can have both a physical and a logical topology. *Physical topology* refers to the physical layout of the devices and media. A physical topology can be a bus, ring, star, extended star, or mesh design (see Figure 4-1).

Figure 4-1   *Physical Topologies*

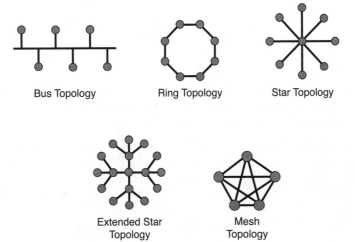

Logical topology refers to the logical paths that signals travel from one point on the network to another (that is, the way in which data accesses media and transmits packets across it). See Figure 4-2.

Figure 4-2   *Logical Topologies*

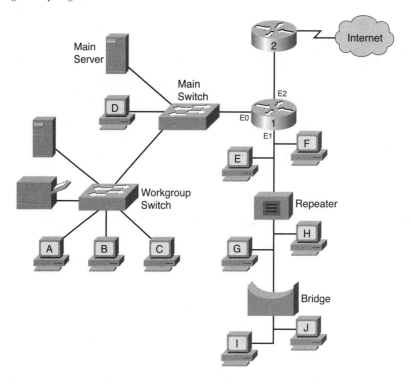

The physical and logical topologies of a network can be the same. For instance, in a network physically shaped as a linear bus, the data travels along the length of the cable. Therefore, it has both a *physical* bus topology and a *logical* bus topology.

A network can also have physical and logical topologies that are quite different. For example, a physical topology in the shape of a star, in which cable segments can connect all computers to a central hub, can have a logical ring topology. Remember that in a ring, the data travels from one computer to the next; inside the hub, the wiring connections are such that the signal actually travels around in a circle from one port to the next, creating a logical ring. Therefore, you cannot always predict how data travels in a network by simply observing its physical layout.

Token Ring uses a logical ring topology in either a physical ring or a physical star, whereas Ethernet uses a logical bus topology in either a physical bus or a physical star.

The following sections discuss the different types of topologies, including bus, star, ring, and mesh topologies.

Bus

Commonly referred to as a linear bus, a *bus topology* connects all the devices by one single cable. This cable proceeds from one computer to the next like a bus line going through a city (see Figure 4-3).

Figure 4-3   *Bus Topology*

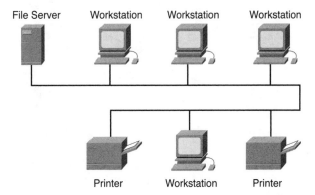

With a physical bus topology, the main cable segment must end with a terminator that absorbs the signal when it reaches the end of the line or wire. If there is no terminator, the electrical signal representing the data bounces back at the end of the wire, causing errors in the network.

With a logical bus topology, only one packet of data can be transmitted at a time. If more than one packet is transmitted, the packets will collide and must be resent. A logical bus topology with many hosts can be very slow because of the collisions.

Star and Extended Star

The *star topology* is the most commonly used physical topology in Ethernet LANs. When installed, the star topology resembles spokes in a bicycle wheel. The star topology is made up of a central connection point that is a device such as a hub, a switch, or a router, where all the cabling segments actually meet. Each host in the network is connected to the central device with its own cable (see Figure 4-4).

Although a physical star topology costs more to implement than the physical bus topology, the advantages of a star topology make this type worth the additional costs. Because each host is connected to the central device with its own wire, when that cable has a problem, only that host is affected and the rest of the network is operational. This benefit is extremely important and is why virtually every newly designed Ethernet LAN has a physical star topology.

Figure 4-4   *Star Topology*

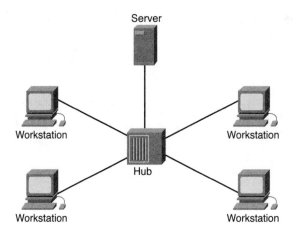

The use of a central connection point might be desirable for security or restricted access, but this is also a main disadvantage of a star topology. If the central device fails, the whole network becomes disconnected.

When a star network is expanded to include an additional networking device that is connected to the main networking device, it is called an *extended-star topology* (see Figure 4-5).

Figure 4-5   *Extended-Star Topology*

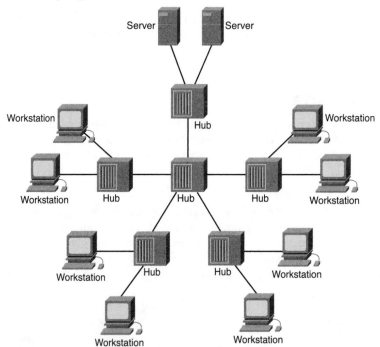

Ring

The logical *ring topology* is another important topology in LAN connectivity. As the name implies, hosts are connected in the form of a ring or circle. Unlike the physical bus topology, the ring topology has no beginning or end that needs to be terminated. Data is transmitted in a way unlike the logical bus topology. A frame travels around the ring, stopping at each node. If a node wants to transmit data, it is permitted to add that data as well as the destination address to the frame. The frame then continues around the ring until it finds the destination node, which takes the data out of the frame. The advantage of using this type of method is that there are no collisions of data packets.

Two types of rings exist:

- Single ring

- Dual ring

In a *single ring*, all the devices on the network share a single cable, and the data travels in one direction only (see Figure 4-6). Each device waits its turn to send data over the network.

Figure 4-6   *Ring Topology*

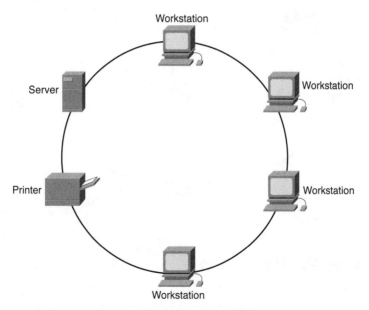

In a *dual ring*, two rings allow data to be sent in both directions (see Figure 4-7). This setup creates redundancy (fault tolerance), meaning that if one ring fails, data can be transmitted on the other ring. Also, if both rings fail, a "wrap" at the fault can heal the topology back into a ring.

Figure 4-7 *Dual-Ring Topology*

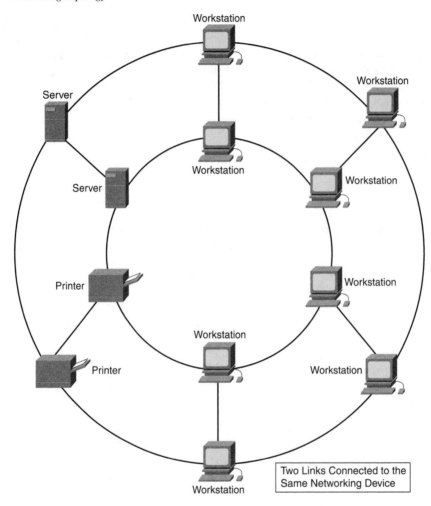

Full Mesh and Partial Mesh

The *full-mesh topology* connects all devices (nodes) to each other for redundancy and fault tolerance (see Figure 4-8). The wiring in a full-mesh topology has very distinct advantages and disadvantages. The advantage is that every node is connected physically to every other node, which creates a redundant connection. If any link fails, information can flow through many other links to reach its destination. The primary disadvantage is that for anything more than a small number of nodes, the amount of media for the links and the number of the connections on the lines becomes overwhelming. Implementing the full-mesh topology is expensive and difficult.

Figure 4-8   *Full-Mesh Topology*

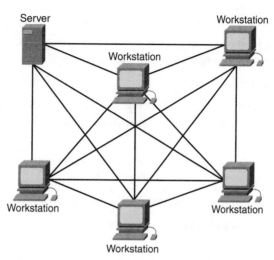

In a *partial-mesh topology*, at least one device maintains multiple connections to others, without being fully meshed (see Figure 4-9). A partial-mesh topology still provides redundancy by having several alternative routes. If one route cannot be used, the data takes another route, even if it is longer. The partial-mesh topology is used for many telecommunications backbones, as well as the Internet.

Figure 4-9   *Partial-Mesh Topology*

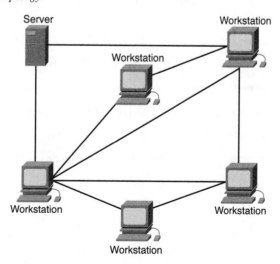

Summary

In this chapter, you learned the following key points:

- A physical topology describes the plan for wiring the physical devices. A logical topology describes how information flows through a network.

- In a physical bus topology, a single cable connects all the devices.

- The most commonly used architecture in Ethernet LANs is the physical star topology. In a star topology, each host in the network is connected to the central device with its own cable.

- When a star network is expanded to include additional networking devices that are connected to the main networking device, it is called an extended-star topology.

- In a ring topology, all the hosts are connected in the form of a ring or circle.

- A full-mesh topology connects all devices to each other.

Review Exercises

1   Which of the following correctly describes networking topology?

a. The network topology defines the way in which the computers, printers, network devices, and other devices are connected.

b. Networks can have either a physical or a logical topology.

c. A physical topology describes the paths that signals travel from one point on the network to another.

d. A logical topology defines the layout of the device and media.

2   Which of the following statements best describes a bus topology?

a. All of its nodes connect directly to a central point.

b. All of its nodes connect directly to one physical link.

c. All of its nodes connect to each other.

d. All of its nodes connect to exactly two other nodes.

3   Which topology has all its nodes connected directly to one center point and has no other connections between nodes?

a. Bus

b. Ring

c. Star

d. Mesh

4 What is the purpose of the second ring in a dual-ring network?

   a. Duplex

   b. Signaling

   c. Redundancy

   d. None of the above

5 In a complete, or full-mesh topology, every node:

   a. Is linked directly to every other node.

   b. Is connected to two central nodes.

   c. Is linked wirelessly to a central node.

   d. None of the above.

Network Types

Upon completing this chapter, you will be able to:

- Describe LAN standards

- Describe the function and operation of Fast Ethernet, Gigabit Ethernet, and 10-Gigabit Ethernet

- Explain how Ethernet LANs work

CHAPTER 5

Understanding Ethernet Technologies

Ethernet is one of the most widely used local-area network (LAN) technologies. Ethernet was designed to fill the middle ground between long-distance, low-speed networks and specialized, computer-room networks carrying data at high speeds for very limited distance.

Ethernet is well suited to applications in which a local communication medium must carry sporadic, occasionally heavy traffic at high-pack data rates. It was designed to enable sharing resources on a local workgroup level. Design goals include simplicity, low cost, compatibility, fairness, low delay, and high speed.

This chapter discusses different types of Ethernet technologies, including Fast Ethernet, Gigabit Ethernet, and 10-Gigabit Ethernet. It also explains how these technologies work.

LAN Standards

*LAN*s are high-speed, low-error data networks that cover a relatively small geographic area (up to a few thousand meters). LANs connect workstations, peripherals, terminals, and other devices in a single building or other geographically limited area.

LAN standards define the physical media and the connectors used to connect devices to media at the physical layer of the OSI reference model. LAN standards also define the way devices communicate at the data link layer. Because they are widely adhered to, the Ethernet and IEEE 802.3 LAN standards are covered in this book. Figure 5-1 shows how Ethernet and IEEE 802.3 LAN standards map to the OSI reference model physical and data link layers.

Figure 5-1   *LAN Standards*

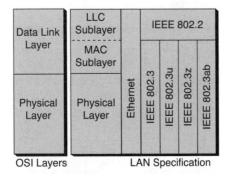

The Institute of Electrical and Electronic Engineers (IEEE) is a professional organization that defines network standards. The IEEE standards are the predominant and best-known LAN standards in the world today. IEEE divides the OSI data link layer into two separate sublayers: Media Access Control (MAC) and Logical Link Control (LLC). As shown in Figure 5-1, the IEEE 802.3 standard defines the physical layer (Layer 1) and the MAC sublayer of the data link layer. The IEEE 802.2 standard defines the LLC sublayer of the data link layer.

The following sections discuss the MAC and LLC sublayers in more detail.

MAC

The *Media Access Control (MAC)* sublayer deals with the protocols that a host follows to access the physical media. The IEEE 802.3 MAC specification defines MAC addresses, which enable multiple devices to uniquely identify one another at the data link layer. The MAC sublayer maintains a table of MAC addresses (physical address) of devices. Each device is assigned and must have a unique MAC address if the device is to participate on the network.

MAC addresses are 48 bits in length and always are expressed as 12 hexadecimal digits. The first six hexadecimal digits (reading left to right), which the IEEE administers, identify the manufacturer or the vendor and thus comprise the Organizationally Unique Identifier (OUI). The remaining six hexadecimal digits comprise the interface serial number or another value administered by the specific vendor.

LLC

The IEEE created the LLC sublayer to allow part of the data link layer to function independently of existing technologies. The *LLC* manages communications between devices over a single link on a network. This layer provides services to network layer protocols that are above it, while communicating effectively with the variety of MAC and Layer 1 technologies below it. The LLC, as a sublayer, participates in the encapsulation process. (Refer to Chapter 2, "Networking Fundamentals," if you need to reacquaint yourself with the encapsulation process.)

An LLC header tells the data link layer what to do with a packet when it receives a frame. For example, a host receives a frame and then looks in the LLC header to understand that the packet is destined for the IP protocol at the network layer.

The LLC adds to the network protocol data more control information to help deliver the packet to its destination. It adds two addressing components of the 802.2 specification: the Destination Service Access Point (DSAP) and the Source Service Access Point (SSAP), which identify the upper-layer protocol at each end. This repackaged packet then travels to the MAC sublayer for handling by the required specific technology, such as Ethernet, for further encapsulation and data.

NOTE   The original Ethernet header, Ethernet_II (prior to IEEE 802.2 and 802.3), does not use an LLC header. Instead, it uses a Type field in the Ethernet header to identify the Layer 3 protocol being carried in the Ethernet frame.

Figure 5-2 illustrates the IEEE 802.3 frame header (inside that frame an IEEE 802.2 header is carried) and Ethernet_II frame header.

Figure 5-2   *IEEE 802.3 Header and Ethernet_II header*

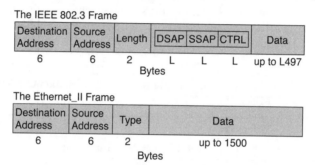

Ethernet

Ethernet was first developed in the early 1970s. Ethernet refers to the family of LAN implementations that includes the following four main categories:

- **Ethernet and IEEE 802.3**—These LAN specifications operate at 10 megabits per second (Mbps) over coaxial cable, twisted-pair cable, or fiber-optic cable.

- **Fast Ethernet, or 100-Mbps Ethernet**—Fast Ethernet, or 100-Mbps Ethernet, is a single LAN specification (IEEE 802.3u). Fast Ethernet operates at 100 Mbps over twisted-pair cable or fiber-optic cable.

- **Gigabit Ethernet**—An extension of the IEEE 802.3 Ethernet standard, Gigabit Ethernet increases speed tenfold over Fast Ethernet to 1000 Mbps, or 1 gigabit per second (Gbps). Two IEEE 802.3 standards, IEEE 802.3z and IEEE 802.3ab, define Gigabit Ethernet operations over fiber-optic or twisted-pair cable.

- **10-Gigabit Ethernet, or 10000-Mbps Ethernet**—In the process of being standardized in IEEE 802.3ae, 10-Gigabit Ethernet is a developing telecommunication technology that offers data speeds up to 10 billion bits per section, or 10 Gbps. 10-Gigabit Ethernet will be operated on fiber-optics cable.

The following sections describe each category of Ethernet in more detail.

Ethernet and IEEE 802.3

When Ethernet was developed, it was designed to fill the middle ground between long-distance, low-speed networks and specialized computer-room networks that carried data at high speeds for limited distances. Ethernet is well suited to applications in which a local communication medium must carry sporadic, occasionally heavy traffic at high-peak data rates.

The Ethernet and IEEE 802.3 standards define a bus-topology LAN that operates at a baseband signaling rate of 10 Mbps, which is referred to as 10BASE. Table 5-1 shows a summary of Ethernet specifications.

The 10BASE2, known as thin Ethernet, and 10BASE5, known as thick Ethernet, standards provide access for multiple stations on the same segments. Because the 10BASE-T standard provides access for a single station only, stations attached to an Ethernet LAN by 10BASE-T are connected to a switch or a hub.

Table 5-1   *Ethernet Specifications*

Protocol	Transmission Medium	Maximum Segment Length
10BASE2	Thin coax	185 m
10BASE5	Thick coax	500 m
10BASE-T	UTP Category 3, 4, 5, and 5e, 2-pair	100 m

NOTE   The designation of the specification is an IEEE standard identifier. The 10 refers to the transmission speed of 10 Mbps. The "BASE" refers to baseband signaling, which means that only Ethernet signals are carried on the medium. The 2 and 5 refer to the coaxial cable segment length (the 185-meter length has been rounded up to 2, for 200), and the *T* represents twisted-pair cable.

Fast Ethernet

Ethernet protocols are usually described as a function of data rate, maximum segment length, and medium. As faster types of Ethernet are used, more users can be added to the network without degrading network performance.

The *Fast Ethernet standard (IEEE 802.3u)* raises the Ethernet speed limit from 10 Mbps to 100 Mbps with only minimal changes to the existing cable structure.

Data can move from 10 Mbps to 100 Mbps without protocol translation or changes to application and networking software (see Table 5-2).

Table 5-2   *Fast Ethernet Specifications*

Protocol	Transmission Medium	Maximum Segment Length
100BASE-FX	Two strands of multimode fiber-optic cable	400 m
100BASE-T	Unshielded twisted-pair (UTP)	100 m
100BASE-T4	Four pairs Category 3 to 5 UTP	100 m
100BASE-TX	Two pairs UTP or shielded twisted-pair (STP)	100 m

Gigabit Ethernet

Gigabit Ethernet is an extension of the IEEE 802.3 Ethernet standard. IEEE 802.3z specifies operations over fiber optics, and IEEE 802.3ab specifies operations over twisted-pair cable.

Gigabit Ethernet builds on the Ethernet protocol but increases speed tenfold over Fast Ethernet to 1000 Mbps, or 1 Gbps. It is currently being deployed as the backbone in both corporate and public data networks. Because Gigabit Ethernet uses Ethernet to significant advantage, network managers can take advantage of their existing knowledge base to manage and maintain gigabit networks.

The Gigabit Ethernet specification addresses five forms of transmission media, as shown in Table 5-3.

Table 5-3   *Gigabit Ethernet Specifications*

Protocol	Transmission Medium	Maximum Segment Length
1000BASE-LX	Long-wavelength laser over single-mode and multimode fiber	3 km (single mode) 10 km (multimode)
1000BASE-SX	Short-wavelength laser over multimode fiber	220 m (62.5 micro) 550 m (50 micro)
1000BASE-CS	Balanced shielded 150-ohm two-pair STP copper cable	25 m
1000BASE-T	Category 5 four-pair UTP copper wiring	100 m
1000BASE-ZX	Extended wavelength single-mode fiber	100 km

The key application of Gigabit Ethernet is in the building backbone for interconnection of wiring closets. A gigabit multilayer switch in the building data center aggregates the traffic in the building and provides connection to servers by way of Gigabit Ethernet or Fast Ethernet. WAN connectivity can be provided by either traditional routers or ATM switching.

Gigabit Ethernet also can be used for connecting buildings on the campus to a central multilayer gigabit switch located at the campus data center. Servers located at the campus data center also are connected to the same gigabit multilayer switch that provides connectivity to the entire campus.

Gigabit Interface Converter

As the demand for faster network speed has grown, Ethernet has been adapted to handle these higher speeds. A gigabit interface converter (GBIC) is a device that is gaining popularity because of the demand and deployment of Gigabit Ethernet.

A *GBIC* is a transceiver that converts digital electric currents to optical signals and also converts optical signals to digital electric currents. GBIC is a hot-swappable input/output device that plugs into a Gigabit Ethernet port (slot), linking the port with the fiber-optic network. (A *hot swap* involves replacing a device with a similar device while the computer system remains in operation.)

GBICs eliminate the necessity for replacing entire boards at the system level, so they are considered economical. With GBIC, upgrading can be done easily, from an individual module to all the modules at a time in a system.

Figure 5-3 shows a Cisco GBIC.

Figure 5-3   *Gigabit Interface Converter*

10-Gigabit Ethernet

Built on the Ethernet technology used in most of today's LANs, *10-Gigabit Ethernet* is described as a technology that offers a more efficient and less expensive approach to moving data on backbone connections between networks, while also providing a consistent technology end to end. Ethernet can now step up to offering data speeds at 10 Gbps.

10-Gigabit Ethernet is expected to be used to interconnect local-area networks (LANs), wide-area networks (WANs), and metropolitan-area networks (MANs). 10-Gigabit Ethernet uses the familiar IEEE 802.3 Ethernet Media Access Control (MAC) protocol and its frame format and size.

Even though 10-Gigabit Ethernet was built on the Ethernet technology, the standard for 10-Gigabit Ethernet is different in some respects from earlier Ethernet standards. The difference is primarily in that 10-Gigabit Ethernet will function only over optical fiber and only in full-duplex mode. On multimode fiber, 10-Gigabit Ethernet will support distances up to 300 meters; on single-mode fiber, it will support distances up to 40 kilometers.

As a full duplex–only and fiber-only technology, 10-Gigabit Ethernet does not need the carrier sense multiple access collision detect (CSMA/CD) protocol. Using optical fiber, 10-Gigabit Ethernet can replace existing networks that use Asynchronous Transfer Mode (ATM) switches and Synchronous Optical Network (SONET) multiplexers on an OC-48 SONET ring with a simpler network of 10-Gigabit Ethernet switches. At the same time, this improves the data rate from 2.5 Gbps to 10 Gbps. (ATM is discussed more in Chapter 22, "Traditional WAN Services," and SONET is discussed more in Chapter 31, "Optical Transmission and Multiplexing.")

How Ethernet Works

Today the term *Ethernet* is often used to refer to all *carrier sense multiple access collision detect (CSMA/CD)* LANs that generally conform to Ethernet specifications. CSMA/CD is an access method that allows only one station to transmit at a time on a shared medium. The goal of standard Ethernet is to provide a best-effort delivery service. However, standard Ethernet using CSMA/CD takes into consideration all the transmission requests and determines what devices can transmit and when they can transmit for all the devices to receive adequate services.

The following subsections describe how CSMA/CD works and introduce you to simplex, half-duplex, and full-duplex transmission.

Carrier Sense Multiple Access Collision Detect

Ethernet signals, or frames, are transmitted to every station connected to the network. Before transmitting, a computer listens to the channel. If the channel is idle, the computer sends its data. After a transmission has been sent, the computers on the network again compete for the next available idle time to send another frame. This contention for idle channel time means that no station has an advantage over another on the network.

Ethernet uses a set of rules (or protocol) called *carrier sense multiple access collision detect (CSMA/CD)* to determine which station on the network can talk at any particular time. Stations on a CSMA/CD LAN can access the network at any time. Figure 5-4 depicts how CSMA/CD works in a network.

Figure 5-4   *CSMA/CD*

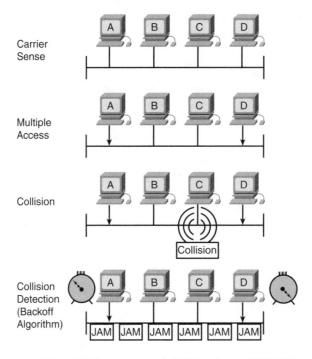

Carrier Sense Multiple Access with Collision Detect (CSMA/CD)

Before sending data, CSMA/CD stations listen to the network to determine whether it is already in use. If it is, they wait. If the network is not in use, the stations transmit. A collision occurs when two stations listen for network traffic, hear none, and transmit simultaneously. In this case, both transmissions are damaged and the stations must retransmit at some later time. CSMA/CD stations can detect collisions, so they know when they must retransmit.

When a station transmits, the signal is referred to as a carrier. The *network interface card (NIC)* "senses" the carrier and consequently restrains itself from broadcasting a signal. If there is no carrier, a waiting station knows that it is free to transmit. This is the "carrier sense" part of the protocol.

Because priorities are not assigned to particular stations, all stations on the network have equal access. This is the "multiple access" part of the protocol. If two or more stations attempt a transmission simultaneously, a collision occurs. The stations are alerted of the collision, and they execute a backoff algorithm that randomly reschedules transmission of the frame. This scenario prevents the machines from repeatedly attempting to "talk" at the same time. Collisions are normally resolved in microseconds. This is the "collision detect" part of the protocol. Figure 5-5 summarizes the CSMA/CD processes.

Figure 5-5   *CSMA/CD Processes*

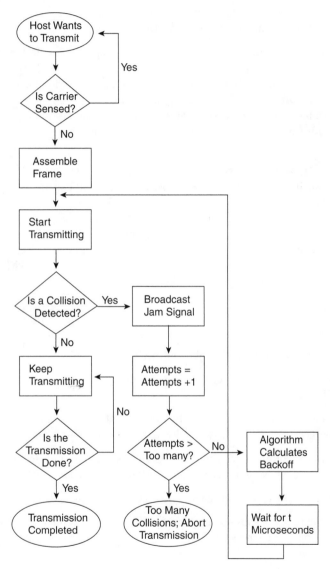

Simplex, Half-Duplex, and Full-Duplex Operation

The data channels over which a signal is sent can operate in one of three ways: simplex, half duplex, or full duplex. The distinction among these is in the way the signal can travel.

Simplex transmission, as its name implies, is simple. It is also called unidirectional because the signal travels in only one direction, just like traffic flows on a one-way street. Television transmission is an example of simplex communication.

Half-duplex transmission is an improvement over simplex transmission; the traffic can travel in both directions. Half-duplex transmission enables signals to travel in either direction, but not in both directions simultaneously. Half-duplex Ethernet, defined in the original 802.3 Ethernet, uses only one wire with a digital signal running in both directions on the wire. It allows data transmission in only on direction at a time between a sending station and a receiving station. It also uses the CSMA/CD protocol to help prevent collisions and retransmit if a collision does occur.

Full-duplex transmission operates like a two-way, two-lane street. Traffic can travel in both directions at the same time. Full-duplex networking technology increases performance because data can be sent and received at the same time. Full-duplex Ethernet uses two pairs of wires, which allow simultaneous data transmission between a sending station and a receiving station. There are no collisions in full-duplex Ethernet because it has two pairs of wires; one is used for transmission and the other is used for receiving. Full-duplex Ethernet is supposed to offer 100 percent efficiency in both directions. This means that you can get 20 Mbps with a 10-Mbps Ethernet running in full-duplex operation.

Summary

In this chapter, you learned the following key points:

- LAN standards specify cabling and signaling at the physical and data link layers of the OSI model.

- Several types of Ethernet exist: Ethernet, Fast Ethernet, Gigabit Ethernet, and 10-Gigabit Ethernet. Each type is associated with a different transfer rate.

- Cisco Gigabit Interface Converter (GBIC) is a hot-swappable input/output device that plugs into a Gigabit Ethernet port (slot), linking the port with the fiber-optic network.

- Ethernet uses carrier sense multiple access collision detect (CSMA/CD).

- Half-duplex transmission enables signals to travel in either direction, but not in both directions simultaneously. Full-duplex transmission enables data to be sent and received at the same time.

Review Exercises

1 Which of the following is *not* one of the recognized IEEE sublayers?

   a. Media Access Control

   b. Data Link Control

   c. Logical Link Control

   d. None of the above

2 What is the name of the method used in Ethernet that explains how Ethernet works?

   a. TCP/IP

   b. CSMA/CD

   c. CMDA/CS

   d. CSMA/CA

3 Fast Ethernet supports up to what transfer rate?

   a. 5 Mbps

   b. 10 Mbps

   c. 100 Mbps

   d. 1000 Mbps

4 Identify two Gigabit Ethernet cable specifications.

   a. 1000BASE-TX

   b. 1000BASE-FX

   c. 1000BASE-CS

   d. 1000BASE-LX

   e. 1000BASE-X

Upon completing this chapter, you will be able to:

- Describe the global Internet
- Describe WAN technology
- Describe WAN connection types
- Describe WAN devices
- Describe WAN provider service types and commonly used service terms
- Describe WAN signaling standards
- Describe WAN physical layer protocols
- Describe WAN data link layer protocols

CHAPTER 6

WANs

A *wide-area network (WAN)* operates at the physical layer, data link layer, and network layer of the OSI reference model. A WAN interconnects local-area networks (LANs), which are usually separated by large geographic areas. WANs provides for the exchange of data packets/frames between routers/bridges and the LANs they support.

The major characteristics of WANs are the following:

- WANs operate beyond the local LAN's geographic scope.
- WANs use the services of carriers such as regional Bell operating companies (RBOCs) and Sprint.
- WANs provide full-time and part-time connectivity.
- WANs use serial connections of various types to access network bandwidth.

This chapter provides an overview of WAN technology and discusses WAN devices, provider services, common WAN service terms, WAN signaling standards, and WAN physical and data link layer standards.

The Global Internet

To understand one example of a WAN, consider the Internet. By definition, an *internet* is a network of networks, and the *Internet* is the interconnection of thousands of large and small networks all over the world. Using an analogy, the telephone system is really a collection of interconnected local phone service providers. At that level, the Internet is practically the same thing: It is a collection of networks.

It sometimes seems that the Internet is a lot of chaos, but there really is a hierarchy in the Internet and the way it is deployed. In fact, the largest component of the Internet is commonly referred to as the Internet *backbone*. The backbone is not a single entity; instead, it is a collection of large transit networks by many different network service providers. The backbone provides the highest level of connectivity in the Internet. From the backbone, the Internet branches down to many lower layers to individual Internet service providers (ISPs), which, in turn, resell access to businesses and also resell access to individual dialup consumers. The established hierarchy in the Internet is a combination of routers and circuits combined with many data paths that exist between any given source and destination. Figure 6-1 illustrates the Internet hierarchy.

Figure 6-1   *Internet Hierarchy*

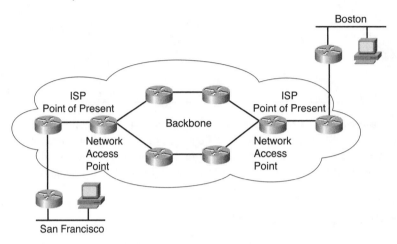

WAN Technology Overview

A WAN connects the locations of an organization to each other, to locations of other organizations, to external services (such as databases), and to remote users. Therefore, a WAN operates globally, unlike a LAN, which operates regionally. The most significant difference between LANs and WANs is the dependency on third-party WAN service providers to provide wide-area carrier services. To connect the various global locations, WAN members must subscribe to an outside WAN service provider, such as a regional Bell operating company (RBOC), to use WAN carrier network services. A WAN uses data link layer protocols, such as Integrated Services Digital Network (ISDN) and Frame Relay, that are provided by carrier services to access bandwidth over wide-area geographies. ISDN is discussed more in Chapter 23, "Dialup Access Technologies," and Frame Relay is discussed more in Chapter 22, "Traditional WAN Services."

As a data communications network, a WAN generally carries a variety of traffic types, such as voice, data, and video.

WAN technologies function at the three lowest layers of the OSI reference model: the physical layer, the data link layer, and the network layer. Figure 6-2 illustrates the relationship between the common WAN technologies and the OSI reference model.

Figure 6-2   *WAN Technologies*

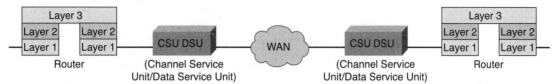

WAN Connection Types

Different WAN connection types can be used to interconnect LANs. This section gives a brief description of the common WAN connection types: dedicated connection, circuit switching, packet switching, and cell switching. Those connection types are discussed more in Chapter 22.

- **Dedicated connection**—Dedicated connection is typically referred to as a *point-to-point* or *leased line*. It provides a single pre-established WAN communication path from the customer premises, through a carrier network (the telephone company), to a remote network. The established path is permanent and is fixed for each remote network reached through the carrier facilities.

- **Circuit switching**—Circuit switching is a WAN switching method in which a dedicated physical circuit through a carrier network is established, maintained, and terminated for each communication session. ISDN is an example of a circuit-switched WAN technology.

- **Packet switching**—Packet switching is a WAN switching method in which network devices share a single point-to-point link to transport packets from a source to a destination across a carrier network. Frame Relay is an example of a packet-switched WAN technology.

- **Cell switching**—Cell switching is similar to packet switching. The real difference is that a packet is of variable size and a cell is a fixed size. An example of a cell-switched WAN technology is ATM.

WAN Provider Services

Telephone and data services are the most commonly used WAN services. Telephone and data services are connected from the building point of presence (POP), which is the point of interconnection between the communication facilities provided by the telephone company and the building's main distribution facility, to the WAN provider's central office (CO). WAN provider services are of the following three main types, as depicted in Figure 6-3:

- Call setup

- Time-division multiplexing (TDM)

- Frame Relay

Figure 6-3   *Three Types of WAN Provider Services*

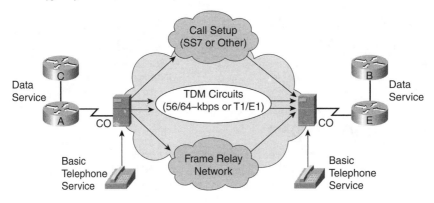

You learn more about each of these three WAN provider services in the following sections.

Call Setup

The *call setup* service feature sets up and clears calls between telephone users. Also called *signaling*, call setup uses a separate channel not used for other traffic. The most commonly used call setup is *Signaling System 7 (SS7)*, which uses call-control messages and signals between the transfer points along the way to the called destination.

Time-Division Multiplexing (TDM)

TDM is a method that allocates bandwidth for information from many sources on a single medium. This method combines signals for transmission on a single communications line and breaks each signal into segments with short durations. The signals then are carried over the line in alternating time slots, one after another. TDM uses a circuit-switching signal to determine the *call route*, which is a dedicated path between the sender and the receiver. By multiplexing traffic into fixed time slots, TDM avoids congested facilities and variable delays. Basic telephone service and ISDN use TDM circuits.

Frame Relay

In *Frame Relay* service, information contained in frames shares bandwidth with other WAN Frame Relay subscribers. Frame Relay is a statistical multiplexed service, which dynamically allocates bandwidth to any communications line that has information to transmit. Unlike TDM, Frame Relay uses data-link connection identifiers (DLCIs) and permanent virtual circuits (PVCs). A *DLCI* is a number that identifies the logical circuit between the source and the destination device. A *PVC* is a permanently established virtual circuit, which saves bandwidth associated with circuit establishment. Refer to Chapter 22 for more discussion on Frame Relay.

WAN Devices

WANs use several types of devices:

- Routers, which offer many services, including LAN and WAN interface ports

- WAN switches, such as an ATM switch used for voice, data, and video communication

- Modems and channel service units/data service units (CSUs/DSUs), which are used to interface the end-user device (such as a PC or a router) to the service provider switch

- An access server, which acts as a concentration point for dial-in and dial-out connections

The following sections describe these WAN devices in more detail.

Routers

Routers are devices that implement the network layer services. They provide a wide range of interfaces, such as Ethernet, Fast Ethernet, and Gigabit Ethernet for LAN connections, and serial and ATM interfaces for WAN connections.

The Internet contains many thousands of routers, for example. Routers are the "traffic cops" in the Internet that direct how a packet should travel through the Internet to reach a particular destination.

WAN Switches

A *WAN switch* is a multiport networking device that switches such traffic as Frame Relay, X.25, and ATM. WAN switches typically operate at the data link layer of the OSI reference model. Figure 6-4 illustrates two routers at remote ends of a WAN that are connected by ATM WAN switches.

Figure 6-4   *WAN Switches—Example: ATM Switches*

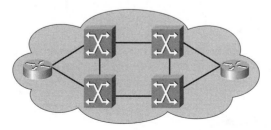

WAN switches use a virtual circuit to logically connect the two routers. It is called a virtual circuit because the routers do not have a physical connection to each other. Each router has only one physical connection to the ATM switch that it connects to directly.

Modems

A *modem* is a device that interprets digital and analog signals by modulating and demodulating the signal, enabling data to be transmitted over voice-grade telephone lines. At the transmitting source, digital signals are converted to an analog form that is suitable for transmission over analog communication facilities. At the destination, a modem returns these analog signals to digital form. Figure 6-5 illustrates a simple modem-to-modem connection through the Public Switched Telephone Network (PSTN).

Figure 6-5   *Modems*

CSUs/DSUs

A CSU/DSU is a digital-interface device (or sometimes two separate digital devices) that adapts the physical interface on a data terminal equipment (DTE) device (such as a terminal) to the interface of a data communication equipment (DCE) device (such as a switch) in a switched-carrier network. A CSU/DSU is like a digital modem: It converts from one digital format to another digital format. Figure 6-6 illustrates the placement of the CSU/DSU in a WAN implementation. Sometimes CSUs/DSUs are integrated in the router interface.

Figure 6-6   *CSU/DSU*

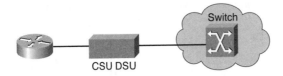

Access Servers

Access servers are used to concentrate modem users' connections. For example, an Internet service provider (ISP) needs access servers so that its dialup customers can call in and connect to its services. Access servers usually contain many built-in modems. Figure 6-7 illustrates an access server concentrating dial-out connections into a WAN.

Figure 6-7   *Access Server*

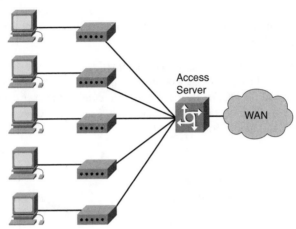

WAN Service Providers and WAN Service Terms

Advances in technology over the past decade have made numerous additional WAN solutions available to network designers. When selecting an appropriate WAN solution, you need to discuss the costs and benefits of each with the service providers.

When an organization subscribes to an outside WAN service provider for network resources, the provider gives connection requirements to the subscriber, such as the type of equipment to be used to receive services.

The following are the most commonly used terms associated with the main parts of WAN services:

- **Customer premises equipment (CPE)**—Devices physically located on the subscriber's premises. These include both devices owned by the subscriber and devices leased to the subscriber by the service provider.

- **Demarcation (or demarc)**—The point at which the CPE ends and the local-loop portion of the service begins. This often occurs at the point of presence (POP) of a building. The demarc point is the point where the WAN provider's support responsibility ends and the customer's begins. It typically ends at the local-loop termination point, but it can include the CPE in some cases.

- **Local loop (or "last mile")**—Cabling (usually copper wiring) that extends from the demarcation into the WAN service provider's central office.

- **Central office (CO)**—The WAN service provider's office to which all local loops in a given area connect and in which circuit switching of subscriber lines occurs.

- **CO switch**—A switching facility that provides the nearest POP for the provider's WAN service.

- **Toll network**—The collective switches and facilities (called trunks) inside the WAN provider's cloud. The caller's traffic can cross a trunk to a primary center, then to a sectional center, and then to a regional or international carrier center as the call travels the long distance to its destination.

- **DTE/DCE**—A key interface in the customer's site occurs between the data terminal equipment (DTE) and the data communication equipment (DCE). Typically, the DTE is the router and the DCE is the device used to convert the user data from the DTE into a form acceptable to the facility providing WAN services. As shown in Figure 6-8, the DCE is the attached modem or CSU/DSU.

Figure 6-8   *DTE/DCE*

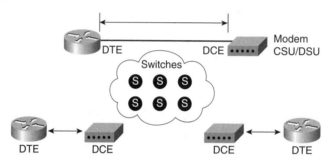

The WAN path between the DTE is called the link, circuit, channel, or line (refer to Figure 6-8). The DCE primarily provides an interface for the DTE into the communication link in the WAN cloud.

As shown in Figure 6-9, the two routers can be connected by the service provider using either a dialup (circuit-switched) connection or a permanent leased-line (point-to-point) connection. The choice of which type of connection to use most often depends on the cost, availability of the service, and the traffic requirements.

Figure 6-9   *WAN Service Providers*

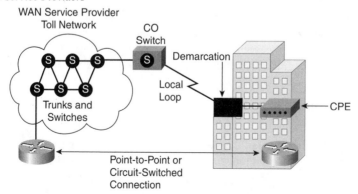

WAN Signaling Standards and Capacity

WAN links can be ordered from the WAN provider at various speeds, which are stated in bits per second (bps) capacity. This bps capacity determines how fast data can be moved across the WAN link.

Signaling is the process of sending a transmission signal over a physical medium for the purposes of communication. Like any other standard networking technology, WAN transmission facilities feature standardized signaling schemes. Such schemes define transmission rates and media types. WAN bandwidth is often provisioned in the United States by using the North American Digital Hierarchy, shown in Table 6-1.

Table 6-1   *WAN Link Types and Bandwidth*

Line Type	Signal Standard	Bit Rate Capacity
56	DS0	56 kbps
64	DS0	64 kbps
T1	DS1	1.544 Mbps
E1	ZM	2.048 Mbps
E3	M3	34.064 Mbps
J1	Y1	2.048 Mbps
T3	DS3	44.736 Mbps
OC-1	SONET	51.84 Mbps
OC-3	SONET	155.54 Mbps
OC-9	SONET	466.56 Mbps
OC-12	SONET	622.08 Mbps
OC-18	SONET	933.12 Mbps
OC-24	SONET	1244.16 Mbps
OC-36	SONET	1866.24 Mbps
OC-48	SONET	2488.32 Mbps

WANs and the Physical Layer

The WAN physical layer protocols describe how to provide electrical, mechanical, operational, and functional connections for WAN services. Most WANs require an interconnection that is provided by a communications service provider (such as an RBOC), an alternative carrier (such as an Internet service provider), or a Post, Telephone, and Telegraph (PTT) agency.

The WAN physical layer also describes the interface between the DTE and the DCE. A DTE is a user device with an interface connecting to the WAN link. A DCE is the end of the WAN provider's side of the communication facility. Typically, the DCE is the service provider and the DTE is the attached device.

Several physical layer standards define the rules governing the interface between the DTE and the DCE:

- **EIA/TIA-232**—This common physical layer interface standard, developed by the Electronic Industries Association (EIA) and Telecommunications Industries Association (TIA), supports signal speeds of up to 64 kbps. It was formerly known as RS-232. This standard has been in place for many years.

- **EIA/TIA-449**—This popular physical layer interface, developed by the EIA and TIA, is essentially a faster (up to 2 Mbps) version of EIA/TIA-232, capable of longer cable runs.

- **EIA/TIA-612/613**—This standard describes High-Speed Serial Interface (HSSI), which provides access to services at T3 (45 Mbps), E3 (34 Mbps), and Synchronous Optical Network (SONET) STS-1 (51.84 Mbps) rates. The actual rate of the interface depends on the external DSU and the type of service to which it is connected.

- **V.24**—This standard is an International Telecommunication Union–Telecommunication Standardization Sector (ITU-T) standard for a physical layer interface between the DTE and the DCE.

- **V.35**—This ITU-T standard describes a synchronous, physical layer protocol used for communication between a network access device and a packet network. V.35 is most commonly used in the United States and Europe.

- **X.21**—This ITU-T standard for serial communications over synchronous digital lines is used primarily in Europe and Japan.

- **G.703**—This ITU-T electrical and mechanical specification for connections between telephone company equipment and the DTE uses British naval connectors (BNCs) and operates at E1 data rates.

In Figure 6-10, the services offered to the DTE are made available through a modem or a CSU/DSU. (Note that WAN service providers typically do not provide and manage the CSU/DSU.)

Figure 6-10 *WAN and the Physical Layer*

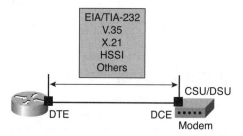

WANs and the Data Link Layer

Data link layer protocols are designed to operate over dedicated point-to-point, multipoint, and multiaccess-switched services such as Frame Relay (see Figure 6-11). The common data link layer encapsulations associated with synchronous serial lines include the following:

- **Cisco High-Level Data Link Control (HDLC)**—This Cisco standard is not compatible with the industry-standard HDLC protocol. Cisco's HDLC contains a protocol field to identify the network layer protocol being carried in Cisco's HDLC frame.

- **Point-to-Point Protocol (PPP)**—This protocol is described by RFC 1661, "The Point-to-Point Protocol." The PPP contains a protocol field to identify the network layer protocol being carried in the PPP frame.

- **Synchronous Data Link Control Protocol (SDLC)**—This protocol is an IBM-designed WAN data link protocol for Systems Network Architecture (SNA) environments. It is largely being replaced by the more versatile HDLC.

- **Serial Line Interface Protocol (SLIP)**—This was once a very popular WAN data link protocol for carrying IP packets only. However, it is being replaced in many applications by the more versatile PPP.

- **Link Access Procedure, Balanced (LAPB)**—This data link protocol is used by X.25. It has extensive error-checking capabilities.

- **Link Access Procedure on the D channel (LAPD)**—This WAN data link protocol is used for signaling and call setup on an ISDN D channel. Data transmissions take place on the ISDN B channels.

- **Link Access Procedures to Frame mode bearer services (LAPF)**—This protocol is for Frame Relay mode bearer services. Similar to LAPD, this WAN data link protocol is used with Frame Relay technologies.

Figure 6-11   *WAN and the Data Link Layer*

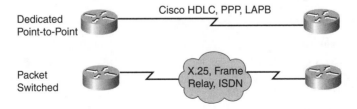

Cisco HDLC, PPP, LAPB

Dedicated
Point-to-Point

Packet
Switched

X.25, Frame
Relay, ISDN

Summary

In this chapter, you learned the following the key points:

- The Internet is the interconnection of thousands of large and small networks all over the world.

- A WAN is used to interconnect LANs that are separated by a large geographic distance.

- Dedicated line, circuit switching, packet switching, and cell switching are some of the common WAN connection types.

- Many types of WAN services are available to the WAN subscriber, who must know how to interface to the WAN provider's service.

- WAN devices include routers, WAN switches, modems, CSUs/DSUs, and access servers.

- WAN physical layer protocols describe how to provide electrical, mechanical, operational, and functional connection for WAN services.

- WAN data link layer protocols describe how frames are carried between systems on a single data link.

Review Exercises

1 Which of the following statements best describes a WAN?

   a. Connects LANs that are separated by a large geographic area

   b. Connects workstations, terminals, and other devices in a metropolitan area

   c. Connects LANs within a large building

   d. Connects workstations, terminals, and other devices within a building

2 What is a group of networks that are networked to each other called?

   a. An internet

   b. A WAN

   c. A LAN

   d. A workgroup

3 A CSU/DSU is generally used as what type of equipment?

   a. Router

   b. DTE

   c. Switch

   d. DCE

4 DCE or DTE equipment is found at which layer of the OSI reference model?

   a. Network layer

   b. Data link layer

   c. Physical layer

   d. Transport layer

5 Which of the following is a circuit-switched WAN technology?

   a. Frame Relay

   b. ISDN

   c. PPP

   d. ATM

Upon completing this chapter, you will be able to:

- Describe the features of a metropolitan-area network (MAN)

- Describe the features of a storage-area network (SAN)

- Describe the features of a content network (CN)

- Describe the functions, benefits, and technologies of virtual private networks (VPNs)

CHAPTER 7

Other Types of Networks

This chapter introduces the basic features of metropolitan-area networks (MANs), storage-area networks (SANs), content networks (CNs), and virtual private networks (VPNs). This chapter also describes VPN benefits and technologies.

Metropolitan-Area Networks (MANs)

A *metropolitan-area network (MAN)* is a network that spans a metropolitan area, such as a city or a suburban area. A MAN usually consists of two or more LANs in a common geographic area (see Figure 7-1). For example, a bank with multiple branches might utilize a MAN. Typically, a service provider is used to connect two or more LAN sites using T1 private lines or optical services. A MAN also can be created using wireless bridge technology by beaming signals across public areas. The higher optical bandwidths that are currently available make MANs a more functional and economically feasible option than in the past.

Figure 7-1 *Metropolitan-Area Network*

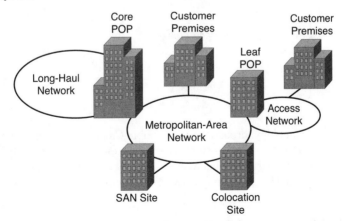

Many MANs have been designed using either Synchronous Optical Network (SONET) or a similar technology known as Synchronous Digital Hierarchy (SDH). SONET and SDH are self-healing network architectures that prevent interruption in service by rerouting traffic almost instantaneously if a fiber is cut.

The following features differentiate MANs from LANs or WANs:

- MANs interconnect users in a geographic area or region larger than that covered by LAN but smaller than the area covered by MAN.

- A MAN often acts as a high-speed network to allow sharing of resources. A MAN also is used to provide a shared connection to other networks using a link to a WAN.

Storage-Area Networks (SANs)

A *storage-area network (SAN)* is a dedicated, high-performance network used to move data between heterogeneous servers and storage resources. As a separate dedicated network, it avoids any traffic conflict between clients and servers (see Figure 7-2).

Figure 7-2   *A Storage-Area Network*

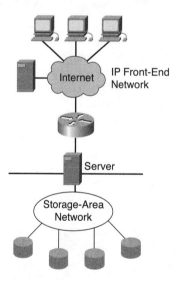

Adopting SAN technology through the use of Fibre Channel, hubs, and switches allows high-speed server-to-storage, storage-to-storage, or server-to-server connectivity. This method uses a separate network infrastructure that relieves any problems, such as large packet overhead and high latency, associated with existing network connectivity.

NOTE   Fibre Channel is a technology for transmitting data between computer devices at a data rate of up to 1 Gbps, which is a billion bits per second. Fibre Channel is especially suitable for connecting computer servers to shared storage devices and for interconnecting storage controllers and drives.

SANs also have the potential to allow cable lengths up to 10 km (6.2 miles) so that servers in different buildings can share external storage devices.

SANs offer the following features:

- **Performance**—SANs enable concurrent access of disk or tape arrays by two or more servers at high speeds across Fibre Channel, providing enhanced system performance.

- **Availability**—SANs have disaster tolerance built in because data can be mirrored using a Fibre Channel SAN up to 10 km (6.2 miles) away.

- **Cost**—Because a SAN is an independent network, initial costs to set up the infrastructure are higher. However, the potential exists for rapid cost erosion as the SAN installed base increases.

- **Scalability**—Scalability is natural to SAN architecture, depending on the SAN network-management tools used for interoperability. Like a LAN/WAN, a SAN can use a variety of technologies. This allows easy relocation of backup data, restore operations, file migration, and data replication between heterogeneous environments.

- **Manageability**—SANs are data centric. They use thin protocol, which means it does not take up much bandwidth on the network, for low latency.

Cisco SN 5420 Storage Router

The Cisco SN 5420 Storage Router is based on both IP and SAN standards. It provides interoperability with existing LAN, WAN, optical, and SAN equipment. Network administrators familiar with IP networking will be instantly familiar with the Cisco SN 5420 Storage Router and its management interfaces. Figure 7-3 illustrates a SAN utilizing the Cisco SN 5420 Storage Router.

Figure 7-3   *A SAN Utilizing Cisco SN 5420 Storage Router*

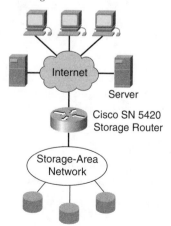

The Cisco SN 5420 Storage Router enables Internet Small Computer Systems Interface over IP (iSCSI), which is the first storage networking implementation based on IP standards and interoperability. It has the capability to automatically discover the storage devices on the attached Fibre Channel and SCSI networks. It also allows easy mapping of servers to storage devices.

Content Networks

A *content network (CN)* is a globally coordinated network of devices designed to accelerate the delivery of information over the Internet infrastructure. By taking advantage of services in the core IP network and the content-aware capabilities of Layers 4 through 7, enterprises and service providers can accelerate and improve the use of rich content such as broadband streaming media (see Figure 7-4). Content networks improve network performance and eliminate the stream of rich media on the infrastructure.

Figure 7-4   *Content Networks*

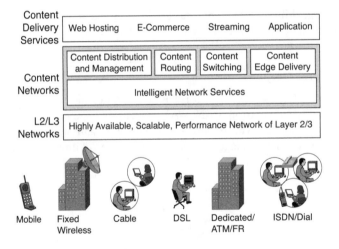

CNs bypass potential sources of congestion by distributing the load across a collection of content engines, which are located close to the viewing audience. Rich web and multimedia content is copied to the content engines, and users are routed to an optimally located content engine.

For example, when downloading a movie from an ISP, instead of waiting for hours for the big movie file to download, the same movie may take only minutes to download if the ISP is using the CN technology because a CN can accelerate the delivery of information.

The Cisco content networks solution is a tiered solution that starts with highly reliable Layer 2 and Layer 3 networks delivered by the Cisco IOS Software core network. The Cisco content networks solution is defined in the following five major technology categories:

- **Content distribution and management**—Distributes content to the network edge and provides the business/operations support system (BSS/OSS) for the content networks service.

- **Content routing**—Locates the optimum site to serve a specific content request based on network topology, network latency, server load, and policy.

- **Content switching**—Selects the best server within that site to deliver the content request based not only on server availability and load, but also on verification of content and application availability. It provides content services based on end-user sessions and the specific content requested.

- **Content edge delivery**—Delivers static and streaming content at the network edge, and keeps the content continuously fresh.

- **Intelligent network services**—Augments the content networks with IP core services, such as Layer 3 quality of service (QoS), VPNs, security, and multicast.

Intranets and Extranets

One common configuration of a LAN is an intranet. Intranet web servers differ from public web servers in that the public does not have access to an organization's intranet without the proper permissions and passwords. Intranets are designed to be accessed by users who have access privileges to an organization's internal LAN. Within an intranet, web servers are installed in the network, and browser technology is used as the common front end to access information such as financial data or graphical, text-based data stored on those servers.

The addition of an intranet on a network is just one of many application and configuration features that can cause an increase in the amount of bandwidth needed. Because network administrators must add bandwidth to the network backbone, they also should consider acquiring robust desktop computers for faster access into intranets. New desktops and servers should be outfitted with 10/100-Mbps Ethernet network interface cards (NICs) to provide the most configuration flexibility, thus enabling network administrators to dedicate bandwidth to individual end stations as needed. Some high-traffic servers might need to be outfitted with a Gigabit Ethernet NIC.

Extranets refer to applications and services that are intranet based but that employ extended, secure access to external users or enterprises. This access usually is accomplished through passwords, user IDs, and other application-level security mechanisms. Therefore, an extranet is the extension of two or more intranet strategies, with a secure interaction between participant enterprises and their respective intranets.

The extranet maintains control of access to those intranets within each enterprise in the deployment. Extranets link customers, suppliers, partners, or communities of interest to a corporate intranet over a shared infrastructure using dedicated connections. Businesses use the same policies as a private network, including security, quality of service (QoS), manageability, and reliability. See Figure 7-5.

Figure 7-5   *Intranet and Extranet*

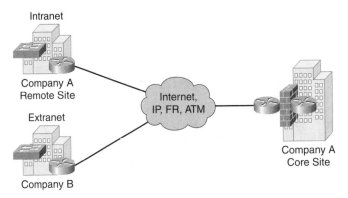

Virtual Private Network (VPN)

A *virtual private network (VPN)* is a communications environment in which access is controlled to permit peer connections within only a defined community of interest. A VPN is constructed by partitioning a common underlying communications medium. This communications medium provides services to the network on a nonexclusive basis. A simpler definition of a VPN follows:

> A VPN is a secure private network that is constructed within a public network infrastructure such as the global Internet.

VPNs maintain the same security and management policies as a private network. They are the most cost-effective method of establishing a point-to-point connection between remote users and an enterprise customer's network. For example, using a VPN, a telecommuter can access the company headquarters' network through the Internet by utilizing a secure tunnel between the telecommuter's PC and a VPN router in the main office.

Three main types of VPNs exist, as illustrated in Figure 7-6:

- **Access VPNs**—Access VPNs provide remote access to a mobile worker and small office/home office (SOHO) to the headquarters' intranet or extranet over a shared infrastructure. Access VPNs use analog, dialup, ISDN, digital subscriber line (DSL), mobile IP, and cable technologies to securely connect mobile users, telecommuters, and branch offices.

- **Intranet VPNs**—Intranet VPNs link regional and remote offices to the headquarters' internal network over a shared infrastructure using dedicated connections. Intranet VPNs differ from extranet VPNs in that they allow access only to the enterprise customer's employees.

- **Extranet VPNs**—Extranet VPNs link business partners to the headquarters' network over a shared infrastructure using dedicated connections. Extranet VPNs differ from intranet VPNs in that they allow access to users outside the enterprise.

Figure 7-6   *VPN Technologies*

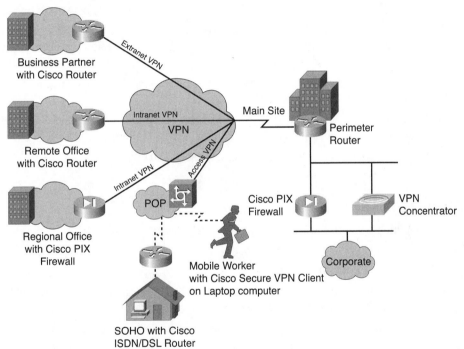

Virtual private networking offers significant advantages over previous forms of channel encryption and alternatives. Two of these advantages follow:

- A single virtual private networking technology can provide privacy for multiple TCP/IP applications. Providing privacy for multiple TCP/IP applications is especially important in environments in which you want to provide secure access for partners or telecommuters.

- Encryption services can be provided for all TCP/IP communications between the trusted client and the virtual private networking server. This scenario has the advantage of being transparent to the end user. Because encryption is turned on, the server can enforce it.

Summary

In this chapter, you learned the following the key points:

- A MAN consists of two or more LANs spanning a common geographic area.

- A SAN provides enhanced system performance, is scalable, and has disaster tolerance built in.

- A CN is a globally coordinated network of devices designed to accelerate the delivery of information over the Internet infrastructure.

- A VPN is a private network that is constructed within a public network infrastructure.

- The benefits of using VPNs include providing privacy for multiple TCP/IP applications and providing encryption services for all TCP/IP communications between a trusted client and the VPN server.

- Intranets are designed to be accessed by users who have access privileges to an organization's internal network.

- Extranets are designed to deliver applications and services that are intranet based but that employ extended, secure access to external users or enterprises.

- Three main types of VPNs are access, intranet, and extranet VPNs.

Review Exercises

1 Which of the following statements correctly describes a MAN?

 a. A MAN is a network that connects workstations, peripherals, terminals, and other devices in a single building.

 b. A MAN is a network that serves users across a broad geographic area and that often uses transmission devices provided by common carriers.

 c. A MAN is a network that spans a metropolitan area such as a city or suburban area.

 d. A MAN is a network that is interconnected by routers and other devices and that functions as a single network.

2 Which of the following does *not* correctly describe the features of content networks?

 a. Content networks accelerate and improve the use of rich content and eliminate the stream of rich content on the infrastructure.

 b. Content networks utilize a collection of content engines located close to the audience to distribute the content.

 c. The content network was designed to accelerate the delivery of information over the MAN infrastructure.

 d. The Cisco content networks solution is a tiered solution.

3 What service offers secure, reliable connectivity over a shared public network infrastructure?

   a. Internet

   b. Virtual private network

   c. Virtual public network

   d. Wide-area network

4 What links enterprise customer headquarters, remote offices, and branch offices to an internal network over a shared infrastructure?

   a. Access VPNs

   b. Intranet VPNs

   c. Extranet VPNs

   d. Internet VPNs

5 What is the name for the part of the company's LAN that is made available to select parties such as suppliers, customers, or partners?

   a. The Internet

   b. The extranet

   c. The intranet

   d. The LAN

6 Which of the following is *not* one of the features of a storage-area network?

   a. SANs enable concurrent access of disk or tape arrays, providing enhanced system performance.

   b. SANs provide a reliable disaster-recovery solution.

   c. SANs are scalable.

   d. SANs minimize the system and data availability.

Network Media

Upon completing this chapter, you will be able to:

- Describe the primary types and uses of twisted-pair cables
- Describe the primary types and uses of coaxial cables
- Describe the primary types and uses of fiber-optic cables
- Describe the primary types and uses of wireless media
- Compare and contrast the primary types and uses of different media

CHAPTER 8

Network Media Types

Network media is the actual path over which an electrical signal travels as it moves from one component to another. This chapter describes the common types of network media, including twisted-pair cable, coaxial cable, fiber-optic cable, and wireless.

Twisted-Pair Cable

Twisted-pair cable is a type of cabling that is used for telephone communications and most modern Ethernet networks. A pair of wires forms a circuit that can transmit data. The pairs are twisted to provide protection against crosstalk, the noise generated by adjacent pairs. When electrical current flows through a wire, it creates a small, circular magnetic field around the wire. When two wires in an electrical circuit are placed close together, their magnetic fields are the exact opposite of each other. Thus, the two magnetic fields cancel each other out. They also cancel out any outside magnetic fields. Twisting the wires can enhance this cancellation effect. Using cancellation together with twisting the wires, cable designers can effectively provide self-shielding for wire pairs within the network media.

Two basic types of twisted-pair cable exist: unshielded twisted pair (UTP) and shielded twisted pair (STP). The following sections discuss UTP and STP cable in more detail.

UTP Cable

UTP cable is a medium that is composed of pairs of wires (see Figure 8-1). UTP cable is used in a variety of networks. Each of the eight individual copper wires in UTP cable ¥is covered by an insulating material. In addition, the wires in each pair are twisted around each other.

Figure 8-1   *Unshielded Twisted-Pair Cable*

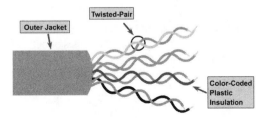

UTP cable relies solely on the cancellation effect produced by the twisted wire pairs to limit signal degradation caused by electromagnetic interference (EMI) and radio frequency interference (RFI). To further reduce crosstalk between the pairs in UTP cable, the number of twists in the wire pairs varies. UTP cable must follow precise specifications governing how many twists or braids are permitted per meter (3.28 feet) of cable.

UTP cable often is installed using a Registered Jack 45 (RJ-45) connector (see Figure 8-2). The RJ-45 is an eight-wire connector used commonly to connect computers onto a local-area network (LAN), especially Ethernets.

Figure 8-2   *RJ-45 Connectors*

When used as a networking medium, UTP cable has four pairs of either 22- or 24-gauge copper wire. UTP used as a networking medium has an impedance of 100 ohms; this differentiates it from other types of twisted-pair wiring such as that used for telephone wiring, which has impedance of 600 ohms.

UTP cable offers many advantages. Because UTP has an external diameter of approximately 0.43 cm (0.17 inches), its small size can be advantageous during installation. Because it has such a small external diameter, UTP does not fill up wiring ducts as rapidly as other types of cable. This can be an extremely important factor to consider, particularly when installing a network in an older building. UTP cable is easy to install and is less expensive than other types of networking media. In fact, UTP costs less per meter than any other type of LAN cabling. And because UTP can be used with most of the major networking architectures, it continues to grow in popularity.

Disadvantages also are involved in using twisted-pair cabling, however. UTP cable is more prone to electrical noise and interference than other types of networking media, and the distance between signal boosts is shorter for UTP than it is for coaxial and fiber-optic cables.

Although UTP was once considered to be slower at transmitting data than other types of cable, this is no longer true. In fact, UTP is considered the fastest copper-based medium today. The following summarizes the features of UTP cable:

- **Speed and throughput**—10 to 1000 Mbps

- **Average cost per node**—Least expensive

- **Media and connector size**—Small

- **Maximum cable length**—100 m (short)

Commonly used types of UTP cabling are as follows:

- **Category 1**—Used for telephone communications. Not suitable for transmitting data.

- **Category 2**—Capable of transmitting data at speeds up to 4 megabits per second (Mbps).

- **Category 3**—Used in 10BASE-T networks. Can transmit data at speeds up to 10 Mbps.

- **Category 4**—Used in Token Ring networks. Can transmit data at speeds up to 16 Mbps.

- **Category 5**—Can transmit data at speeds up to 100 Mbps.

- **Category 5e** —Used in networks running at speeds up to 1000 Mbps (1 gigabit per second [Gbps]).

- **Category 6**—Typically, Category 6 cable consists of four pairs of 24 American Wire Gauge (AWG) copper wires. Category 6 cable is currently the fastest standard for UTP.

Shielded Twisted-Pair Cable

Shielded twisted-pair (STP) cable combines the techniques of shielding, cancellation, and wire twisting. Each pair of wires is wrapped in a metallic foil (see Figure 8-3). The four pairs of wires then are wrapped in an overall metallic braid or foil, usually 150-ohm cable. As specified for use in Ethernet network installations, STP reduces electrical noise both within the cable (pair-to-pair coupling, or crosstalk) and from outside the cable (EMI and RFI). STP usually is installed with STP data connector, which is created especially for the STP cable. However, STP cabling also can use the same RJ connectors that UTP uses.

Figure 8-3   *Shielded Twisted-Pair Cable*

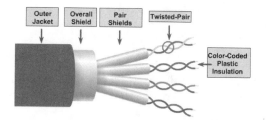

Although STP prevents interference better than UTP, it is more expensive and difficult to install. In addition, the metallic shielding must be grounded at both ends. If it is improperly grounded, the shield acts like an antenna and picks up unwanted signals. Because of its cost and difficulty with termination, STP is rarely used in Ethernet networks. STP is primarily used in Europe.

The following summarizes the features of STP cable:

- **Speed and throughput**—10 to 100 Mbps
- **Average cost per node**—Moderately expensive
- **Media and connector size**—Medium to large
- **Maximum cable length**—100 m (short)

When comparing UTP and STP, keep the following points in mind:

- The speed of both types of cable is usually satisfactory for local-area distances.
- These are the least-expensive media for data communication. UTP is less expensive than STP.
- Because most buildings are already wired with UTP, many transmission standards are adapted to use it, to avoid costly rewiring with an alternative cable type.

Coaxial Cable

Coaxial cable consists of a hollow outer cylindrical conductor that surrounds a single inner wire made of two conducting elements. One of these elements, located in the center of the cable, is a copper conductor. Surrounding the copper conductor is a layer of flexible insulation. Over this insulating material is a woven copper braid or metallic foil that acts both as the second wire in the circuit and as a shield for the inner conductor. This second layer, or shield, can help reduce the amount of outside interference. Covering this shield is the cable jacket. (See Figure 8-4.)

Figure 8-4 *Coaxial Cable*

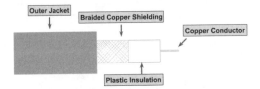

Coaxial cable supports 10 to 100 Mbps and is relatively inexpensive, although it is more costly than UTP on a per-unit length. However, coaxial cable can be cheaper for a physical bus topology because less cable will be needed. Coaxial cable can be cabled over longer distances than twisted-pair cable. For example, Ethernet can run approximately 100 meters (328 feet) using twisted-pair cabling. Using coaxial cable increases this distance to 500m (1640.4 feet).

For LANs, coaxial cable offers several advantages. It can be run with fewer boosts from repeaters for longer distances between network nodes than either STP or UTP cable. Repeaters regenerate the signals in a network so that they can cover greater distances. Coaxial cable is less expensive than fiber-optic cable, and the technology is well known; it has been used for many years for all types of data communication.

When working with cable, you need to consider its size. As the thickness, or diameter, of the cable increases, so does the difficulty in working with it. Many times cable must be pulled through existing conduits and troughs that are limited in size. Coaxial cable comes in a variety of sizes. The largest diameter (1 centimeter [cm]) was specified for use as Ethernet backbone cable because historically it had greater transmission length and noise-rejection characteristics. This type of coaxial cable is frequently referred to as *Thicknet*. As its nickname suggests, Thicknet cable can be too rigid to install easily in some situations because of its thickness. The general rule is that the more difficult the network medium is to install, the more expensive it is to install. Coaxial cable is more expensive to install than twisted-pair cable. Thicknet cable is almost never used except for special-purpose installations.

A connection device known as a *vampire tap* was used to connect network devices to Thicknet. The vampire tap then was connected to the computers via a more flexible cable called the attachment unit interface (AUI). Although this 15-pin cable was still thick and tricky to terminate, it was much easier to work with than Thicknet.

In the past, coaxial cable with an outside diameter of only 0.35 cm (sometimes referred to as *Thinnet*) was used in Ethernet networks. Thinnet was especially useful for cable installations that required the cable to make many twists and turns. Because it was easier to install, it was also cheaper to install. Thus, it was sometimes referred to as *Cheapernet*. However, because the outer copper or metallic braid in coaxial cable comprises half the electrical circuit, special care had to be taken to ensure that it was properly grounded. Grounding was done by ensuring that a solid electrical connection existed at both ends of the cable. Frequently, however, installers failed to properly ground the cable. As a result, poor shield connection was one of the biggest sources of connection problems in the installation of coaxial cable. Connection problems resulted in electrical noise, which interfered with signal transmittal on the networking medium. For this reason, despite its small diameter, Thinnet no longer is commonly used in Ethernet networks.

The most common connectors used with Thinnet are BNC, short for British Naval Connector or Bayonet Neill Concelman, connectors (see Figure 8-5). The basic BNC connector is a male type mounted at each end of a cable. This connector has a center pin connected to the center cable conductor and a metal tube connected to the outer cable shield. A rotating ring outside the tube locks the cable to any female connector. BNC T-connectors are female devices for connecting two cables to a network interface card (NIC). A BNC barrel connector facilitates connecting two cables together.

Figure 8-5   *Thinnet and BNC Connector*

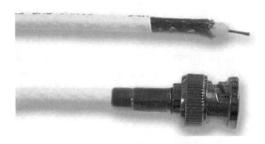

The following summarizes the features of coaxial cables:

- **Speed and throughput** — 10 to 100 Mbps

- **Average cost per node** — Inexpensive

- **Media and connector size** — Medium

- **Maximum cable length** — 500 m (medium)

Plenum Cable

Plenum cable is the cable that runs in plenum spaces of a building. In building construction, a plenum (pronounced PLEH-nuhm, from Latin meaning "full") is a separate space provided for air circulation for heating, ventilation, and air-conditioning (sometimes referred to as HVAC), typically in the space between the structural ceiling and a drop-down ceiling. In buildings with computer installations, the plenum space often is used to house connecting communication cables. Because ordinary cable introduces a toxic hazard in the event of fire, special plenum cabling is required in plenum areas.

In the United States, typical plenum cable sizes are AWG sizes 22 and 24. Plenum cabling often is made of Teflon and is more expensive than ordinary cabling. Its outer material is more resistant to flames and, when burning, produces less smoke than ordinary cabling. Both twisted-pair and coaxial cable are made in plenum cable versions.

Fiber-Optic Cable

Fiber-optic cable used for networking consists of two fibers encased in separate sheaths. If you were viewing it in a cross-section, you would see that each optical fiber is surrounded by layers of protective buffer material, usually a plastic shield, then a plastic such as Kevlar, and finally an outer jacket. The outer jacket provides protection for the entire cable, while the plastic conforms to appropriate fire and building codes. The Kevlar furnishes additional cushioning and protection for the fragile, hair-thin glass fibers (see Figure 8-6). Wherever buried fiber-optic cables are required by codes, a stainless-steel wire sometimes is included for added strength.

Figure 8-6 *Fiber-Optic Cable*

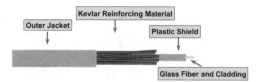

The light-guiding parts of an optical fiber are called the *core* and the *cladding*. The core is usually very pure glass with a high index of refraction. When a cladding layer of glass or plastic with a low index of refraction surrounds the core glass, light can be trapped in the fiber core. This process is called *total internal reflection*. It allows the optical fiber to act like a light pipe, guiding light for tremendous distances, even around bends. Fiber-optic cable is the most expensive of the four media discussed in this chapter, but it supports line speeds of more than 1 Gbps.

Two types of fiber-optic cable exist:

- **Single-mode**—Single-mode fiber cable allows only one mode (or wavelength) of light to propagate through the fiber. It is capable of higher bandwidth and greater distances than multimode, and it is often used for campus backbones. This type of fiber uses lasers as the light-generating method. Single-mode cable is much more expensive than multimode cable. Its maximum cable length is more than 10 km (32808.4 feet).

- **Multimode**—Multimode fiber cable allows multiple modes of light to propagate through the fiber. It is often used for workgroup applications and intrabuilding applications such as risers. It uses light-emitting diodes (LEDs) as a light-generating device. The maximum cable length is 2 km (6561.7 feet).

The characteristics of the different transport media have a significant impact on the speed of data transfer. Fiber-optic cable is a networking medium capable of conducting modulated light transmissions. Compared to other networking media, it is more expensive. However, it is not susceptible to EMI, and it is capable of higher data rates than any of the other types of networking media discussed in this chapter. Fiber-optic cable does not carry electrical impulses as other forms of networking media that use copper wire do. Instead, signals that represent bits are converted into beams of light.

NOTE   Even though light is an electromagnetic wave, light in fibers is not considered wireless because the electromagnetic waves are guided in the optical fiber. The term *wireless* is reserved for radiated, or unguided, electromagnetic waves.

Fiber-optic connectors come in single-mode and multimode varieties. The greatest difference between single-mode connectors and multimode connectors is the precision in the manufacturing process. The hole in the single-mode connector is slightly smaller than in the multimode connector. This ensures tighter tolerances in the assembly of the connector. The tighter tolerances make field assembly slightly more difficult.

A number of different types of fiber-optic connectors are used in the communications industry. The following list briefly describes two of the commonly used connectors:

- **SC**—SC type connectors feature a push-pull connect and disconnect method. To make a connection, the connector is simply pushed into the receptacle. To disconnect, the connector is simply pulled out.

- **ST**—ST fiber-optic connector is a bayonet type of connector. The connector is fully inserted into the receptacle and is then twisted in a clockwise direction to lock it into place (see Figure 8-7).

Figure 8-7   *ST Fiber-Optic Connector*

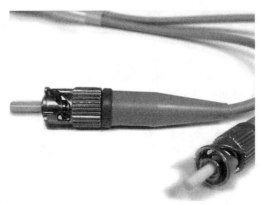

The following summarizes the features of fiber-optic cables:

- **Speed and throughput**—More than 1 Gbps
- **Average cost per node**—Expensive
- **Media and connector size**—Small
- **Maximum cable length**—More than 10 km for single mode; up to 2 km for multimode

Wireless Communication

Wireless communication uses radio frequencies (RF) or infrared (IR) waves to transmit data between devices on a LAN. For wireless LANs, a key component is the wireless hub, or access point, used for signal distribution (see Figure 8-8).

Figure 8-8   *Wireless Network*

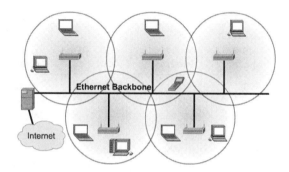

To receive the signals from the access point, a PC or laptop must install a wireless adapter card (wireless NIC). *Wireless signals* are electromagnetic waves that can travel through the vacuum of outer space and through a medium such as air. Therefore, no physical medium is necessary for wireless signals, making them a very versatile way to build a network. Wireless signals use portions of the RF spectrum to transmit voice, video, and data. Wireless frequencies range from 3 kilohertz (kHz) to 300 gigahertz (GHz). The data-transmission rates range from 9 kilobits per second (kbps) to as high as 54 Mbps.

The primary difference between electromagnetic waves is their frequency. Low-frequency electromagnetic waves have a long wavelength (the distance from one peak to the next on the sine wave), while high-frequency electromagnetic waves have a short wavelength.

Some common applications of wireless data communication include the following:

* Accessing the Internet using a cellular phone

* Establishing a home or business Internet connection over satellite

* Beaming data between two hand-held computing devices

* Using a wireless keyboard and mouse for the PC

Another common application of wireless data communication is the wireless LAN (WLAN), which is built in accordance with Institute of Electrical and Electronics Engineers (IEEE) 802.11 standards. WLANs typically use radio waves (for example, 902 megahertz [MHz]), microwaves (for example, 2.4 GHz), and IR waves (for example, 820 nanometers [nm]) for communication. Wireless technologies are a crucial part of the today's networking. See Chapter 28, "Wireless LANs," for a more detailed discuss on wireless networking.

Comparing Media Types

Presented in Table 8-1 are comparisons of the features of the common network media. This chart provides an overview of various media that you can use as a reference. The medium is possibly the single most important long-term investment made in a network. The choice of media type will affect the type of NICs installed, the speed of the network, and the capability of the network to meet future needs.

Table 8-1   *Media Type Comparison*

Media Type	Maximum Segment Length	Speed	Cost	Advantages	Disadvantages
UTP	100 m	10 Mbps to 1000 Mbps	Least expensive	Easy to install; widely available and widely used	Susceptible to interference; can cover only a limited distance
STP	100 m	10 Mbps to 100 Mbps	More expensive than UTP	Reduced crosstalk; more resistant to EMI than Thinnet or UTP	Difficult to work with; can cover only a limited distance
Coaxial	500 m (Thicknet) 185 m (Thinnet)	10 Mbps to 100 Mbps	Relatively inexpensive, but more costly than UTP	Less susceptible to EMI interference than other types of copper media	Difficult to work with (Thicknet); limited bandwidth; limited application (Thinnet); damage to cable can bring down entire network
Fiber-Optic	10 km and farther (single-mode) 2 km and farther (multimode)	100 Mbps to 100 Gbps (single mode) 100 Mbps to 9.92 Gbps (multimode)	Expensive	Cannot be tapped, so security is better; can be used over great distances; is not susceptible to EMI; has a higher data rate than coaxial and twisted-pair cable	Difficult to terminate

Summary

In this chapter, you learned the following key points:

- Coaxial cable consists of a hollow outer cylindrical conductor that surrounds a single inner wire conductor.

- UTP cable is a four-pair wire medium used in a variety of networks.

- STP cable combines the techniques of shielding, cancellation, and wire twisting.

- Fiber-optic cable is a networking medium capable of conducting modulated light transmission.

- Wireless signals are electromagnetic waves that can travel through the vacuum of outer space and through a medium such as air.

Review Exercises

1 What is the maximum cable length for STP?

   a. 100 feet

   b. 150 feet

   c. 100 meters

   d. 1000 meters

2 Which connector does UTP use?

   a. STP

   b. BNC

   c. RJ-45

   d. RJ-69

3 What is an advantage that coaxial cable has over STP or UTP?

   a. It is capable of achieving 10 Mbps to 100 Mbps.

   b. It is inexpensive.

   c. It can run for a longer distance unboosted.

   d. None of the above.

4 A _____ fiber-optic cable transmits multiple streams of LED-generated light.

   a. multimode

   b. multichannel

   c. multiphase

   d. None of the above

5 Wireless communication uses which of the following to transmit data between devices on a LAN?

   a. Radio frequencies

   b. LED-generated light

   c. Fiber optics

   d. None of the above

6 What is one advantage of using fiber-optic cable in networks?

   a. It is inexpensive.

   b. It is easy to install.

   c. It is an industry standard and is available at any electronics store.

   d. It is capable of higher data rates than either coaxial or twisted-pair cable.

Upon completing this chapter, you will be able to:

- Describe the LAN physical layer implementations

- Describe the main principle of implementing Ethernet in the campus LAN

- Identify different types of connectors specified for Ethernet use

- Describe the UTP wiring standards

CHAPTER 9

Cabling the LAN

The cabling aspect of the LAN exists at Layer 1 of the OSI reference model. To understand the types of cabling used to assemble and cable networking devices, you need to understand the LAN physical layer implementation of Ethernet, which is a LAN technology specified at the data link layer.

It is very important that you be able to identify the usages of different types of cable and to differentiate among the types of connectors that can be used to connect Ethernet.

This chapter addresses the LAN physical layer implementation and the main principle of implementing Ethernet in a campus LAN. This chapter also discusses the different types of connectors specified for Ethernet use as well as the UTP wiring standards.

LAN Physical Layer

Ethernet is the most widely used LAN technology. Ethernet was first implemented by a group called DIX (Digital, Intel, and Xerox). DIX created and implemented the first Ethernet LAN specification, which was used as the basis for the Institute of Electrical and Electronics Engineers (IEEE) 802.3 specification released in 1980. Later, the IEEE extended the 802.3 committee to three new committees known as 802.3u (Fast Ethernet), 802.3z (Gigabit Ethernet over Fiber), and 802.3ab (Gigabit Ethernet over UTP).

The cabling aspect of the LAN exists at Layer 1 of the Open System Interconnection (OSI) reference model. Many topologies support LANs as well as different physical media. Figure 9-1 shows a subset of physical layer implementations that you can deploy to support Ethernet.

Figure 9-1   *LAN Physical Layer Implementation*

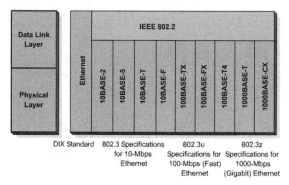

For a refresher on different Ethernet technologies, refer to Chapter 5, "Understanding Ethernet Technologies."

Ethernet in the Campus LAN

Given the variety of Ethernet speeds that you can deploy in the campus, you need to determine when, if, and where to upgrade to one or more of the Fast Ethernet implementations. With the correct hardware and cabling infrastructure, 10- or 100-Mbps Ethernet can be run anywhere in the network. As noted in Table 9-1, 10-Mbps Ethernet typically is implemented at the end-user level to connect to desktops, and faster technologies are used to interconnect network devices, such as routers and switches.

Table 9-1   *Ethernet Connectivity Recommendations*

	Ethernet 10BASE-T Position	Fast Ethernet Position	Gigabit Ethernet Position
End-user Level (End-user device to workgroup device)	Provides connectivity between the end-user device and the user-level switch.	Gives high-performance PC workstations 100-Mbps access to the server.	Not typically used at this level.
Workgroup Level (Workgroup device to backbone)	Not typically used at this level.	Provides connectivity between the end user and workgroups. Provides connectivity from the workgroup to backbone. Provides connectivity from the server block to the backbone layer.	Provides high-performance connectivity from the workgroup to backbone. Provides high-performance connectivity to the enterprise server.
Backbone Level	Not typically used at this level.	Provides interswitch connectivity for low- to medium-volume applications.	Provides backbone and interswitch connectivity.

In today's installations, although customers are considering providing Gigabit Ethernet from the backbone to the end user, costs for cabling and switch ports can make this prohibitive. Before making this decision, network requirements must be determined. For example, a network running at traditional Ethernet speeds of 10 Mbps can be easily overwhelmed with the new generation of multimedia, imaging, and database products.

In general, you can use Ethernet technologies in a campus LAN in several different ways:

- An Ethernet speed of 10-Mbps or 100-Mbps Fast Ethernet can be used at the user level to provide good performance. Also, 100-Mbps Fast Ethernet or Gigabit Ethernet can be used for clients or servers that consume high bandwidth.

- Fast Ethernet is often used as the link between the user-level and network devices, supporting the aggregate traffic from each Ethernet segment on the access link.

- Many client/server networks suffer from too many clients trying to access the same server, creating a bottleneck where the server attaches to the LAN. To enhance client/server performance across the campus LAN and avoid bottlenecks at the server, you can use Fast Ethernet or Gigabit Ethernet links to connect enterprise servers. Fast Ethernet or Gigabit Ethernet creates an effective solution for avoiding slow networks.

- You also can use Fast Ethernet links to provide the connection between the workgroup level and the backbone. Because the campus LAN model supports dual links between each workgroup router and backbone switch, you can load-balance the aggregate traffic from multiple-access switches across the links.

- You can use Fast Ethernet (or Gigabit Ethernet) between switches and the backbone. The fastest medium affordable should be implemented between backbone switches.

Ethernet Media and Connector Requirements

In addition to network need, and before selecting an Ethernet implementation, you must consider the media and connector requirements for each implementation. The cables and connector specifications used to support Ethernet implementations are derived from the Electronic Industries Association and Telecommunications Industry Association (EIA/TIA) standards body. The categories of cabling defined for the Ethernet are derived from the EIA/TIA-568 (SP-2840) Commercial Building Telecommunications Wiring Standards. The EIA/TIA specifies an RJ-45 connector for unshielded twisted-pair (UTP) cable. The letters "RJ" stand for "registered jack," and the number 45 refers to the physical connector that has eight conductors.

Table 9-2 compares the cable and connector specifications for the most popular Ethernet implementations. The important difference to note is the medium used for 10-Mbps Ethernet versus 100-Mbps and 1000-Mbps Ethernet. In today's networks, in which you will see a mix of 10- and 1000-Mbps requirements, you must be aware of the need to change over to UTP Category 5 to support Fast Ethernet.

Table 9-2 *Comparing Ethernet Media Requirements*

	10BASE2	10BASE5	10BASE-T	100BASE-TX	100BASE-FX	1000BASE-CX	1000BASE-T	1000BASE-SX	1000BASE-LX
Media	50-ohm coaxial (Thinnet)	50-ohm coaxial (Thicknet)	EIA/TIA Category 3, 4, 5 UTP, two pair	EIA/TIA Category 5 UTP, two pair	62.5/125 micro multimode fiber	STP	EIA/TIA Category 5 UTP, four pair	62.5/50 micro multimode fiber	62.5/50 micro multimode fiber; 9-micron single-mode fiber
Maximum Segment Length	185 m (606.94 feet)	500 m (1640.4 feet)	100 m (328 feet)	100 m (328 feet)	400 m (1312.3 feet)	25 m (82 feet)	100 m (328 feet)	275 m (853 feet) for 62.5 micro fiber; 550 m (1804.5 feet) for 50 micro fiber	440 m (1443.6 feet) for 62.5 micro fiber; 550 m (1804.5 feet) for 50 micro fiber; 3 to 10 km (1.86 to 6.2 miles)on single-mode fiber
Topology	Bus	Bus	Star	Star	Star	Star	Star	Star	Star
Connector	BNC	Attachment unit interface (AUI)	ISO 8877 (RJ-45)	ISO 8877 (RJ-45)	Duplex media interface connector (MIC) ST or SC connector	ISO 8877 (RJ-45)	ISO 8877 (RJ-45)	SC connector	SC connector

Figure 9-2 illustrates some of different connection types used by the physical layer implementation.

Figure 9-2   *Differentiating Among Connections*

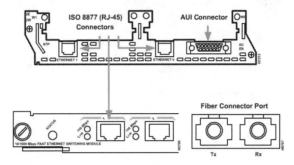

Connection Media

This section briefly discusses the connection types use by physical layer implementation and an interface device, GBIC, used between the Ethernet and fiber-optic systems. This section covers the following topics:

- **RJ-45**—A connector commonly used for finishing a twisted-pair cable
- **AUI**—A connector that interfaces between a computer's NIC and an Ethernet cable
- **GBIC**—A device used as an interface between the Ethernet and fiber-optic systems

RJ-45

The RJ-45 connector and jack are the most prevalent. RJ-45 connectors are discussed in more detail in the section "UTP Implementation."

Attachment Unit Interface

In some cases, the type of connector on a NIC does not match the type of media that it needs to connect to. As shown in Figure 9-2, an interface exists for the attachment unit interface (AUI) connector. The AUI is the 15-pin physical connector interface between a computer's NIC and Ethernet cable. On 10BASE5 (Thicknet) Ethernet, a short cable is used to connect the AUI on the computer with a transceiver on the main cable. In 10BASE2 (Thinnet) Ethernet networks, the NIC connects directly to the Ethernet coaxial cable at the back of the computer.

Gigabit Interface Converter

A *Gigabit Interface Converter (GBIC)* is a hot-swappable input/output device that plugs into a Gigabit Ethernet port. A key benefit of using GBIC is that GBICs are interchangeable. This gives users the flexibility to deploy other 1000BASE-X technology without needing to change the physical interface/module on the router or switch.

The fiber-optic GBIC is a transceiver that converts serial electric currents to optical signals and that also coverts optical signals to digital electric currents. Some of the optical GBICs include the following:

- Short wavelength (1000BASE-SX)
- Long wavelength/long haul (1000BASE-LX/LH)
- Extended distance (1000BASE-ZX)

Typically, the GBIC is used as an interface between the Ethernet and fiber-optic systems, such as Fibre Channel and Gigabit Ethernet. Figure 9-3 shows a photograph of the Cisco Catalyst 6000 series Supervisor with GBICs, and Figure 9-4 shows a Cisco WS-X2931 Gigabit Ethernet Module with the GBIC out.

Figure 9-3   *Catalyst 6000 Series Supervisor with GBICs*

Figure 9-4   *Cisco WS-X2931 Gigabit Ethernet Module with GBIC Out*

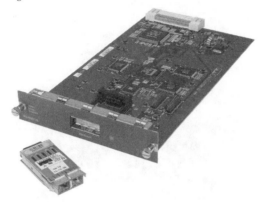

UTP Implementation

If you look at the RJ-45 transparent end connector, you can see eight colored wires. These wires are twisted into four pairs. Four of the wires (two pairs) carry the positive, or true, voltage and are considered "tip" (T1 through T4); the other four wires carry the inverse, or false, voltage grounded and are called "ring" (R1 through R4). *Tip* and *ring* are terms that originated in the early days of the telephone. Today these terms refer to the positive and the negative wire in a pair. The wires in the first pair in a cable or a connector are designated as T1 and R1, the second pair is T2 and R2, and so on.

The RJ-45 plug is the male component, crimped at the end of the cable. As you look at the male connector from the front, the pin locations are numbered from 8 on the left down to 1 on the right (see Figure 9-5). The jack is the female component in a network device, wall or cubicle partition outlet, or patch panel. As you look at the device port, the corresponding female pin locations are 1 on the left up to 8 on the right (see Figure 9-6). For electricity to run between the connector and the jack, the order of the wires must follow EIA/TIA-568-A and EIA/TIA-568-B standards, as shown in Figure 9-7.

Figure 9-5   *RJ-45 Plug*

Figure 9-6   *RJ-45 Jack*

Figure 9-7   *EIA/TIA 568 Standards*

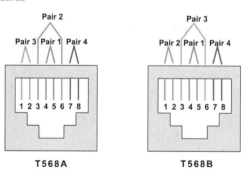

In addition to identifying the correct EIA/TIA category of cable to use for a connecting device (this depends on what standard is being used by the jack on the network device), you will need to determine which of the following to use:

- **A straight-through cable**—A cable that maintains the pin connection all the way through the cable. Thus, the wire connected to pin 1 is the same on both ends of the cable.

- **A crossover cable**—A cable that crosses the critical pair to properly align, transmit, and receive signals on the device with line connections.

If the two RJ-45 ends of a cable are held side by side in the same orientation, the colored wires (or strips or pins) will be seen at each connector end. If the order of the colored wires is the same at each end, the cable is straight-through. Figure 9-8 illustrates that the RJ-45 connectors on both ends show all the wires in the same order.

Specified for Ethernet, in a Category 5 UTP cable, only wires 1, 2, 3, and 6 are used for transmit (TD) and receive (RD) signals. The other four wires are not used. As shown on the left of Figure 9-8, in a straight-through cable, the RJ-45 pins 1, 2, 3, and 6 at one end are connected to pins 1, 2, 3, and 6 at the other end of the connection.

Figure 9-8   *UTP Implementation—Straight-Through*

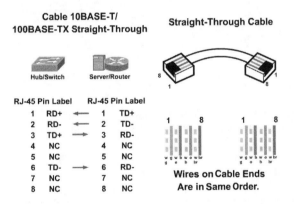

You can use a straight-through cable to connect devices such as PCs or routers to other devices used as hubs or switches. As Figure 9-9 shows, you should use straight-through when only one port is designated with an *x*.

With crossover cable, the RJ-45 connectors on both ends show that some of the wires on one side of the cable are crossed to a different pin on the other side of the cable. Specifically for Ethernet, pin 1 at one RJ-45 end should be connected to pin 3 at the other end. Pin 2 at one end should be connected to pin 6 at the other end, as shown in Figure 9-10.

Figure 9-9 *Interconnecting Devices Using Straight-Through Cable*

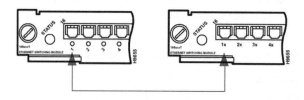

Figure 9-10 *UTP Implementation—Crossover*

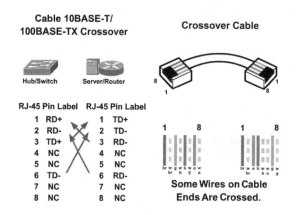

You can use a crossover cable to connect similar devices, switch to switch or switch to hub. Figure 9-11 shows that you should use a crossover cable when both ports are designated with an *x* or when neither port is designated with an *x*.

Figure 9-11 *Interconnecting Devices Using Crossover Cable*

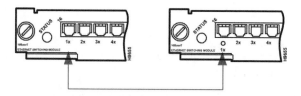

The following are the guidelines for the type of cable to use when interconnecting networking devices.

Use straight-through cables for the following cabling:

- Switch to router

- Switch to PC or server

- Hub to PC or server

Use crossover cables for the following cabling:

- Switch to switch

- Switch to hub

- Hub to hub

- Router to router

- PC to PC

- Router to PC

Cabling the Campus

Figure 9-12 illustrates how a variety of cable types might be required in a given network. Note that the category of UTP required is based on the type of Ethernet that you choose to implement. In general, you must determine the physical medium used—10 Mbps, 100 Mbps, or 1000 Mbps. This indicates what category of cable is required. Finally, locate the interface and determine whether you need a crossover or straight-through cable.

Figure 9-12   *Cabling the Campus*

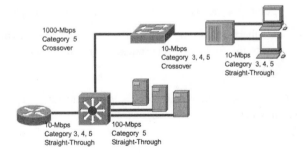

Summary

In this chapter, you learned the following key points:

- The three principle LAN implementation categories are Ethernet, Fast Ethernet, and Gigabit Ethernet.

- Use a crossover cable to connect between similar devices (switch to switch, router to router, PC to PC, and hub to hub).

- Use a straight-through cable to connect between dissimilar devices (switch to router, switch to PC, hub to router, and hub to PC).

- A Gigabit Interface Converter (GBIC) is a hot-swappable input/output device that plugs into a Gigabit Ethernet port.

Review Exercises

1 Which of the following is an 802.3u specification?

   a. 10BASE-F

   b. 10BASE-T

   c. 100BASE-TX

   d. 1000BASE-CX

2 Which of the following is the most appropriate choice for Ethernet connectivity?

   a. Use 10-Mbps Ethernet as a connection between server and LAN.

   b. Use Gigabit Ethernet as the link at the user level to provide good performance.

   c. Use Fast Ethernet as a link between the user level and network devices to support the aggregate traffic from each Ethernet segment on the access link.

   d. None of the above.

3 Which standards body created the cables and connector specification used to support Ethernet implementation?

   a. ISO

   b. ANSI

   c. EIA/TIA

   d. IETF

4 Which of the following statements does *not* correctly describe a media connector?

  a. An RJ-45 connector is an 8-pin connector used mainly for terminating coaxial cable.

  b. An AUI is a 15-pin connector used between a NIC and an Ethernet cable.

  c. The GBIC is a transceiver that converts serial electric currents to optical signals, and vice versa.

  d. None of the above.

5 For which of the following would you *not* need to provide a crossover cable?

  a. Connecting uplinks between switches

  b. Connecting routers to switches

  c. Connecting hubs to switches

  d. None of the above

Upon completing this chapter, you will be able to:

- Describe the WAN physical layer implementations
- Identify the different types of WAN serial connections
- Describe how to cable routers for serial connections
- Describe how to cable routers for ISDN BRI connections
- Describe how to cable routers for DSL connections
- Describe how to cable routers for cable connections
- Describe how to set up console connections for Cisco devices

CHAPTER 10

Cabling the WAN

To connect one network to other remote networks, it is sometimes necessary to utilize wide-area network (WAN) services. WAN services provide different connection methods, and the cabling standards differ from those of LANs. It is therefore important to understand the types of cabling needed to connect to these services.

This chapter explains the cabling and connectors that are used to interconnect switches and routers in a LAN or WAN. This chapter also discusses how to cable routers for serial connection, ISDN BRI connection, DSL connection, and cable connection, as well as how to set up console connection.

WAN Physical Layer

Many physical implementations carry traffic across the WAN. Needs vary, depending on the distance of the equipment from the services, the speed, and the actual service itself. Figure 10-1 lists a subset of physical implementations that support some of the more prominent WAN solutions today. The type of physical layer you will choose depends on the distance, speed, and the type of interface in which you need to connect.

Figure 10-1   *WAN Physical Layer Implementations*

Cisco High-level Data Link Control (HDLC)	PPP	Frame Relay	ISDN BRI (with PPP)	DSL Modem	Cable Modem
EIA/TIA-232 EIA/TIA-449 X.21 V.24 V.35			RJ-45 *Note:* ISDN BRI Cable Pinouts Are Different than the Pinouts for Ethernet	RJ-11 *Note:* Works over Telephone Line	F *Note:* Works over Cable TV Line

Serial connections are used to support WAN services such as dedicated leased lines that run the Point-to-Point Protocol (PPP) or Frame Relay. The speed of these connections ranges from 2400 bits per second (bps) to T1 (1.544 megabits per second [Mbps]).

Other WAN services, such as the ISDN, offer dial-on-demand connections or dial-backup services. An ISDN Basic Rate Interface (BRI) is composed of two 64-kbps bearer channels

(B channels) for data, and one delta channel (D channel) at 16 kilobits per second (kbps) used for signaling and other link-management tasks. PPP typically is used to carry data over the B channels.

With the increasing demand for residential broadband (high-speed) services, digital subscriber line (DSL) and cable modem connections are becoming more popular. For example, typical residential DSL service can offer a speed of up to 1.5 Mbps over the existing telephone line. Cable services, which work over the existing coaxial cable TV line, also offer high-speed connectivity matching or surpassing that of DSL. DSL is discussed in more detail in Chapter 25, "Digital Subscriber Line (DSL)," and cable modems are covered in Chapter 26, "Cable Modems."

WAN Serial Connections

Serial transmission is a method of data transmission in which bits of data are transmitted over a single channel. This one-at-a-time transmission contrasts with parallel data transmission, which transmits several bits at a time. For long-distance communication, WANs use serial transmission. To carry the energy represented in bits, serial channels use a specific electromagnetic or optical frequency range.

Frequencies, described in terms of their cycles per second (hertz), function as a band or spectrum for communication. For example, the signals transmitted over voice-grade telephone lines use up to 3 kHz (kilohertz, or thousand hertz). The size of this frequency range is called the *bandwidth*.

Another way to express bandwidth is to specify the amount of data in bits per second that the serial channel can carry.

Table 10-1 compares physical standards for EIA/TIA-232 and EIA/TIA-449, V.35, X.21, and EIA-530 WAN serial connection options.

Table 10-1 *Comparison of Physical Standards*

Data bps	Distance (Meters) EIA/TIA-232	Distance (Meters) EIA/TIA-449, V.35, X.21, EIA-530
2400	60	1250
4800	30	625
9600	15	312
19,200	15	156
38,400	15	78
115,200	3.7	—
T1 (1.544 Mbps)	—	15

Several types of physical connections enable you to connect to serial WAN services. You must select the correct serial cable type to use with the router, depending on the physical implementation that you choose or the physical implementation that your service provider imposes. Figure 10-2 shows all the different serial connector options available. Serial connectors are used to connect end-user devices and service providers. Note that serial ports on Cisco routers use a proprietary 60-pin connector or smaller "smart serial" connector, which enables two serial connections on a WAN interface card. The type of connector on the other end of the cable is dependent on the service provider or end-device requirements.

Figure 10-2   *WAN Serial Connection Options*

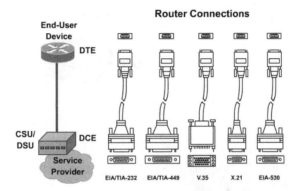

Routers and Serial Connections

In addition to determining the cable type, you will need to determine whether you need data terminal equipment (DTE) or data communications equipment (DCE) connectors for your equipment. The DTE is the endpoint of the user's device on the WAN link. The DCE is the device used to convert the user data from the DTE into a form acceptable to the facility providing WAN services.

As shown in Figure 10-3, if connecting directly to a service provider or to a device that will perform signal clocking (such as a channel service unit/data service unit [CSU/DSU]), the router is a DTE and needs a DTE serial cable. This is typically the case for routers.

NOTE   *Clocking* is a method used to synchronize data transmission between devices. In a WAN serial connection, the CSU/DSU controls the clocking of the transmitted data.

Figure 10-3   *Serial Implementation of DTE and DCE*

However, in some cases the router must be the DCE. For example, if performing a back-to-back router scenario (meaning that routers are used at both ends of the connection) in a test environment, one of the routers will be a DTE and the other will be a DCE (see Figure 10-4).

Figure 10-4   *Back-to-Back Serial Connection*

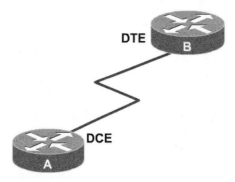

When you are cabling routers for serial connectivity, the routers will have either fixed or modular ports. The type of port being used affects the syntax that you use later to configure each interface.

Figure 10-5 shows an example of a router with fixed serial ports (interfaces). Each port is given a label of port type and port number—for example, serial 0. To configure a fixed interface, you specify the interface using the port type and port number convention.

Figure 10-6 shows examples of routers with modular serial ports. Usually each port is given a label of port type, slot (the location of the module), and port number. To configure a port on a modular card, you are asked to specify the interface using the convention "port type slot number/port number"—for example, serial 1/0, in which the type of interface is a serial interface, the slot number where the serial interface module is installed is slot 1, and the specific port that you are referencing on that serial interface module is port 0.

Figure 10-5   *Fixed Interfaces*

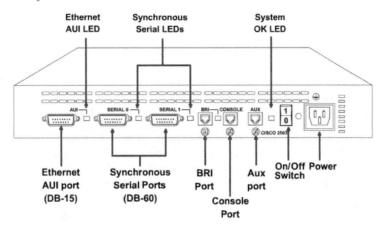

Figure 10-6   *Modular Serial Port Interfaces*

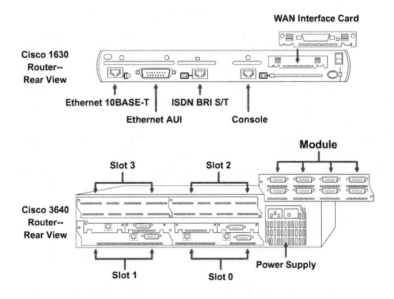

Routers and ISDN BRI Connections

With ISDN BRI, you can use two types of interfaces: BRI S/T and BRI U. In ISDN BRI service, a user (U) interface is the electrical interface for the twisted-pair wire connection from a user to a Network Termination 1 (NT1) device. A terminal (T) interface is the electrical interface between an NT1 device and an NT 2 device, which is usually a private branch exchange (PBX).

A system (S) interface is the electrical interface between an NT1 and ISDN devices such as a computer or a telephone. In BRI, the T interface is electrically identical to the S interface. Thus, the two interfaces are typically combined in a single interface, referenced as an S/T interface.

To determine which interface type you need, you must determine whether you or the service provider will provide an NT1 device. An NT1 device is an intermediate device between the router and the service-provider ISDN switch (cloud) that is used to connect four-wire subscriber wiring to the conventional two-wire local loop. In North America, the customer typically provides the NT1; in the rest of the world, the service provider provides the NT1 device.

If the NT1 device needs to be provided by the customer, an ISDN BRI with a U interface can be used. A U interface has an NT1 built in. If an external NT1 device is used, or if the service provider uses an NT1 device, the router needs an ISDN BRI S/T interface. Because routers can have multiple ISDN interface types, the interface needed must be determined when the router is purchased. The type of ISDN connector that the router has can be determined by looking at the port label. Figure 10-7 shows the different port types for the ISDN interface.

Figure 10-7   *Cabling Routers for ISDN Connections*

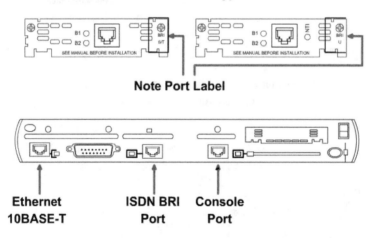

To interconnect the ISDN BRI port to the service-provider device, use a UTP Category 5 straight-through cable with RJ-45 connectors. Note that the ISDN BRI cable pinouts are different than the pinouts for Ethernet. Table 10-2 shows the ISDN BRI S/T interface connector pinouts.

CAUTION   It is important to insert a cable running from an ISDN BRI port only to an ISDN jack or an ISDN switch. ISDN BRI uses voltages that can seriously damage non-ISDN devices.

Table 10-2   *SDN BRI S/T Interface Connector Pinouts*

Pin	Signal
1	Unused
2	Unused
3	Transmit (Tx+)
4	Receive (Rx+)
5	Receive (Rx-)
6	Transmit (Tx-)
7	Unused
8	Unused

Routers and DSL Connections

DSL technology is a modem technology that enables inexpensive, high-speed digital transmission over existing twisted-pair telephone lines. For most small offices or home offices today, DSL technology is a good choice for many business applications such as file transfer and access to a corporate Intranet. Asymmetric Digital Subscriber Line (ADSL) is part of a larger family of DSL technologies generically referred to as *xDSL*.

The Cisco 800 series of fixed-configuration routers provides enhanced security, low cost of ownership, proven reliability, and safe investment through the power of Cisco IOS Software tailored for small offices and telecommuters.

The Cisco 827-4V ADSL router has one ADSL interface (see Figure 10-8) that can connect users to the Internet or to a corporate LAN via DSL.

Figure 10-8   *Cisco 827-4V Router*

To connect an ADSL line to the ADSL port on a router, perform the following simple steps:

Step 1   Connect the phone cable to the ADSL port on the router.

Step 2   Connect the other end of the phone cable to the external wall phone jack.

To connect a router for DSL service, you will need a phone cable with RJ-11 connectors. DSL works over standard telephone lines. It uses only two pins on the RJ-11 connector, as shown in Table 10-3.

Table 10-3   *Telephone Connector Pinouts (RJ-11)*

Pin	Signal
1	Unused
2	Unused
3	Transmit (Tx)
4	Receive (Rx)
5	Unused
6	Unused

NOTE   If you are connecting non-DSL devices to a phone line with DSL service, you need to install a filter to prevent interference between data and voice services.

Routers and Cable Connections

Cable modems enable two-way, high-speed data transmissions using the same coaxial lines that transmit cable television. Some cable service providers are promising data speeds up to six and a half times that of T1 leased lines. With the demand for broadband services, cable modem connection is becoming more popular.

Cisco's uBR905 cable access router provides high-speed network access on the cable television system to residential and small office, home office (SOHO) subscribers. The uBR905 router has a coaxial cable (F-connector) interface that can be connected to a cable system. Coaxial cable and an F connector are used to connect the router and cable system. The coaxial cable may be either radio grade 59 (RG-59) or RG-6, although RG-6 is recommended.

To connect the Cisco uBR905 cable access router to the cable system, follow these steps:

Step 1   Verify that the router is not connected to power.

Step 2   Locate the radio frequency (RF) coaxial cable coming from the coaxial cable CATV wall outlet.

NOTE   RF coaxial cable is used to connect RF to antennas. The majority of cable TV systems use coaxial cable as their wiring system. The main trunk lines that run from the cable provider to a neighborhood distribution boxes may be fiber-optic, but coaxial cables are likely to be used in runs between the distribution boxes and the end user.

Step 3   Install a cable splitter/directional coupler, if needed, to separate signals for TV and computer use (see Figure 10-9). If necessary, also install a high-pass filter to prevent interference between the TV and computer signals.

Figure 10-9   *Two-Way Splitter*

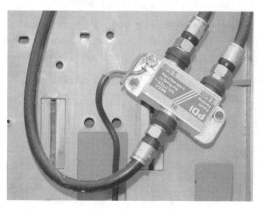

Step 4   Connect the coaxial cable to the F connector of the router (see Figure 10-10). Hand-tighten the connector, making sure that it is finger-tight, and then give it a 1/6 turn with a wrench.

Figure 10-10 *Connecting a Coaxial Cable to an ADSL Router*

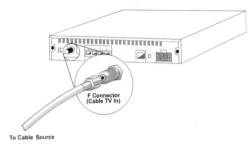

Step 5 Make sure that all other coaxial cable connectors—all intermediate splitters, couplers, or ground blocks—are securely tightened from the distribution tap to the Cisco uBR905 router, following the instructions in Step 4.

CAUTION Do not overtighten the connector; doing so can break off the connector. Use of a torque wrench is not recommended because of the danger of tightening the connector more than the recommended 1/6 turn after it is finger-tight.

Setting Up Console Connections

To initially configure your Cisco device, you will need to provide a management connection directly to the device. For Cisco equipment, this management attachment is called a *console port*. The console port enables you to monitor and configure a Cisco hub, switch, or router.

The cable used between a terminal and a console port is a *rollover cable* with RJ-45 connectors, as illustrated in Figure 10-11.

Figure 10-11 *Setting Up a Console Connection*

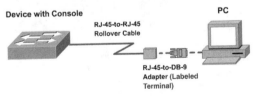

The rollover cable, also known as a *console cable*, has a different pinout than the straight-through or crossover RJ-45 cables used with Ethernet or the ISDN BRI. The pinout for a rollover is as follows:

1 to 8

2 to 7

3 to 6

4 to 5

5 to 4

6 to 3

7 to 2

8 to 1

To set up a connection between your terminal and the Cisco console port, you must perform the following steps:

Step 1 Cable the devices using a rollover cable. You might need an RJ-45-to-DB-9 or an RJ-45-to-DB-25 adapter for your PC or terminal.

Step 2 Configure your terminal emulation application with the following common equipment (COM) port settings:

- 9600 bps
- 8 data bits
- No parity
- 1 stop bit
- No flow control

NOTE   The AUX port is used to provide remote management through a modem. The AUX port must be configured using the console port before it can be used. The AUX port also uses the settings of 9600 bps, 8 data bits, no parity, 1 stop bit, and no flow control. The speed can be set up to 38,400 bps.

Summary

In this chapter, you learned the following key points:

- WANs use serial data transmission.

- A router is usually the DTE and needs a DTE serial cable to connect to a DCE device such as a CSU/DSU.

- The ISDN BRI has two types of interfaces: S/T and U. To interconnect the ISDN BRI port to the service-provider device, a UTP Category 5 straight-through cable is used.

- A phone cable and an RJ-11 connector are used to connect a router for DSL service.

- Coaxial cable and an F connector are used to connect a router for cable service.

- Rollover cable is used to connect a terminal and the console port of a router.

Review Exercises

1   Which of the following is not a physical WAN implementation?

  a. DSL

  b. ISDN

  c. Frame Relay

  d. Ethernet

2   What type of data-transmission method is used by a WAN?

  a. Parallel

  b. Serial

  c. Single

  d. None of above

3   What best describes a DCE?

  a. User device at the end of a network

  b. Equipment that serves as the data source or destination

  c. Physical devices such as protocol translators and multiplexers

  d. Devices that make up the network end of the user-to-network interface

4 Which of the following media is used to interconnect the ISDN BRI port to the service-provider device?

a. Category 5 UTP straight-through

b. Category 5 UTP crossover

c. Coaxial

d. Fiber-optic

5 What type of connector is used for DSL connection?

a. RJ-45

b. RJ-11

c. F

d. DB-9

6 What type of connector is used to connect a router and a cable system?

a. RJ-45

b. RJ-11

c. F

d. AUI

7 What type of cable is used to connect a terminal and a console port?

a. Straight-through

b. Rollover

c. Crossover

d. Coaxial

PART IV

Switching Fundamentals

Upon completing this chapter, you will be able to:

- Identify traditional LAN technology
- Identify the problems when using a hub in a network
- Define a collision in an Ethernet LAN
- Identify the features of hub-based network
- Identify the features of a bridge-based network
- Identify the features of a switch-based network
- Compare and contrast the features of switched-based and hub-based networks
- Identify the typical causes of network congestion
- Describe the features of today's LAN

CHAPTER 11

Shared LAN Technology

Nowadays, network designers are moving away from using hubs and bridges and primarily are using switches and routers to build networks. This chapter discusses the basic concepts and problems of traditional hub-based LANs, bridge-based LANs, and switch-based LAN.

In this chapter, you also learn about LAN congestion, its effect on network performance, and the advantage of LAN segmentation in a network. In addition, this chapter discusses the advantages and disadvantages of using bridges and switches for LAN segmentation.

Early Local-Area Networks

The earliest local-area network (LAN) technologies that were installed widely were either Thicknet (10BASE5) or Thinnet (10BASE2) infrastructures. It is important to understand some of the limitations of these infrastructures to see where LAN switching stands today. The early Thicknet installations had some important limitations, such as distance. Early Thicknet networks were limited to only 500 m (1640.4 feet) before the signal degraded. For distances beyond that, repeaters were required to boost and amplify that signal.

Limitations also were placed on the number of stations and servers that could be on a network, as well as on the placement of those workstations on the network. The cable itself was relatively expensive. It was also large in diameter, making it difficult to install throughout the building because it had to be pulled through the walls and ceilings. Adding new users was relatively difficult. A vampire tap had to be added at the correct location on the cable to avoid reflections, and the tap was intrusive and could damage the cable and bring down the whole infrastructure if not done correctly. The Thicknet network provided a capacity of 10 megabits per second (Mbps), but this bandwidth was shared among all users on a given segment.

A slight improvement to Thicknet was Thinnet technology, commonly referred to as Cheapernet because this technology was less expensive. Thinnet also required less space in terms of installation than Thicknet because it was thinner in diameter. It was still relatively challenging to install because it sometimes required a direct run from a workstation back to a hub or concentrator. Adding users required a momentary interruption in the network because a cable segment had to be broken to add a new server or workstation. Thinnet networks were limited to only 185 m (606.9 feet) before the signal degraded. Table 11-1 compares Thicknet and Thinnet.

Table 11-1 *Thicknet Versus Thinnet*

Thick Ethernet	Thin Ethernet
Relatively expensive and large in diameter	Less expensive and requires less space than thick Ethernet
Requires repeaters every 500 m	Requires repeaters every 185 m
Limitations on number and placement of stations	Limitations on number and placement of stations
Difficult to pull through buildings	Difficult to pull through buildings
Adding users is relatively difficult	Adding users requires network interruption
Provides 10-Mbps shared bandwidth	Provides 10-Mbps shared bandwidth

Hubs

Adding hubs, or concentrators, into the network offered an improvement on Thinnet and Thicknet technology. Hubs sometimes are referred to as *Ethernet concentrators* or *Ethernet repeaters*. Hubs, operating at Layer 1, are basically self-contained Ethernet segments within a box. As shown in Figure 11-1, Ethernet is fundamentally a shared technology, meaning that all users of a given LAN segment compete for the same amount of bandwidth. This situation is analogous to cars all trying to get onto the same one-lane freeway at once. Because the freeway has only one lane, only one car can get on the freeway at any one time. In the network, even though each device has its own cable segment that connects into the hub, they all share the same fixed amount of bandwidth. Frames, or packets, in a network all compete for bandwidth. Only one station can transmit at any one time.

Figure 11-1 *Shared Bandwidth with Hubs*

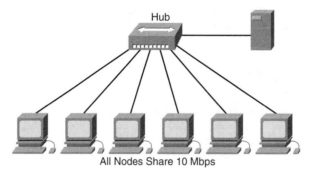

Hub

All Nodes Share 10 Mbps

Although physically it looks like all the users have their own segment to their workstation, they are all interconnected inside the hub. Therefore, the hub is a shared Ethernet technology.

Each individual workstation or server in the network has an individual desktop connection, allowing centralization of all cabling back to a wiring closet. This setup makes any adds, moves, and changes easier because cables can just be moved around in the wiring closet.

Hubs also are passive, meaning that they are virtually transparent to the end users. Working like a repeater, a hub amplifies incoming data signals and propagates the signals to entire network, regardless of whether the data needs to go there. In addition, hubs do not filter or switch network traffic, nor do they provide any segmentation within the network because they work at Layer 1 in the OSI framework. A hub-based LAN offers very little security because on a hub or concentrator, all traffic in the network is available on all ports.

In a hub-based network, the physical hub plugged into a router determines the workgroup segment. A router can be used to interconnect the hubs to separate the workgroup segments into different subnetworks at Layer 3. This is analogous to creating two separate freeways: one freeway for the users on the first floor, and another freeway for the users on the second floor. The router is used to interconnect the traffic flow between the two freeways (see Figure 11-2).

Figure 11-2   *Hub-Based LANs*

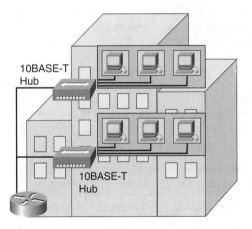

Collisions

Collisions are by-products of an Ethernet network. In an Ethernet network, many stations share the same segment (they are on the same collision domain), so any one of these stations can transmit at any given time. If two or more stations try to transmit at the same time, a collision results (see Figure 11-3). This situation is analogous to two cars merging onto a single lane at the same time, resulting in a collision and backing up all traffic behind the collision until the collision can be cleared.

Figure 11-3 *Collisions*

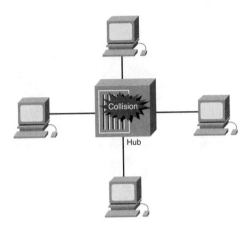

When the number of collisions in the network becomes excessive (for example, more than 100 collisions per second), sluggish network response times result, indicating that the network is becoming too congested or that too many users are on the same segment. An increasing number of user complaints, such as "File transfers take forever," "I could have walked to Finance by now," or "I'm waiting all the time," reported to the network manager is a good indication that the network is sluggish.

Transmission Ways

Understanding how transmissions can occur in the network is important because each transmission method has a different impact on the network data flow. As illustrated in Figure 11-4, LAN data transmission falls into three classifications:

- **Unicast transmissions**—Unicast is the most common method of transmission. In a unicast transmission, one transmitter tries to reach one receiver.

- **Broadcast transmissions**—In broadcast transmission, one transmitter tries to reach all the receivers in the network. As shown in Figure 11-4, the server station is sending out one message and everyone on that segment is receiving it.

- **Multicast transmissions**—In multicast transmission, one transmitter tries to reach only a subset, or a group, of the entire segment. Multicast is based on the concept of a group. A *multicast group* consists of hosts that have joined the group and want to receive traffic sent to this group. As shown in Figure 11-4, the transmitter reaches two stations, the other two workstations do not participate, so they are not in the multicast group.

Figure 11-4   *Transmission Methods*

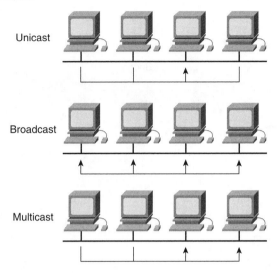

Unicast

Broadcast

Multicast

Bridges

Segmentation is used to scale networks. One way to scale hub-based networks is to add routers. Another way is to add bridges, which provide segmentation by adding intelligence into the network.

Bridges operate at Layer 2, whereas hubs operate at Layer 1. Operating at Layer 2 offers the capability to make forwarding decisions. Bridges are more intelligent than hubs because bridges can listen in on the traffic going through, analyze incoming frame packets, and forward (or drop) them based on Media Access Control address information. Bridges can look at source and destination Media Access Control (MAC) addresses, and they can build a MAC address table that enables them to make forwarding decisions at Layer 2. Bridges actually collect and pass frames between two network segments. As a result, bridges can provide greater control of the traffic within a network.

Unlike the hub, in which all ports on the hub belong to the same collision domain, the ports on the bridge belong to separate collision domains. In Figure 11-5, the bridge has two ports. Stations 123, 124, and 125 are on one collision domain, and stations 126 and 127 are on a different collision domain. Therefore, station 126 can transmit to station 127 while station 123 is transmitting to station 124. However, station 126 and station 127 cannot transmit at the same time because they are on the same collision domain. Stations 126 and 127 are connected to the same port on the bridge using a hub.

Figure 11-5 *Bridges*

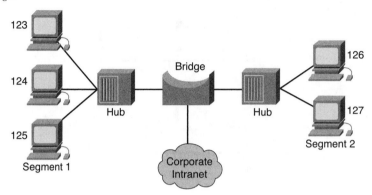

Layer 2 Switches

Like bridges, switches function at Layer 2. However, with switches, frame forwarding is handled by specialized hardware called application-specific integrated circuits (ASICs). The ASIC technology engineered for switches allows for scalability up to gigabit speeds, with low latency at a cost significantly less than that of Ethernet bridges. With bridges, frame forwarding is handled in software. Switches also have more advanced features than bridges, including the following:

- **High-speed backplane**—Backplane is a printed circuit board that provides internal busing to distribute data, clocking, and power among the various modules. A switch has a high-speed backplane and enables multiple simultaneous conversations to occur by forwarding several packets over the switch backplane at the same time, thereby increasing network capacity by the number of conversations supported.

- **Data-buffering capabilities**—Buffer is a memory storage area used for handling data in transit. A LAN switch uses a buffering technique to store and forward packets to the correct port or ports. The area of memory where the switch stores the destination and transmission data is called the *memory buffer*.

- **Higher port density**—Port density refers to the number of available ports on a device. A switch can have more than 100 Fast Ethernet ports available.

- **Lower latency**—Latency, sometimes called *propagation delay*, is the time that a frame, or packet, of data takes to travel from the source station or node to its final destination on the network. LAN switches have lower latency than routers.

As shown in Figure 11-6 the model of traffic going through the network has been improved. Returning to the traffic analogy, the main highway has been subdivided so that each car appears to have its own lane to drive in on the highway. Fundamentally, this functionality can be provided in data networks as well. In a switched-based LAN, each workstation is directly connected to one of the switch ports or to a segment that is connected to a switch's port.

Figure 11-6   *Layer 2 Switches*

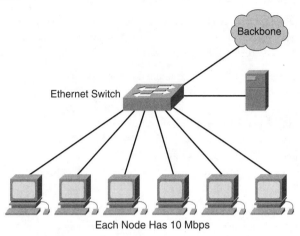

Each Node Has 10 Mbps

Then, with functionality known as *microsegmentation*, each workstation gets its own dedicated segment (collision domain) to the switch. Microsegmentation and data buffering within the switch enable the travel of multiple, simultaneous conversations through the switch at any given time (see Figure 11-7).

Figure 11-7   *Segmentation with LAN Switches*

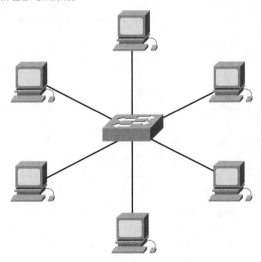

Remember that if two stations try to communicate in a hubbed environment, collisions will result. However, in a switched environment the number of collisions is minimized because each workstation has its own dedicated path (collision domain) through the network. With switches, the network has dramatically more effective bandwidth, and each station has a dedicated 10-Mbps worth of bandwidth.

Typical Causes of Network Congestion

How do congestion problems manifest themselves in a network? Remember that shared LAN segments have a fixed amount of bandwidth. As users are added, the amount of bandwidth per user decreases. The result is collisions, and collisions reduce performance.

Now consider the newer technologies used in workstations. With early LAN technologies, workstations were relatively limited in terms of the amount of traffic that could be delivered to the network. However, with faster CPUs, faster buses, faster peripherals, and so on, it is much easier for a single workstation to fill up a network segment. With faster PCs, network applications can be better used, but at the expense of available bandwidth. In particular, bandwidth-intensive applications that are used today, such as desktop publishing, engineering applications, imaging applications, and even multimedia applications, deplete available bandwidth faster than ever.

Another cause of network congestion is excessive broadcast or multicast traffic. LAN switches do not block the broadcast traffic. Therefore, when receiving a broadcast message, LAN switches forward the message to all the ports except the port on which it came in. Broadcasts are used by most networking protocols to provide a mechanism for providing all interested network devices with information such as where a specific service is and what route to take to reach that service. Performance of lower-end network stations can be adversely affected when the number of broadcasts per second reaches 100 or so. But even higher-performance systems experience an increase in processor utilization as the number of broadcasts increases.

When many broadcasts are sent simultaneously across all network segments, it is called a *broadcast storm*. A broadcast storm uses substantial network bandwidth and typically causes network timeouts.

Today's LANs

Switched infrastructures are the most commonly implemented LANs today. Because the price of deploying switches is becoming affordable, many companies are bypassing the shared-hub or bridged technologies and are moving directly to switches. Even within switched networks, at some point routers are needed to provide scalability. Routers can be used to separate the traffic among different workgroups (Layer 3 networks). With switches, the grouping of users is largely determined by their physical location (see Figure 11-8).

For example, all the users connected to the switch in the first floor belong to the same workgroup (Layer 3 network example IP network 10.0.0.0), and all the users connected to the switch in the second floor belong to a different workgroup (Layer 3 network example IP network 192.168.1.0).

This chapter discussed the limitations of traditional shared LAN technologies. See Chapter 12, "LAN Switching Basics," to learn how to improve performance in some of these areas.

Figure 11-8   *Today's LANs*

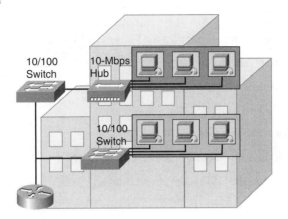

Summary

In this chapter, you learned the following key points:

- The earliest LAN technologies that were installed widely were either Thicknet or Thinnet infrastructures.

- Hubs also are known as Ethernet concentrators or Ethernet multiport repeaters. Hubs are Layer 1 devices.

- When two nodes on an Ethernet network try to send data at the same time, a collision happens.

- Three common transmission methods exist: unicast, broadcast, and multicast transmission.

- In a hub-based LAN, all resources are shared.

- Bridges operate at Layer 2. Bridges use MAC addresses to filter traffic passed to it.

- Switches are Layer 2 devices. A switch segments a LAN into microsegments.

- Some of the typical causes of network congestions are too many users, too many network-intensive applications in use, too many users trying to access the same server, and so on.

Review Exercises

1 What is the maximum distance for Thicknet without using a repeater?

  a. 185 m (606.95 feet)

  b. 250 m (820.2 feet)

  c. 500 m (1640.4 feet)

  d. 800 m (2624.64 feet)

2 Which of the following does not describe a hub?

  a. It works at the OSI model physical layer.

  b. It is a passive device.

  c. It is also known as an Ethernet concentrator.

  d. It filters the traffic passed through it.

3 What term is used if two or more stations on a network try to transmit simultaneously?

  a. Propagation

  b. Retransmission

  c. Collision

  d. Backoff

4 Which of the following is not a common method of transmission in a network?

  a. Unicast

  b. Bicast

  c. Broadcast

  d. Multicast

5 Which of the following is *not* a characteristic of hub-based LANs?

  a. All resources are shared.

  b. Security is very high within each segment.

  c. Adding, moving, and changing users in a hub-based network is easier than in Thinnet and Thicknet.

  d. Desktop connections are wired to centralized closets.

6 Which of the following is *not* a feature of bridges?

  a. They operate at Layer 2 of the OSI model.

  b. They are more intelligent than hubs.

  c. They do not make any forwarding decisions.

  d. They build and maintain address tables.

7 Which of the following statements is true of microsegmentation?

  a. Each workstation gets its own dedicated segment through the network.

  b. All the workstations are grouped as one segment.

  c. Microsegmentation increases the number of collisions on a network.

  d. None of the above.

8 Which of the following statements is true?

  a. In a hubbed network, multiple devices can send data at the same time.

  b. In a switched network, only one device can send data at a time.

  c. Switches can improve the traffic flow of a network.

  d. None of the above.

9 Which of the following is *not* a cause of network congestion?

  a. Too many users

  b. Most of the users accessing the same server

  c. Too many bandwidth-intensive applications installed

  d. Too many segments

10 Which of the following technologies is the most commonly implemented LAN today?

  a. Hubbed network

  b. Switched network

  c. Shared network

  d. None of the above

Upon completing this chapter, you will be able to:

- Define microsegmentation

- Describe how a local-area network (LAN) switch operates

- Describe full-duplex transmission

- Identify three common switching methods: cut-through, store-and-forward, and fragment-free

- Describe the functions and features of the Spanning-Tree Protocol (STP)

- Describe how STP works

- Describe the different STP port states

CHAPTER 12

LAN Switching Basics

Switching is a technology that decreases congestion in LANs by reducing traffic and increasing bandwidth. LAN switches often replace shared hubs and are designed to work with existing cable infrastructures so that they can be installed without disrupting existing network traffic.

LAN switches use microsegmentation to reduce the number of collisions in a LAN and increase the bandwidth. LAN switches also support features such as full-duplex communication and multiple simultaneous conversations. Full-duplex communication enables two devices to communicate with each other simultaneously. Full-duplex communication effectively doubles the throughput that the LAN switch can translate. In a full-duplex switched LAN, no collision occurs.

Three switching modes can be used to forward a frame through a switch: store-and-forward, cut-through, and fragment-free switching. The latency of each switching mode depends on how the switch forwards the frames. The faster the switching mode is, the smaller the latency in the switch is.

LAN switches and bridges, operating at Layer 2 of the OSI reference model, forward frames based on the MAC addresses to perform the switching function. If the Layer 2 MAC address is unknown, the device floods the frame in an attempt to reach the desired destination. LAN switches and bridges also forward all broadcast frames. The result could be storms of traffic being looped endlessly through the network. A Spanning-Tree Protocol (STP) is a loop-prevention protocol. It is a technology that enables switches to communicate with each other to discover physical loops in the network.

This chapter discusses the functions of microsegmentation, operation of LAN switches, full-duplex transmission, and switching modes. This chapter also introduces the STP, tells how STP works, and covers the STP switch port states.

Microsegmentation

The fundamental concept behind LAN switching is that it provides microsegmentation. *Microsegmentation* facilitates the creation of a dedicated segment and provides dedicated bandwidth to each user on the network (see Figure 12-1). Each user receives instant access to the full bandwidth and does not have to contend for available bandwidth with other users. This means that pairs of devices on the same switch can communicate in parallel with a minimum number of collisions. Microsegmentation reduces collisions in a network and effectively increases the capacity for each station connected to the network.

Figure 12-1 *Microsegmentation of a LAN Network*

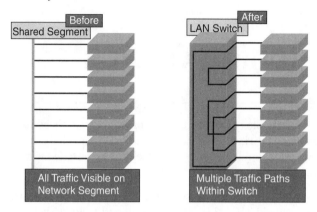

Using ASICs, high port-density LAN switches can support multiple simultaneous conversations at any given time. Multiple simultaneous conversations can occur by forwarding or switching several frame packets at the same time, therefore increasing network capacity by the number of conversations supported. This results in a dramatic improvement in available bandwidth and scalability.

LAN Switch Operation

This section discusses the fundamental operation of a LAN switch. Figure 12-2 shows a LAN with three workstations, a LAN switch, and the LAN switch's address table. The LAN switch has four *interfaces* (or network connections). Stations A and C are connected to the switch's interface 3, and Station B is on Interface 4. As indicated, Station A needs to transmit data to Station B.

Figure 12-2 *LAN Switch Operation*

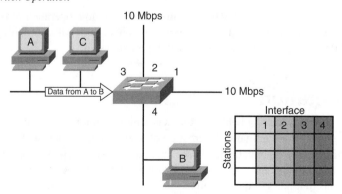

Remember that as this traffic goes through the network, the switch operates at Layer 2, meaning that the switch can look at the Media Access Control (MAC) layer address. When Station A transmits and the switch receives the frames, the switch assesses the traffic as it goes through to discover the source MAC address and store it in the address table (see Figure 12-3).

Figure 12-3   *Building an Address Table*

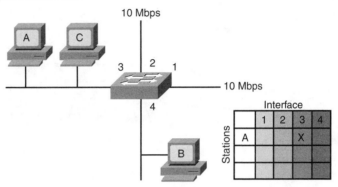

As the traffic goes through the switch, an entry is made in the address table identifying the source station and the interface that it's connected to on the switch. The switch now knows where Station A is connected. When that frame of data is in the switch, it floods to all ports because the destination station is unknown (see Figure 12-4).

Figure 12-4   *Flooding Data to All Switch Ports*

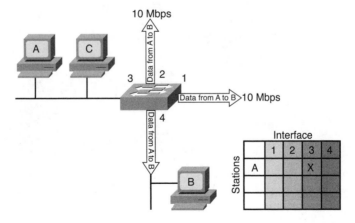

After the address entry is made in the table, however, a response comes back from Station B to Station A. The switch now knows that Station B is connected to Interface 4 (see Figure 12-5).

Figure 12-5 *Responding to the Flooding Message*

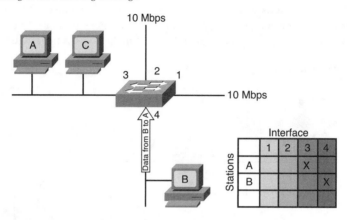

The data is transmitted into the switch, but notice that the switch does not flood the traffic this time. The switch sends the data out of only Interface 3 because it knows where Station A is on the network (see Figure 12-6).

Figure 12-6 *Transmitting Data to a Known Station*

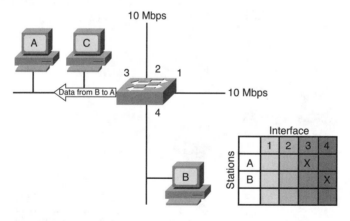

The original transmission indicated where that MAC address came from, enabling the switch to more efficiently deliver traffic in the network.

Full-Duplex Transmission

Another function of LAN switching that dramatically improves bandwidth is full-duplex transmission, which effectively doubles the amount of bandwidth between nodes. Full-duplex transmission between stations is achieved by using point-to-point Ethernet connections. This feature can be important, for example, between high-bandwidth consumers such as a connection between a switch and a server. Full-duplex transmission provides a collision-free transmission environment. Because both nodes can transmit and receive at the same time, there are no negotiations for bandwidth.

In 10-Mbps connections, for example, full-duplex transmission effectively provides 10 Mb of transmit capacity and 10 Mb of receive capacity, for effectively 20 Mb of capacity on a single connection. Likewise, a 100-Mbps connection offers effectively 200 Mbps of throughput (see Figure 12-7). Full-duplex communication also supports two data transmission paths, with speeds up to 1 Gbps.

Figure 12-7   *Full-Duplex Transmission*

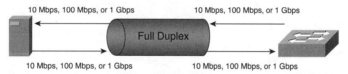

Modes of Switching

The three modes of switching—store-and-forward, cut-through, and fragment-free switching—offer different performance and latency. *Latency*, sometimes called *propagation delay*, is the time that a frame, or packet, of data takes to travel from the source station or node to its final destination on the network.

Store-and-Forward Switching

In *store-and-forward switching*, the switch reads the entire frame of data, checks the frame for errors, decides where it needs to go, and then sends it on its way (see Figure 12-8). The obvious trade-off here is that it takes the switch longer to read the entire frame. As the switch reads the entire frame, however, it detects any errors on that frame. If the frame is in error, the frame is not forwarded and is discarded. Although cut-through switching is faster, it offers no error detection. The latency introduced by store-and-forward switching is usually not a significant issue.

Figure 12-8 *Store-and-Forward Switching*

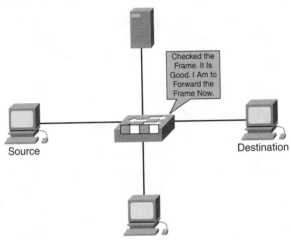

Cut-Through Switching

In *cut-through switching*, the switch reads the beginning of the frame up to the destination MAC address as the traffic flows through the switch and "cuts through" to its destination without continuing to read the rest of the frame (see Figure 12-9).

Cut-through switching decreases the latency of the transmission. However, cut-through switching has no error detection.

Figure 12-9 *Cut-through Switching*

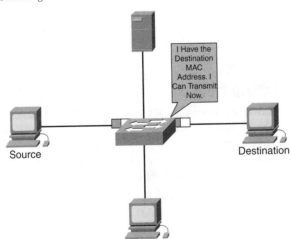

Fragment-Free Switching

Fragment-free switching is a modified form of cut-through switching. Fragment-free switching filters out collision fragments, which are the majority of packet errors, before forwarding begins. In a properly functioning network, a collision fragment must be smaller than 64 bytes. Anything greater than 64 bytes is a valid packet and usually is received without error. Fragment-free switching waits until the received packet has been determined not to be a collision fragment before forwarding the packet.

The Need for Spanning Tree

In large networks, one of the problems at Layer 2 in the OSI model is that if forwarding decisions are made only at this layer, the network cannot have any physical layer loops. Thus, in a simple network with redundant switches/bridges in parallel, as shown in Figure 12-10, when a switch has any multicast, broadcast, or unknown traffic, that traffic will be flooded out to all ports except the incoming port. The result will be storms of traffic being looped endlessly through the network.

Figure 12-10   *Using Bridging Loops for Redundancy*

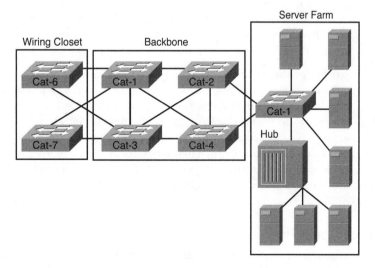

One way to eliminate the loops is to physically disconnect those segments, but that is not a good solution because the network would have no physical redundancy. Instead, the STP enables you to logically cut out the loops in the network so that you can re-enable them dynamically, if necessary (see Figure 12-11).

Figure 12-11 *Introducing the STP*

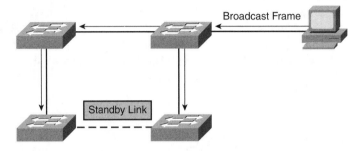

Digital Equipment Corporation (DEC) originally developed STP. The DEC STP protocol subsequently was revised by the Institute of Electrical and Electronics Engineers (IEEE) 802 committee. The IEEE 802 committee published an industry-standard STP protocol known as the *802.1d Spanning-Tree Protocol*. The DEC and the IEEE 802.1d protocols are not compatible.

Logically disconnecting the loops allows dynamic re-establishment of a connection if a failure occurs within the network. Switches and bridges can disconnect loops simply by communicating back and forth with hello messages. *Hello messages* are status messages that the bridges and switches exchange periodically so that they know the status of those logical connections and disconnections.

If a switch or bridge stops hearing a given communication from a certain device on the network, that network device has failed. When a network failure occurs, STP re-establishes the link to maintain redundancy. Technically, these exchanges are known as bridge protocol data units (BPDUs). Although STP works well, it can take from 30 seconds to a full minute for the network to fully converge (re-establish the traffic flow through an alternate path after a network failure). STP can become unstable and inadvertently can enable loops, causing network traffic to endlessly loop and causing the network to fail. These failures usually occur when heavy network traffic causes BPDUs to get delayed or lost.

Spanning-Tree Operation

The main function of the STP is to ensure a loop-free topology while allowing redundant/ duplicate paths in case of failures. A loop-free path is accomplished when a device recognizes a loop in the topology and blocks one or more redundant ports.

Figure 12-12 illustrates a loop-free network as created by the STP.

Figure 12-12 *Spanning-Tree Operation*

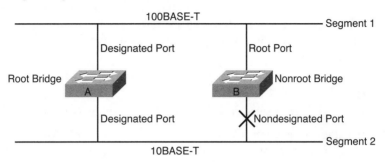

The STP provides a loop-free network topology by doing the following:

1 Electing a root bridge—Each of the switches or bridges in a LAN participating in the Spanning-Tree Protocol is assigned an 8-byte unique identifier. The switch or bridge that has the lowest identifier among all switches and bridges is elected as a *root bridge*, which acts as the "root" of the spanning tree and decides on the network topology. Other switches in that network are called *nonroot bridges*. Only one root bridge can exist in a given broadcast domain. In Figure 12-12, Switch A is elected the root bridge.

NOTE   Cisco bridges utilize the configured priority and MAC address of the switch for the root bridge election. If the priorities are equal, the lowest MAC address becomes the root bridge. You can influence the root bridge election by setting a priority value. (The lowest priority wins.) All ports on the root bridge are put into forwarding mode.

2 Electing a root port—After electing the root bridge, each switch or bridge in the network calculates the path cost (an accumulated cost based on bandwidth). The port with the lowest coast to the root bridge is called a *root port*. The root path cost is the total cost to the root. In Figure 12-12, from Switch B, the lowest-cost path to the root bridge is through the 100BASE-T Fast Ethernet link.

3 Electing a designated port on each segment—On each segment, all the participating switches or bridges then elect a designated port. A designated port is selected on the switch or bridge that has the lowest-cost path to the root bridge. A designated port is the only port that is allowed to forward frames to and from the segment toward the root. In Figure 12-12, the designated ports for both segments are on the root bridge because the root bridge is directly connected on both segments. The 10BASE-T Ethernet port on Switch B is a nondesignated port because there is only one designated port per segment, and 100BASE-T segments would have a lower cost than 10BASE-T segments (by default).

4 Removing loops—Using the preceding steps, only the switch or bridge ports directly connected to each LAN segment are allowed to forward the frames to and from the segment toward the root. All the other redundant switch or bridge ports are placed in a blocking state, thereby removing the loops in a network.

Spanning-Tree Protocol Port States

The ports on a bridge or switch using STP exist in one of the following five states:

- **Blocking**—A port in blocking state sends and listens to BPDUs but does not forward frames. By default, all ports are in blocking state when the switch is turned on.

- **Listening**—In listening state, a port listens to the BPDUs to make sure there are no loops on the network. No frames are forwarded in this state.

- **Learning**—In this state, a port learns MAC addresses and builds a address table, but it does not forward frames.

- **Forwarding**—A port in the forwarding state forwards frames. BPDUs are sent and listened to.

- **Disabled**—A port in the disabled state does not participate in the operation of STP. Therefore, it does not listen to BPDUs or forward frames.

Typically, switch ports that participate in STP operation are in either blocking or forwarding state. Ports can be configured to immediately enter Spanning-Tree Protocol forwarding mode when a connection is made instead of following the usual sequence of blocking, listening, learning, and forwarding. The capability to quickly switch states from blocking to forwarding rather than going through the traditional port states is useful in situations when immediate access to a server is required.

NOTE The capability to quickly switch states from blocking to forwarding is referred to as *portfast* and is recommended only on switch ports connecting to workstations and servers, *not* ports connecting to switches or routers.

The following web link provides a link to the article "Understanding Spanning-Tree Protocol," which presents a more detailed discussion on Spanning-Tree Protocol: www.cisco.com/univercd/cc/td/doc/product/rtrmgmt/sw_ntman/cwsimain/cwsi2/cwsiug2/vlan2/stpapp.htm.

Summary

In this chapter, you learned the following key points:

- Switches can provide dedicated access to improve the shared LAN technologies.

- A switch segments a LAN into microsegments. Microsegmentation reduces the number of collisions to a minimum and increases the effective bandwidth.

- Switches achieve high-speed transfer by reading the destination Layer 2 MAC address of the frame packet.

- Full-duplex communication allows two devices to communicate with each other simultaneously and effectively doubles the throughput that the LAN switch can translate.

- Switches can support multiple simultaneous conversations in a network.

- Three switching modes can be used to forward frames through a switch: store-and-forward, cut-through, and fragment-free switching.

- The main task of the Spanning-Tree Protocol (STP) is to prevent the occurrence of network loops on a Layer 2 network.

- The ports on a bridge or switch using STP exist in one of the following five states: blocking, listening, learning, forwarding, or disabled.

Review Exercises

1   Which of the following is *not* a feature of microsegmentation?

    a. It enables dedicated access.

    b. It supports multiple conversations at any given time.

    c. It increases the capacity for each workstation connected to the network.

    d. It increases collisions.

2   Which of the following is used by LAN switches for making the forwarding decision?

    a. IP address

    b. MAC address

    c. Network address

    d. Host address

3 Which of the following is a feature of full-duplex transmission?

    a. It offers two 10- to 1-Gbps data-transmission paths.

    b. It doubles bandwidth between nodes.

    c. It provides collision-free transmission.

    d. All of the above.

4 The three types of switching methods are _____ , _____ , and _____.

5 The Spanning-Tree Protocol allows which of the following?

    a. Bridges to communicate Layer 3 information

    b. A redundant network path without suffering the effects of loops in the network

    c. Static network paths for loop prevention

    d. None of the above

6 Which of the following is *not* one of the STP port states?

    a. Blocking

    b. Learning

    c. Listening

    d. Transmitting

Upon completing this chapter, you will be able to:

- Identify and describe the switching devices used in OSI Layer 2

- Identify and describe the switching devices used in OSI Layer 3

- Identify and describe the switching devices used in OSI Layer 4

CHAPTER 13

Multilayer Switching Devices

Switching technology is increasing the efficiency and speed of networks. To optimize a network's switching performance, it is important for a networking technician to understanding the different switching techniques and devices. Many different techniques exist for switching network traffic. The switching techniques can be categorized according to the OSI layer at which they filter and forward (or switch) the data. These categories are Layer 2, Layer 3, and Layer 4 switching.

A Layer 2 LAN switch, like a bridge, performs switching and filtering based on the data link layer MAC address. However, unlike bridges, which switch traffic through software, Layer 2 switches uses hardware to switch network traffic.

Layer 3 switching provides the same advantages as routing, with the added performance boost from packet forwarding handled by specialized hardware, application-specific integrated circuit (ASIC). Layer 3 switches determine forwarding paths based on Layer 3 information.

Layer 4 switching is Layer 3 hardware-based routing that uses Layer 4 information. In addition to MAC addresses (Layer 2) and source/destination IP addresses (Layer 3), Layer 4 switches can make forwarding decision based on TCP/UDP (Layer 4) application port numbers.

This chapter describes OSI Layers 2, 3, and 4 switching devices and technologies.

Layer 2 Switching Devices

A Layer 2 switch is operationally similar to a multiport bridge, but it has a much higher capacity and supports many features, such as full-duplex communication, dedicated communication between devices, and multiple simultaneous conversations. Full-duplex communication effectively doubles the throughput. Dedicated communication between network devices increases file-transfer throughput, while multiple simultaneous conversations increase network capacity by the number of conversations supported.

A Layer 2 LAN switch performs switching and filtering based on the OSI data link layer (Layer 2) MAC address. Like bridges, Layer 2 switches are completely transparent to network protocols and user applications.

Bridges and switches analyze incoming frames, make forwarding decisions based on information contained in the frames, and forward the frames toward the destination. Upper-layer protocol transparency is a primary advantage of both bridging and switching. Because both device types operate at the data link layer, they are not required to examine upper-layer information. Bridges are also capable of filtering frames based on any Layer 2 fields.

Although bridges and switches share most relevant attributes, several distinctions characterize these technologies. Switches are significantly faster because they switch in hardware, while bridges switch through software. Switches also can support higher port densities than bridges. Some switches support cut-through switching, reducing latency and delays in the network, while bridges support only store-and-forward traffic switching.

In a Layer 2 switch, frame forwarding is handled by specialized hardware called ASICs. ASIC technology allows a silicon chip to be programmed to perform a specific function as it is built. This technology allows functions to be performed at much higher rates of speed than those of a chip that is programmed by software. Because of ASIC technology, switches provides scalability up to gigabit speeds with low latency, at costs not significantly higher than Ethernet bridges.

Figure 13-1 illustrates a network with Layer 2 switching.

Figure 13-1   *Sample Network with Layer 2 Switching*

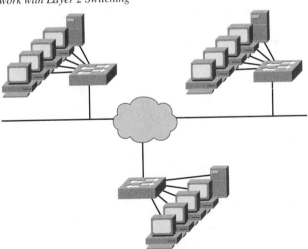

Layer 2 switches give network managers the ability to increase bandwidth without adding complexity to the network. Layer 2 data frames consist of both control information, such as MAC addresses, and end-user content. At Layer 2, no modification of the frame control information is required when moving between similar Layer 1 interfaces such as Ethernet and Fast Ethernet. However, changes to control information might occur when bridging between unlike LAN types such as Token Ring and Ethernet.

Workgroup connectivity and network segmentation are the two primary uses of Layer 2 switches. The high performance of a Layer 2 switch allows for network designs that significantly decrease the number of hosts per physical segment. Decreasing the number of hosts per segment leads to a flatter design with more segments in the campus network (see Figure 13-2).

Figure 13-2   *A Flat Network Design*

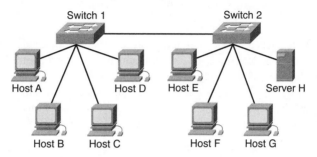

A network design that emphasizes Layer 2 switching is commonly characterized as "flat" because it avoids the logical and hierarchical structure provided by routers. With a flat network design, there is no hierarchy. Each internetworking device has essentially the same job, and the network is not divided into layers or modules. A flat network design works well in a small network. A flat network topology is easy to design and implement, and it is easy to maintain.

Despite the advantages of Layer 2 switching, it has all the same characteristics and limitations of legacy bridging. One of those limitations is that all the ports on a bridge or a Layer 2 switch belong to the same Layer 3 network (for example, the same IP network), so a broadcast by one station is forwarded by all the Layer 2 switches or bridges to all other stations. Think of it this way: Instead of having multiple freeways in the transportation system, only a single freeway connects every city.

Layer 2 switches also are discussed in Chapter 11, "Shared LAN Technology." Refer to Chapter 11 for an introduction to Layer 2 switching.

Layer 3 Switching Devices

Layer 3 switches are basically a cross between a LAN switch and a router. Each port on the switch is a separate LAN port, but the forwarding engine actually calculates and stores routes based on Layer 3 addresses (IP addresses), not Layer 2 MAC addresses. A Layer 3 switch is a switch that performs hardware-based routing using Layer 3 (network) addresses.

The Layer 3 switches that are available today tend to support only IP or both IP and Internetwork Packet Exchange (IPX), the Novell NetWare Layer 3 protocol used to route packets through interconnected network, to the exclusion of other network layer protocols. Similarly, selection of LAN port technologies is frequently limited to 10-, 100-, or 1000-Mbps Ethernet.

Because Layer 3 switching offers hardware-based routing, packet forwarding is handled by specialized hardware ASICs. The goal of Layer 3 switching is to capture the speed of switching and the scalability of routing.

A Layer 3 switch acts on a packet in the same way that a traditional router does. For example, a Layer 3 switch can determine the forwarding path based on Layer 3 information and can validate the integrity of the Layer 3 header via checksum (a method for checking the integrity of transmitted data). Layer 3 switches also can apply security controls, if required, and can implement quality of service (QoS). (QoS is a measure of performance for a transmission system that reflects its transmission quality and service availability.)

The primary difference between the packet-switching operation of a router and a Layer 3 switch lies in the physical implementation. In general-purpose routers, microprocessor-based engines typically perform software-based packet switching. A Layer 3 switch performs packet switching with hardware (ASIC engines). Because it is designed to handle high-performance LAN traffic, a Layer 3 switch can be placed anywhere within the network, offering a cost-effective alternative to the traditional router (see Figure 13-3).

Figure 13-3   *Layer 3 Switching*

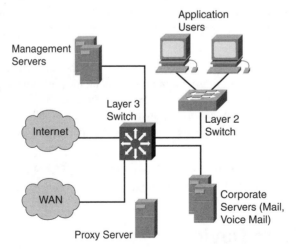

Layer 4 Switching Devices

Layer 4 switching refers to Layer 3 hardware-based routing that accounts for Layer 4 control information. Information in packet headers typically includes Layer 3 addressing, the Layer 3 protocol type, and more fields relevant to Layer 3 devices, such as Time To Live (TTL)—a field in an IP header that indicates how long a packet is considered valid—and checksum. The packet also contains information relevant to the higher layers within the communicating hosts, such as the protocol type and port number.

A simple description of Layer 4 switching is that it has the capability to make forwarding decisions based not just on the MAC address or source/destination IP addresses, but on Layer 4 parameters such as port numbers as well. In TCP or User Datagram Protocol (UDP) flows, the application is encoded as a port number in the TCP or UDP header (see Figure 13-4). (Refer to Chapter 16, "Transport Layer," for more information on the TCP and UDP header format.)

Figure 13-4   *TCP and UDP Header*

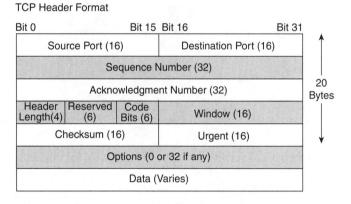

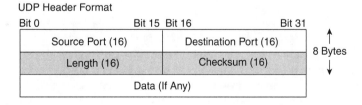

Figure 13-5 illustrates a network with Layer 4 switches integrated.

Figure 13-5 *Layer 4 Switching*

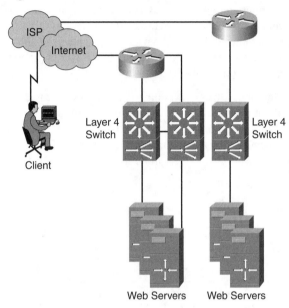

Routers are capable of controlling traffic based on Layer 4 information. One method of controlling Layer 4 traffic is to use extended access lists. Another method of providing Layer 4 accounting of flows is to use NetFlow switching, which is utilized on the Cisco Catalyst 5000 and 6000 switch platforms and the Cisco 7200 and 7500 router platforms.

NOTE   NetFlow switching is developed by Cisco Systems, Inc., as a technique to reduce per-packet overhead associated with routing. NetFlow switching identifies flows by using both network layer and transport layer information, and it switches packets between subnets by using advanced ASIC switching hardware. NetFlow switching uses standard routing protocols such as Open Shortest Path First (OSPF), Enhanced Interior Gateway Routing Protocol (EIGRP), Routing Information Protocol (RIP), and Intermediate System-to-Intermediate System (IS-IS) for route determination. (For more information on routing protocols, see Chapter 21, "Routing Protocols.")

Finally, when performing Layer 4 functions, a switch reads the TCP and UDP fields within the headers to determine what type of information the packet is carrying. The network manager can program the switch to prioritize traffic by application. This function enables network managers to define a QoS for end users. When used for QoS purposes, Layer 4 switching might grant a videoconferencing application more bandwidth than an e-mail message or File Transfer Protocol (FTP) packet because video data is more sensitive to delay.

Layer 4 switching is necessary if policy dictates granular control of traffic by application or if the accounting of traffic itemized in terms of applications is required. However, note that switches performing Layer 4 switching need the capability to identify and store large numbers of forwarding-table entries, especially if the switch is within the core of an enterprise network. Many Layer 2 and Layer 3 switches have forwarding tables that are sized in proportion to the number of network devices.

With Layer 4 switches, the number of network devices must be multiplied by the number of different application protocols and conversations in use in the network. Thus, the size of the forwarding table can grow quickly as the number of end devices and types of applications increase. This large table capacity is essential to creating a high-performance switch that supports wire-speed Layer 4 traffic forwarding.

Summary

In this chapter, you learned the following key points:

- Layer 2 switches enable network managers to increase the effective bandwidth without adding complexity to the network.

- Layer 3 switching is basically hardware-based routing. Because it is designed to handle high-performance LAN traffic, a Layer 3 switch can be placed anywhere within the network, offering a cost-effective alternative to the traditional router.

- Layer 4 switching refers to Layer 3 hardware-based routing that accounts for Layer 4 control information.

Review Exercises

1 Which of the following is true for LAN switches?

   a. They repair network fragments known as microsegments.

   b. They are very high-speed multiport bridges.

   c. Lower bandwidth makes up for higher latency.

   d. They require new network interface cards on attached hosts.

2 What does ASIC stand for?

   a. Application-specific interface card

   b. Asymmetrical integrated circuit

   c. Application-specific integrated circuit

   d. Automatically scalable interchange circuit

3 Which of the following best describes Layer 3 switching?

   a. Hardware-based bridging

   b. Hardware-based routing

   c. Software-based switching

   d. Software-based routing

4 How does the packet-switching function of a router differ from that of a Layer 3 switch?

   a. The router uses network layer information to determine the forwarding path, whereas the Layer 3 switch uses data link layer information.

   b. The router performs its operation in software, whereas the Layer 3 switch uses hardware.

   c. The router can implement QoS, whereas the Layer 3 switch cannot.

   d. The router operates faster than the Layer 3 switch, but the switch is more scalable.

5 Using Layer 4 switching enables prioritization of traffic based on _____.

   a. the application

   b. source and destination

   c. source only

   d. the network layer protocol

Upon completing this chapter, you will be able to:

- Identify the limitations of shared LANs

- Define VLAN

- Identify the functions and benefits of VLANs

- Identify the functions of VLAN components

- Identify different ways of establishing VLAN membership

- Identify the features of port-based VLANs and MAC address-based VLANs

- Identify the connectivity types used between VLANs

CHAPTER 14

Virtual LANs

A typical shared LAN is configured according to the physical infrastructure that it is connecting. Users are grouped based on their location in relation to the hub they are plugged into. A *virtual LAN (VLAN)* is a switched network that is logically segmented by functions, project teams, or applications, without regard to the physical location of users.

VLANs provide several benefits. VLANs reduce administration costs related to solving problems associated with moves, additions, and changes to user. Creating VLANs improves network security by controlling broadcast propagation. VLANs also improve the network scalability and performance.

This chapter provides an introduction to VLANs, compares traditional shared LANs and VLANs, and discusses the benefits of VLANs. In addition, this chapter discusses VLAN components and tells how a VLAN membership is established. Finally, this chapter describes the communication between VLANs.

Constraints of Shared LANs

To understand the purpose of VLANs, you must first understand the limitations of traditional, shared local-area networks (LANs). In traditional LANs, users generally are grouped not logically, but physically, by where they sit and where they gain their physical connectivity. That is, the actual port or hub that the users plug into determines what resources they can connect to and how they are grouped together in a LAN.

Shared LAN networks offer very little security because, on a hub or concentrator, all traffic in the network is available on all ports. A broadcast sent out by a host on a single segment would propagate to all segments, saturating the bandwidth of the entire network. This limits the amount of security that could be enforced on the network.

In shared LAN networks, routers are used to divide the networks into multiple broadcast domains. Because routers do not forward broadcasts, each interface is in a different broadcast domain.

Also, the physical layout and requirements in the shared-technology environment limit flexibility in moving, adding, or changing the user locations. Many moves require recabling either on a patch panel or in a wiring closet wherever the hubs or concentrators reside, and almost all moves require new station addressing and hub and router reconfiguration.

Finally, routers are needed to connect different segments. If separation occurs, router ports might not be available—or, if they are, they are relatively expensive compared to some of the alternatives. Figure 14-1 illustrates a shared LAN.

Figure 14-1 *A Shared LAN*

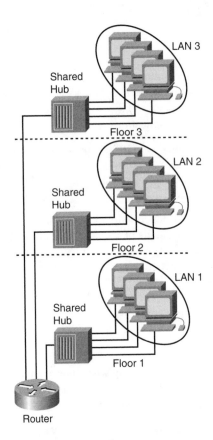

The limitations discussed in this section are some of the reasons for implementing virtual LANs, or VLANs.

Virtual LANs

As mentioned in the preceding section, a typical shared LAN is configured according to the physical infrastructure it is connecting. Users are grouped based on their location in relation to the hub they are plugged into and how the cable is run to the wiring closet. The router interconnecting each shared hub typically provides segmentation and can act as a broadcast firewall. The segments created by switches do not do this. Traditional LAN segmentation does not group users according to their workgroup association or need for bandwidth. Therefore, they share the same segment (broadcast domain/Layer 3 network) and contend for the same bandwidth, although the bandwidth requirements might vary greatly by workgroup or department.

A VLAN is a switched network that is logically segmented by functions, project teams, or applications, without regard to the physical location of users (see Figure 14-2). For example, several end stations might be grouped as a department, such as Engineering or Accounting, and have the same attributes as a LAN even though they are not all on the same physical LAN segment.

Figure 14-2   *Virtual LANs Grouping Users Logically*

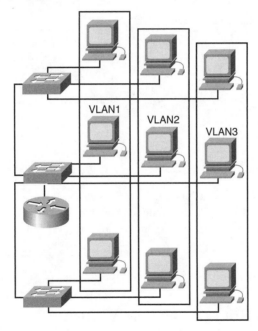

To accomplish this logical grouping, a VLAN-capable switching device must be used. Each switch port can be assigned to a VLAN. Ports in a VLAN share broadcast traffic and belong to the same broadcast domain. A VLAN is a broadcast domain. Broadcast traffic in one VLAN is not transmitted outside that VLAN. In Figure 14-3, the broadcast traffic in VLAN1 will not be transmitted to VLAN2 or VLAN3. This segmentation improves the overall performance of the network.

Figure 14-3   *Virtual LANs*

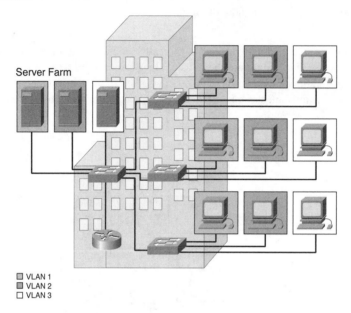

VLAN configuration is done at the switch through software. VLANs use standardized trunking protocols such as 802.1Q so that multivendor VLAN networks can be built. You learn more about 802.1Q later in this chapter in the section "Trunking."

A port on a switch can be assigned to a particular VLAN in different ways, as discussed later in this chapter in the section "Establishing VLAN Membership."

Removing Physical Boundaries with VLANs

Conceptually, VLANs provide greater segmentation and organizational flexibility. VLAN technology allows switch ports, and the users connected to them, to be grouped into logically defined communities of interest. These groupings can be coworkers within the same department, a cross-functional product team, or diverse users sharing the same network application or software.

Grouping these ports and users into communities of interest (referred to as *VLAN organizations*) can be accomplished within a single switch or, more powerfully, between connected switches within the enterprise. By grouping ports and users across multiple switches, VLANs can span single-building infrastructures or interconnected buildings. As shown in Figure 14-4, VLANs completely remove the physical constraints of workgroup communications across the enterprise.

Figure 14-4   *Removing the Physical Boundaries with VLANs*

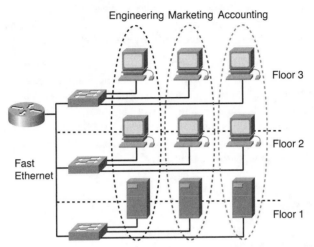

Routers remain vital for switched architectures configured as VLANs because they provide the communication between logically defined workgroups (VLANs). Layer 3 communication, either embedded in the Layer 3 switch or provided externally by a traditional router, is an integral part of any high-performance switching architecture.

VLAN Benefits

The original motivation for using VLANs was to reduce the administrative costs associated with managing a routine shared network. VLANs provided a way to simplify the moves, adds, and changes commonly associated with most organizations as their networks evolved. If a group of VLAN users moves but remains in the same VLAN connected to a switch port, the network addresses do not change. Router configuration is left intact; a simple move for a user from one location to another does not create any configuration changes in the router if the user stays in the same VLAN.

VLANs also offer other benefits, including better bandwidth control. Segmenting a switch into multiple VLANs limits the size of broadcast domains. In other words, VLANs limit how far and to how many ports the broadcast traffic is propagated.

Another benefit of VLANs is improved network security. VLANs can be separated on the switch so that traffic from one VLAN is not communicated to another VLAN. Servers also can be relocated into secured locations, with connectivity provided to only those workstations that need it.

VLANs can improve scalability and performance, and microsegmentation can dramatically improve some key performance aspects in a LAN. You can assign users that require high-performance networking to their own VLANs. For example, you might assign an engineer who is testing a multicast application and the servers that the engineer uses to a single VLAN. The engineer experiences improved network performance by being on a "dedicated LAN," and the rest of the engineering group experiences improved network performance because the traffic generated by the network-intensive application is isolated on another VLAN.

Finally, VLANs can be used to distribute the traffic load more efficiently throughout the LAN. VLANs provide segmentation and organizational flexibility. Using VLAN technology, you can group switch ports and their connected users into logically defined communities of interest or diverse user groups sharing the same network application. Each group's traffic is largely contained within the VLAN, reducing extraneous traffic and improving the efficiency and performance of the whole network. Additionally, less traffic will need to be routed, and the latency added by routers will be reduced.

VLAN Components

This section introduces some of the major components and concepts that are essential for implementing VLANs. Those components and concepts include switches, routers, interoperability concerns, transport protocols, and VLAN management.

Switches

Switches are a primary component of VLAN communication. They perform critical VLAN functions by acting as the entry point for end-station devices into the switched fabric, facilitating communication across the organization, and providing the intelligence to group users, ports, MAC addresses, or logical addresses (Layer 3 information) into common communities of interest.

Routers

For inter-VLAN communication, you must use routers that extend VLAN communications between workgroups. Routers provide broadcast management and route processing and distribution. Routers also provide VLAN access to shared resources such as servers and hosts. In addition, routers connect to other parts of the network—either parts that are logically segmented with the more traditional subnet approach or parts that require access to remote sites across wide-area links.

Interoperability

VLANs provide system compatibility with previously installed systems, such as shared-hub devices. Although many of these devices are being replaced with newer switching technologies, previously installed concentrators still perform useful functions. With VLANs, you can configure devices such as shared hubs as a part of the VLAN architecture and can share traffic and network resources that directly attach to switching ports with VLAN designations.

Transport Protocols

The VLAN transport enables information to be exchanged between interconnected switches and routers residing on the corporate backbone. Transport capabilities remove physical boundaries, increase flexibility of a VLAN solution, and provide mechanisms for interoperability between backbone system components.

VLAN Management

Network-management solutions offer centralized control, configuration, and traffic-management functions.

Establishing VLAN Membership

VLAN membership describes how a port on the switch is assigned to belong to a particular VLAN. VLAN membership can be established in several ways. The common VLAN membership options implemented today are as follows:

- **Port-driven membership**—VLANs are determined by the port into which a given workstation plugs. For example, on a 12-port switch, ports 1 through 6 are VLAN 1, and ports 7 through 12 are VLAN 2.

- **MAC address membership**—The switch looks at a MAC address and then dynamically determines which VLAN a station belongs to. MAC address VLAN membership offers a mechanism for dynamic VLAN membership that is similar to network address VLAN membership.

- **Layer 3–based membership**—VLANs are defined based on information contained in the network layer header of the packet, such as the protocol type or the network layer address.

Membership by Port

Providing the maximum forwarding performance, membership by port is the simplest mechanism of VLAN membership. VLAN membership by port is defined by assigning a specific VLAN to a port or a group of ports. No address lookups are required in the application-specific integrated circuits (ASICs) because the administrator manually defines the VLAN a particular port that it belongs to. Port-based VLANs are also known as *static VLANs*.

Administration of port-based VLANs is relatively easy with either the command-line interface (CLI) or a graphical user interface (GUI). Port-based VLANs can be created to ensure that the packets do not leak into other domains, thereby maximizing the security between VLANs. When a user is moved to a different port of the switch, the administrator can simply reassign the new port to the user's old VLAN. Network administration easily is controlled across the entire network with port membership (see Figure 14-5).

Figure 14-5   *Membership by Port*

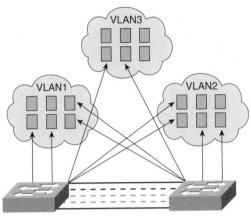

Membership by MAC Addresses

VLAN membership also can be determined by the MAC address. This scenario requires filtering because the switch must look at the traffic as it goes through the switch, a process that impacts performance. In addition, the switch must look up in a MAC address table to determine which VLAN that traffic belongs to.

Although membership by MAC addresses offers flexibility, it also adds to the switch-processing overhead. It offers flexibility to support mobile users and dynamically determines their VLAN membership based on the MAC address of their PC (see Figure 14-6).

Figure 14-6   *Membership by MAC Addresses*

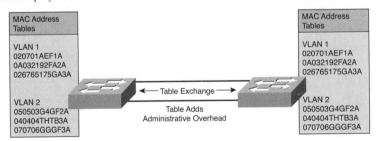

When a station initially is connected to an unassigned switch port, the appropriate switch checks the MAC address entry in the VLAN management database and dynamically configures the port with the corresponding VLAN configuration. The advantage of membership by MAC addresses is less administration within the wiring closet when a user is added or moved, and centralized notification when an unrecognized user is added to the network. However, more administration is required up front to set up the database within the VLAN management software and to maintain an accurate database of all network users. Also, a single MAC address cannot easily be a member of multiple VLANs. This can be a significant limitation, making it difficult to share server resources between more than one VLAN.

Layer 3–Based VLANs

A Layer 3–based VLAN is constructed using information contained in the network layer header of packets, such as the protocol type or the network layer address (see Figure 14-7). Defining VLANs using Layer 3 information is restricted to routers and switches that support a Layer-3 routing.

Figure 14-7   *Layer 3–Based Membership*

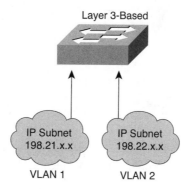

Several advantages exist when defining VLANs at Layer 3. A Layer 3–based VLAN provides flexibility and easy configuration. There is no need to reconfigure the network address of each workstation when a user moves to a new location. Another benefit of defining a VLAN at Layer 3 is that it can eliminate the need for frame tagging to communicate VLAN membership between switches, therefore reducing transport overhead.

However, inspecting Layer 3 addresses in packets is more time consuming than looking at MAC addresses in frames. For this reason, switches that use Layer 3 information for VLAN definition are generally slower than those that use Layer 2 information (MAC addresses).

Communicating Between VLANs

VLANs perform traffic separation within a shared-network environment. VLANs can span multiple connected switches. A router is needed to provide connectivity between VLANs.

Inter-VLAN connectivity can be achieved in two ways: logical connectivity or physical connectivity. Logical connectivity involves a single connection (a trunk) from the switch to the router, and that trunk can support multiple VLANs. This configuration sometimes is referred to as a "router on a stick" because there is a single connection to the router but multiple logical connections within that physical connection (see Figure 14-8). The router also performs the routing among the multiple VLANs. You learn more about trunking in next section, "Trunking."

Figure 14-8 *Trunking*

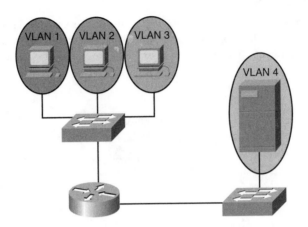

Another connectivity option is to have a separate physical connection for each VLAN. The obvious trade-off is that this configuration requires a separate physical port for each of the VLANs. Although this setup might provide better separation and better performance, the trade-off is the requirement for more resources, namely the individual interfaces on the router.

With regard to VLAN support on the router, Cisco IOS Software can support 255 VLANs or greater (depending on router platform and IOS revision) on a given router (see Figure 14-9). Thus, there is flexibility in terms of routing between VLANs.

NOTE   Inter-VLAN communication most commonly works by using a switch that routes between VLANs by way of a special "router engine" card or an embedded Layer 3 router.

Figure 14-9 *Multiple Links*

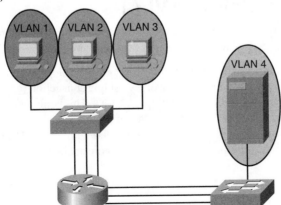

Trunking

If a VLAN spans multiple devices, a trunk is used to interconnect the devices. A *trunk* carries traffic for multiple VLANs. For example, a trunk can connect a switch to another switch, a switch to the inter-VLAN router, or a switch to a server with a special network interface card (NIC) installed that supports trunking. Cisco routers require a Fast Ethernet interface to do trunking. To keep track of frames traversing a switch fabric, VLAN identification is used to identify which frames belong to which VLANs. The most common trunking methods for Ethernet segments follow:

- **Inter-Switch Link (ISL)**—ISL is a Cisco proprietary protocol for interconnecting multiple switches and maintaining VLAN information as traffic travels between switches. ISL provides VLAN capabilities while maintaining full wire-speed performance over Fast Ethernet links in full- or half-duplex mode. Running a trunk in full-duplex mode is efficient and highly recommended. ISL operates in a point-to-point environment. It has been implemented for connections among switches, routers, and NICs used on nodes such as servers.

- **IEEE 802.1Q**—IEEE 802.1Q, "Standard for Virtual Bridged Local-Area Networks," is an open-standard (IEEE) VLAN tagging mechanism that predominates in modern switching installations. The IEEE 802.1Q protocol relates to the capability to carry the traffic of more than one subnet down a single cable. The IEEE 802.1Q committee defined this method of multiplexing VLANs in an effort to provide multivendor VLAN support.

Summary

In this chapter, you learned the following key points:

- In shared LAN networks, users physically are grouped together in the same broadcast domain. All traffic in the network is available on all ports. Therefore, networks offer very little security.

- A VLAN is a logical grouping of devices or users. A VLAN is a broadcast domain or a Layer 3 network such as an IP network or subnetwork.

- VLAN membership can be established in several ways, such as by port, MAC address, network address, and application type.

- VLANs remove the physical constraints of workgroup communications across the enterprise.

- VLANs enable logical (instead of physical) groups of users on a switch.

- VLANs address the needs for mobility and flexibility.

- VLANs reduce administrative overhead, improve security, and provide more efficient bandwidth utilization by limiting the broadcast traffic.

- If a VLAN spans multiple devices, a trunk is used to interconnect the devices.

- The most common trunking methods for Ethernet segments are ISL and IEEE 802.1Q.

Review Exercises

1 Which of the following is a limitation of traditional, shared LANs?

   a. Routers are needed to connect segments.

   b. Shared LAN networks offer very little security.

   c. Users usually are bound by their physical locations.

   d. All of the above.

2 A VLAN can be thought of as _____.

   a. a broadcast domain

   b. an IP network or subnetwork

   c. a Layer 3 network

   d. All of the above

3 Which of the following statements is true of using VLANs?

   a. Switches do not need to be configured.

   b. The broadcast domain is increased.

   c. Physical boundaries that prevent user groupings can be removed.

   d. None of the above.

4 Which of the following is *not* a beneficial effect of adding a VLAN?

   a. Broadcasts can be controlled.

   b. Confidential data can be protected.

   c. Relocation of users is not easy.

   d. Administration costs can be reduced.

5 Why is a trunk used?

   a. To carry traffic from multiple VLANs

   b. To carry traffic from a single VLAN

   c. To carry network-management traffic

   d. To connect a user PC to a switch port

6 Which of the following is *not* an approach for establishing VLAN membership?

   a. Port driven

   b. MAC address driven

   c. Layer 3 information driven

   d. Device type driven

7 What is port-based VLAN membership also known as?

   a. Local VLANs

   b. Dynamic VLANs

   c. Geographic VLANs

   d. Static VLANs

8 Which of the following is true of a MAC address-based VLAN?

   a. Offers flexibility

   b. Reduces overhead

   c. Improves performance, scalability, and administration

   d. None of the above

9 Inter-VLAN connectivity can be achieved in two ways: _____ connectivity and _____ connectivity.

10 Which protocol is Cisco proprietary and designed to carry traffic from multiple VLANs?

   a. ISL

   b. IEEE 802.1Q

   c. HDLC

   d. IEEE 802.3

TCP/IP

Upon completing this chapter, you will be able to:

- Describe a communication protocol

- Describe the TCP/IP protocol stack

- Describe the functions of IP

- Describe the characteristics of TCP

- Identify the TCP/IP applications

CHAPTER 15

TCP/IP Overview

To understand how to configure the functions of network devices, you must have a solid understanding of the protocols and their functions. The most common protocol used in data networks today is the Transmission Control Protocol/Internet Protocol (TCP/IP) protocol stack.

The TCP/IP protocol stack was developed as part of the research done by the Defense Advanced Research Projects Agency (DARPA). Later, TCP/IP was included with the Berkeley Software Distribution of UNIX. Now TCP/IP is a universally available protocol and is used to interconnect devices in corporate networks; it also is the protocol of the Internet.

This chapter defines protocols and, specifically, communication protocols. It discusses the TCP/IP protocol stack and introduces TCP/IP application layer protocols.

Communication Protocol

A *protocol* is a standard set of rules that determine how computers communicate with each other across networks. When network devices communicate with one another, they exchange a series of messages. To understand and act on these messages, network devices must agree on what a message means.

A protocol describes the following:

- The format that a message must take

- The way in which computers must exchange a message within the context of a particular activity, such as sending messages across networks, exchanging e-mail, establishing remote connections, or transferring files

A *communication protocol* handles errors in transmission, manages the routing and delivery of data, and controls the actual transmission by the use of predetermined status signals. TCP/IP is a software-based communication protocol used in the Internet. The name *TCP/IP* implies that the entire scope of the product is a combination of two protocols—the Transmission Control Protocol (TCP) and the Internet Protocol (IP). However, the term TCP/IP refers not to a single entity combining two protocols, but to a larger set of software programs that provide network services information from one machine to another. The TCP/IP protocol stack ensures communication across any set of interconnected networks (see Figure 15-1). The following section describes the TCP/IP protocol stack in more detail.

Figure 15-1 *Communication Protocol*

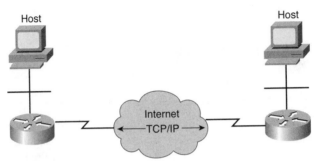

TCP/IP Protocol Stack

TCP/IP is a suite of communication protocols that define rules for how packets or information is moved across a network. To move information across a network, you need to have applications that are defined, an addressing scheme, and a way to deal with errors. The TCP/IP protocol stack can be used to communicate across any set of interconnected networks. It is equally well suited for LAN and WAN communication.

Of the TCP/IP protocol stack, IP (Layer 3) and TCP (Layer 4) are the best-known protocols. However, the TCP/IP protocol suite not only includes Layer 3 and Layer 4 protocols, but it also specified common applications such as e-mail, terminal emulation, and file transfer.

The TCP/IP protocol stack maps closely to the lower layers of the Open System Interconnection (OSI) reference model. Figure 15-2 compares the TCP/IP model to the OSI reference model. For a refresher on the similarities and differences between the TCP/IP protocol stack and the OSI model, refer to Chapter 2, "Networking Fundamentals."

Figure 15-2 *TCP/IP Stack*

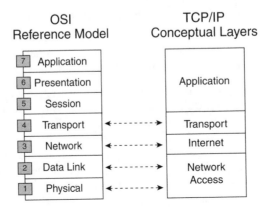

Internet Protocol

The *Internet Protocol (IP)* is a Layer 3 protocol that offers a connectionless service that provides best-effort delivery across a network. In a connectionless communication, the destination is not contacted before a packet is sent. An analogy for a connectionless service is a postal system; the recipient is not contacted before a letter is sent.

IP is not concerned with the content of the packets. Instead, it looks for a way to move the packets to their destination. IP determines where packets are routed, based on their destination address. IP basically breaks down the application information (for example, a 10-megabit [Mb] file that you are transferring) into smaller packets and then pushes those packets out on the network. Each packet finds the best path at the time. Then when the packets get to the other side of the network, they are put together in any order. Therefore, IP is packet-based networking.

TCP

TCP is a Layer 4 protocol that offers a connection-oriented service as well as reliability. In a connection-oriented environment, a connection is established between both ends before transfer of information can begin. An example of a nontechnical connection-oriented communication is a conversation between two people. First, a protocol lets the participants know that they have connected and can begin communication. This would be an initial conversation of "Hello."

In addition to being connection oriented, TCP has the following characteristics:

- It is reliable.
- It divides outgoing messages into segments.
- It reassembles messages from incoming segments at the destination station.
- It resends anything not received.

TCP sets up a connection, sometimes called a *virtual circuit*, between end-user applications.

TCP/IP Applications

The application layer of the TCP/IP protocols combines the functionality found in the OSI session, presentation, and application layers. TCP/IP has protocols to support file transfer, e-mail, and remote login, including the following (see Figure 15-3):

- **File Transfer Protocol (FTP)**—FTP is a reliable, connection-oriented service that uses TCP to transfer files between systems that support FTP. It supports bidirectional binary file and ASCII file transfers.

- **Trivial File Transfer Protocol (TFTP)** — TFTP is a connectionless service that uses the User Datagram Protocol (UDP). TFTP is used on the router to transfer configuration files and Cisco IOS Software images, and to transfer files between systems that support TFTP.

- **Network File System (NFS)** — NFS is a distributed file-system protocol suite developed by Sun Microsystems that allows remote file access across a network.

- **Simple Mail Transfer Protocol (SMTP)** — SMTP governs the transmission of e-mail over computer networks. It does not provide support for transmission of data other than plain text.

- **Terminal emulation (Telnet)** — Telnet provides the capability to remotely access another computer. It enables a user to log into an Internet host and execute commands. A Telnet client is referred to as a local host; a Telnet server is referred to as a remote host.

- **Simple Network Management Protocol (SNMP)** — SNMP is a protocol that provides a means to monitor and control network devices, and to manage configurations, statistics collection, performance, and security.

- **Domain Name System (DNS)** — DNS is a system used on the Internet for translating names of domains and their publicly advertised network nodes into IP addresses.

Figure 15-3 *TCP/IP Applications*

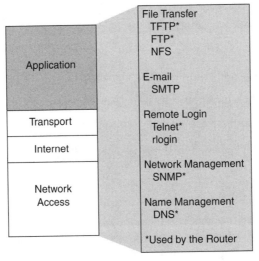

Summary

In this chapter, you learned the following key points:

- Computers use protocols to communicate on a network. The protocols define the rules of communication between devices.

- The function of the TCP/IP protocol stack is the transfer of information from one network device to another.

- IP is a connectionless protocol that provides best-effect delivery of packets.

- TCP is a reliable, connection-oriented protocol.

- TCP application layer protocols include FTP, TFTP, NFS, SMTP, Telnet, SNMP, and DNS.

Review Exercises

1 Which of the following statements best describes a protocol?

   a. A tool that lets Macintosh and PC computers communicate with each other

   b. A universal translator that allows different kinds of computers to share data

   c. A standard set of rules and conventions that determine how computers communicate with each other across networks

   d. The language that all the computers on a network must use to communicate with each other

2 Which of the following statements best describes TCP/IP?

   a. It is a suite of protocols that define rules for how packets or information is moved across a Internet.

   b. It is a suite of protocols that allow LANs to connect into WANs.

   c. It is a suite of protocols that allow for data transmission across a multitude of networks.

   d. It is a suite of protocols that allow different devices to be shared by interconnected networks.

3 Which of the following statements is true of IP?

   a. It determines where packets are routed based on their source address.

   b. It breaks packets into smaller packets, sends the packets to the destination, and reassembles them.

   c. It is a Layer 4 protocol.

   d. All of the above.

4 Which of the following is *not* a characteristic of TCP?

    a. TCP is a connectionless protocol.

    b. TCP is reliable.

    c. TCP divides outgoing messages into segments and reassembles messages at the destination station.

    d. TCP resends anything that is not received by the destination station.

5 Which of the following protocols was developed by Sun Microsystems and allows remote file access across a network?

    a. SMTP

    b. TFTP

    c. NFS

    d. SNMP

Upon completing this chapter, you will be able to:

- Describe the functions of the TCP/IP transport layer
- Describe flow control
- Identify and describe transport layer protocols
- Describe TCP and UDP header formats
- Describe TCP and UDP port numbers
- Describe the processes of establishing a TCP connection
- Describe acknowledgment
- Describe the functions of TCP sequence and acknowledgment numbers
- Describe the functions of TCP windowing

CHAPTER 16

Transport Layer

The transport layer uses the services provided by the network layer, such as best-path selection and logical addressing, to provide end-to-end communication between source and destination. The transport layer regulates the flow of information from source to destination reliably and accurately.

The TCP/IP protocol suite has two protocols at the transport layer: TCP and UDP. TCP is a connection-oriented protocol that provides reliable data transport. UDP is a connectionless, unreliable protocol.

This chapter describes the functions and services of the transport layer. It discusses how TCP and UDP use port numbers to keep track of different conversations that cross the network at the same time. In addition, it describes the process of establishing a TCP connection and covers the functions of TCP windowing, sequence numbers, and acknowledgment.

Transport Layer Functions

The transport layer provides transport services from the source host to the destination host through a logical connection between endpoints. Transport services enable users to segment and reassemble data from several upper-layer applications onto the same transport layer data stream. This transport layer data stream provides *end-to-end transport services*.

The primary services provided by the transport layer are as follows:

- **Segmenting upper-layer application data**—The transport layer enables users to assemble and disassemble multiple upper-layer segments into the same transport layer data stream. This is accomplished by assigning upper-layer application identifiers, also known as *port numbers*. You learn more about port numbers in the section "TCP and UDP Port Numbers," later in this chapter.

- **Establishing end-to-end operations**—The transport layer defines the end-to-end connectivity between two end stations.

- **Sending segments from one end host to another end host**—The transport layer provides transport services from the source host to the destination host.

- **Providing flow control and ensuring data reliability**—The transport layer ensures data integrity by maintaining flow control and enabling users to request reliable data transport between communicating end stations. Flow control is a mechanism that allows the communicating hosts to negotiate how much data is transmitted each time. To obtain such reliable data transport, a connection-orientated relationship is used between the communicating end stations.

The transport layer, Layer 4, assumes that it can use the network as a "cloud," as shown in Figure 16-1, to send data packets from the sender source to the receiver destination. A router in the cloud deals with issues such as "Which of several paths is best for a given route?" You can start to see the role that routers perform in this process.

NOTE   The "cloud" symbol suggests another network, or perhaps the entire Internet. When a cloud is used between two networks, it indicates that there is a way to connect from one network to another network, but it does not supply all the details of either the connection or the network.

Figure 16-1   *Transport Layer Functions*

Flow Control

As the transport layer sends its data segments, it can also ensure the integrity of the data. One method of doing this is called *flow control*. Flow control avoids the problem of a transmitting host at one side of the connection overflowing the buffers in the receiving host at the other side. Overflows can present serious problems because they can result in the loss of data.

Transport layer services also enable users to request reliable data transport between hosts and destinations. To obtain such reliable transport of data, a connection-oriented relationship is used between the communicating end systems. Reliable transport can accomplish the following:

- Ensures that the segments delivered will be acknowledged to the sender
- Provides for retransmission of any segments that are not acknowledged
- Put segments back into their correct sequence at the destination
- Provides congestion avoidance and control

TCP and UDP

The TCP/IP protocol suite provides two protocols at the transport layer: TCP and UDP. (See Figure 16-2.)

Figure 16-2   *TCP and UDP*

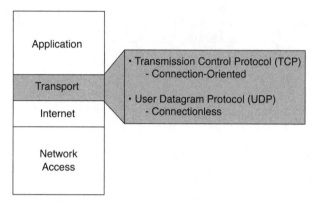

TCP is a connection-oriented, reliable protocol. In a connection-oriented environment, a connection is established between both ends before transfer of information can begin. TCP is responsible for breaking messages into segments, reassembling them at the destination station, resending anything that is not received, and reassembling messages from the segments. TCP supplies a virtual circuit between end-user applications.

UDP is a connectionless, unreliable protocol. Although UDP is responsible for transmitting messages, no software checking for segment delivery is provided at this layer. UDP depends on the application layer protocols for reliability. UDP is designed for applications that provide their own error-recovery process. It trades reliability for speed. UDP does not provide flow control and does not reassemble incoming messages.

The following sections describe the header formats of TCP and UDP.

TCP Header Format

Figure 16-3 illustrates the TCP segment header format. The fields in the header provide the communication between end stations to control conversation.

Figure 16-3   *TCP Segment Header Format*

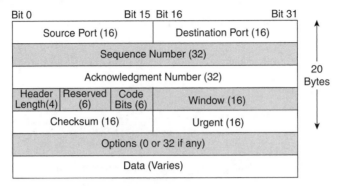

Field definitions in the TCP segment follow:

- **Source port**—Number of the calling port (16 bits)

- **Destination port**—Number of the called port (16 bits)

- **Sequence number**—Number used to ensure correct sequencing of the arriving data (32 bits)

- **Acknowledgment number**—Next expected TCP octet (32 bits)

- **Header length**—Number of 32-bit words in the header (4 bits)

- **Reserved**—Set to 0 (6 bits)

- **Code bits**—Control functions such as setup and termination of a session (6 bits)

- **Window**—Number of octets that the device is willing to accept (16 bits)

- **Checksum**—Calculated checksum of the Header and Data fields (16 bits)

- **Urgent**—The end of the urgent data (16 bits)

- **Options**—One currently defined: maximum TCP segment size (0 or 32 bits, if any)

- **Data**—Upper-layer protocol data (varies)

UDP Header Format

UDP transports data unreliably between hosts. Figure 16-4 illustrates the UDP segment header format. UDP has no sequence or acknowledgment fields. The fields in the UDP heads provide the communication between end stations.

Figure 16-4   *UDP Segment Header Format*

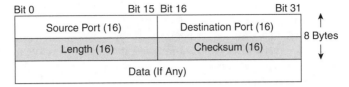

The UDP header length is always 64 bits. Field definitions in the UDP segment follow:

- **Source port**—Number of the calling port (16 bits)
- **Destination port**—Number of the called port (16 bits)
- **Length**—Length of UDP header and UDP data (16 bits)
- **Checksum**—Calculated checksum of the header and data fields (16 bits)
- **Data**—Upper-layer protocol data (varies)

Protocols that use UDP include the Trivial File Transfer Protocol (TFTP), the Simple Network Management Protocol (SNMP), the Network File System (NFS), and the Domain Name System (DNS). Refer to Chapter 15, "TCP/IP Overview," for a brief explanation of these protocols.

TCP and UDP Port Numbers

Both TCP and UDP use port (or socket) numbers to pass information to the upper layers (see Figure 16-5). Port numbers are used to keep track of different conversations crossing the network at the same time.

Figure 16-5   *Port Numbers*

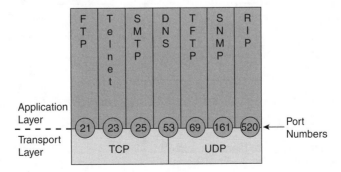

Application software developers use well-known port numbers that are controlled by the Internet Assigned Numbers Authority (IANA). For example, any conversation bound for the FTP application uses the standard port numbers 20 and 21 (20 for the data and 21 for control). Conversations that do not involve an application with a well-known port number are assigned port numbers randomly chosen from within a specific range instead. Some ports are reserved in both TCP and UDP, but applications might not be written to support them. Table 16-1 lists some of the well-known TCP and UDP port numbers.

Table 16-1   *Reserved TCP and UDP Port Numbers*

Decimal	Keyword	Description
7	echo	Echo
9	discard	Discard
11	user	Active users
20	ftp-data	File Transfer Protocol (data)
21	ftp	File Transfer Protocol
23	telnet	Terminal connection
25	smtp	Simple Mail Transfer Protocol
42	nameserver	Host name server
53	domain	Domain Name Server
67	bootps	Bootstrap Protocol server
68	bootpc	Bootstrap Protocol client
69	tftp	Trivial File Transfer Protocol
80	www-http	World Wide Web HTTP
110	pop3	Post Office Protocol, version 3
161	snmp	Simple Network Management Protocol
213	ipx	Internet Package Exchange
556	remotefs	Remote File System Server

Port numbers have the following assigned ranges:

- Numbers below 1024 are considered well-known ports.

- Numbers 1024 and above are dynamically assigned ports.

- Registered ports are those registered for vendor-specific applications. Most are above 1024.

As shown in Figure 16-6, end systems use port numbers to select the proper application. Originating source port numbers dynamically are assigned by the source host some number greater than 1023.

Figure 16-6   *TCP Port Numbers*

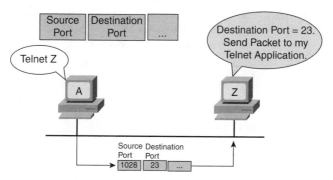

Establishing a TCP Connection

Connection-oriented services involve three phases: the connection establishment phase, the data transfer phase, and the connection termination phase. In the connection establishment phase, a connection or session is set up between the source and the destination. Resources typically are reserved at this time to ensure a consistent grade of service. During the data transfer phase, data is transmitted sequentially over the established path, arriving at the destination in the order in which it was sent. The connection termination phase consists of terminating the connection between the source and the destination when it is no longer needed.

Three-Way Handshake

TCP is connection oriented, so it requires connection establishment before data transfer begins. For a connection to be established or initialized, the two hosts must synchronize on each other's initial sequence numbers (ISNs). Sequence numbers, randomly chosen by TCP hosts, are used to track the order of packets and to ensure that no packets are lost in transmission. The ISN is the starting number used when a TCP connection is established. Exchanging the ISN during the connection sequence ensures that lost data can be recovered.

Synchronization is done in an exchange of connection-establishing segments that carry a control bit called SYN (for synchronize) and the ISNs. Segments that carry the SYN bit are also called SYNs. Hence, establishing a TCP connection requires a suitable mechanism for picking an ISN and a slightly complicated three-way handshake to exchange the ISNs.

The synchronization requires each side to send its own ISN and to receive a confirmation of it in an acknowledgment (ACK) from the other side. Each side also must receive the other side's

ISN and send a confirming ACK. The three-way handshake sequence follows, and Figure 16-7 illustrates this process:

1   **Host A–to–Host B SYN**—In the SYN segment, Host A tells Host B that its sequence number (SEQ) is X.

2   **Host B–to–Host A SYN**—Host B receives the SYN, records the sequence number X, and replies by acknowledging the SYN with an ACK = X + 1 and its own sequence number (SEQ = Y). ACK = X + 1 means that a host (in this case, Host B) has received X and expects X + 1 next. This technique is called *forward acknowledgment*.

3   **Host A–to–Host B ACK**—Host A then acknowledges the data that Host B sent with an acknowledgment indicating that Host A expects Y + 1 next (ACK = Y + 1).

After completing these three steps, a connection is established. At this point, either side can begin data transfer.

Figure 16-7   *Three-Way Handshake*

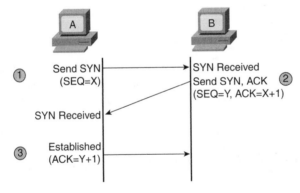

A three-way handshake is necessary because sequence numbers are not tied to a global clock in the network, and TCP protocols might have different mechanisms for picking the ISN. The receiver of the first SYN has no way of knowing whether the segment was an old delayed one, unless it remembers the last sequence number used on the connection (which is not always possible). Thus, it must ask the source to verify this SYN.

Acknowledgment

Reliable delivery guarantees that a stream of data sent from one machine is delivered through a data link to another machine without duplication or data loss. Positive acknowledgment and retransmission, or PAR, is a common technique that many protocols use to provide reliability. With PAR, the source sends a packet, starts a timer, and waits for an acknowledgment before sending the next segment. If the timer expires before the source receives an acknowledgment, the source retransmits the segment and starts the timer again.

Window size determines the amount of data that you can transmit at one time before receiving an acknowledgment from the destination. The larger the window size number (bytes) is, the greater the amount of data the host can transmit. After a host transmits the window-sized number of bytes, the host must receive an acknowledgment that the data has been received before it can send any more messages. For example, with a window size of 1, each individual (1) segment must be acknowledged before you can send the next segment (see Figure 16-8). You learn more about windowing in the section "TCP Windowing," later in this chapter.

Figure 16-8   *TCP Simple Acknowledgment*

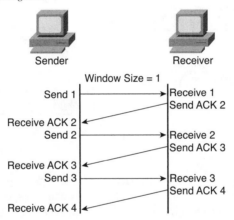

TCP Sequence and Acknowledgment Numbers

TCP provides sequencing of segments with a forward reference acknowledgment. Each segment is numbered by the source station before transmission (see Figure 16-9). At the receiving station, TCP reassembles the segments into a complete message. If a sequence number is missing in the series, that segment is retransmitted. Segments that are not acknowledged within a given time period result in retransmission.

Figure 16-9   *TCP Sequence and Acknowledgment Numbers*

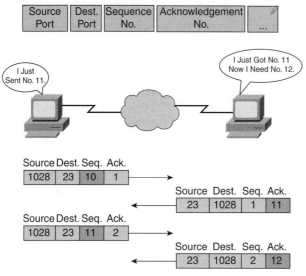

TCP Windowing

To govern the flow of data between devices, TCP uses a *flow-control* mechanism. The receiving TCP reports a "window" to the sending TCP. This window specifies the number of octets, starting with the acknowledgment number, that the receiving TCP currently is prepared to receive.

For example, with a window size of 3, the source device can send three octets to the destination. It then must wait for an acknowledgment. If the destination receives the three octets, it sends an acknowledgment to the source device, which can now transmit three more octets. If the destination does not receive the three octets—for example, because of overflowing buffers—it does not send an acknowledgment. Because the source does not receive an acknowledgment, it knows that the octets should be retransmitted and that the transmission rate should be slowed.

TCP window sizes are variable during the lifetime of a connection. Each acknowledgment contains a window advertisement indicating the number of bytes that the receiver can accept. TCP also maintains a congestion-control window, which is normally the same size as the receiver's window but is cut in half when a segment is lost (for example, when there is congestion). This approach permits the window to be expanded or contracted as necessary to manage buffer space and processing. A larger window size enables more data to be processed.

In Figure 16-10, the source sends three segments before expecting an ACK. The receiver received only up to segment 2 because it can handle a window size of only two segments. So,

it specifies 3 as the next segment and specifies a new window size of 2. The source sends the
next two segments but still specifies its own window size of 3 (for example, it still can accept
three segments from the receiver). The receiver replies by requesting segment 5 and specifying
a window size of 2.

Figure 16-10 *TCP Windowing*

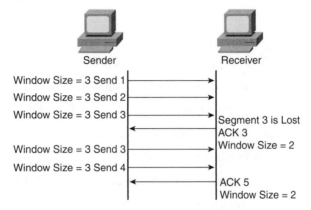

Summary

In this chapter, you learned the following key points:

- The transport layer provides transport service from the source host to the destination host.

- TCP uses a connection-oriented relationship between communicating end systems to
  ensure data-transfer reliability.

- The transport layer has two primary protocols: TCP and UDP.

- TCP and UDP use port numbers to keep track of different conversations that cross the
  network at the same time to pass information to the upper layers.

- The synchronization between the endpoints of a TCP connection is known as a *three-way
  handshake*.

- Positive acknowledgment and retransmission (PAR) is a common technique that many
  protocols use to provide reliability.

- TCP windowing is a flow-control mechanism.

Review Exercises

1 Which of the following is a basic service of the transport layer?

   a. To provide reliability by using sequence numbers and acknowledgments

   b. To segment upper-layer application data

   c. To establish end-to-end operations

   d. All of the above

2 Which of the following phrases best describes flow control?

   a. A device at the destination side that controls the flow of incoming data

   b. A buffer at the source side that monitors the outflow of data

   c. A technique that ensures that the source does not overwhelm the destination with data

   d. A suspension of transmission until the data in the source buffers has been processed

3 Which of the following statements best describes positive acknowledgment?

   a. Positive acknowledgment requires a recipient to communicate with the source, sending back an acknowledgment message when it receives data.

   b. If a recipient does not receive one of the packets, it sends a negative acknowledgment to the sender with the numbers of the packets received.

   c. Positive acknowledgment is the retransmission of guaranteed and reliable delivery of data.

   d. If a sender does not receive a negative acknowledgment within a certain time, the sender retransmits the data.

4 What layer do TCP and UDP reside in?

   a. Network layer

   b. Data link layer

   c. Transport layer

   d. Internet layer

5 What does the Window field in a TCP segment indicate?

   a. Number of 32-bit words in the header

   b. Number of the called port

   c. Number used to ensure correct sequencing of the arriving data

   d. Number of octets that the device is willing to accept

6 What do TCP and UDP use to keep track of different conversations crossing a network at the same time?

   a. Port numbers

   b. IP addresses

   c. MAC addresses

   d. Sequence numbers

7 Which range of port numbers is unregulated?

   a. Below 255

   b. Between 256 and 512

   c. Between 256 and 1023

   d. 1024 and above

8 How does TCP synchronize a connection between the source and the destination before data transmission?

   a. Two-way handshake

   b. Three-way handshake

   c. Four-way handshake

   d. Holton functions

9 What do the TCP sequence and acknowledgment numbers do?

   a. They break segments into their binary coefficients, number them sequentially, and send them to their destination, where the sender acknowledges their recipient.

   b. They break down messages into datagrams that are numbered and then sent to a host according to the sequence set by the source TCP.

   c. They provide a system for sequencing datagrams at the source and acknowledging them at the destination.

   d. They provide sequencing of segments with a forward reference acknowledgment, number segments before transmission, and reassemble the segments into a complete message.

10 What flow-control method does TCP implement?

   a. Acknowledgment

   b. Buffering

   c. Windowing

   d. Port numbers

Upon completing this chapter, you will be able to:

- Identify the protocols that operate at the TCP/IP Internet layer

- Identify the definitions of different fields in an IP datagram

- Identify the function of the Protocol field in an IP datagram

- Describe the functions of the Internet Control Message Protocol (ICMP)

- Describe the functions of the Address Resolution Protocol (ARP)

- Describe the functions of the Reverse Address Resolution Protocol (RARP)

- Describe the functions of the Bootstrap Protocol (BOOTP)

- Describe the functions of the Dynamic Host Configuration Protocol (DHCP)

CHAPTER 17

TCP/IP Internet Layer Overview

The Internet layer of the TCP/IP protocol stack corresponds to the network layer of the OSI model. The network layer is responsible for getting packets through a network using IP addressing. This is the layer that routers operate at to identify paths in the network, but there are many other functions at the Internet layer. Several protocols operate at the TCP/IP Internet layer: the Internet Protocol (IP), ICMP, ARP, and RARP.

This chapter describes the protocols that operate at the TCP/IP Internet layer and their functions. In addition, this chapter discusses two protocols used to dynamically assign IP addresses: BOOTP and DHCP.

TCP/IP Internet Layer and the OSI Network Layer

The Internet layer of the TCP/IP model corresponds to the OSI network layer, which designates the protocol relating to the logical transmission of packets over the entire network. The network layer takes care of the addressing of the host by giving the host an IP address, and it handles the routing of packets among multiple networks. The network layer also controls the communication flow between two hosts.

The following protocols operate at the TCP/IP Internet layer (see Figure 17-1):

- **IP**—Provides connectionless, best-effort delivery routing of datagrams. IP is not concerned with the content of the datagrams. Instead, it looks for a way to move the datagrams to their destination.

- **ICMP**—Provides messages to report errors and other information regarding IP datagram processing back to the source host.

- **ARP**—Determines the data link layer address (Media Access Control [MAC] addresses) for known IP addresses.

- **RARP**—Determines IP addresses when data link layer addresses (MAC addresses) are known.

Figure 17-1   *Internet Layer Overview*

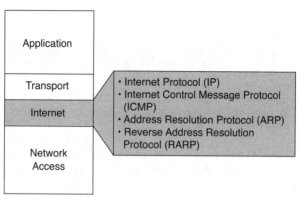

IP Datagram

IP is a network layer (Layer 3) protocol that contains addressing information and some control information that enables packets to be routed. IP provides connectionless, best-effort delivery of datagram through an internetwork.

When IP receives segments from the transport layer, it fragments them into *datagrams* (packets). (The term *packet* often is used interchangeably with *datagram*.) IP then reassembles datagrams back into segments on the receiving side. Each IP datagram contains the IP address of the sender and the recipient. Each router that receives an IP datagram makes the routing decisions based on the destination IP address in the datagram.

Figure 17-2 illustrates the format of an IP datagram. Field definitions within this IP datagram are as follows:

- **Version**—Version number (4 bits).

- **Header Length**—Header length in 32-bit words (4 bits).

- **Priority and Type of Service**—How the datagram should be handled. The first 3 bits are priority bits (8 bits).

- **Total Length**—Total length (header + data) (16 bits).

- **Identification**—Unique IP datagram value (16 bits).

- **Flags**—Whether fragmenting should occur (3 bits).

- **Fragment Offset**—Fragmentation of datagrams to allow differing maximum transmission units (MTUs) in the Internet (13 bits). (MTU refers to the maximum packet size, in bytes, that a particular interface can handle.)

- **Time To Live (TTL)**—How long a packet is considered valid (8 bits).

- **Protocol**—Upper-layer (Layer 4) protocol sending the datagram (8 bits).

- **Header Checksum**—Integrity check on the header (16 bits).

- **Source IP Address**—The 32-bit source IP addresses (32 bits).

- **Destination IP Addresses**—The 32-bit destination IP addresses (32 bits).

- **IP Options**—Network testing, debugging, security, and others (0 or 32 bits, if any).

- **Data**—Upper-layer protocol data (varies).

Figure 17-2   *IP Datagram*

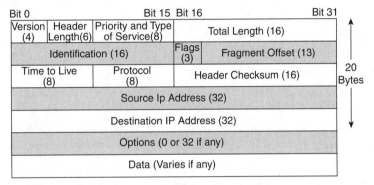

Protocol Field

The Protocol field determines the transport layer protocol being carried within an IP datagram. Each IP header must identify the destination transport layer (Layer 4) protocol for the datagram. If the header didn't carry the protocol information for the transport layer, IP would not know what to do with the data carried in the datagram.

Transport layer protocols are numbered, similar to port numbers. IP includes the protocol number in the Protocol field. As shown in Figure 17-3, the Protocol field determines the Layer 4 protocol being carried within an IP datagram. The figure also shows that the protocol number of TCP is 6 and that the protocol number of UDP is 17.

Figure 17-3   *Protocol Field*

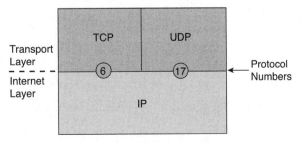

Although most IP traffic uses TCP or UDP, other protocols can use IP. Table 17-1 lists some sample protocols and their numbers that can be specified in the Protocol fields.

Table 17-1   *Protocol Numbers*

Protocol	Protocol Number
Internet Control Message Protocol (ICMP)	1
Interior Routing Gateway Protocol (IGRP)	9
IP version 6 (IPv6)	41
Generic Routing Encapsulation (GRE)	47
Internetwork Packet Exchange in Internet Protocol (IPX in IP)	111
Layer 2 Tunneling Protocol (L2TP)	115

ICMP

The ICMP is implemented by all TCP/IP hosts. ICMP messages are carried in IP datagrams and are used to send error and control messages. ICMP uses the following types of defined messages:

- **Destination unreachable**—Informs the source host that an IP datagram cannot be delivered

- **Time exceeded**—Indicates that the Time To Live (TTL) of an IP datagram has expired

- **Parameter problem**—Informs the source host that there is an incorrect parameter on the datagram

- **Source quench**—Informs the source host that it is sending the data too fast for the receiver

- **Redirect**—Informs the source host that there is a better route for a particular IP datagram

- **Echo request**—Sent by any host to test host reachability across an internetwork

- **Echo reply**—Replies to an ICMP echo request

- **Timestamp request**—Requests a round-trip time to a particular destination

- **Timestamp reply**—Replies to a timestamp request

- **Information request**—Enables a host to learn the network portion of an IP address on its subnet

- **Information reply**—Replies to an information request

- **Address request**—Requests that the correct subnet mask be used

- **Address reply**—Replies to an address mask request

ICMP Testing

If a router receives a packet that it cannot deliver to its final destination, the router sends an ICMP destination unreachable message to the source, as shown in Figure 17-4.

Figure 17-4   *ICMP Testing*

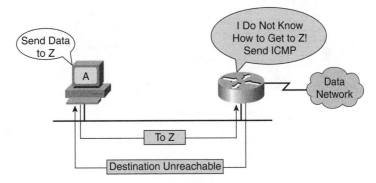

The message might be undeliverable because there is no known route to the destination. In Figure 17-5, an echo reply is a successful reply to a **ping** command, or echo request. The **ping** command often is used to test connectivity between IP hosts. If the ping fails, results could include other ICMP messages, such as destination unreachable and timeout messages.

Figure 17-5   *ICMP Echo Request and Echo Reply*

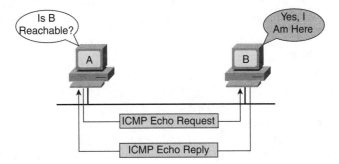

ARP

ARP is used to resolve or map a known IP address to a MAC sublayer address to allow communication on a multiaccess medium such as Ethernet. To determine a destination MAC address for a datagram, the ARP cache table is checked. If the destination MAC address associated with the destination IP address is not in the ARP cache table, the device sends an ARP request, which is a broadcast looking for the MAC address of the destination station.

Every station on the network receives the broadcast. If a station recognizes that the IP address in the ARP broadcast is its own IP address, it sends an ARP response indicating its MAC address (see Figure 17-6). The term *local ARP* describes the process of resolving an address when both the requesting host and the destination host share the same medium or wire.

Figure 17-6   *Address Resolution Protocol*

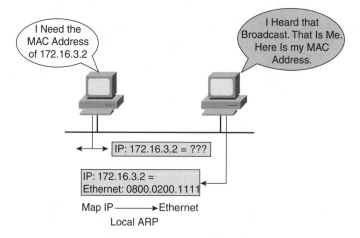

The ARP cache table in a host running TCP/IP maintains recent mappings of IP addresses to MAC addresses. As a host contacts other hosts or routers on its attached network, new entries are added. Normally, the entries "time out" after some time interval and are removed from the cache.

RARP

RARP relies on the presence of a RARP server with a table entry or some other means to respond to these RARP requests. On the local segment, you can use RARP to initiate a remote operating system load sequence. ARP and RARP are implemented directly on top of the data link layer. RARP binds MAC addresses to IP addresses. This binding allows network devices to encapsulate data before sending the data out on the network. A network device, such as a diskless workstation, might know its MAC address but not its IP address. The RARP request is a broadcast packet. Devices using RARP require the presence of a RARP server on the network to answer RARP requests. Figure 17-7 illustrates how RARP works so that workstations can identify their own IP addresses.

Figure 17-7   *RARP*

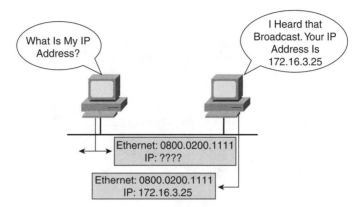

BOOTP and DHCP

In a TCP/IP environment, end stations communicate seamlessly with servers or other end stations. This communication occurs because each node using the TCP/IP protocol suite has a unique 32-bit logical IP address assigned to it. You will learn more about IP addressing in Chapter 18, "Networking Addressing."

Besides RARP, you can use a few different methods to assign IP addresses dynamically. The Bootstrap Protocol (BOOTP) and the Dynamic Host Configuration Protocol (DHCP) are examples of these.

A device uses BOOTP when it starts up to obtain an IP address. BOOTP uses UDP to carry messages; the UDP message is encapsulated in an IP datagram. A computer uses BOOTP to send a broadcast IP datagram using a destination IP address of all 1s—255.255.255.255. A BOOTP server receives the broadcast and then sends a broadcast. The client receives a datagram and checks the MAC address. If it finds its own MAC address in the destination address field, it takes the IP address in that datagram.

Like RARP, BOOTP operates in a client/server environment and requires only a single packet exchange. However, unlike RARP, which sends back only a four-octet IP address, BOOTP datagrams can include the IP address, the address of a router (default gateway), the address of a server, and a vendor-specific field. One of the problems with BOOTP is that it was not designed to provide dynamic address assignment. With BOOTP, you create a configuration file that specifies the parameters for each device.

BOOTP is an old program that is still around. However, BOOTP is surpassed in popularity by DHCP, which is discussed in next section.

DHCP is a newer and more sophisticated from of BOOTP. Unlike BOOTP, DHCP allows a host to obtain an IP address quickly and dynamically. All that is required using DHCP is a defined range of IP addresses on a DHCP server. As hosts come online, they contact the DHCP server and request an address. The DHCP server chooses an address and allocates it to that host (see Figure 17-8). With DHCP, the entire computer's configuration can be obtained in one message (for example, along with the IP address, subnet mask, domain name, default gateway, and DNS, the server can provide Windows Internet Naming Service [WINS] information).

Figure 17-8 *DHCP*

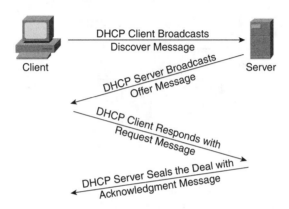

Client

DHCP Client Broadcasts
Discover Message

DHCP Server Broadcasts
Offer Message

Server

DHCP Client Responds with
Request Message

DHCP Server Seals the Deal with
Acknowledgment Message

Summary

In this chapter, you learned the following key points:

- The TCP/IP Internet layer corresponds to the OSI network layer.

- The Protocol field in the IP datagram determines the destination upper-layer (transport layer) protocol.

- ICMP is implemented by all TCP/IP hosts.

- ARP is used to resolve or map a known IP address to a MAC address. RARP is used to map a known MAC address to an IP address.

- BOOTP and DHCP are different methods that you can use to assign IP addresses dynamically.

Review Exercises

1 Which of the following protocols operate at the TCP/IP Internet layer?

  a. IP

  b. ICMP

  c. ARP

  d. All of the above

2 Which of the following *best* describes TTL?

  a. Field in the datagram header that determines how long the data is valid

  b. Field in the IP datagram that indicates how long a packet is considered valid

  c. Field within an IP datagram that indicates the upper-layer protocol sending the datagram

  d. Field in a datagram header that indicates when the next data packet will arrive

3 What is the function of Protocol field in an IP datagram?

  a. To specify the application layer protocol

  b. To specify the physical layer protocol

  c. To specify the upper-layer (transport layer) protocol

  d. To specify the lower-layer (data link layer) protocol

4 What does the acronym ICMP stand for?

  a. Internetwork Connection Model Protocol

  b. Internet Connection Monitor Protocol

  c. Internet Control Message Protocol

  d. Internetwork Control Mode Protocol

5 What is the purpose of ICMPs?

  a. They put the internetwork in control mode so that protocols can be set up.

  b. They are messages that the network uses to monitor connection protocols.

  c. They are standard binary messages that act as model internetwork protocols.

  d. They are messages carried in IP datagrams used to send error and control messages.

6 What is the function of ARP?

    a. It is used to map a given MAC address to an IP address.

    b. It is used to develop a cached address resource table.

    c. It is used to map an IP address to a MAC address.

    d. It sends a broadcast message looking for the router address

7 What is the function of the RARP?

    a. It is a protocol in the TCP/IP stack that provides a method for finding IP addresses based on MAC addresses.

    b. It is a protocol used to map a 32-bit IP address to a MAC address.

    c. It is a protocol used to develop a cached address resource table for the router.

    d. It a protocol that is used for maintaining the ARP cache in an IP host.

8 Which of the following statements is true?

    a. All that is required using DHCP is an undefined range of IP addresses on a DHCP server.

    b. Unlike BOOTP, DHCP allows a host to obtain an IP address quickly and dynamically.

    c. BOOTP is designed to provide dynamic address assignment.

    d. With BOOTP, you cannot create a configuration file that specifies the parameters for each device.

IP Addressing and Routing

Upon completing this chapter, you will be able to:

- Describe the IP addressing scheme
- Describe the types of IP address classes
- Describe the reserved IP address space
- Describe the functions of private addresses
- Describe the differences between IPv4 and IPv6 standards
- Describe the functions of classless interdomain routing (CIDR)

CHAPTER 18

Networking Addressing

The network layer is responsible for navigating data through a network. The function of the network layer is to find the best path through a network. Devices use the network-layer addressing scheme to determine the destination of data as it moves through the network.

The TCP/IP protocol suite has a network-layer addressing scheme known as *IP addressing*. The original version of IP, IP version 4 (IPv4), uses a 32-bit binary address. To accommodate different network sizes, the IPv4 addressing was broken down into five classes, from Class A to Class E. In 1980s, IPv4 offered an addressing strategy that, although scalable for a time, resulted in an inefficient allocation of addresses. Over the past two decades, networking engineers have successfully modified IPv4 so that it could survive the Internet's exponential growth. Meanwhile, a more extendible and scalable version of IP, IP version 6 (IPv6), has been defined and developed.

This chapter examines IP addressing and the five classes of IP addresses. This chapter also discusses the reserved IP addresses, which are the IP addresses that have been set aside and cannot be assigned to any network on the Internet.

Finally, this chapter explores the evolution and extension of IPv4, including one of the key scalability features that engineers have added to it over the years—classless interdomain routing (CIDR).

IP Addressing

In an IP network, end stations communicate with servers or other end stations. This communication requires a way to identify the two sides of the conversation. The TCP/IP protocol suite uses a 32-bit address. This address is known as the *IP address*. IP addressing is a hierarchical addressing. An IP address has two parts, as follows:

- **The network number portion (network ID)**—The network number portion of an IP address identifies the network to which a device is attached.

- **The host number portion (host ID)**—The host number portion of an IP address identifies a specific device on a network.

Together, those two parts of addresses could uniquely identify any and all devices connected via the Internet. It is the unique combination of both the host number and the network number that make it possible to access any given host in an internetwork. IP addresses are like postal mail addresses, which describe a person's location by providing a country, a state, a city, a street, and a street number. The IP packet, which carries the information between network devices, is like an envelope containing the information a user wants to send. Outside the envelope, we need an address for delivery.

A network number functions like a postal code. A postal code enables the postal system to direct your mail to your local post office and to your neighborhood. From there, the street address directs the carrier to the proper destination.

For example, if you have a letter that is addressed to "150 Tasman Drive, Los Angeles, CA 90210," the postal code 90210 directs the mail to a local post office in Los Angeles, California. Then the carrier uses the street address 150 Tasman Drive to deliver the letter to the proper house. In this example, the postal code (90210) represents the network number, or network ID, and the street address (150 Tasman Drive) represents the host number, or host ID.

It is important to understand the significance of the network ID and host ID. The following sections discuss the network ID and host ID in more detail.

Network ID

A *network ID* helps the router find a path through the internetwork to the destination network. Hosts on a network can communicate directly only with devices that have the same network ID. They might share the same physical segment, but if they have different network numbers, they usually cannot communicate with each other unless there is another device that can make a connection between the networks.

A network ID enables a router to put a packet onto the appropriate network segment.

Host ID

In addition to the network ID, network protocols use the host ID. The *host ID* refers to the device port on the network.

The host ID helps the router deliver the Layer 2 frame (such as an Ethernet frame) encapsulating the packet to a specific host on the network. As a result, the IP address is mapped to the correct Media Access Control (MAC) address, which is needed by the Layer 2 process on the router to create the Ethernet frame. Recall from Chapter 17, "TCP/IP Internet Layer Overview," that the Address Resolution Protocol (ARP) is used for determining the MAC address of a device, given its IP address.

From some network layer protocols, a network administrator assigns host numbers according to a predetermined network-addressing plan developed by the network administrator. For other network layer protocols, assigning the host number is partially or completely dynamic or automatic. Figure 18-1 shows three devices in Network 1 (two workstations and a router), each with a unique host number. Figure 18-1 also shows that the router is connected to two other networks, Networks 2 and 3. (Note that the addresses used in Figure 18-1 are for illustration of the concept; they are not valid IP addressing.)

Figure 18-1   *Network Numbers and Host Numbers*

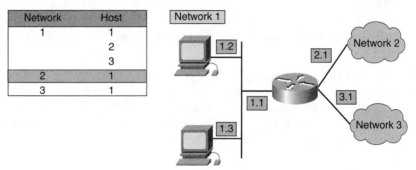

IP Address Classes

IP addresses are globally unique 32-bit numbers. Globally unique addresses permit IP devices anywhere in the world to communicate with each other. For simplicity and clarity, these bits are normally represented as four sets of octets (8 bits [or 1 byte per octet]). Each octet is then represented as a decimal number between 0 and 255, separated by a period, or dot. This scenario is known as *dotted-decimal notation*. As shown in the following list, the IP address 10000100101000111000000000010001 can be written as 132.163.128.17 and spoken as "132 dot 163 dot 128 dot 17":

- An IP address is a 32-bit binary number:

   10000100101000111000000000010001

- This binary number can be divided into four octets:

   10000100 10100011 10000000 00010001

- Each octet (or byte) can be represented in decimal:

   132   163   128   17

- The address can be written in dotted-decimal notation:

   132.163.128.17

To accommodate different sizes of networks and aid in classifying them, IP addresses are divided into categories called *classes*. This scenario is known as *classful addressing*. Each IP address is broken down into a network number (or network ID) and a host number (or host ID). A bit or bit sequence at the start of each address determines the class of the address. There are five IP address classes, ranging from Class A to Class E.

The following sections describe each IP address class in more detail.

Class A Address

The Class A address was designed to support extremely large networks. A Class A IP address uses only the first octet to indicate the network number. The remaining three octets are used for host number.

The first bit of a Class A address is always 0 (see Figure 18-2). With that first bit as 0, the lowest number that can be represented is 00000000 (decimal 0), and the highest number that can be represented is 01111111 (decimal 127). However, these two network numbers, 0 and 127, are reserved and cannot be used as a network address. Any address that starts with a value between 1 and 126 in the first octet is a Class A address.

Figure 18-2   *Class A IP Address*

Number of Bits | 1 | 7 | 24 |
Class A: 0 Network Number   Host Number

NOTE   The 0.0.0.0 network is reserved for use by routers to designate the default route. A default router associates a specific router's interface with all unknown destination address. The 127.0.0.0 network is reserved for loopback testing (routers or local machines can use this address to send packets to themselves). Therefore, the 0.0.0.0 network or 127.0.0.0 network cannot be assigned to a network.

Class B Address

The Class B address was designed to support the needs of moderate- to large-size networks. A Class B IP address uses two of the four octets to indicate the network address. The other two octets specify host addresses.

The first 2 bits of the first octet of a Class B address are always 10 (see Figure 18-3). The remaining 6 bits may be populated with either 1s or 0s. Therefore, the lowest number that can be represented with a Class B address is 10000000 (decimal 128), and the highest number that can be represented is 10111111 (decimal 191). Any address that starts with a value in the range of 128 to 191 in the first octet is a Class B address.

Figure 18-3   *Class B IP Address*

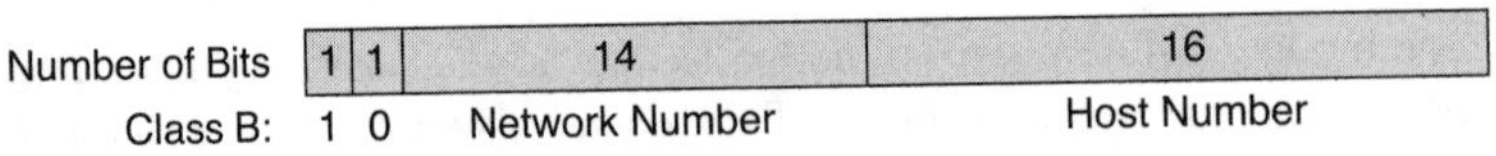

Number of Bits | 1 | 1 | 14 | 16 |
Class B: 1 0   Network Number   Host Number

Class C Address

The Class C address space is the most commonly used of the original address classes. This address space was intended to support a lot of small networks. A Class C address begins with binary 110 (see Figure 18-4). Therefore, the lowest number that can be represented is 11000000 (decimal 192), and the highest number that can be represented is 11011111 (decimal 223). If an address contains a number in the range of 192 to 223 in the first octet, it is a Class C address.

Figure 18-4   *Class C IP Address*

Number of Bits	1	1	1	21	8
Class C:	1	1	0	Network Number	Host Number

Class D Address

The Class D address class was created to enable multicasting in an IP address. A *multicast address* is a unique network address that directs packets with that destination address to predefined groups of IP addresses. Therefore, a single station can simultaneously transmit a single stream of datagrams to multiple recipients.

The Class D address space, much like the other address spaces, is mathematically constrained. The first 4 bits of a Class D address must be 1110 (see Figure 18-5). Therefore, the first octet range for Class D addresses is 11100000 to 11101111, or 224 to 239. An IP address that starts with a value in the range of 224 to 239 in the first octet is a Class D address.

Figure 18-5   *Class D IP Address*

Number of Bits	1	1	1	1	28
Class D:	1	1	1	0	Address

NOTE   Class D addresses are used for multicast groups. Therefore, there is no need to allocate octets or bits to separate network number and host number.

Class E Address

A Class E address has been defined; however, the Internet Engineering Task Force (IETF) reserves these addresses for its own research. Therefore, no Class E addresses have been released for use in the Internet. The first 4 bits of a Class E address are always set to 1s (see Figure 18-6). Therefore, the first octet range for Class D addresses is 11110000 to 11111111, or 240 to 255.

Figure 18-6   *Class E IP Address*

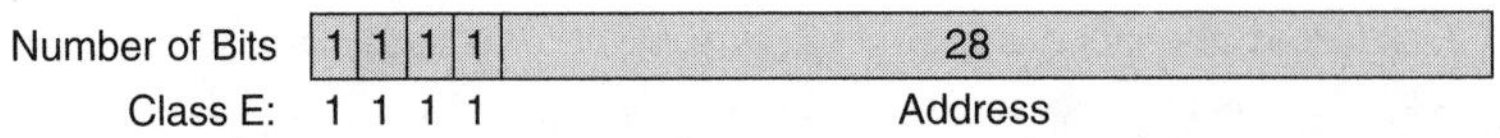

To summarize, Table 18-1 shows the IP address range of the first octet (in decimal and binary) for each of the five IP address classes.

Table 18-1   *IP Address Ranges*

IP Address Class	IP Address Range (First Octet Decimal Value)
Class A	1 to 126 (00000001 to 01111110) *
Class B	128 to 191 (10000000 to 10111111)
Class C	192 to 223 (11000000 to 11011111)
Class D	224 to 239 (11100000 to 11101111)
Class E	240 to 255 (11110000 to 11111111)

* Technically, 127 (01111111) is a Class A address. However, it is reserved and cannot be used for network addresses.

Reserved IP Address

Certain host addresses are reserved and cannot be assigned to devices on a network. These reserved host addresses include the following:

- **Network address**—Used to identify the network itself
- **Broadcast address**—Used for broadcasting packets to all the devices on a network

The following sections describe network addresses and broadcast addresses in more detail.

Network Address

An IP address that has binary 0s in all host bit positions is reserved for the network address. Therefore, as a Class A network example, 113.0.0.0 is the IP address of the network containing the host 113.1.2.3. A router uses the network IP address when it searches its IP routing table for the destination network location. As a Class B network example, the IP address 176.10.0.0 is a network address, as shown in Figure 18-7.

Figure 18-7   *Network Address*

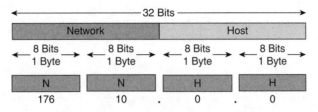

Network Address (Host Bits = All Zeros)

The decimal numbers that fill the first two octets in a Class B network address are assigned. The last two octets contain 0s because those 16 bits are for host numbers and are used for devices that are attached to the network. The IP address in the example 176.10.0.0 is reserved for the network address; it is never used as an address for any device that is attached to it. An example of an IP address for a device on the 176.10.0.0 network is 176.10.16.1. In this example, 176.10 is the network number portion and 16.1 is the host number portion.

Broadcast Address

If you wanted to send data to all the devices on a network, you would need to use a *broadcast address*. Broadcast addresses are never valid as source addresses—only as destination addresses. Different types of broadcast addresses exist as follows:

- **Local broadcast**—If an IP device wants to communicate with all devices on the local network, it sets the destination address to all 1s—for example, 255.255.255.255—and transmits the packet. This form of broadcast is *never* capable of being routed and will never be forwarded by routers onto other network segments.

- **Directed broadcast**—A directed broadcast is a local broadcast within a particular subnetwork, which is a smaller division of a local network. (You will learn more about subnetworks in Chapter 19, "IP Subnetting and Calculation.") A directed broadcast address contains a valid network ID and the broadcast host ID. The directed broadcast is capable of being routed. However, this behavior is not the default for Cisco routers. The directed broadcast addresses are discussed more detail in next section, "Directed Broadcast Address."

Directed Broadcast Address

A directed broadcast occurs when a source sends out data to all devices on a subnetwork. To ensure that all the devices on the network pay attention to the broadcast, the sender must use a destination IP address that all of the devices can recognize and pick up. Directed broadcast IP addresses end with binary 1s in the entire host part of the address.

For the network in the example 176.10.0.0, in which the last 16 bits make up the host part of the address, the broadcast that would be sent out to all devices on that network would include a destination address of 176.10.255.255 (because 255 is the decimal value of an octet containing 11111111), as shown in Figure 18-8.

Figure 18-8   *Directed Broadcast Address*

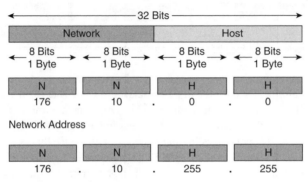

Directed Broadcast Address (Host Bits = All Ones)

A directed broadcast address is quite similar to a bulk postal mailing. The postal code directs the mail to the appropriate area, and the broadcast address of "Current Resident" further directs the mail to every address. An IP broadcast address uses the same concept. The network number designates the segment, and the rest of the address tells every IP host in that network that this is a broadcast message and that the device needs to pay attention to the message. All devices on a network recognize their own host IP address as well as the broadcast address for their network.

Hosts for Classes of IP Addresses

Each class of network allows a fixed number of hosts. In a Class A network, the first octet is assigned for the network, leaving the last three octets (24 bits) to be assigned to hosts. Remember that the first host address in each network (all 0s) is reserved for the actual network address, and the final host address in each network (all 1s) is reserved for broadcasts. The maximum number of hosts in a Class A network is $2^{24} - 2$ (subtracting the network and broadcast reserved addresses), or 16,777,214 hosts.

In a Class B network, the first two octets are assigned for the network, leaving the final two octets (16 bits) to be assigned to hosts. The maximum number of hosts in a Class B network is $2^{16} - 2$, or 65,534 hosts.

In a Class C network, the first three octets are assigned for the network. This leaves the final octet (8 bits) to assign to hosts, so the maximum number of hosts is $2^8 - 2$, or 254 hosts.

Private IP Addresses

Internet stability depends directly on the uniqueness of publicly used network addresses. Therefore, some mechanism was needed to ensure that addresses were, in fact, unique. This responsibility originally rested within an organization known as the Internet Network Information Center (InterNIC). This organization is now defunct and has been succeeded by the Internet Assigned Numbers Authority (IANA). IANA carefully manages the remaining supply of IP addresses to ensure that duplication of publicly used addresses does not occur. Such duplication would cause instability in the Internet and compromise its capability to deliver datagrams to networks using the duplicated addresses.

Internet hosts require a globally unique routable IP address, or *public IP address*. (You learn more about public IP address later in this chapter.) However, private hosts that are not connected to the Internet can use any valid address, as long as it is unique within the private network. These address are called *private IP addresses*. Because many private networks exist alongside public networks, grabbing just any address is strongly discouraged. RFC 1918, "Address Allocation for Private Internets," sets aside three blocks of IP addresses (that is, a Class A, a Class B, and a Class C range) for private, internal use (see Table 18-2). Private IP addresses are defined as not routable on the Internet and are used exclusively in a private network. Addresses in this range are not routed on the Internet backbone; Internet routers immediately discard private addresses.

Table 18-2   *Private IP Addresses*

Class	RFC 1918 Internal Address Range
A	10.0.0.0 to 10.255.255.255
B	172.16.0.0 to 172.31.255.255
C	192.168.0.0 to 192.168.255.255

NOTE   You can find all RFCs online at www.isi.edu/in-notes/rfc*xxxx*.txt, where *xxxx* is the number of the RFC. If you do not know the number of the RFC, you can find it by doing a topic search at www.rfc-editor.org/rfcsearch.html.

If you are addressing a nonpublic intranet, a test lab, or a home network, these private addresses can be used instead of globally unique addresses.

Connecting a network using private addresses to the Internet requires a translation of the private addresses to public addresses. This translation process is referred to as *Network Address Translation (NAT)*. A router or a firewall is usually the device that performs NAT.

Using RFC 1918 addresses and NAT ensures that all addresses on the Internet will be reachable. If an address were just grabbed, the section of the Internet using that registered address would be confused with the local intranet and thus unreachable.

NOTE   NAT, as defined by RFC 1631, is the process of swapping one address for another in the IP packet header. In practice, NAT is used to allow hosts with private IP addresses to access the Internet.

A NAT-enabled device, such as a Cisco router or firewall, operates at the border of a stub domain (an internetwork that has a single connection to the outside world). When a host inside the stub domain wants to transmit to a host on the outside, it forwards the packet to the NAT-enabled device. The NAT process then looks inside the IP header and, if appropriate, replaces the local IP (inside, or private IP) address with a globally unique IP address. When an outside host sends a response, the NAT process receives it, checks the current table of network address translations, and replaces the destination address with the original inside source address.

Public IP Addresses

Public IP addresses are unique. No two machines that connect to a public network can have the same IP address: Public IP addresses are global and standardized, and all machines connected to the Internet agree to adhere to the system. Public IP addresses must be obtained from an Internet service provider (ISP) or a registry at some expense.

With the rapid growth of the Internet, public IP addresses are beginning to run out, so new addressing schemes such as classless interdomain routing (CIDR) and IPv6 (IP version 6) have been developed to help solve the problem. CIDR and IPv6 are discussed in the following two sections.

IPv4 vs. IPv6

When TCP/IP was first introduced in the 1980s, it relied on a two-level addressing scheme, which at the time offered adequate scalability. Unfortunately, the architects of TCP/IP could not have predicted that their protocol would eventually sustain a global network of information, commerce, and entertainment. Twenty years ago, IP version 4 (IPv4) offered an addressing strategy that, although scalable for a time, resulted in an inefficient allocation of addresses.

The Class A and B addresses make up 75 percent of the IPv4 address space, but a relative handful of organizations (fewer than 17,000) can be assigned a Class A or B network number. Class C network addresses are far more numerous than Class A and Class B addresses, although they account for only 12.5 percent of the possible 4 billion IP addresses available in IPv4, as shown in Figure 18-9.

Figure 18-9   *IPv4 Address Allocation*

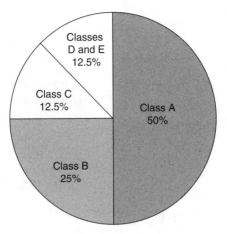

Unfortunately, Class C addresses are limited to 254 hosts, which does not meet the needs of larger organizations that cannot acquire a Class A or B address. Even if more Class A, B, and C addresses existed, too many network addresses would cause Internet routers to grind to a halt under the weight of the enormous size of routing tables required to store the routes to reach the networks.

As early as 1992, the Internet Engineering Task Force (IETF) identified two specific concerns:

- **Exhaustion of the remaining, unassigned IPv4 network addresses**—In the early 1990s, the Class B space was on the verge of depletion.

- **The rapid and substantial increase in the size of Internet routing tables**—As more Class C networks came online, the resulting flood of new network information threatened the capability of Internet routers to process the information effectively.

Over the past two decades, numerous extensions to IPv4 have been developed that are specifically designed to improve the efficiency with which the 32-bit address space can be used. Two of the most important of these are subnet masks and classless interdomain routing (CIDR), which are discussed in more detail in the following section and in Chapter 19.

Meanwhile, an even more extendable and scalable version of IP, IP version 6 (IPv6), has been defined and developed. IPv6 uses 128-bit binary values that can be displayed as 32 hexadecimal digits. IPv6 provides 3.4×10^{38} IP addresses. This version of IP should provide sufficient addresses for future needs, if used wisely.

Table 18-3 compares the characteristics of IPv4 and IPv6.

Table 18-3   *Comparing IPv4 and IPv6*

IPv4	IPv6
4 octets: 11010001.10011100.11001001.01110001	16 octets: 10100101.00100100.01110010.11010011. 00101100.10000000.11011101.00000010. 00000000.00101001.11101100.01111010. 00000000.00101011.11101010.01110011
209.156.201.113	A524:72D3:2C80:DD02:0029:EC7A:002B:EA73 (32 hexadecimal digits)
4,294,467,295 IP addresses	3.4×10^{38} IP addresses

IPv6 is slowly being implemented in certain networks. Eventually, IPv6 may replace IPv4 as the dominant Internet protocol.

CIDR

As you learned in the previous section, the original IPv4 defines IP addresses in five major classes of address structure, Classes A through E. Using IPv4, the Internet was running out of address space very quickly.

Classless interdomain routing (CIDR) is a new addressing scheme for the Internet that allows for more efficient allocation of IP addresses than the old Class A, B, and C address scheme.

First introduced in 1993 by RFCs 1517, 1518, 1519, and 1520, and later deployed in 1994, CIDR dramatically improves scalability and efficiency of IPv4 by providing the following:

- The replacement of classful addressing with a more flexible and less wasteful classless scheme.

- Enhanced route aggregation, also known as *supernetting*. As the Internet grows, routers on the Internet require huge memory tables to store all the routing information. Supernetting helps reduce the size of router memory tables by combining and summarizing multiple routing information entries into one single entry. This reduces the size of router memory tables and also allows for faster table lookup.

A CIDR network address looks like this: 207.21.54.0/23.

The 207.21.54.0 is the network address itself. The /23 means that the first 23 bits are the network part of the address, leaving the last 9 bits for specific host addresses. As compared to the classful approach, this would be a Class C address, with the network part 24 bits long and the host part 8 bits long.

With the CIDR approach, if you need more than 254 host addresses, you can be assigned a /23 address instead of wasting a whole Class B address that supports 65,534 hosts. For example, in Figure 18-10, using CIDR, company XYZ asks for an address block from its ISP, not a central authority. The ISP assesses XYZ's needs and allocates address space from its own large *CIDR block* of addresses. In this example, the ISP owns the 207.21.0.0/16 address block. The ISP announces only this single 207.21.0.0/16 address to the Internet (even though this address block actually consists of many Class C networks). The ISP assigns the smaller 207.21.54.0/23 address block within the larger 207.21.0.0/16 address block to the XYZ company. This allows the XYZ company to have a network that can have up to 510 hosts ($2^9 - 2 = 510$), or that network can be subdivided into multiple smaller subnets by the XYZ company. Chapter 19 discusses subnetting in more detail.

Figure 18-10   *Addressing with CIDR*

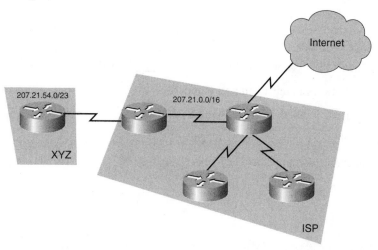

ISPs assume the burden of managing address space in a classless system. With this system, Internet routers keep only one summary route, or supernet route, to the provider's network, and only the individual provider keeps routes that are more specific to its own customer networks. This method drastically reduces the size of Internet routing tables.

Summary

In this chapter, you learned the following key points:

- Network addresses consist of two parts: the network number portion and the host number portion. IPv4 addresses have 32 bits and are generally shown in dotted-decimal form—for example, 132.17.141.19.

- IPv4 addresses are divided primarily into A, B, and C classes. Other classes (D and E) exist but are reserved for special uses (multicasting and research, respectively). Addressing space as defined by IPv4 is limited and has been mostly exhausted.

- When written in a binary format, the first bit of a Class A address is always 0, the first 2 bits of a Class B address are always 10, and the first 3 bits of a Class C address are always 110.

- The more flexible IPv6 will replace IPv4 in the future. IPv6 offers 128 bits of addressing, compared to the 32-bit addressing available in IPv4.

- Classless interdomain routing (CIDR) is an addressing scheme for the Internet that allows for more efficient allocation of IP addresses than the old Class A, B, and C addressing scheme.

Review Exercises

1 The IP address consists of two parts: _____ and _____.

    a. Network number and host number

    b. Host number and MAC address

    c. Network number and MAC address

    d. Network number and subnetwork address

2 How many bits are in an IPv4 address?

    a. 16

    b. 32

    c. 48

    d. 64

3 In a Class B address, which octets are the host number portion and are assigned locally?

    a. The first octet is assigned locally.

    b. The first and second octets are assigned locally.

    c. The second and third octets are assigned locally.

    d. The third and fourth octets are assigned locally.

4 The following address is of which class? 129.21.89.75

  a. Class A

  b. Class B

  c. Class C

  d. Class D

5 Which of the following is true of a directed broadcast address?

  a. A directed broadcast address is an address that has all 0s in the Host field.

  b. Any IP address in a network can be used as a broadcast address.

  c. A directed broadcast address is an address that has all 1s in the Host field.

  d. None of the above.

6 According to RFC 1918, which is a private Internet address?

  a. 10.215.34.124

  b. 192.32.146.23

  c. 172.34.221.18

  d. 119.12.73.215

7 How many bits are there in an IPv6 address?

  a. 32

  b. 48

  c. 96

  d. 128

8 Which of the following is a feature of CIDR?

  a. Classful addressing

  b. No supernetting

  c. More entries in the routing table

  d. Route aggregation

Upon completing this chapter, you will be able to:

- Describe the purpose of a subnetwork

- Describe the use of a subnet mask

- Interpret addressing requirements for a given scenario

- Calculate subnetwork addresses and masks for Class B and Class C

- Given an classful IP address class and networking requirements, calculate the appropriate subnetworks and hosts per subnet needs

- Given an classful IP address and the network requirements, determine the subnetwork address, the directed broadcast address, and the range of host addresses

CHAPTER 19

IP Subnetting and Calculation

When the Internet Protocol was first proposed in the early 1980s, IPv4 classful addressing seemed to provide a limitless amount of address space. However, it became quickly apparent that there were limitations. The major drawback to the system is that, although the scheme is easy to understand and implement, the boundaries set by the Class A, B, and C addresses do not provide efficient use of the available addresses.

To address these problems, a modification to the system was needed that allowed the addresses to be used more efficiently. In 1985, RFC 950, "Internet Standard Subnetting Procedure," was written to standardize a procedure for dividing Class A, B, and C networks into smaller, more manageable sections. This procedure is known as *subnetting*.

This chapter discusses how to plan and create subnets for Class B and C IP addresses.

Subnetworks

The original two-level Internet hierarchy (network ID and host ID) assumed that each site would have only a single network. Therefore, each site would need only a single connection to the Internet. Initially, these were safe assumptions. Over time, however, network computing matured and expanded. By 1985, it was no longer safe to assume that an organization would have only a single network, nor that it would be satisfied with a single connection to the Internet.

As sites began to develop multiple networks, it became obvious to the Internet Engineering Task Force (IETF) that some mechanism was needed to differentiate among the multiple logical networks that were emerging as subsets of the second tier of the Internet. Otherwise, there could be no efficient way to route data to specific end systems in sites with multiple networks. This is illustrated in Figure 19-1.

Figure 19-1 *Multiple Networks*

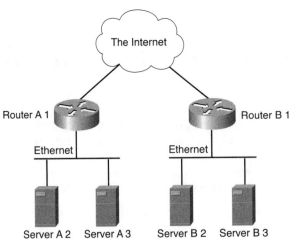

In 1985, the IETF released RFC 950, "Internet Standard Subnetting Procedure," which enabled the network number of IP address Class A, B, and C networks to be subdivided into smaller, more manageable sections. This procedure is known as *subnetting*. The smaller divisions are called *subnetworks*, and they provide addressing flexibility. Normally, subnetworks are simply referred to as *subnets*. The concept of subnetting is based on the need for a third level in the Internet addressing hierarchy. As internetworking technologies matured, their acceptance and use increased dramatically. As a result, it became common for medium- and large-size organizations to have multiple subnets.

Network administrators might want to subnet a network for several reasons. A primary reason for using subnets is to reduce the size of a broadcast domain. Broadcasts are sent to all hosts on a network or subnetwork. When broadcast traffic begins to consume too much of the available bandwidth, network administrators might choose to reduce the size of the broadcast domain. In these situations, routers are used to separate networks. The router breaks the network into multiple subnets.

In such multiple-network environments, each subnetwork could be connected to other IP networks via a single router (see Figure 19-2). In this example, the Class B address (172.16.0.0) is subdivided into multiple subnetworks (172.16.1.0, 172.16.2.0, 172.16.3.0, and 172.16.4.0). The actual details of the internal network environment and how the network is divided into multiple subnetworks are inconsequential to other IP networks. The router connected to other IP network announces only the 172.16.0.0 network toward other IP networks.

Figure 19-2   *Subnetworks*

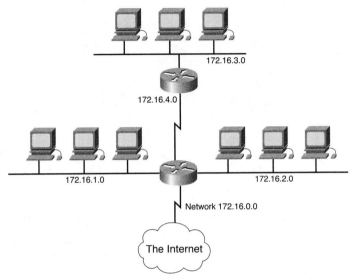

Because the subnet address is taken from the host number portion of Class A, Class B, and Class C addresses, it is assigned locally, usually by the network administrator. Also, like IP addresses, each subnet address must be unique.

When you configure routers, you can connect each interface to a different network or subnet segment. You must select an available host address from each different network or subnet to assign to the interface of the router that connects to that network or subnet (see Figure 19-3). In this example, the router has two Ethernet interfaces (E0 and E1). The interface that is connected to the 172.16.2.0 subnetwork is assigned the IP address of 172.16.2.1, and the other interface that is connected to the 172.16.3.0 subnetwork is assigned the IP address of 172.16.3.1.

Figure 19-3 *Subnet Address*

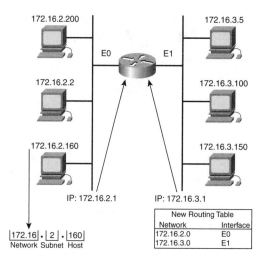

The idea to subnet a network is very similar to the street address of a multilevel building. For example, in a two-story building, each floor has nine cubicles. The street address of the first and second floor number 9 cubicle can be written as shown here. The street number 150 Tasman Drive can be thought of as the network number. The floor number would be the subnet, and the cubicle number would be the host number:

   150 Tasman Drive, 1st Floor, Cube 9

   Network number = 150 Tasman Drive

   Subnet = 1st Floor

   Host number = Cube 9

   150 Tasman Drive, 2nd Floor, Cube 9

   Network number = 150 Tasman Drive

   Subnet = 2nd Floor

   Host number = Cube 9

Subnet Masks

Subnet addresses include the Class A, Class B, or Class C network number portion, plus a Subnet field and a Host field. The Subnet field and the Host field are created from the original host number portion for the entire network. The capability to decide how to divide the original host number portion into the new Subnet and Host fields provides addressing flexibility for the network administrator.

To create a subnet address, you borrow bits from the original host number portion and designate them as the Subnet field.

A single-bit subnet is seldom used because the only possible values are 0 and 1. Subnets consisting of all 0s or all 1s are discouraged because of possible confusion with the network address, which has all 0s in the host number portion, or the network directed broadcast address, which has all 1s in the host number portion.

NOTE   The Cisco routers enable a network administrator to use subnet 0. However, this can create problems with older TCP/IP software. Configuring addresses in the subnet 0 range is generally not recommended because of the confusion inherent in having a network and a subnet with indistinguishable addresses. The use of subnet 0 is discouraged.

The maximum number of bits that you can borrow can be any number that leaves at least 2 bits remaining for the host number. The subnet mask is not an IP address. The function of a subnet mask is to tell devices which part of an address is the network number, including the subnet, and which part is the host number.

Subnet masks use the same format as IP addresses. In other words, each is 32 bits long, is divided into four octets, and is usually represented in the dotted-decimal notation like IP addresses. Subnet masks have all 1s in the network number and subnetwork portions, and all 0s in the host number portion.

For example, in a Class C IP address without subnetting, 24 bits are used for the network number portion and 8 bits are used for the host number portion. As shown in the Class C subnetting example in Figure 19-4, 3 bits from the original Host field have been borrowed for the Subnet field, leaving the 5 remaining bits for the new Host field. Therefore, the subnet mask expressed in dotted-decimal notation is 255.255.255.224.

Figure 19-4   *Subnet Mask*

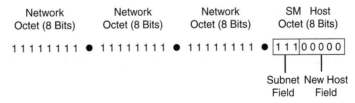

By default, if no bits are borrowed to represent a subnet, the default subnet masks for Class A, B, and C networks are as follows:

- **Class A**—Default subnet mask = 255.0.0.0 (8 network bits, 24 host bits)

- **Class B**—Default subnet mask = 255.255.0.0 (16 network bits, 16 host bits)

- **Class C**—Default subnet mask = 255.255.255.0 (24 network bits, 8 host bits)

To determine the subnetwork number, given an IP address and subnet mask, perform the following steps (see Table 19-1):

Step 1   Express the IP address in binary form.

Step 2   Express the subnet mask in binary form.

Step 3   Perform a logical AND operation on the IP address and the subnet mask. The result of the logical AND operation is the subnetwork number.

NOTE   The network or subnet address has all 0s in the host number portion. To route a data packet, the router must first determine the destination network/subnet address by performing a logical AND using the destination host's IP address and the subnet mask.

Performing an AND operation means that anytime you AND a 0 value to another 0 or a 1 value, the result is 0. Only a 1 ANDed with another 1 value will result in a 1 value. Here's how it works:

   0 AND 0 is 0

   0 AND 1 is 0

   1 AND 1 is 1

Performing the logical AND operation with the IP address and the subnet mask sets the host number portion of the IP address to all 0s, while the network portion number remains unchanged.

Step 4   Express the subnetwork number in dotted-decimal notation.

Table 19-1   *IP Address 192.5.34.139 with a Subnet Mask of 255.255.255.224*

IP address in decimal	192.	5.	34.	139
IP address in binary	11000000	00000101	00100010	10001011
Logical AND				
Subnet mask in binary	111111111	111111111	111111111	11110000
Subnetwork address in binary	11000000	00000101	00100010	10000000
Subnetwork address in decimal	192.	5.	34.	128

As an illustration, given a Class B network address, if you borrow 8 bits to represent a subnet, the subnet mask for the same Class B network would be 255.255.255.0, as shown in Figure 19-5.

Figure 19-5   *Eight-Bit Subnet Mask*

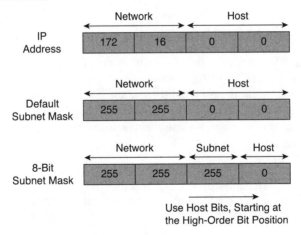

To create subnets, you must extend the network portion of the address. That means you need to borrow bits from the Host field. However, the number of bits to be borrowed depends on both of the following requirements:

- How many subnetworks are required

- How many hosts are required on each subnetwork

Because there are three octets in the Host field of a Class A network, up to 22 bits can be borrowed in Class A networks to create subnetworks. (Remember that the maximum number of bits that can be borrowed can be any number that leaves at least 2 bits remaining for the host number.)

A Class B network has two octets in the Host field. Therefore, up to 14 bits can be borrowed to create subnetworks. A Class C network has only one octet in the Host field. Therefore, up to only 6 bits can be borrowed in Class C networks to create subnetworks.

The Subnet field always immediately follows the network number. That is, the borrowed bits must be the first n bits directly following the network ID, where n is the desired size of the new Subnet field (see Figure 19-6). The subnet mask is the tool used by the router to determine which bits are network/subnet bits and which bits are host bits.

Figure 19-6 *A Class B Subnet Field*

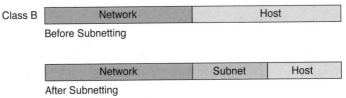

Class B

Network | Host
Before Subnetting

Network | Subnet | Host
After Subnetting

Network Addressing Planning

One of the decisions that you must make whenever you create subnets is the optimal number of subnets and hosts (see Table 19-2). The number of lost IP addresses with a Class C network and the number of subnetwork host IP addresses available depend on the number of bits borrowed for subnetting. When you create subnets, you lose many potential addresses. For this reason, network administrators must pay close attention to the percentage of addresses that they lose by creating subnets.

Table 19-2 *Network Addressing Planning—Class C Subnetting Example*

Number of Bits Borrowed	Number of Efficient Subnets Created	Number of Usable Hosts per Subnet	Total Number of Hosts	Percent Used (out of 254)
2	$2^2 - 2 = 2$	$2^6 - 2 = 62$	124	49%
3	$2^3 - 2 = 6$	$2^5 - 2 = 30$	180	71%
4	$2^4 - 2 = 14$	$2^4 - 2 = 14$	196	77%
5	$2^5 - 2 = 30$	$2^3 - 2 = 6$	180	71%
6	$2^6 - 2 = 62$	$2^2 - 2 = 2$	124	49%

Note: This table does not use the all 0s and all 1s subnets, trading safety for address usage efficiency.

For example, if you borrow 2 bits with a Class C network, you create 4 subnets, each with 64 hosts. However, only 2 of the subnets are efficient (4 minus the all 0s and all 1s subnets), and only 62 (64 minus subnet address and directed broadcast address) hosts are usable per subnet, giving 124 usable out of 254 that were possible before you chose to use subnets. This means that you are losing 51 percent of your addresses. Whenever you create subnets, you need to take into consideration future network growth and the percentage of addresses that you lose by creating subnets.

Computing Usable Subnetworks

Whenever you borrow bits from the Host field, it is important to note the number of additional subnets that are being created each time you borrow 1 more bit. Borrowing 2 bits creates four possible subnets (2^2), but remember that there are always two discouraged subnets (all 0s and all 1s subnets). Each time you borrow another bit from the Host field, the number of subnets created increases by a power of 2.

For example, using 3 bits for the Subnet field results in eight possible subnets, six of which are usable ($2^3 = 8$, $8 - 2$ discouraged subnets = 6 usable subnets).

Using 4 bits for the Subnet field results in 16 possible subnets, 14 of which are usable ($2^4 = 16$, $16 - 2$ discouraged subnets = 14 usable subnets).

In general, you can use the following formula to calculate the number of usable subnets, given the number of subnet bits used:

Number of subnets = $2^n - 2$ (where n is the number of subnet bits)

Computing Hosts per Subnetwork

Each time you borrow 1 bit from a Host field, there is 1 less bit remaining in the Host field that can be used for host numbers. The number of host addresses that you can assign decreases by a power of 2.

To help you understand how this works, consider a Class C network address as an example. If there is no subnet mask, all 8 bits in the last octet are used for the Host field. Therefore, there are 256 (2^8) possible addresses available to assign to hosts (254 usable addresses, after you subtract the 2 addresses [the directed broadcast and the subnet address] that you cannot use).

Now imagine that this Class C network is divided into subnets. If you borrow 2 bits from the default 8-bit Host field, the size of the Host field decreases to 6 bits. If you write out all the possible combinations of 0s and 1s that could occur in the remaining 6 bits, you discover that the total number of possible hosts that could be assigned in each subnet decreases to 64 (2^6). The number of usable host numbers decreases to 62 ($64 - 2$).

In the same Class C network, if you borrow 3 bits, the size of the Host field decreases to 5 bits, and the total number of hosts that you could assign to each subnet decreases to 32 (2^5). The number of usable host numbers decreases to 30 ($32 - 2$).

The number of possible host addresses that can be assigned to a subnet is related to the number of subnets that have been created. In a Class C network, for example, if you apply a subnet mask of 255.255.255.224, you have to borrow 3 bits (224 = 11100000) from the Host field. The usable subnets created are 6 (8 – 2), each having 30 (32 – 2) usable host addresses.

In general, the following formula can be used to calculate the number of usable host addresses, given the number of host bits used:

Number of host addresses $= 2^n - 2$ (where n is the number of host bits)

Subnetting Class C Addresses

Imagine that you are a network administrator. Your company has a Class C network address of 200.10.57.0. You want to subdivide your network into 3 subnets, and you need at least 20 hosts per subnet. Because you have a Class C network address, you have 8 bits in the fourth octet available, for a total of 256 possible hosts. To create a custom subnet mask, you need to borrow bits from the host portion of the address. The following steps help accomplish this:

Step 1   The first step in subnetting is to determine how many subnets are needed. In this case, you need three subnets. To see how many bits you should borrow from the host portion of the network address, add the bit values from *right to left* until the total (decimal value) is *greater* than the number of subnets you need. Because you need three subnets, add the 1 bit through the 3 bit, which equals 7. This is more than the number of subnets you need, so you need to borrow at least 3 bits from the host number starting from the *left* side of the octet that contains the host number. Remember that the Subnet field always immediately follows the network number.

Step 2   When you know how many bits to borrow, borrow them from the left side of the first octet of the host address. Remember that every bit you borrow from the host portion leaves fewer bits for the hosts. Because you need to borrow 3 bits from the left side, you must show that new value in your subnet mask. The default subnet mask for Class C network address is 255.255.255.0, and your new custom subnet mask is 255.255.255.224. The 224 comes from the value of the first 3 bits from the left (128 + 64 + 32 = 224). These bits now become 1s and are part of the overall subnet mask. This leaves 5 bits for host IP addresses, or $2^5 - 2 = 30$ usable hosts per subnet (see Table 19-3).

Table 19-3   *Determining How Many Bits to Borrow*

Network Address	200.10.57.0
Subnets Needed	3
Host per Subnet Needed	20
Bits Value (Fourth Octet)	128 64 32 16 8 **4 2 1** (4 + 2 + 1 = 7, which is greater than 3)
Bits to Borrow	3

Table 19-3   *Determining How Many Bits to Borrow (Continued)*

Network Address with Borrowed Bits	11001000 00001010 00111001 **00**000000
Default Class C Subnet Mask	11111111 11111111 11111111 00000000
Required Subnet Mask	11111111 11111111 11111111 **111**00000
Required Subnet Mask in Dotted-Decimal Notation	255.255.255.224

Step 3   With this information, you can build Tables 19-4 and 19-5.

Table 19-4 illustrates how to determine the subnet and host addresses of Class C network address 200.10.57.0. In previous steps, you determined that you need to borrow 3 bits for subnets. As shown in Table 19-4, the first 3 bits of the fourth octet are the subnet bits, and the last 5 bits are the host bits. By borrowing 3 bits from the 8 bits of the host address, you can create 8 subnets with 32 hosts each. The 8 networks created are the 0, 32, 64, 96, 128, 160, 192, and 224 subnets. The 0 subnet and the 224 subnet are discouraged subnets because the 0 subnet has all 0s (**000**00000) in the subnet portion of the address and the 224 subnet has all ones (**111**00000) in the subnet portion of the address.

Table 19-4   *Determining the Subnet and Host Addresses*

IP Network in Decimal	200.	10.	57.	0
IP Network in Binary	11001000	00001010	00111001	00000000
Subnet Mask	11111111	11111111	11111111	**111**00000
First Subnet	11001000	00001010	00111001	**000**00000
Second Subnet	11001000	00001010	00111001	**001**00000
First Host	11001000	00001010	00111001	**001**00001
Second Host	11001000	00001010	00111001	**001**00010
Third Host	11001000	00001010	00111001	**001**00011
:				
Last Host	11001000	00001010	00111001	**001**11111
Third Subnet	11001000	00001010	00111001	**010**00000
:				
Last Subnet	11001000	00001010	00111001	**111**00000

Note: The bold digits identify the Subnet field, and the italicized digits represent the Host field.

Table 19-5 shows the subnets of 200.10.57.0, possible host IP address range of each subnet, and the directed broadcast address of each subnet. Notice that the first subnet always starts at 0 and, in this case, increases by 32, which is the number of hosts on each subnet. One way to determine the number of hosts on each subnet or the start of each subnet is to take the remaining host bits to the power of 2. Because you borrowed 3 of the 8 bits for subnets and have 5 bits left, the number of hosts per subnet is 2^5, or 32. Another way to figure the number of hosts per subnet, or the "increment" from one subnet to the next, is to subtract the subnet mask value in decimal (224 in the fourth octet) from 256 (which is the maximum number of possible combinations of 8 bits), which equals 32. This means that you start at 0 for the first network and add 32 for each additional subnetwork. Consider the second subnet (the 32 subnet) as an example; the IP address of 200.10.57.32 cannot be used for a host ID because it is the subnetwork ID of the 32 subnet (the host portion is all 0s).

Table 19-5 *Calculating Class C Subnets and Host Ranges*

Subnet Number	Network Address	Subnet Mask	Subnet Addresses	Range of Possible Host IP Addresses	Directed Broadcast Addresses
0	200.10.57.0	255.255.255.224	200.10.57.0	200.10.57.1 to 30	200.10.57.31
1	200.10.57.0	255.255.255.224	200.10.57.32	200.10.57.33 to 62	200.10.57.63
2	200.10.57.0	255.255.255.224	200.10.57.64	200.10.57.65 to 94	200.10.57.95
3	200.10.57.0	255.255.255.224	200.10.57.96	200.10.57.97 to 126	200.10.57.127
4	200.10.57.0	255.255.255.224	200.10.57.128	200.10.57.129 to 158	200.10.57.159
5	200.10.57.0	255.255.255.224	200.10.57.160	200.10.57.161 to 190	200.10.57.191
6	200.10.57.0	255.255.255.224	200.10.57.192	200.10.57.193 to 222	200.10.57.223
7	200.10.57.0	255.255.255.224	200.10.57.224	200.10.57.225 to 254	200.10.57.255

Step 4 After you have all the subnetwork addresses, you can determine the directed broadcast address and the ranges of possible host IP addresses for each subnet.

Consider the third subnet, 200.10.57.64, as an example. If you borrow 3 bits from the Host field, the last 5 bits left in the fourth octets are the host bits. As you learned in Chapter 18, "Networking Addressing," the directed broadcast address has all the 1s in the host portion. As shown in Table 19-6, when you place all 1s in the host bits, the directed broadcast address for 200.10.57.64 subnetwork is 200.10.57.95.

Table 19-6   *Determining Directed Broadcast Address*

Subnet Address	200.	10.	57.	64
Subnet Address in Binary	11001000	00001010	00111001	01*000000*
Bits Borrowed	3			
Network and Host Portions	**11001000** N	**00001010** N	**00111001** N	**010***000000* N H
Directed Broadcast Address	**11001000** N	**00001010** N	**00111001** N	**010***11111* N H
Subnet Broadcast Address in Decimal	200.	10.	57.	95

Step 5   Now that you know thedirected broadcast addresst for the 200.10.57.64 subnetwork, you are ready to determine the host range of this network.

Because 200.10.57.64 has all the 0s in the host portion, it is a subnetwork address. The first address of this subnetwork is 200.10.57.65 (11001000.00001010.00111001.01000001), and the last address of this subnetwork is 200.10.57.95 (11001000.00001010.00111001.01011111). However, because this address is used as the subnet's directed broadcast address, the last usable host address is 200.10.57.94 (11001000.00001010.00111001.01011110). Therefore, the host address range for the 200.10.57.64 subnetwork is 200.10.57.65 to 200.10.57.94.

Table 19-7 illustrates a Class C network that is subnetted to provide 6 host addresses and 30 subnets. The IP host address is 192.168.5.121. The subnet mask is 255.255.255.248 (5 bits of subnetting).

Table 19-7   *Subnetting a Class C Address*

	Network	Network	Network	Subnet	Host
192.168.5.121	11000000	10101000	00000101	01111	001
255.255.255.248	11111111	11111111	11111111	11111	000
Subnet	11000000	10101000	00000101	01111	000
Directed Broadcast	11000000	10101000	00000101	01111	111

In Table 19-7, the subnet address, host range, and directed broadcast address are as follows:

Subnet address: 192.168.5.120

Host range: 192.168.5.121 to 192.168.5.126

Directed broadcast address: 192.168.5.127

Table 19-8 is an example table used for Class C subnet planning.

Table 19-8   *Class C Subnet Planning*

Number of Bits Borrowed	Subnet Mask	Number of Subnets	Number of Hosts
2	255.255.255.192	2	62
3	255.255.255.224	6	30
4	255.255.255.240	14	14
5	255.255.255.248	30	6
6	255.255.255.252	62	2

Note: Subnets of all 0s and all 1s are excluded. Hosts of all 0s and all 1s are excluded.

Now that you have learned how to subnet a Class C network address, the next section teaches you how to subnet a Class B network address.

Subnetting Class B Addresses

Imagine that you are a network administrator and your company has a Class B network address of 150.193.0.0. This Class B network address will be subdivided to accommodate your physical network; you will need at least 12 subnets interconnected with routers, and each subnet needs to be capable of handling at least 750 hosts.

Because you have a Class B network address, you have 16 bits in the third and fourth octets available, for a total of 65536 possible hosts. To create a custom subnet mask, you need to borrow bits from the host portion of the address. The following steps help accomplish this:

Step 1   The first step in subnetting is to determine how many subnets are needed. In this case, you need 12 subnetworks. To see how many bits you should borrow from the host portion of the network address, add the bit values from *right to left* until the total (decimal value) is *greater* than the number of subnets you need. Because you need 12 subnets, add the 1 bit through the 4 bit, which equals 15. This is more than the number of subnets you need, so you need to borrow at least 4 bits from the host address, starting from the *left* side of the Host field (see Table 19-9).

Table 19-9 *Determining How Many Bits to Borrow*

Network Address	150.193.0.0
Subnets Needed	12
Hosts per Subnet Needed	750
Bits Value (3rd and 4th octets, 16 bits)	32768 16384 8192 4096 2048 1024 512 256 128 64 32 16 **8 4 2 1** (8 + 4 + 2 + 1 = 15, which is greater than 12)
Bits to Borrow	4
Network Address with Borrowed Bits	10010110 11000001 **0000**0000 00000000
Default Class B Subnet Mask	11111111 11111111 00000000 00000000
Required Subnet Mask	11111111 11111111 **1111**0000 00000000
Required Subnet Mask in Dotted-Decimal Notation	255.255.240.0

Step 2   When you know how many bits to borrow, borrow them from the *left* side of the first octet of the host address.

Remember that every bit you borrow from the host leaves fewer bits for the hosts. Even though you increase the number of subnets, you decrease the number of hosts per subnet. Because you need to borrow 4 bits from the left side, you must show that new value in the subnet mask. Your existing default subnet mask was 255.255.0.0, and your new custom subnet mask is 255.255.240.0. The 240 comes from the value of the first 4 bits from the left (128 + 64 + 32 + 16 = 240). These bits now become 1s and are part of the overall subnet mask. This leaves 12 bits for host IP addresses, or $2^{12} - 2 = 4094$ usable hosts per subnet.

Step 3   With this information, you can build Tables 19-10 and 19-11. Table 19-10
illustrates how to determine the subnets and host addresses range of Class B
network address 150.193.0.0.

Table 19-10   *Determining the Subnet and Host Addresses*

IP Network in Decimal	150.	193.	0.	0
IP Network in Binary	10010110	11000001	*00000000*	*00000000*
Subnet Mask	11111111	11111111	**1111**0000	00000000
First Subnet	10010110	11000001	**0001**0000	*00000000*
Second Subnet	10010110	11000001	**0001**0000	*00000000*
First Host	10010110	11000001	**0001**0000	*00000001*
Second Host	10010110	11000001	**0001**0000	*00000010*
Third Host	10010110	11000001	**0001**0000	*00000011*
		:		
Last Host	10010110	11000001	**0001***1111*	*11111111*
Third Subnet	10010110	11000001	**0010**0000	*00000000*
		:		
Last Subnet	10010110	11000001	**1111**0000	*00000000*

Note: The bold digits identify the Subnet field, and the italicized digits represent the Host field.

In previous steps, you determined that you need to borrow 4 bits for subnet.
As shown in Table 19-10, the first 4 bits of the third octet are the subnet binary
value, and the last 12 bits are the host bits. By borrowing 4 bits from the 16
bits of the host address, you can create 16 subnets with 4096 hosts each. The
16 networks created are the 0, 16, 32, 48, 64, 80, 96, 112, 128, 144, 160, 176,
192, 208, 224, and 240 subnets. The 0 subnet and the 240 subnet are
discouraged subnets because the 0 subnet has all 0s (**0000**0000) in the subnet
portion of the address and the 240 subnet has all 1s (**1111**0000) in the subnet
portion of the address.

Table 19-11 shows the subnets of 150.193.0.0, possible host IP ranges of each subnet and the directed broadcast address of each subnet.

Table 19-11   *Calculating the Subnets and Host Ranges*

Subnet Number	Network Address	Subnet Mask	Subnet Addresses	Range of Possible Host IP Addresses	Directed Broadcast Addresses
0	150.190.0.0	255.255.240.0	150.190.0.0	150.190.0.1 to 150.190.15.254	150.190.15.255
1	150.190.0.0	255.255.240.0	150.190.16.0	150.190.16.1 to 150.190.31.254	150.190.31.255
2	150.190.0.0	255.255.240.0	150.190.32.0	150.190.32.1 to 150.190.47.254	150.190.47.255
3	150.190.0.0	255.255.240.0	150.190.48.0	150.190.48.1 to 150.190.63.254	150.190.63.255
4	150.190.0.0	255.255.240.0	150.190.64.0	150.190.64.1 to 150.190.79.254	150.190.79.255
5	150.190.0.0	255.255.240.0	150.190.80.0	150.190.80.1 to 150.190.95.254	150.190.95.255
6	150.190.0.0	255.255.240.0	150.190.96.0	150.190.96.1 to 150.190.111.254	150.190.111.255
7	150.190.0.0	255.255.240.0	150.190.112.0	150.190.112.1 to 150.190.127.254	150.190.127.255
8	150.190.0.0	255.255.240.0	150.190.128.0	150.190.128.1 to 150.190.143.254	150.190.143.255
9	150.190.0.0	255.255.240.0	150.190.144.0	150.190.144.1 to 150.190.159.254	150.190.159.255
10	150.190.0.0	255.255.240.0	150.190.160.0	150.190.160.1 to 150.190.175.254	150.190.175.255
11	150.190.0.0	255.255.240.0	150.190.176.0	150.190.176.1 to 150.190.191.254	150.190.191.255
12	150.190.0.0	255.255.240.0	150.190.192.0	150.190.192.1 to 150.190.207.254	150.190.207.255
13	150.190.0.0	255.255.240.0	150.190.208.0	150.190.208.1 to 150.190.223.254	150.190.223.255
14	150.190.0.0	255.255.240.0	150.190.224.0	150.190.224.1 to 150.190.239.254	150.190.239.255
15	150.190.0.0	255.255.240.0	150.190.240.0	150.190.240.1 to 150.190.254.254	150.190.254.255

Step 4   After you have all the subnetwork addresses, you can determine the directed
broadcast address and the ranges of possible host IP addresses for each
subnet.

Consider the second subnet, 150.193.16.0, as an example. If you borrow 4
bits from the Host field, the last 12 bits left in the third and fourth octets are
the host bits. As you learned earlier, the directed broadcast address has all 1s
in the host portion. As shown in Table 19-12, when you place all 1s in the host
bits, the directed broadcast address for 150.193.16.0 network is
150.193.31.255.

Table 19-12   *Subnetting Class B Addresses*

Subnet Address	150.	190.	16.	0
Subnet Address in Binary	10010110	11000001	00010000	00000000
Bits Borrowed	4			
Network and Host Portions	**10010110** N	**11000001** N	**0001**0000 N H	00000000 H
Directed Broadcast Address	**10010110** N	**11000001** N	**0001**1111 N H	11111111 H
Subnet Broadcast Address in Decimal	150.	190.	31.	255

Step 5   Now that you know the directed broadcast address for the 150.193.16.0
subnetwork, you are ready to determine the host range of this subnetwork.

Because 150.193.16.0 has all the 0s in the host portion, it is a subnetwork
address. The first usage host address of this subnetwork would be
150.193.16.1 (10010110.11000001.00010000.00000001). The last host
address of this subnetwork would be 150.193.31.255
(10010110.11000001.00011111.11111111). However, because this address is
used as the subnet directed directed boradcast address address, the last usable
host address is 150.193.31.254 (10010110.11000001.00011111.11111110).
Therefore, the host address range for the 150.193.16.0 subnetwork is
150.193.16.1 to 150.193.31.254.

Table 19-13 shows an example of a Class B IP network that has 8 bits of subnetting that provide up to 254 subnets and 254 host addresses. The IP host address is 172.16.2.121. The subnet mask is 255.255.255.0 (8 bits of subnetting).

Table 19-13   *Subnetting Class B Addresses*

	Network	Network	Subnet	Host
172.16.2.121	10101100	00010000	00000010	01111001
255.255.255.0	11111111	11111111	11111111	00000000
Subnet	10101100	00010000	00000010	00000000
Directed Broadcast	10101100	00010000	00000010	11111111

In Table 19-13, the subnet address, host range, and directed broadcast address are as follows:

Subnet address: 172.16.2.0

Host range: 172.16.2.1 to 172.16.2.254

Directed broadcast address: 172.16.2.255

Table 19-14 is an example of a table used for Class B subnet planning.

Table 19-14   *Class B Subnet Planning*

Number of Bits	Subnet Mask	Number of Subnets	Number of Hosts
2	255.255.192.0	2	16,382
3	255.255.224.0	6	8190
4	255.255.240.0	14	4094
5	255.255.248.0	30	2046
6	255.255.252.0	62	1022
7	255.255.254.0	126	510
8	255.255.255.0	254	254
9	255.255.255.128	510	126
10	255.255.255.192	1022	62
11	255.255.255.224	2045	30
12	255.255.255.240	4096	14
13	255.255.255.248	8190	6
14	255.255.255.252	16,382	2

Note: Subnets of all 0s and all 1s are excluded. Hosts of all 0s and all 1s are excluded.

Identifying Subnet, Directed Broadcast, and Usable Addresses

If given an IP address and subnet mask, you should be able to use the information given to identify the subnet address, the directed broadcast address, and the range of the host addresses (see Table 19-15).

Table 19-15   *Identifying Subnet, Direct Broadcast, and Host Addresses*

Subnet host address: 172.16.2.160	10101100 00010000 00000010 10100000
Subnet mask: 255.255.255.192	**11111111 11111111 11111111 11***000000*
Subnet address: 172.16.2.128	**10101100 00010000 00000010 10***000000*
Directed broadcast address: 172.16.2.191	**10101100 00001000 00000010 10***111111*
First usable host address: 172.16.2.129	**10101100 00001000 00000010 10***000001*
Last usable host address: 172.16.2.190	**10101100 00001000 00000010 10***111110*

For example, imagine that you have a subnet host address 172.16.2.160 with a 255.255.255.192 subnet mask. The following steps will help you determine the subnet address, the directed broadcast address, and the range of the host IP addresses.

Step 1   Write the 32-bit address in binary notation for 172.16.2.160, which would be 10101100.00010000.00000010.10100000.

Step 2   Then write the 32-bit subnet mask 255.255.255.192 in binary just below, which would be 11111111.11111111.11111111.11000000. The subnet number can be calculated by logical ANDing.

As you learned in the section "Subnet Masks" earlier in this chapter, the default subnet mask for a Class B address (without subnetting) is 255.255.0.0. To subnet a network, you need to borrow the bits from the Host field. Those bits borrowed become part of the network address. With the subnet mask 255.255.255.192 (11111111.11111111.11111111.11000000), you can see that 10 bits in the third and fourth octets were in 1s. This means that 10 bits were borrowed from the Host field for subnetting.

Step 3   Now look at the binary equivalent of the subnet host addresses you have written down, 10101100.00010000.00000010.10100000. You know that the last 6 bits in the fourth octet make up the host address, and the subnet address has 0s in all the Host fields. If you replace the last 6 bits with 0s, you get 10101100.00010000.00000010.10000000, which is the subnet address (172.16.2.128 in decimal).

Step 4 After you have all the subnetwork addresses, you can determine the directed broadcast address. To determine the directed broadcast address, simply place all the 1s in the Host field. In this example, the directed broadcast address is 10101100.00010000.00000010.10111111 (172.16.2.191 in decimal).

Step 5 Now that you know the directed broadcast for the 172.16.2.128 network, you are ready to determine the host range of this network.

Because 172.16.2.128 has all the 0s in the host portion, it is a subnetwork address. The first usage host address of this subnetwork is 172.16.2.129 (10101100.00010000.00000010.10000001), and the last host address of this subnetwork is 172.16.2.191 (10101100.00010000.00000010.10111111). However, because this address is used as the subnet directed broadcast address, the last usable host address is 172.16.2.190 (10101100.00010000.00000010.10111110). Therefore, the host range of 172.16.2.128 network is 172.16.2.129 to 172.16.2.190.

Summary

In this chapter, you learned the follow key points:

- To provide extra flexibility for the network administrator, networks—particularly large ones—are often divided into smaller networks called subnetworks or subnets.

- Subnetting allows a network administrator to get around the limitations of IPv4 by dividing a single network address into many subnets visible only within that single network.

- The function of a subnet mask is to tell devices which part of an address is the network number, including the subnet, and which part is the host.

- Internetworking functions of the network layer include network addressing and best-path selection for data traffic.

Review Exercises

1 Originally, the Internet Protocol used how many levels of hierarchy addressing?

   a. Two

   b. Three

   c. Four

   d. Five

2 How many bits are in a subnet mask?

    a. 16

    b. 32

    c. 48

    d. 64

3 What is the primary function of a subnet mask?

    a. To determine which part of the IP address is the network/subnetwork part and which part is the host part

    b. To conceal outside networks from subnetworks

    c. To determine the numbers of subnetworks that can be created

    d. To determine the numbers of hosts within a subnetwork

4 What is the minimum number of bits that should be borrowed to form a subnet?

    a. 1

    b. 2

    c. 3

    d. 4

5 If you were going to borrow 5 bits to create a subnet mask for a Class B address, what would the subnet mask be?

    a. 255.255.0.0

    b. 255.255.192.0

    c. 255.255.248.0

    d. 255.255.254.0

6 How many host addresses can be used in a Class C network?

    a. 253

    b. 254

    c. 255

    d. 256

7 How many bits can be borrowed to create a subnet for a Class C network?

   a. 2

   b. 4

   c. 6

   d. 8

8 What is the largest number of host bits you can borrow from a Class A address for subnetting?

   a. 24

   b. 22

   c. 16

   d. 14

Upon completing this chapter, you will be able to:

- Describe routing and tell how routers perform routing to determine the best path
- Define routing protocol and routed protocol
- Describe the basic decision-making processes involved in path determination
- Describe the purpose and use of network routing tables
- Describe different types of routing algorithms and metrics

CHAPTER 20

Routing Basics

The network layer is responsible for navigating data through a network. The function of the network layer is to find the best path through a network. Devices use the network-layer addressing scheme to determine the destination of data as it moves through the network.

Routing is the act of moving information across an internetwork from a source to a destination. A router is an internetworking device that passes data between networks. To be capable of routing packets of information, a router needs to know information such as the source address, the destination address, and the possible paths to the intended destination. The routing information that a router learns from its routing sources is placed in its *routing table*. The router relies on the routing table to determine which path to use when forwarding a packet toward its destination.

This chapter describes the router's use and operations in performing the key internetworking function of the OSI reference model's network layer, Layer 3. This chapter discusses the difference between routing and routed protocols. The design goals of routing algorithms can affect the resulting routing protocols. This chapter presents design goals of routing algorithms as well as routing metrics used by routing algorithms to determine the optimal route between networks. Finally, this chapter discusses the administrative distance, which defines the reliability of routing protocols.

Routing Overview

A *router* has two key functions. First, it must maintain its routing tables and make sure that other routers know of changes in the network. It does this by using a routing protocol to communicate network information from its routing table with other routers.

Second, when packets arrive at an interface, the router must use the routing table to determine where to send them. It switches them to the appropriate interface, adds the necessary framing for the particular interface, and then actually sends the packet. In some cases, a router applies quality of service (QoS) and security functions.

How a Router Works

A *router* is a network layer device that uses one or more routing metrics to determine the optimal path along which network traffic should be forwarded. The *routing metric* is a factor used in determining the desirability of the route. Different routing protocols use different criteria for determining the routing metric of a route.

Routers tie together, or interconnect, network segments or entire networks. They pass data packets between networks based on Layer 3 information. Routers use the network address (IP address) to identify the destination network of a packet within an internetwork. Routers make logical decisions based on the routing table regarding the best path for the delivery of data on an internetwork. Then they direct packets to the appropriate output port and segment. Routers forward packets from LAN devices (for example, workstations) through the network, based on Layer 3 information (such as destination IP address) (see Figure 20-1).

Figure 20-1 *Network Layer Protocol Operation*

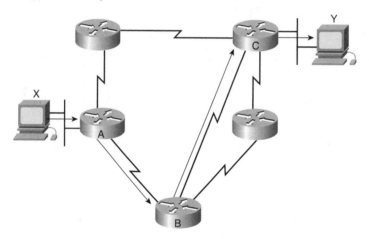

Encapsulation

The de-encapsulation and encapsulation process occurs each time the packet transfers through a router. The following steps describe the de-encapsulation and encapsulation process:

1 The router de-encapsulates and examines the frame to determine what type of network layer data is being carried. The network layer data is sent to the appropriate network layer process, and the frame (data link layer) header/trailer is discarded.

2 The network layer process examines the network layer header to determine the destination network and then references the routing table that associates networks with outgoing interfaces.

3 The packet is again encapsulated in the data link layer frame for the selected interface and is sent on.

Routed Versus Routing

Protocols that provide support for the network layer are called *routed* or *routable protocols*.

A routed protocol is distinguished by the following:

- Includes any network protocol suite that provides enough information in its network layer address to allow a packet to direct user traffic.

- Defines the format and use of the fields within a packet. Packets generally are conveyed from end system to end system.

The Internet Protocol (IP) and Novell's Internetwork Packet Exchange (IPX) are examples of routed protocols. Other examples include DECnet, AppleTalk, Banyan VINES, and Xerox Network Systems (XNS).

Routed protocols are used between routers to direct user traffic (see Figure 20-2).

Figure 20-2   *Routed Protocols*

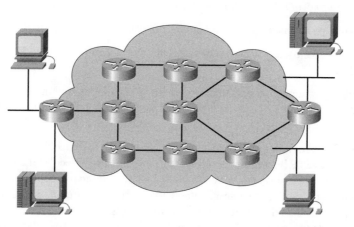

Routers use routing protocols to exchange routing tables and share routing information. In other words, *routing* protocols determine how *routed* protocols are routed. Routing protocols are used between routers to determine paths and maintain routing tables (see Figure 20-2).

Figure 20-3 *Routing Protocols*

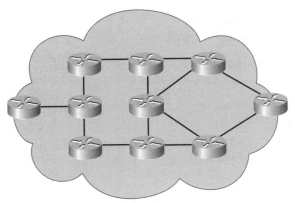

A routing protocol has the following characteristics:

- Supports a routed protocol by providing mechanisms for sharing routing information

- Allows the routers to communicate with other routers to update and maintain the routing tables

Examples of routing protocols that support the IP routed protocol include Routing Information Protocol (RIP), Interior Gateway Routing Protocol (IGRP), Open Shortest Path First (OSPF), Border Gateway Protocol (BGP), and Enhanced IGRP (EIGRP).

Examples of a routing protocol that support other routed protocols such as Novell NetWare (IPX) are Novell RIP, the Novell NetWare Link Services Protocol (NLSP), and EIGRP. Using the postal system as an example, you can think of the routing protocol as the postal system used between the post offices to determine how to best route your mail via the postal system. The routed protocol then defines the format of the address on the envelope and the format of the content inside the envelope. For example, each letter should have a date, some content, and a signature at the bottom.

Path Determination

Routers use routing tables and network addresses to transmit data packets through the network. Routing involves two basic activities:

- Determining optimal routing paths

- Transporting packets through an internetwork

During path determination, routers evaluate the available paths to a destination and establish the preferred handling of a packet as follows (see Figure 20-4):

- Routing services use internetwork topology information when evaluating network paths. This information can be configured onto each router by the network administrator statically (static routing), or it can be learned dynamically (dynamic routing) by the routers using a routing protocol.

- After the router determines which path to use, it can proceed with switching the packet by forwarding the packet it accepted on one interface to another interface or port that reflects the best path toward the packet destination.

Figure 20-4   *Path Determination*

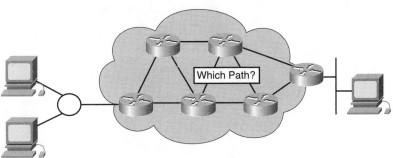

Routing Tables

To aid in the process of path determination, routing protocols build and maintain routing tables, which contain route information. Route information varies, depending on the routing protocol used. Routing protocols fill routing tables with a variety of information.

Figure 20-5 shows how routers keep tables of information to aid in traffic management and path determination.

Figure 20-5 *Routing Tables*

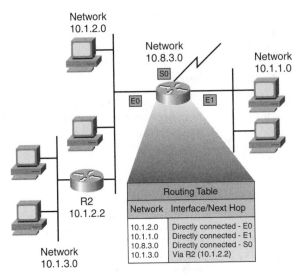

Routing Table Information

Routers keep track of important information in their routing tables, such as destination/next-hop addresses and routing metrics. Destination/next-hop associations tell a router that a particular destination either is directly connected to the router or can be reached through another router called the "next-hop" router on the way to the final destination. When a router receives an incoming packet, it checks the destination address and attempts to associate this address with either a directly connected interface or the next-hop router.

Different routing protocols use different routing metrics. Routing metric is used to determine the desirability of the route. For example, the Routing Information Protocol (RIP) routing protocol uses hop count as its routing metric. A hop represents an intermediate router that a packet must goes through before reaching the destination. Therefore, a route with a lower total hop count is more desirable than another route with a higher total hop count because the lower hop count route has to go through fewer intermediate routers.

Routing Update Messages

Routers communicate with one another and maintain their routing tables through the transmission of routing update messages. Routing update messages are exchanged between routers. Depending on the particular routing protocol, routing update messages can be sent periodically or only when there is a change in the network topology. Some of the information contained in the routing update messages includes the destination networks that the router can reach, along with the routing metric to reach each destination. By analyzing the routing updates from the neighboring routers, a router can build and maintain its routing table.

Routing Algorithms

Routing algorithms can be designed with different goals. The particular goals of algorithm designers affect the operation of resulting routing protocol. Routing metrics are used by a routing algorithm to determine the optimal routes. The following sections describe routing algorithm design goals and routing metrics.

Design Goals

Routing algorithms often have one or more of the following design goals:

- **Optimization**—Optimization describes the capability of the routing protocol/algorithm to select the best route, depending on metrics and metric weightings used in the calculation. For example, one algorithm might use hop count and delay for its metric but might weigh delay more heavily in the calculation.

- **Simplicity and low overhead**—Ideally, efficient routing algorithm functionality is achieved if the routers have minimum CPU and memory overhead. This is important so that the network can scale to large proportions, such as the Internet.

- **Robustness and stability**—A routing algorithm should perform correctly in the face of unusual or unforeseen circumstances, such as hardware failures, high load conditions, and implementations errors.

- **Rapid convergence**—Convergence is the process of agreement by all routers on optimal routes. When a network event causes changes in link or router availability, recalculations are needed to re-establish network connectivity. Routing algorithms that converge slowly can cause routing loops or long network outages.

- **Flexibility**—A routing algorithm should quickly and accurately adapt to a variety of network circumstances. Changes of consequence include router availability, changes in network bandwidth, queue size, and network delay.

Routing Metrics

When a routing algorithm updates a routing table, its primary objective is to determine the best information to include in the table. Routing algorithms have used many different metrics to determine the best route. Each routing algorithm interprets what is best in its own way. The routing algorithm generates a number, called the *metric value*, for each path through the network. Sophisticated routing algorithms can base route selection on multiple metrics, combining them in a single (hybrid) metric (see Figure 20-6). Typically, the smaller the metric number is, the better the path is.

Figure 20-6   *Routing Metrics*

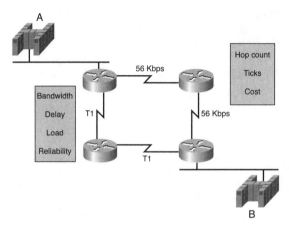

Metrics can be based on a single characteristic of a path or several characteristics of a path. The metrics that are most commonly used by routing protocols are as follows:

- **Bandwidth**—The data capacity of a link. (Normally, a 10-Mbps Ethernet link is preferable to a 64-kbps leased line.)

- **Delay**—The length of time required to move a packet along each link from source to destination. Delay depends on the bandwidth of intermediate links, port queues at each router, network congestion, and physical distance.

- **Load**—The amount of activity on a network resource such as a router or a link.

- **Reliability**—Usually a reference to the error rate of each network link.

- **Hop count**—The number of routers that a packet must travel through before reaching its destination.

- **Ticks**—The delay on a data link using IBM PC clock ticks (1 tick is approximately 55 milliseconds, or 1/18 second).

- **Cost**—An arbitrary value, usually based on bandwidth, monetary expense, or other measurement, that is assigned by a network administrator.

Administrative Distance

Routers are capable of supporting multiple independent routing protocols and maintaining routing tables for several routed protocols. This capability allows a router to deliver packets from several routed protocols over the same data links.

Most routing protocols have metric structures and algorithms that are not compatible with other protocols. In a network in which multiple routing protocols are present, the exchange of route information and the capability to select the best path across the multiple protocols are critical.

Administrative distance is the feature used by routers to select the best path when there are two or more different routes to the same destination from two different routing protocols. Administrative distance defines the reliability of a routing protocol. Each routing protocol is prioritized in order of most to least reliable using an administrative distance value.

The smaller the administrative distance value is, the more reliable the protocol is. For example, if a router receives a route to a certain network from both the Routing Information Protocol (RIP) and the Interior Gateway Routing Protocol (IGRP), the router will choose IGRP because it is more reliable. This means that the IGRP version of the route would be added to the routing table. RIP and IGRP are discussed in Chapter 21, "Routing Protocols."

In Cisco routers, administrative distance is expressed as a numerical value between 0 and 255. Table 20-1 lists the administrative distance default values of the protocols that Cisco supports.

Table 20-1   *Default Administrative Distance Value*

Route Source	Default Administrative Distance Value
Connected interface	0
Static route	1
Enhanced Interior Gateway Routing Protocol (EIGRP)	5
External Border Gateway Protocol (BGP)	20
Internal EIGRP	90
Interior Gateway Routing Protocol (IGRP)	100
Intermediate System-to-Intermediate System (IS-IS)	115
Routing Information Protocol (RIP)	120
Exterior Gateway Protocol (EGP)	140
On-demand routing (ODR)	160
External EIGRP	170
Internal BGP	200
Unknown	255

Summary

In this chapter, you learned the following key points:

- Routers operate at the network layer. The de-encapsulation and encapsulation process occurs each time the packet transfers through a router.

- Routers make decisions regarding the best path for the delivery of data on an internetwork and then direct packets to the appropriate output port and segment.

- Routed protocols define the format and use of the fields within a packet. Packets generally are conveyed from end system to end system.

- Routing protocols are used between routers to determine paths and maintain routing tables. Routed protocols are used to direct user traffic.

- Routing involves two basic activities: determining the best routing paths and transporting packets through an internetwork.

- Routing algorithms process the received updates and populate the routing table with the best routes.

- Routing algorithms use different metrics to determine the best route.

- Routing tables contain the best path to all known networks.

- Administrative distance defines the reliability of a routing protocol.

Review Exercises

1 What function allows routers to evaluate available routes to a destination and to establish the preferred handling of a packet?

   a. Data linkage

   b. Path determination

   c. SDLC interface protocol

   d. Frame Relay

2 Which best describes a routed protocol?

   a. Provides enough information in its network layer address to allow a packet to be forwarded from host to host

   b. Provides information necessary to pass data packets up to the next highest network layer

   c. Allows routers to communicate with other routers to maintain and update address tables

   d. Allows routers to bind MAC and IP address together

3 Routing involves which of the following basic activities? (Choose all that apply.)

   a. Determining optimal routing paths

   b. Determining the source MAC address

   c. Transporting information packets

   d. Configuring router interfaces

   e. Determining the source IP address

4 Which of the following contains routing information that helps a router in determining the routing path?

   a. IP address

   b. MAC address

   c. Routing table

   d. Routing protocol

5 Which of the following is *not* a common routing metric?

   a. Delay

   b. Bandwidth

   c. Length

   d. Cost

6 Administrative distance defines the _____ of a routing protocol.

   a. Scalability

   b. Flexibility

   c. Speed

   d. Reliability

Upon completing this chapter, you will be able to:

- Describe the difference between interior and exterior routing protocols
- Describe the primary types of routing protocols and provide examples of each
- Describe the features of and routing metrics used by RIPv1 and RIPv2
- Describe the features of and routing metrics used by IGRP
- Identify the four basic components used by EIGRP to enhance its capability
- Describe the routing algorithm and metrics used by OSPF
- Describe the routing algorithm and metrics used by IS-IS
- Describe the functions of BGP

CHAPTER 21

Routing Protocols

Routing protocols determine the paths that routed protocols follow to their destinations. Routers use routing protocols to exchange routing tables and share routing information. Routing protocols can be classified in many ways, including according to their operational characteristics, such as the relationship of a router to other autonomous systems, the way in which they discover and calculate routes, and so on.

Depending on the relationship of a router with other autonomous systems, routing protocols can divided into two classes: exterior gateway protocols (EGPs) and interior gateway protocols (IGPs). EGPs route data between autonomous systems. IGPs route data within an autonomous system.

However, according to the way routing protocols discover and calculate routes, routing protocols can be categorized into three classes: distance-vector, link-state, and hybrid routing protocols.

This chapter describes EGP and IGP. In addition, this chapter discusses distance-vector, link-state, and hybrid routing protocols.

IGP and EGP

An *autonomous system* is a network or set of networks that is under common administrative control. An autonomous system consists of routers that present a consistent view of routing to the external world. Autonomous system numbers are allocated to the regional registries by the Internet Assigned Numbers Authority (IANA). These regional registries include the following:

- American Registry for Internet Numbers (ARIN) for North America, South America, South Africa, and the Caribbean

- Réseaux IP Européennes (RIPE) Network Coordination Centre (NCC) for Europe

- Asia Pacific Network Information Centre (APNIC) for the Asia Pacific region

Autonomous system numbers can be obtained from the registry in your region. An autonomous system number is a 16-bit number. A routing protocol such as the Border Gateway Protocol (BGP) requires that you specify this unique, assigned autonomous system number in your configuration.

Routers use routing protocols to exchange routing information. In other words, routing protocols determine how routed protocols are routed. Routing protocols can be classified in many ways, such as by the role that they perform in an internetwork, the way that they discover and calculate routes, and so on.

Depending on the relationship of the router with other autonomous systems, there are two main classes of routing protocols: interior gateway protocols (IGPs) and exterior gateway protocols (EGPs) (see Figure 21-1).

IGPs route data within an autonomous system. Examples of IGPs include the following:

- Routing Information Protocol (RIP)

- Interior Gateway Routing Protocol (IGRP)

- Enhanced Interior Gateway Routing Protocol (EIGRP)

- Open Shortest Path First (OSPF)

- Intermediate System-to-Intermediate System protocol (IS-IS)

EGPs route data between autonomous systems. The Border Gateway Protocol is an example of an EGP.

Figure 21-1   *Interior and Exterior Routing Protocols*

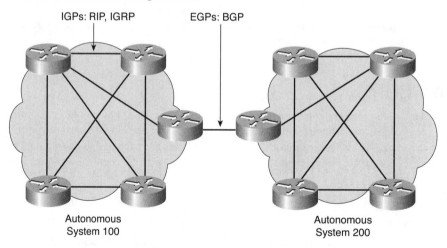

IGPs: RIP, IGRP   EGPs: BGP

Autonomous
System 100

Autonomous
System 200

Routing Protocols

Depending on the way in which routing protocols discover and calculate routes, routing protocols can be categorized into three classes: distance-vector, link-state, and hybrid routing protocols. The following sections describe each in detail.

Distance-Vector Protocols

The distance-vector routing approach determines the direction (vector) and distance (hop count) to any link in the internetwork. Distance-vector algorithms periodically (such as every 30 seconds) send all or some portion of their routing table only to their adjacent neighbors. Routers running the distance-vector routing protocol send periodic updates even if there are no changes in the network. By receiving a neighbor's routing table, a router can verify all the known routes and make changes to the local routing table based upon updated information received from the neighboring router. This process is also known as *routing by rumor* because the understanding that a router has of the network is based upon the neighbor's perspective of the network topology.

For example, in Figure 21-2, Router B receives information from Router A. Router B adds a distance-vector number (such as a number of hops), which increases the distance vector and passes this new routing table to its other neighbor, Router C. This same step-by-step process occurs in all directions between direct-neighbor routers.

Figure 21-2   *Distance-Vector Routing Protocols*

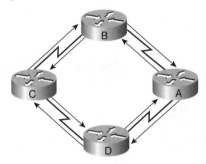

Examples of distance-vector protocols include the following:

- **Routing Information Protocol (RIP)**—A commonly used IGP in the Internet, RIP uses hop count as its routing metric. You learn more about RIP in the section "RIPv1 and RIPv2," later in this chapter.

- **Interior Gateway Routing Protocol (IGRP)**—This IGP was developed by Cisco to address the issues associated with routing in large, heterogeneous networks. You learn more about IGRP later in this chapter in the section "IGRP."

Distance-vector protocols are less complex than link-state approaches, but they suffer from significant limitations. In particular, the small hop-count limit (15) of RIP places a limitation on the size of internetworks, and its single metric does not allow for routing flexibility in complex environments. In addition, RIP can take a long time (minutes) to response to topology changes. Because of those limitations, complex networks require a more sophisticated routing protocol.

Routing Loops and Convergence

Whenever the topology of a network changes because of growth, reconfiguration, or failure, the network knowledge base must also change. The knowledgebase needs to reflect an accurate, consistent view of the new topology. This view is called *convergence*. Fast convergence is a desirable network feature because it reduces the period of time in which routers would continue to make incorrect routing decisions.

Routing loops can occur if a network's slow convergence on a new configuration causes inconsistent routing entries. Distance-vector algorithms use the following mechanisms to avoid routing loop:

- **Split horizon**—Split horizon is a technique used to reduce routing loops and speed convergence. Split horizon ensures that information about a route is never sent back in the direction from which the original packet came. For example, Router A initially advertises that the route to Network 1 is unreachable to Router B and Router D. As a result, there is no reason for Router B and Router D to send this route back to Router A (see Figure 21-3). The split horizon rule helps prevent routing loops.

Figure 21-3   *Split Horizon*

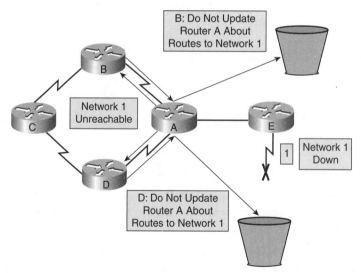

- **Hold-down timers**—When a router learns that a network is farther away than was previously known or learns that the network is down, the router marks that route as inaccessible and starts a hold-down timer. During the hold-down period, the route is advertised, but incoming advertisements about that network from any router other than the one that originally advertised the network's new metric are ignored. This mechanism is often used to help avoid routing loops in the network, but it increases the topology convergence time.

- **Poison reverse updates**—Whereas split horizons should prevent routing loops between adjacent routers, poison reverse updates are intended to defeat larger routing loops. Increases in routing metrics generally indicate routing loops. Poison reverse updates are then sent to remove the route and place it in holddown. A router poisons the route by sending an update with a metric of infinity to a router that originally advertised a route to a network. Poisoning the route can help speed convergence.

Link-State Protocols

Link-state routing protocols were designed to overcome the limitations of distance-vector routing protocols. Link-state routing protocols respond quickly to network changes, send trigger updates only when a network change has occurred, send periodic updates (known as *link-state refreshes*) at long time intervals (such as every 30 minutes), and send "hellos" to neighbor routers to verify the links are functional.

When a link changes state, the device that detected the change creates a link-state advertisement (LSA) concerning that link (route), and that LSA is propagated to all devices. Each routing device takes a copy of the LSA, updates its link-state (topological) database, and forwards the LSA to all neighboring devices. This flooding of the LSA is required to ensure that all routing devices update their databases before creating an updated routing table that reflects the new topology (see Figure 21-4).

Figure 21-4   *Link-State Routing Protocols*

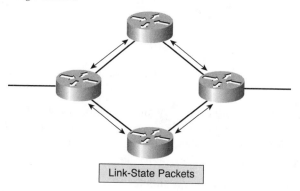

Link-State Packets

The link-state database is used to calculate the best paths through the network. Link-state routers find the best paths to destinations by applying the Dijkstra Shortest Path First (SPF) algorithm against the link-state database to build the Shortest Path First tree. The best (shortest) paths are then selected from the Shortest Path First tree and placed in the routing table (see Figure 21-5).

Figure 21-5   *Shortest Path First Tree*

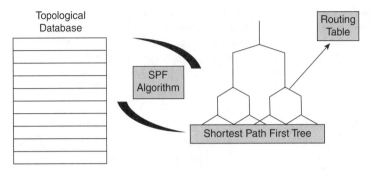

Examples of a link-state protocol are as follows:

- **Open Shortest Path First (OSPF)**—OSPF was proposed as a successor to RIP in the Internet community. OSPF features include least-cost routing, multipath routing, and load balancing. You learn more about OSPF in the section "OSPF," later in this chapter.

- **Intermediate System-to-Intermediate System (IS-IS)**—IS-IS was developed by the International Organization for Standardization (ISO) as part of its Open System Interconnection (OSI) model. IS-IS is a routing protocol that dynamically routes packets between routers, or *intermediate systems*. You learn more about IS-IS in the section "IS-IS", later in this chapter.

Hybrid Protocols

A third classification of protocols, called *hybrid*, combines aspects of distance-vector and link-state protocols.

An example of a hybrid protocol is Enhanced Interior Gateway Routing Protocol (EIGRP). EIGRP is an advanced version of IGRP developed by Cisco. It provides rapid convergence and operating efficiency, and it combines the advantages of link-state protocols with those of distance-vector protocols. You learn more about EIGRP later in this chapter.

There is no single best routing algorithm for all internetworks. Network administrators must weigh technical and nontechnical aspects of their network to determine what is best.

RIPv1 and RIPv2

RIP uses distance-vector algorithms to determine the direction and distance to any link in the internetwork. If there are multiple paths to a destination, RIP selects the path with the least number of hops. However, because hop count is the only routing metric used by RIP, it does not necessarily select the fastest path to a destination.

RIP allows routers to update their routing tables at programmable intervals; the default interval is every 30 seconds. Because RIP is constantly sending routing updates to its neighboring routers, this process can cause network traffic to build.

To prevent a packet from looping infinitely, RIP has a hop-count limitation of 15 hops. If the destination network is more than 15 routers away, it is considered unreachable and the packet is dropped. This limitation creates a scalability issue when routing in large, heterogeneous networks (see Figure 21-6).

Figure 21-6   *Hop Count*

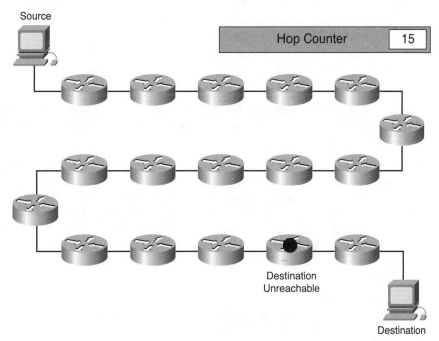

Despite these limitations, RIP, one of the earliest routing protocols to be developed, remains very popular and is still widely implemented because it is easy to configure. Many hosts (such as UNIX host) can also run RIP.

RIP is available in the following two versions:

- **RIP version 1 (RIPv1)**—Uses only classful routing. This means that all devices in the network must use the same subnet mask because RIPv1 does not include the subnet information with the routing update.

- **RIP version 2 (RIPv2)**—Provides prefix routing and sends subnet mask information with the route updates. In prefix routing, the forwarding decisions are based on a "longest prefix match" algorithm on arbitrary bit boundaries, without any knowledge of the internal structure of addresses. RIPv2 supports the use of *classless routing*. With classless routing protocols, different subnets within the same network can have different subnet masks. The use of different subnet masks within the same network is referred to as a *variable-length subnet mask (VLSM)*. RIPv2 is backward compatible with RIPv1.

RIPv1 was one of the first dynamic routing protocols used in the Internet. However, the Internet has changed significantly since RIPv1 was defined, particularly with the introduction and use of subnets and CIDR. Although RIPv1 is widely used in private networks, it can no longer be considered applicable for use in the global Internet.

As recommended in RFC 1923, "RIPv1 Applicability Statement for Historic Status," if RIP is to be used in a network environment, RIPv2 should be used. RIPv1 itself should be used only in a network with simple topologies and simple reachability.

IGRP

IGRP is a distance-vector routing protocol developed by Cisco. It was developed specifically to address problems associated with routing in large networks that were beyond the scope of protocols such as RIP.

Whereas RIP selects the path with the fewest hops, IGRP can select the fastest path based on the delay, bandwidth, load, and reliability. Network administrators can determine the importance given to any one of these metrics or can allow IGRP to automatically calculate the optimal path. By default, IGRP uses bandwidth and delay metrics. This is called a *composite metric*. IGRP has a maximum hop count of 255, with a default of 100. This allows the network to scale and solves the problem of having only 15 hops maximum possible in a RIP network. Table 21-1 shows a comparison of IGRP and RIP.

NOTE   Cisco does not recommend using any other metrics than delay and bandwidth because the algorithm can become unstable if they are used.

Table 21-1   *IGRP vs. RIP*

	Metric	Maximum Number of Hops	Origins
RIP	Hop count	15	Xerox
IGRP	Bandwidth Delay	255 (successfully run in the largest internetworks in the world)	Cisco

IGRP sends routing updates at 90-second intervals, advertising the network for a particular autonomous system. Some of the IGRP key design characteristics emphasize the following:

- Versatility that enables IGRP to automatically handle indefinite, complex topologies

- Flexibility for segments that have different bandwidth and delay characteristics

- Scalability for functioning in very large networks

EIGRP

Like IGRP, EIGRP is a proprietary Cisco protocol. EIGRP is an advanced version of IGRP. Specifically, EIGRP provides superior operating efficiency, such as faster convergence and lower overhead bandwidth. It combines the advantages of link-state protocols with those of distance-vector protocols; hence, the term *hybrid* is used to describe its algorithm. IGRP and EIGRP are Cisco proprietary routing protocols. No other vendors' routers support these routing protocols. Therefore, IGRP and EIGRP are not suitable for multivendor networks.

EIGRP uses four basic components that enhance its capability to route data beyond IGRP:

- **Neighbor discovery/recovery**—This feature allows routers to learn about neighboring routers dynamically.

- **Reliable Transport Protocol**—This technology guarantees the ordered delivery of EIGRP packets to all neighbors.

- **DUAL finite-state machine**—The Diffusing Update Algorithm (DUAL) tracks all routes advertised by all neighbors so that it can select a loop-free path.

- **Protocol-dependent modules**—These modules are responsible for network layer, protocol-specific requirements needed to make routing decisions. EIGRP supports multiple routed protocols, such as IP, IPX, and AppleTalk.

OSPF

OSPF is a link-state technology, as opposed to a distance-vector technology such as RIP. The Internet Engineering Task Force (IETF) developed OSPF in 1988. The most recent version, known as OSPF version 2, is described in RFC 2328, "OSPF Version 2.". OSPF is an IGP, which means that it distributes routing information between routers belonging to the same autonomous system. OSPF was written to address the needs of large, scalable internetworks that RIP could not. OSPF was derived from an early version of IS-IS.

The issues that OSPF addresses follow:

- **Speed of convergence**—In large networks, RIP convergence can take several minutes as the routing algorithm goes through a hold-down and route-aging period. With OSPF, convergence is faster than with RIP because routing changes are flooded immediately and are computed in parallel.

- **Support for variable-length subnet masks (VLSMs)**—RIPv1 does not support VLSMs. OSPF is a classless routing protocol, and it sends subnet mask information along with the routing updates; therefore, it supports VLSMs. (Note that RIPv2 also supports VLSMs.)

- **Network reachability**—A RIP network that spans more than 15 hops (15 routers) is considered unreachable. OSPF has virtually no reachability limitations.

- **Use of bandwidth**—RIP broadcasts full routing tables to all neighbors every 30 seconds, a situation that can become especially problematic over slow WAN links. OSPF multicasts link-state updates and sends the updates only when there is a change in the network. (Note that OSPF does send updates every 30 minutes to ensure that all routers are synchronized.)

- **Method for path selection**—RIP has no concept of network delays and link costs. Routing decisions are based purely on hop count, a situation that could lead to suboptimal path selection when a longer path (in terms of hop count) has a higher aggregate link bandwidth and shorter delays. OSPF uses a cost value, which for Cisco routers is based on the configured bandwidth of the interface.

IS-IS

The OSI protocol suite supports numerous standard protocols at each of the seven OSI layers. Figure 21-7 illustrates the entire OSI protocol suite and its relation to the layers of the OSI reference model. Intermediate System-to-Intermediate System (IS-IS) is the dynamic link-state routing protocol developed by the ISO as part of the OSI protocol stack.

IS-IS is based on a routing method developed at Digital Equipment Corporation—DECnet Phase V. IS-IS distributes routing information for routing Connectionless Network Protocol (CLNP) data for the ISO Connectionless Network Service (CLNS) environment.

Figure 21-7   *IS-IS*

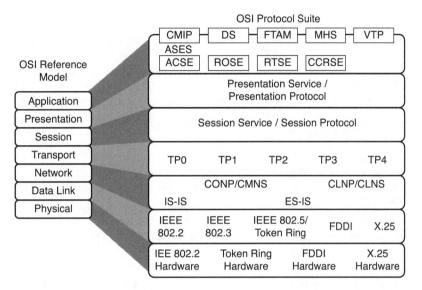

NOTE   CLNP and CLNS are described in the ISO 8473, "ConnectionLess Network Protocol (CLNP)," standard. CLNP is an OSI network-layer protocol that carries upper-layer data and error indications over connectionless links. CLNP provides the interface between CLNS and the upper layers. CLNS provides network layer services to the transport layer via CLNP. CLNS does not perform connection setup or termination because paths are determined independently for each packet that is transmitted through a network. In addition, CLNS provides best-effort delivery, which means that no guarantee exists that data will not be lost, corrupted, misordered, or duplicated. CLNS relies on transport layer protocols to perform error detection and correction.

Integrated IS-IS is an implementation of the IS-IS protocol for routing multiple network protocols. Integrated IS-IS tags CLNP routes with information regarding IP networks and subnets. It provides an alternative to OSPF in the IP world, mixing ISO CLNP and IP routing in one protocol. It can be used purely for IP routing, purely for ISO routing, or for a combination of the two. OSPF on the other hand, supports only IP.

BGP

Most recently defined in RFC 1772, "Application of the Border Gateway Protocol in the Internet," the Border Gateway Protocol (BGP) is an example of an EGP. BGP exchanges routing information between autonomous systems while guaranteeing loop-free path selection. It is the principal route-advertising protocol used by major companies and ISPs on the Internet. BGP4 is the first version of BGP that supports CIDR and route aggregation. Unlike common IGPs such as RIP, OSPF, and EIGRP, BGP does not use metrics such as hop count or bandwidth or delay. Instead, BGP makes routing decisions based on network policies, or rules, using various BGP path attributes.

BGP updates are carried using TCP on port 179. In contrast, RIP updates use User Datagram Protocol (UDP) port 520, whereas OSPF uses neither TCP nor UDP (it has its own network layer protocol number of 89). Because BGP requires TCP, IP connectivity must exist between BGP peers, and TCP connections must be negotiated between them before updates can be exchanged. Thus, BGP inherits the reliable, connection-oriented properties of TCP. To guarantee loop-free path selection, BGP constructs a graph of autonomous systems based on the information exchanged between BGP neighbors. As far as BGP is concerned, the whole internetwork is a graph, or tree, of autonomous systems. The connection between any two autonomous systems forms a path, and the collection of path information is expressed as a sequence of autonomous system numbers (called the *autonomous system path*). This sequence forms a route to reach a specific destination, as shown in Figure 21-8.

Figure 21-8   *BGP*

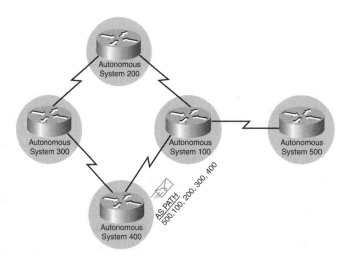

BGP4 is used extensively in the Internet today to connect Internet service providers (ISPs) and to connect enterprises to ISPs.

Summary

In this chapter, you learned the following key points:

- Interior gateway protocols (IGPs) route data within an autonomous system. Exterior gateway protocols (EGPs) route data between autonomous systems.

- Distance-vector routing protocols send all or some portion of their routing table only to neighbors. The distance-vector routing approach determines the direction (vector) and distance to any link in the internetwork.

- Distance-vector algorithms use mechanisms such as split horizon, hold-down timer, and poison reverse updates to avoid routing loops.

- Link-state routing protocols run the Shortest Path First (SPF) algorithms against the link-state database to determine the best paths and then flood routing information about their own links to all the routers in the network. The link-state approach re-creates the exact topology of the entire internetwork (or at least the partition in which the router is situated).

- A hybrid routing algorithm combines aspects of link-state and distance-vector algorithms.

- The Routing Information Protocol (RIP) is a distance-vector protocol that uses the hop-count metric to determine the best path. The Interior Gateway Routing Protocol (IGRP) is a distance-vector protocol that was developed by Cisco. IGRP uses a composite metric.

- The Enhanced Interior Gateway Routing Protocol (EIGRP) is a hybrid routing protocol developed by Cisco. EIGRP supports multiple routed protocols and uses a composite routing metric.

- Open Shortest Path First (OSPF) is a link-state protocol and uses cost as its metric. IS-IS is a link-state protocol that supports both IP and CLNP.

- The Border Gateway Protocol (BGP) is an exterior routing protocol that exchanges routing information between autonomous systems while guaranteeing loop-free path selection. BGP uses a variety of routing policies as its metric.

Review Exercises

1 Which of the following is an example of an EGP?

   a. OSPF

   b. RIP

   c. BGP

   d. EIGRP

2 What are IGPs used for?

   a. To set up a compatibility infrastructure between networks

   b. To communicate between autonomous systems

   c. To transmit between nodes on a network

   d. To deliver routing information within a single autonomous system

3 Which best describes a distance-vector protocol?

   a. It determines the direction and distance to any link in the internetwork.

   b. Each router maintains a complex database of internetwork topology information.

   c. It is computationally complex.

   d. It is a method of routing that prevents loops and minimizes counting to infinity.

4 Which of the following best describes link-state algorithms?

   a. They determine distance and direction to any link on the internetwork.

   b. They require minimal computation.

   c. They re-create the topology of the entire internetwork.

   d. They use little network overhead and reduce overall traffic.

5 In the IP RIP routing protocol, how often are routing updates sent?

   a. Every 30 seconds

   b. Every 60 seconds

   c. Every 90 seconds

   d. Only when the administrator directs the router to do so

6 By default, which of the following is a routing metric used by IGRP?

   a. Bandwidth and delay

   b. MTU size and load

   c. Hop count and delay

   d. Reliability and load

7 Which of the following is *not* a basic component of EIGRP?

    a. Protocol-independent modules

    b. DUAL finite-state machine

    c. Neighbor discover and recovery

    d. Reliable Transport Protocol

8 Which of the following is *not* a feature of OSPF?

    a. Has fast convergence

    b. Processes updates efficiently

    c. Selects paths based on hop count

    d. Supports VLSM

9 Which of the following is true of IS-IS?

    a. IS-IS is a dynamic link-state routing protocol.

    b. Integrated IS-IS is an implementation of the IS-IS protocol for routing multiple network protocols.

    c. Integrated IS-IS can be used for both IP routing and ISO CLNS routing.

    d. All of the above.

10 BGP is an example of which type of protocol?

    a. Internal gateway protocol

    b. External gateway protocol

    c. Routed protocol

    d. None of the above

WAN Technologies

Upon completing this chapter, you will be able to:

- Describe different WAN connection options
- Define packet switching and circuit switching
- Describe the operation of leased lines
- Describe the function of Frame Relay
- Describe features of ATM and define cell switching
- Describe features of SONET

CHAPTER 22

Traditional WAN Services

A wide-area network (WAN) uses data links that are provided by carrier services to access bandwidth over wide-area geographies. Various protocols and technologies are used in a WAN environment. Multiplexing is a technology that enables multiple logical signals to be transmitted simultaneously across a single physical channel.

This chapter introduces various WAN connection options and technologies, including leased line, Frame Relay, ATM, and SONET. In addition, this chapter describes different types of multiplexing techniques used in WANs. Finally, this chapter introduces different WAN switching methods, including packet switching, circuit switching, and cell switching.

For an introduction to WANs, refer to Chapter 6, "WANs."

WAN Connection Options

WAN is a data communications network that covers a relatively broad geographic area and often uses transmission facilities provided by common carriers, such as telephone companies (see Figure 22-1).

Figure 22-1   *WAN Connection*

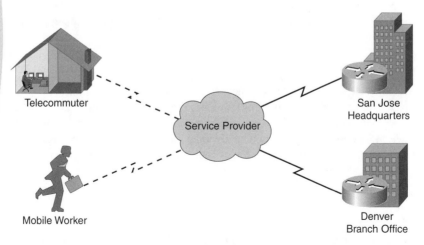

WAN connections can be made through a service provider in several ways, including the following:

- Dialup
- Integrated Services Digital Network (ISDN)
- Leased line
- Frame Relay
- Asynchronous Transfer Mode (ATM)
- Digital subscriber line (DSL)
- Cable
- X.25

The following subsections describe each of these methods in more detail.

Dialup

Usage on dialup lines is paid for only when the lines are used. This means that the line is active only when the user dials up. Dialup lines are often ideal for small offices, branch offices, telecommuters, and mobile workers. The disadvantage of dialup connection is that the connection speed is slow (less than 56 kilobits per second [kbps]).

ISDN

ISDN is an efficient alternative to dialup for connecting over existing telephone wiring systems. ISDN is explained further in Chapter 23, "Dialup Access Technologies."

Leased Line

Service providers also offer leased lines, or point-to-point connections. With leased lines, companies pay for a continuous connection between two remote sites. This means that the line is active 24 hours a day, 7 days a week. With a leased line, the customer is the only user of the bandwidth, as opposed to a "shared bandwidth" model utilizing a Frame Relay or ATM services. The disadvantage of leased lines is that they are generally expensive, and the expense is related to distance.

Frame Relay

Frame Relay provides connection-oriented data link layer communication. This service is implemented using virtual circuits. A *virtual circuit* is a logical circuit created to allow communication between two remote network devices. For example, Figure 22-2 shows a hub-

and-spoke topology used to connect the router at SF Headquarters to three remote routers. Even though the router at SF Headquarters has only one physical connection to the service provider (such as a Frame Relay service provider), that physical connection is divided into three logical connections (virtual circuits), with each virtual circuit connecting to a different remote router. At the remote routers, their physical connection will contain only one virtual circuit because the remote routers need to connect only to the router at SF Headquarters.

Frame Relay works at Layer 2 of the Open System Interconnection (OSI) reference model. Frame Relay does not provide error recovery, which is handled by higher-layer protocols. An identifier (data-link connection identifier [DLCI]) within the Frame Relay (Layer 2) header indicates which virtual circuit a frame belongs to. The Frame Relay service provider also makes its switching decision based on the DLCI. In Figure 22-2, the Frame Relay connection at SF Headquarters is provisioned with three virtual circuits. The SF Headquarters router uses DLCI 102 in the Frame Relay header for sending data to the Los Angeles (LA) router, DLCI 101 for the New York (NY) router, and DLCI 100 for the Chicago router.

Figure 22-2   *Virtual Circuit*

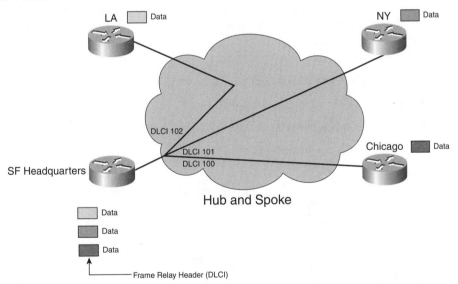

ATM

ATM comprises specifications at both the physical and data link layers. Like Frame Relay, this service is implemented using virtual circuits. With ATM, the data packet is divided into small 53-byte cells before it is transmitted. In the ATM cell header is a field called the virtual path identifier/virtual channel identifier (VPI/VCI) that is used to indicate which virtual circuit an ATM cell belongs to. At the physical layer, ATM can run over a variety of physical media, including fiber optics using Synchronous Optical Network (SONET) framing and coaxial cable using digital signal level 3 (DS3).

Additional WAN Connection Options

Additional WAN connection options include using DSL, cable, wireless, and X.25. WAN technologies generally function at the lowest two layers of the OSI reference model: the physical layer and the data link layer. WAN connections can be purchased or leased in a variety of speeds, or *bandwidths*. Start with the simple DS0 (64 kbps), which is the bandwidth required for a uncompressed typical digitized phone call. Bundle (multiplex) 24 DS0s to get a DS1/T1 line (1.544 megabits per second [Mbps]). Then bundle (multiplex) 28 DS1s to get a DS3/T3 line (44.736 Mbps). The DS technically refers to the rate and format of the signal, whereas the T designation refers to the equipment providing the signals. In practice, DS and T are used synonymously. E1 (2.048 Mbps) and E3 (34.064 Mbps) are European standards similar to T1 and T3, but they possess different bandwidths.

Multiplexing

Multiplexing is a process of sharing, in which multiple data channels are combined into a single data or physical channel at the source. Multiplexing can be implemented at any of the OSI layers. Broadband WAN lines use multiplexing technology (see Figure 22-3). *Demultiplexing* is the process of separating multiplexed data channels at the destination. Four primary types of multiplexing operate at the physical layer:

- Time-division multiplexing (TDM)

- Frequency-division multiplexing (FDM)

- Wave-division multiplexing (WDM) and dense WDM (DWDM)

- Statistical-division multiplexing (SDM)

Figure 22-3   *Multiplexing Technologies*

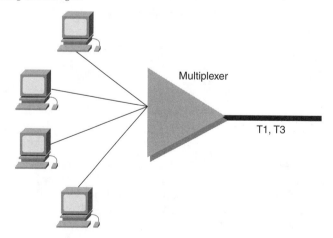

Multiplexer

T1, T3

In the following subsections, you learn more about each type of multiplexing.

TDM

In TDM, information from each data channel is allocated bandwidth based on preassigned time slots, regardless of whether there is data to transmit (see Figure 22-4). As a result, bandwidth is wasted when a data channel has nothing to transmit during its assigned time slot. In TDM, the physical layer attribute used for sharing is based on time.

Figure 22-4   *TDM*

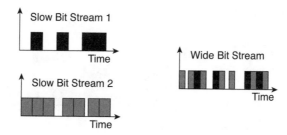

FDM

In FDM, information from each data channel is allocated bandwidth based on the signal frequency of the traffic (see Figure 22-5). For example, FM radio broadcasts use FDM. Each FM station is assigned a specific frequency to use for broadcasting its radio programs. In FDM, the physical layer attribute used for sharing is based on frequency.

Figure 22-5   *FDM*

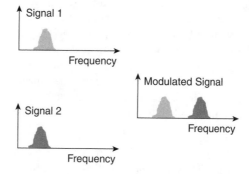

WDM and DWDM

In WDM and DWDM, the physical layer attribute used for sharing is based on wavelength (inverse of frequency). These optical multiplexing technologies are discussed in Chapter 31, "Optical Transmission and Multiplexing."

Statistical Multiplexing

In statistical multiplexing, bandwidth is dynamically allocated to any data channels that have information to transmit (see Figure 22-6).

Figure 22-6   *STM*

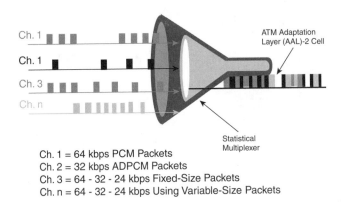

Ch. 1 = 64 kbps PCM Packets
Ch. 2 = 32 kbps ADPCM Packets
Ch. 3 = 64 - 32 - 24 kbps Fixed-Size Packets
Ch. n = 64 - 32 - 24 kbps Using Variable-Size Packets

Packet Switching vs. Circuit Switching

Packet switching is a switching method in which users share common carrier resources. Because this allows the carrier to make more efficient use of its infrastructure, the cost to the customer is generally much better than with point-to-point leased lines. Leased lines are dedicated bandwidth for the customer, and only that customer can use it (which causes it to sit idle for a significant portion of the day, in most cases due to people working 9 to 5.) With packet switching, the carrier does not have to have some of its capacity dedicated to a particular customer, and most customers utilization is sporadic; when a customer's bandwidth is not being used by that customer, the bandwidth is available for other customer to utilize.

In a packet-switching setup, networks have connections into the carrier's network, and many customers share the carrier's network. The carrier can then create virtual circuits between customers' sites by which packets of data are delivered from one to the other through the network (see Figure 22-7).

Figure 22-7 *Packet Switching*

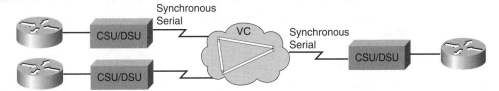

Circuit switching is a WAN switching method in which a dedicated physical circuit is established, maintained, and terminated through a carrier network for each communication session (see Figure 22-8). Circuit switching operates much like a normal telephone call and is used extensively in telephone company networks. ISDN is an example of a circuit-switched WAN access technology.

Figure 22-8 *Circuit Switching*

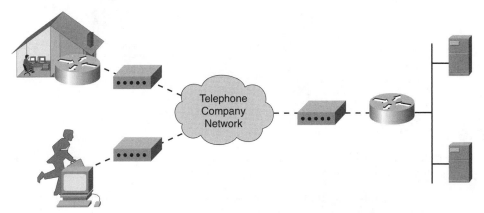

Leased Lines

A point-to-point link provides a single pre-established WAN communications path from the customer premises through a carrier network, such as a telephone company, to a remote network. Point-to-point lines are usually leased from a carrier and thus are often called leased lines. For a point-to-point line, the carrier allocates transport capacity and facility hardware to your circuit only. These circuits are generally priced based on bandwidth required and distance between the two connected points. Point-to-point links are generally more expensive than shared services such as Frame Relay.

When leased-line connections are made, a router serial port is required for each connection. If a serial port is used, a channel/data service unit (CSU/DSU) is also required (see Figure 22-9). The purpose of the CSU/DSU is to provide a clocked signal to the customer equipment interface from the DSU and terminate the carrier's channelized transport media on the CSU. The CSU also provides diagnostic functions (such as loopback). Most T1/E1 TDM interfaces on current routers include approved CSU capabilities. Typically, the CSU/DSU are packaged as a single unit. You can think of it as a very high-powered and expensive modem that connects to a digital line (such as a T1).

NOTE   On the carrier side of the CSU/DSU, there might be no difference between packet and circuit switching because some carriers use statistical multiplexing to maximize backbone bandwidth utilization.

Figure 22-9   *Leased Line*

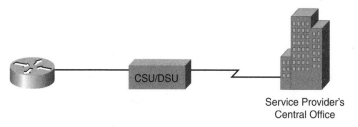

Service Provider's
Central Office

Frame Relay

Frame Relay provides connection-oriented data link layer communication. This service is implemented using virtual circuits. Frame Relay devices have two classes:

- **Data terminal equipment (DTE)**—Terminating equipment for a specific network, typically located on customer premises. An example of a Frame Relay DTE device is a router.

- **Data communications equipment (DCE)**—Carrier-owned internetworking devices that provide clocking and switching services within a network. An example of a Frame Relay DCE device is the Frame Relay switch.

Frame Relay Virtual Circuits

A Frame Relay virtual circuit is a logical connection created between two DTE devices across a network (see Figure 22-10). Virtual circuits provide a bidirectional communication path from one DTE device to another. A data-link connection identifier (DLCI) within the Frame Relay address header uniquely identifies them. The DLCI is specific to the side of virtual circuit. A virtual circuit can pass through any number of intermediate DCE devices located within the network. Numerous virtual circuits can be multiplexed into a single physical circuit for access to and transmission across the network.

Figure 22-10 *Frame Relay Virtual Circuits*

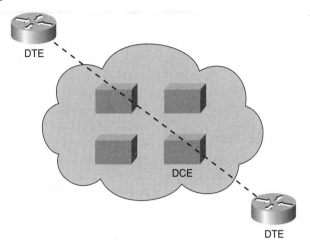

Permanent Virtual Circuits (PVCs)

PVCs are permanently established connections that are used when there is frequent and consistent data transfer between DTE devices across the network. Communication across a PVC does not require the call setup and termination states. DTE devices can begin transferring data whenever they are ready because the circuit is permanently established (see Figure 22-11). A PVC works like a leased-line connection—it is always connected.

Figure 22-11 *Frame Relay PVC*

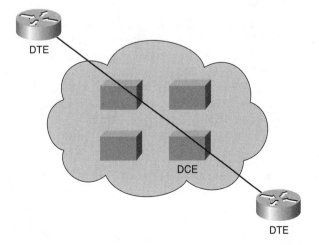

Frame Relay provides a packet-switching network to many different customers at the same time. In Frame Relay networks, customers can purchase different bandwidths for their connections. A committed information rate (CIR) is a bandwidth associated with a logical connection in a PVC. The CIR, provided by the carrier, is the rate, in bits per section, at which the Frame Relay switch agrees to transfer data. It is sometimes possible for a customer to purchase a committed burst, which allows customers to have the bandwidths exceed their CIRs for a specified amount of time.

Local Management Interface (LMI)

LMI is a signaling standard between the customer premises equipment (CPE) device and the Frame Relay switch that is responsible for managing the connection and maintaining status between the devices. LMI messages provide information about the following:

- **Keepalives**—Verifying that data is flowing

- **Multicasting**—Providing the network server with its local DLCI

- **Multicast addressing**—Providing a few DLCIs to be used as multicast addresses and the capability to give DLCIs global significance rather than just local significance

- **Status of virtual circuits**—Providing an ongoing status on the DLCIs known to the switch

Several LMI types exist, and routers need to be told which LMI type is being used. Three types of LMIs supported by routers are Cisco, ANSI, and Q933A.

ATM and Cell Switching

ATM is a technology that is capable of transferring voice, video, and data through private and public networks. ATM is used primarily in enterprise LAN backbones or WAN links. It is built on a cell-based architecture rather than on a frame-based architecture. ATM cells are always a fixed length of 53 bytes, whereas the sizes of frames and packets vary. The 53-byte ATM cell is made up of a 5-byte ATM header followed by 48 bytes of ATM payload (user data). Small fixed-length, 53-byte cells are well suited for carrying data, voice, and video traffic because voice and video traffic are intolerant of delay that can result from having to wait for a larger data packet to be transmitted ahead of a voice or video packet.

An ATM switch is responsible for cell transit through an ATM network. It accepts the incoming cell from an ATM endpoint or another ATM switch. It then reads and updates the cell-header information and quickly switches the cell to an output interface toward its destination (see Figure 22-12).

Figure 22-12   *ATM and Cell Switching*

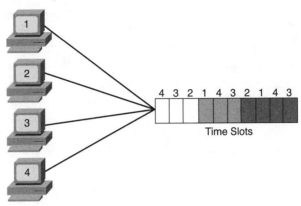

An ATM virtual circuit is a logical connection created between two ATM endpoints across an ATM network. ATM virtual circuits fall into two categories:

• Permanent virtual circuit (PVC)

• Switched virtual circuit (SVC)

Virtual circuits provide a bidirectional communication path from one ATM endpoint to another. The virtual path identifier/virtual channel identifier (VPI/VCI) within the ATM cell header uniquely identifies them. A virtual circuit can pass through any number of intermediate ATM switches in the ATM network. Numerous virtual circuits can be multiplexed into a single physical circuit for transmission across the network.

SONET

SONET, which stands for Synchronous Optical Network, is a physical layer protocol that provides for high-speed transmission using fiber-optic media. ATM can run over SONET to achieve very high data-transfer speeds.

You might see the term Synchronous Digital Hierarchy (SDH) used to refer to the SONET technology outside the United States. The SONET signal rate is measured by Optical Carrier (OC) standards. Table 22-1 illustrates the available transmission rates (called Optical Carrier levels). SONET and SDH are discussed in Part 9, "Optical Networking Fundamentals."

Table 22-1   *SONET Optical Carrier Standards*

SONET OC Level	Signal Transmission Rate
OC-1 (base rate)	51.84 Mbps
OC-3	155.52 Mbps

continues

Table 22-1 *SONET Optical Carrier Standards (Continued)*

SONET OC Level	Signal Transmission Rate
OC-12	622.08 Mbps
OC-24	1.244 Gbps
OC-48	2.488 Gbps
OC-192	10 Gbps
OC-256	13.271 Gbps
OC-768	40 Gbps

Summary

In this chapter, you learned the following key points:

- WAN networks offer access to internetworks and connection between geographically distant nodes.

- WAN customers pay service providers for WAN connections, including dialup, leased lines, ISDN, and Frame Relay.

- WANs have a variety of protocols that all operate at physical and data link layers of the OSI model.

- WAN switching methods include packet switching, circuit switching, and cell switching.

Review Exercises

1 Which of the following is a type of physical layer multiplexing?

   a. TDM

   b. FDM

   c. WDM

   d. All of the above

2 Which of the following best describes a WAN?

   a. Connects LANs that are separated by a large geographic area

   b. Connects workstations, terminals, and other devices in a metropolitan area

   c. Connects LANs within a large building

   d. Connects workstation, terminals, and other devices within a building

3 Which of the following is an example of a circuit-switching protocol?

   a. ISDN

   b. Frame Relay

   c. PPP

   d. HDLC

4 A leased line is a _____ link that provides a single, pre-established WAN communication path from the customer to a remote network.

   a. point-to-point

   b. point-to-multipoint

   c. analog

   d. digital

5 How does Frame Relay handle multiple conversations on the same physical connection?

   a. Frame Relay multiplexes the circuits.

   b. Multiple conversations are not allowed.

   c. Frame Relay duplexes the conversation.

   d. Frame Relay uses WDM.

6 Which of the following is *not* true about ATM technology?

   a. It is capable of transferring voice, video, and data.

   b. ATM is used primarily in enterprise LAN backbones or WAN links.

   c. It is based on a cell-based architecture rather than on a frame-based architecture.

   d. ATM cells are always a fixed length of 35 bytes, whereas the sizes of frames and packets vary.

7 Name the family of very high-speed physical layer technologies that offers a series of data rates with special designations, implemented at different transmission rates ranging from 51.85 Mbps to 40 Gbps.

   a. ADSL

   b. ATM

   c. SONET

   d. ISDN

Upon completing this chapter, you will be able to:

- Describe the function and operation of ISDN

- Describe the function and operation of PPP

- Describe the function and operation of PAP

- Describe the function and operation of CHAP

- Describe the function and operation of HDLC

CHAPTER 23

Dialup Access Technologies

Many types of WAN technologies can be implemented to solve connectivity issues for users who need network access from remote locations. Integrated Services Digital Network (ISDN) is specifically designed to solve the low-bandwidth problems that small offices or dial-in users have with traditional telephone dial-in services.

The Point-to-Point Protocol (PPP), defined in RFC 1661, "Point-to-Point Protocol," was designed for simple links that transport packets between two peers. PPP provides a standard method for transporting multiprotocol datagrams over point-to-point links. High-Level Data Link Control (HDLC) is a WAN data link layer protocol developed by the International Organization for Standardization (ISO). HDLC specifies a data-encapsulation method on synchronous serial links.

This chapter describes the functions and operation of dialup access technologies, including ISDN, PPP, and HDLC. This chapter also discusses the authentication protocols that PPP supports—the Password Authentication Protocol (PAP) and the Challenge Handshake Authentication Protocol (CHAP).

ISDN

ISDN refers to a set of communication protocols proposed by telephone companies to permit telephone networks to carry data, voice, and video (see Figure 23-1). In general, ISDN provides a set of digital services that concurrently deliver voice, data, text, graphics, music, video, and information to end users. ISDN was developed to permit faster access over existing telephone systems without the additional call setup time.

Figure 23-1   *ISDN*

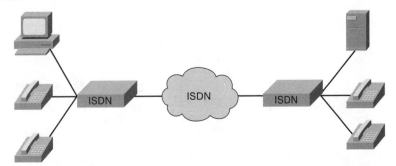

ISDN offers two types of services:

- **Basic Rate Interface (BRI)**—The ISDN BRI service, intended for the home and small enterprise, provides a total bandwidth of 144 kbps in a line with three separate channels: two B channels (64 kbps each) and one D channel (16 kbps). The BRI B channel carries user data and voice traffic, whereas the BRI D channel usually carries control and signaling information.

- **Primary Rate Interface (PRI)**—The ISDN PRI service, intended for larger installations, delivers 23 B channels and 1 D channel in North America, for a total bit rate of up to 1.544 Mbps (T1). In Europe, Australia, and other parts of the world, ISDN PRI provides 30 B channels and 1 D channel, for a total bit rate of up to 2.048 Mbps (E1) (see Figure 23-2). On ISDN PRI, both B and D channels are 64 kbps, as opposed to 16 kbps rate for the D channel on ISDN BRI.

Figure 23-2 *BRI and PRI*

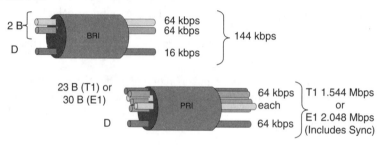

PPP

PPP, defined in RFC 1661, was designed for simple links that transport packets between two peers. PPP provides dynamic assignment of IP addresses and supports multiple routed protocols. PPP provides router-to-router and host-to-network connections over both synchronous and asynchronous circuits (see Figure 23-3). An example of an asynchronous connection is a dialup connection. An example of a synchronous connection is a leased line.

Figure 23-3 *PPP*

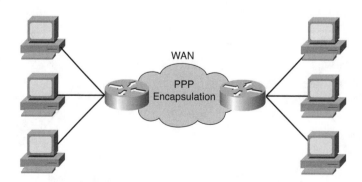

PPP provides a standard method for transporting multiprotocol datagrams over point-to-point links. PPP comprises three main components:

- Method for encapsulating multiprotocol datagrams
- Link control protocol (LCP) for establishing, configuring, and testing the data-link connection
- Family of network control protocols (NCPs) for establishing and configuring different network layer protocols

PPP is designed to allow the simultaneous use of multiple network-layer protocols. PPP supports other protocols besides IP, including Internetwork Protocol Exchange (IPX) and AppleTalk. As shown in Figure 23-4, PPP uses its NCP component to encapsulate multiple protocols.

Figure 23-4   *PPP Components*

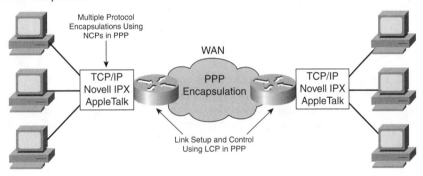

PPP encapsulation is a standard serial-line encapsulation method defined in RFC 1661 (see Figure 23-5). PPP encapsulation provides for multiplexing of different network layer protocols simultaneously over the same link. It has been designed to retain compatibility with most commonly used supporting hardware. PPP encapsulation is nonproprietary. For this reason, it is often used to connect dissimilar vender device.

Figure 23-5   *PPP Encapsulation*

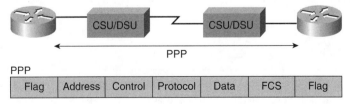

To be sufficiently versatile to be portable to a wide variety of environments, PPP provides an LCP. The LCP is used to automatically agree upon the encapsulation format options, handle varying limits on sizes of packets, detect a looped-back link and other common misconfiguration errors, and terminate the link. Other optional facilities provided by PPP include authenticating the identity of its peer on the link and determining when a link is functioning properly and when it is failing.

After the link has been established and the authentication protocol has been chosen, the peer can be authenticated. If it is used, authentication takes place before the network layer protocol configuration phase begins.

The authentication options require that the calling side of the link enter authentication information to help ensure that the user has the network administrator's permission to make the call. Peer routers exchange authentication messages.

When configuring PPP authentication, you can select PAP or CHAP. In general, CHAP is the preferred protocol. PAP and CHAP are discussed in the following sections.

PAP

PAP provides a simple method for a remote node to establish its identity by using a two-way handshake. After the PPP link-establishment phase is complete, a user name/password pair is repeatedly sent by the remote node across the link until authentication is acknowledged or the connection is terminated, as shown in Figure 23-6.

Figure 23-6 *PAP*

PAP is not a strong authentication protocol. Passwords are sent across the link in clear text (not encrypted), and there is no protection from playback or repeated brute-force attacks. The remote node controls the frequency and timing of the login attempts.

NOTE   Brute force is a trial-and-error technique used by application programs to decode encrypted data such as passwords. In a brute-force attack, every possible combination of letters and numbers is tested one by one until the correct password is found.

CHAP

CHAP is used to periodically verify the identity of the remote node by using a three-way handshake, as shown in Figure 23-7. This handshake is done upon initial link establishment and can be repeated any time after the link has been established. After the PPP link-establishment phase is complete, the host sends a challenge message to the remote node. The remote node responds with a value. The response value is calculated based on the shared password between the two devices. The host checks the response against its own calculated value. If the values match, the authentication is acknowledged. Otherwise, the connection is terminated.

Figure 23-7 *CHAP*

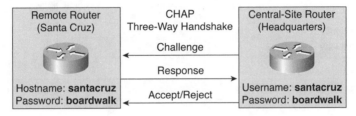

CHAP offers features such as periodic verification to improve security, making CHAP more effective than PAP. PAP verifies only once, making it vulnerable to hacks and modem playback. Furthermore, PAP allows the caller to attempt authentication at will (without first receiving a challenge), making it vulnerable to brute-force attacks; CHAP, on the other hand, does not allow a caller to attempt authentication without a challenge.

CHAP provides protection against playback attacks through the use of a variable challenge value that is unique and unpredictable. The use of repeated challenges is intended to limit the time of exposure to any single attack. The local router (or an external authentication server, such as Cisco Secure Access Control Server [ACS]) controls the frequency and timing of the challenges.

HDLC

HDLC is a standard data link layer protocol. It specifies an encapsulation method for data on synchronous serial data links using frame character and checksum. HDLC supports both point-to-point and multipoint configurations. The HDLC protocol includes a means for authentication. HDLC might not be compatible between different vendors because of the way each vendor has chosen to implement it.

HDLC is Cisco's default encapsulation for serial lines. This implementation is very streamlined; there is no windowing or flow control, and only point-to-point connections are allowed. (For a review on windowing, refer to Chapter 16, "Transport Layer.") The Cisco HDLC implementation includes proprietary extension in the Data field. It will not communicate with another vendor's HDLC implementation.

As shown in Figure 23-8, each vendor has a proprietary HDLC encapsulation method because each vendor has a different way for the HDLC protocol to communicate with the network layer protocols. This proprietary header is placed in the Data field of the HDLC encapsulation. The Address field is always set to all 1s. Furthermore, Cisco's HDLC includes a 2-byte proprietary type code that is inserted after the Control field, meaning that Cisco HDLC framing is not interoperable with other vendors' equipment.

Figure 23-8   *HDLC and Cisco HDLC*

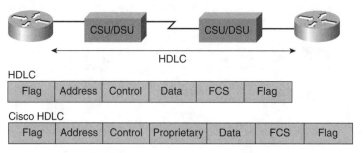

If both ends of a dedicated-line connection are routers or access servers running Cisco IOS Software, Cisco's HDLC encapsulation typically is used. Because HDLC encapsulation methods can vary, you should use PPP with devices that are not running Cisco IOS Software.

Summary

In this chapter, you learned the following key points:

- Two ISDN services exist: BRI and PRI.

- ISDN provides an integrated data, voice, and video capability that uses the public switched network.

- You can select PAP or CHAP when configuring PPP authentication.

- CHAP provides protection against playback attacks through the use of a variable challenge value that is unique and unpredictable.

- WAN encapsulation formats include PPP and HDLC encapsulation.

- HDLC is the default encapsulation for serial lines in the Cisco IOS software.

Review Exercises

1 Which of the following statements pertaining to ISDN is true?

   a. The ISDN BRI offers two B channels and one D channel.

   b. The D channel, operating at 16 kbps, is meant to carry user data.

   c. The ISDN BRI offers 23 B channels and 1 D channel in North America.

   d. The total bit rate of the ISDN BRI is 2.533 Mbps.

2 Which protocol does PPP use for establishing and maintaining point-to-point connections?

   a. HDLC

   b. LCP

   c. LAPD

   d. Cisco IETF

3 What type of handshaking occurs when PAP is your selected authentication when using PPP?

   a. One-way

   b. Two-way

   c. Three-way

   d. Four-way

4 What type of handshaking occurs when CHAP is your selected authentication when using PPP?

   a. One-way

   b. Two-way

   c. Three-way

   d. Four-way

5 What is the default encapsulation type for serial interfaces on a Cisco router?

   a. PPP

   b. HDLC

   c. Frame Relay

   d. X.25

Upon completing this chapter, you will be able to:

- Describe analog modem types

- Describe commonly used analog modem standards

CHAPTER 24

Analog Modems

Analog dialup connections are supported over existing telephone lines, which originally were designed to carry voice using analog signaling. Analog dialup connections are a cheap, readily available remote access solution.

To use analog phone lines for data transmission, a computer's digital signals must be converted to an analog tone that can be carried by ordinary telephone lines. Furthermore, analog signals must be converted back to digital signals so that the receiving computer can decode the information. A modem performs these conversions.

This chapter provides an overview of analog modems and describes different types of analog modems and analog modem standards.

Modem Overview

A *modem* is an electronic device that is used for computer communications through telephone lines. It allows data transfer between one computer and another over the Public Switched Telephone Network (PSTN). Typically, modems send data in blocks of bytes. After each block, basic math is performed to analyze the block, and the computer on the receiving end is asked whether it agrees with the results. If any differences appear, the block is sent again. The modems convert digital data to analog signals and convert analog signals back to digital data.

The term modem derives from the function of this device. The process of converting analog signals to digital and back again is called *modulation/demodulation* (hence the term *modem*).

Modems work at OSI model Layer 1. At Layer 2, a protocol such as PPP, which supports point-to-point connections, is often used. Figure 24-1 depicts a typical modem connection. The modems connect digital computers to the digital telecommunications company (telco) network via analog local loops. When the telco switch receives the analog signal of the modems, it must encode the signals so that it can traverse the digital network.

Figure 24-1 *Modem Transmission*

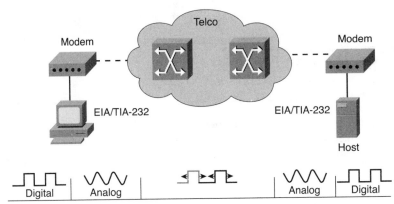

Telcos use a device called a *codec* to encode analog waveforms into digital pulses (analog-to-digital conversion), and vice versa. The name *codec* comes from the words *coder* and *decoder*. The standard for encoding analog to digital is a technique called *pulse code modulation (PCM)*. PCM works by sampling an analog signal thousands of times per second. Each sample is then measured, or quantified, so that it can be encoded as a binary value (typically 8 bits). These approximate values can be used to reconstruct the waveform digitally. Today's telecommunications rely heavily on this kind of digital-to-analog and analog-to-digital conversion.

Modem-based transmission is remarkably accurate, despite the fact that telephone lines can be quite noisy because of clicks, static, and other problems.

Three main types of modems exist:

- Internal
- External
- PC card

The following subsections describe each modem type in more detail.

Internal Modems

Internal modems are the most common type of modem. Internal modems can be built into the motherboard or can be plugged into the expansion slots (Industry-Standard Architecture [ISA] or peripheral component interconnect [PCI]) on the motherboard. Figure 24-2 illustrates a typical internal modem card.

Figure 24-2   *Typical Internal Modem Card*

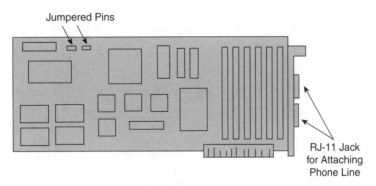

Internal modems allow a communicating device to be connected directly to the telephone network. Internal modems do not take up extra space on the desktop. They also usually cost a little less than the modems that are plugged externally into the computer.

To configure an internal modem, jumpers might have to be set to select the interrupt request (IRQ) line and input/output (I/O) addresses. A modem using a serial (COM) port that is not yet in use must be configured. Additionally, the software drivers that come with the modem must be installed for the modem to work. No configuration is needed for a "plug-and-play" modem, which is installed on a motherboard that supports plug and play.

NOTE   In a computer, a *jumper* is a pair of prongs that are electrical contact points set into the computer motherboard. When you set a jumper, you place a plug on the prongs that completes a contact.

External Modems

You can use external modems with any computer by simply plugging into a serial port (COM1 or COM2) on the back of the computer.

External modems are typically a bit more expensive than the internal modems. The computer case does not have to be opened. Newer Universal Serial Bus (USB) modems are plugged into a USB port or hub. An external modem uses the IRQ and I/O address assigned to the serial port. A status light on the modem indicates whether the modem is online. Figure 24-3 illustrates a typical external modem. Software must be installed for the external modem to work properly.

External modems typically are connected to the other modems using a EIA/TIA 232 serial line (COM port) or USB.

Figure 24-3   *Typical External Modem*

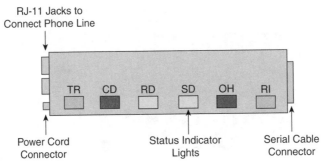

PC Card Modems

PC card modems, also called PCMCIA modems, are a variation of internal modems designed for easy installation in laptop or notebook computers. PC cards look like credit cards, are small, and are very portable. A PC card modem is configured in a manner similar to other modem types. An advantage of the PC card is its small size and portability.

Analog Modem Standards

A modem modulates outgoing digital signals from a computer or other digital device to analog signals for a conventional copper twisted-pair telephone line. It demodulates the incoming analog signal and converts it to a digital signal for the digital device. An analog waveform can be modulated in terms of its amplitude, its frequency, its phase (position of the sine waves), or a combination of these qualities.

International modem standards ensure the interoperability of different types of modems from different vendors. Despite the development of international standards, proprietary techniques are not uncommon. Thus, interoperability among different types of modems is not always easily achieved.

Figure 24-4 lists several modulation standards developed by modem manufacturers and standards organizations including the International Telecommunications Union, Telecommunication Standardization Sector (ITU-T). The ITU-T "V Series Recommendations" are the most commonly used modulation standards and have international acceptance.

Modulation standards typically go through at least one revision. When a second version of a standard is introduced, the Latin suffix *bis* is added to its name. Thus, the second version of the V.32 standard is called V.32bis. The suffix *terbo* is applied to the third release of a modulation standard.

Figure 24-4   *Modem Modulation Standards*

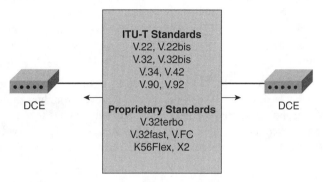

Table 24-1 documents the history of the most commonly used ITU-T modem recommendations and their maximum transfer speeds. Modems accept asynchronous data at one rate measured in bits per second (bps) and transmit analog in other rate measured in baud.

Table 24-1   *Analog Modem Standards*

Standard	Meaning
V.22	V.22 provides 1200 bps at 600 baud. This standard was used mainly outside the United States.
V.22bis	V.22bis is the first true worldwide standard for full-duplex modems sending and receiving data across a telephone line at 2400 bps at 600 baud.
V.32	V.32 is the standard for full-duplex modems. It allows sending and receiving data across phone lines at 4800 or 9600 bps at 2400 baud. V.32 modems automatically adjust their transmission speed based on the quality of the lines.
V.32bis	V.32bis provides throughputs of 14.4 kbps. It also allows fallback onto regular V.32 if the phone line is impaired.
V.34	V.34 is the standard for full-duplex modems sending and receiving data across phone lines at up to 28.8 kbps. V.34 modems automatically adjust their transmission speed based on the quality of the lines. V.34 is backward compatible with V.32.
V.42	V.42 has the same transfer rate as V.32, but with better error correction;, therefore, V.42 is more reliable. V.42 can be used with digital telephone networks.
V.90	V.90 is the standard for full-duplex modems sending and receiving data across phone lines at a downstream data-transmission rate of up to 56 kbps and an upstream data-transmission rate of up to 330 kbps. The V.90 standard is a combination of the X2 technology from US Robotics (now part of 3Com) and the K56Flex technology from Rockwell.
V.92	V.92 is the new dialup modem specification from the ITU-T. It introduces three new features that will add convenience and performance for the modem user: quick connect, modem-on-hold, and PCM upstream.

In recent years, the 2400-bps modem that could carry e-mail has become obsolete. Modems of 14.4- and 28.8-kbps speeds were temporary landing places on the way to much higher bandwidth devices and carriers. From early 1998, most new personal computers came with 56-kbps modems. The 56-kbps downstream rate was standardized by V.90. The maximum upstream rate was increased to 48 kbps in ITU-T recommendation V.92.

In general, when modems initially connect, they "handshake" and agree on the highest standard transfer rate that both can achieve. Modems can achieve throughputs ranging from 300 bps up to 56 kbps, depending on the modulation standard supported. Most modems adapt their transmission rates to achieve the maximum supported speed given several factors, including the best speed supported by the remote modem and the best speed supported by the local loop.

To achieve 56 kbps speed, both the local and remote modems must support the same 56 kbps transmission standard (for example, X2 to X2, K56Flex to K56Flex, V.90 to V.90). However, under current Federal Communications Commission (FCC) rules that place a limit on amplitude (signal strength), 56 kbps modems cannot exceed 53.3 kbps.

Summary

In this chapter, you learned the following key points:

- Several types of analog modems exist. The three main types are internal, external, and PC card modems.

- Modems work at OSI model Layer 1.

- V.22bis is the first true worldwide standard for modems; it allows 2400 bps at 600 baud.

- V.34 is a full-duplex modem standard that allows the modems to send and receive data across phone lines at up to 28.8 kbps.

- V.90 standard allows a downstream data rate of up to 56 kbps.

Review Exercises

1 Which of the following is true of analog modems?

   a. They allow data transfer between two computers over the PSTN.

   b. They convert analog signals to digital bit streams.

   c. They convert digital data to analog signals.

   d. All of the above.

2 Which of the following is the most common type of modem?

   a. Internal

   b. External

   c. PC card

   d. All of the above

3 Which of the following cable standards allows a 56 kbps downstream data-transmission rate?

   a. V.32

   b. V.34

   c. V.42

   d. V.90

4 What was the first true worldwide standard for modems that allowed 2400 bps at 600 baud?

   a. V.12

   b. V.22bis

   c. V.32

   d. V.90

Upon completing this chapter, you will be able to:

- Define DSL

- Identify different types of DSL

- Describe DSL standards

- Describe DSL encapsulation and protocols

- Describe benefits of DSL

CHAPTER 25

Digital Subscriber Line (DSL)

Digital subscriber line (DSL) is a modem technology that uses existing telephone lines to bring high-bandwidth information to home and small businesses. The term *xDSL* refers to different variations of DSL.

xDSL is drawing significant attention from implementers and service providers because it has the potential to deliver high-bandwidth data rates to dispersed locations with relatively small changes to the existing telecommunications company (telco) infrastructure.

This chapter describes the two main types of DSL: asymmetric DSL (ADSL) and symmetric DSL (SDSL). This chapter also introduces DSL standards and DSL encapsulation and protocols. In addition, this chapter discusses the advantages and disadvantages of the DSL technology.

Basic DSL

DSL technology is a modem technology that uses existing twisted-pair telephone lines to transport high-bandwidth data, such as multimedia and video, to service subscribers (see Figure 25-1). Because DSL uses existing phone lines, in most cases there is no need to dig a new trench, as with cable, or install a dish, as with wireless.

Figure 25-1   *DSL*

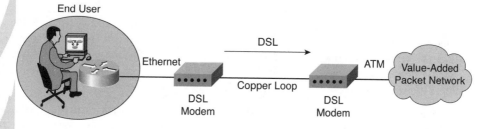

Wherever there is a phone line, there is the potential for getting DSL service. DSL requires central office (CO) access equipment, called DSL access multiplexers (DSLAMs), to connect the DSL line to the network. A *DSLAM* is a network device that receives signals from multiple customer DSL connections and puts the singles on a high-speed backbone line using multiplexing techniques. DSL subscribers must be within a certain distance of the CO, which might limit service availability.

DSL provides a full-time Internet connection. As soon as users turn on their computers, they are connected to the Internet. This setup removes the time and effort of dialing in to establish a connection.

Products such as the Cisco 827 Asymmetric DSL (ADSL) Router integrate a fully functional Cisco IOS Software router and DSL modem into one unit (see Figure 25-2).

Figure 25-2   *Cisco 827 ADSL Router*

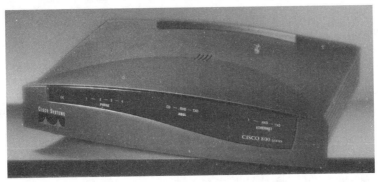

DSL Types

The two basic types of DSL technologies are asymmetric (ADSL) and symmetric (SDSL). All forms of DSL service are categorized as one or the other, and there are numerous varieties of each type. The term *xDSL* sometimes is used to refer generically to any of the various forms of DSL that exist. The DSL transfer speeds often are broken down into *upstream* and *downstream* rates. Asymmetric service provides a higher download or downstream speed (in bits per second, or bps) than upstream speed. Symmetric service provides the same speed in both directions (see Figure 25-3).

Downstream information, such as requested World Wide Web pages, comes from the Internet to the user (from the CO to the subscriber). Upstream information is sent from the user to the Internet (from the subscriber to the CO). Asymmetric types of DSL generally use analog transmission encoding (modulation) technology, whereas symmetric forms generally use digital transmission encoding (modulation) techniques.

ADSL is currently the most commonly used DSL technology. Its fast downstream speed, up to 8 Mbps, appears to work in its favor because most Internet users spend the majority of their time doing tasks that require a lot of downloading, such as checking e-mail and surfing the World Wide Web. The slower upstream rate does not work that well when hosting a web server or FTP server, both of which involve upload-intensive Internet activities.

Figure 25-3   *DSL Service Types Overview*

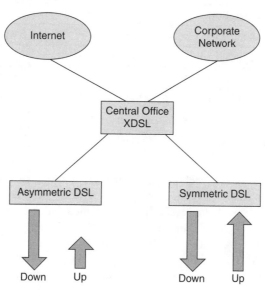

DSL Standards

Standards benefit the consumer and the industry in general. They might take a while to evolve, but they tend to level the playing field, allowing more competition with improved interoperability. Standards also contribute to consumer confidence. Numerous standards organizations and industry consortia have contributed to the evolution of DSL. Among these are the DSL Forum, American National Standards Institute (ANSI), International Telecommunications Union (ITU-T), Digital Audio Video Council (DAVIC), and European Telecommunications Standards Institute (ETSI). Table 25-1 lists industry consortia DSL-focused organizations and their websites. Table 25-2 lists DSL-related standards organizations and their websites.

Table 25-1   *DSL Industry Consortia*

Industry Consortia	URL
DSL Forum	www.dslforum.org
DSL Life	www.dsllife.com
Broadband Reports	www.dslreports.com
Telcordia Technologies, Inc.	www.telcordia.com
Telechoice	www.xdsl.com
International Engineering Consortium (IEC)	www.iec.org

Table 25-2   *DSL Standards Organizations*

Standards Organization	URL
American National Standards Institute (ANSI)	www.ansi.org
Alliance for Telecommunications Industry Standards (ATIS)	www.atis.org
Digital Audio Video Council (DAVIC)	www.davic.org
European Telecommunications Standards Institute (ETSI)	www.etsi.org
Institute for Electrical and Electronics Engineers (IEEE)	www.ieee.org
International Telecommunications Union (ITU-T)	www.itu.int

Table 25-3 lists each DSL technology and the relevant standards organizations and standard numbers associated with those technologies. Not all the DSL technologies listed have a standard associated with them. Also listed is the modulation or encoding standard(s) used by the DSL modems to place digital data bits onto the wire. Several modulation and encoding techniques are used by various kinds of DSL. As mentioned in the "DSL Types" section, earlier in this chapter, ADSL uses analog modem-encoding and transmission technology. Two basic modulation techniques used with ADSL are carrierless amplitude phase (CAP) and discrete multitone (DMT). VDSL also supports single-carrier modulation (SCM). Symmetric versions of DSL use digital techniques to encode data using pulses of electricity representing binary 0s and 1s. An example of digital encoding techniques is 2B1Q (2 binary one quaternary), which is used with IDSL, SDSL, and HDSL. G.SHDSL uses a more advanced encoding technique called trellis-coded pulse amplitude modulation (TC-PAM).

The most important standards listed in Table 25-3 are asymmetric DSL standards G.992.1 (G.DMT) and G.992.2 (G.Lite), as well as symmetric standard G.991.2 (G.SHDSL). All vendors that are currently building DSL support these international standards.

Table 25-3   *DSL Technologies Standards Comparison*

DSL Types	Standards	Modulation/ Encoding Technique	Speed	Distance Limit
Full-rate ADSL /G.DMT	ANSI T1.413 Issue 2	DMT or CAP	Downstream speed of 384 kbps to 8 Mbps; upstream speed slower, up to 1.024 Mbps	18,000 feet
G.Lite	ITU-T G.992.1, ITU-T G.992.2	DMT	Downstream speed up to 1.544 Mbps to 6 Mbps; upstream speed up to 640 kbps	18,000 feet
Very-high-data-rate DSL (VDSL)	ETSI and ANSI in process	DMT/SCM	12.96 Mbps to 52.8 Mbps for both upstream and downstream speed	4500 feet

Table 25-3   *DSL Technologies Standards Comparison (Continued)*

DSL Types	Standards	Modulation/ Encoding Technique	Speed	Distance Limit
ISDN DSL (IDSL)	ANSI ETR 080	2B1Q	144 kbps for both upstream and downstream speed	18,000 feet
SDSL	None	2B1Q	768 kbps for both upstream and downstream speed	22,000 feet
High-data-rate DSL (HDSL)	ITU G.991.1, ANSI TR 28	2B1Q	1.544 or 2.048 Mbps for both upstream and downstream speed	12,000 feet
G.SHDSL	ITU G.991.2	TC PAM	192 kbps to 2.360 Mbps for both upstream and downstream speed	28,000 feet

Encapsulation and Protocols

DSL operates at Layer 1, or the physical layer, of the OSI model. It is basically a bit pump data-transmission technology that relies on higher-layer protocols to encapsulate the data to the CO and the Internet service provider (ISP). Protocols most often include Layer 2 protocols such as Ethernet, ATM, and PPP, as well as the IP Layer 3 protocol. Other higher-layer protocols such as Dynamic Host Configuration Protocol (DHCP) and Domain Name System (DNS), and services such as Remote Access Dial-In User Service (RADIUS) also play a part in the complete DSL picture from subscriber to ISP. The DSL provider and ISP also have a choice of providing bridged or routed service to the subscriber. Figure 25-4 illustrates the relationship of the DSL-related protocols and the OSI reference model.

Figure 25-4   *OSI- and DSL-Related Protocols*

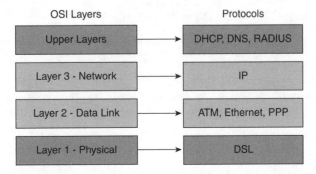

DSL Advantages and Disadvantages

DSL service can be added incrementally in any area. That means that the service provider literally can start up with a handful of clients and upgrade the bandwidth to coincide with the growth in numbers of subscribers. DSL is also backward compatible with analog voice and makes good use of the existing local loop. This means that very little needs to be done to use the cable services simultaneously with normal phone service. In addition, DSL offers the following advantages:

- DSL offers speeds up to and exceeding those of T1, at just a fraction of the cost.

- Both voice and data can be transmitted over the same line at the same time.

- DSL is an always-on technology. This means that users do not need to dial up each time they want to connect to the Internet.

However, DSL suffers from distance limitations. Most DSL service offerings currently require the customer to be within 18,000 feet of the provider's CO location. Additionally, the longer and older loops present problems, and the best form of voice support is still being debated. Also, upstream (upload) speed usually is considerably slower than the downstream (download) speed. Additional drawbacks to DSL include these:

- The availability of DSL presently still is limited, with service for most "flavors" or varieties possible only for areas that fall within a specified number of feeds from the telephone company CO of the service provider.

- The telephone company CO that is servicing the location must have DSL equipment installed.

Summary

This section summarizes the key points you learned in this lesson:

- DSL operates at Layer 1 of the OSI model.

- DSL is a modem technology that uses existing twisted-pair telephone lines to transport data.

- Two basic types of DSL technology exist: asymmetric and symmetric. Asymmetric service provides a higher downstream speed than upstream speed. Symmetric service provides the same speed in both directions.

- G.992.1 and G.992.2 are asymmetric DSL standards, and G.991.2 is a symmetric standard.

- DSL service can be added incrementally as more users subscribe. However, DSL service has distance limitations.

Review Exercises

1 Which of the following media is used by DSL to transport data?

    a. Existing coaxial cable TV lines

    b. Existing twisted-pair telephone lines

    c. Existing Ethernet lines

    d. Wireless transmission

2 What are the two basic types of DSL technology?

    a. Downstream DSL and upstream DSL

    b. xDSL and yDSL

    c. Asymmetric DSL and symmetric DSL

    d. None of the above

3 Which of the following standards organizations and industries have contributed to the evolution of DSL?

    a. ANSI

    b. ITU-T

    c. ETSI

    d. All of the above

4 Which of the following Layer 2 protocols is used often by DSL?

    a. HDLC

    b. IPX

    c. PPP

    d. LLC

5 Which of the following is *not* one of the benefits of DSL?

    a. DSL service can be added incrementally in any area.

    b. DSL is backward compatible with conventional analog voice.

    c. DSL service has no distance limitations.

    d. DSL is an always-on technology.

Upon completing this chapter, you will be able to:

- Describe cable modem types
- Describe how a cable modem works
- Describe benefits of cable modems

CHAPTER 26

Cable Modems

Cable modems enable two-way, high-speed data transmissions using the same coaxial lines that transmit cable television. Some cable service providers are promising data speeds up to 6.5 times those of T1 leased lines. This speed makes cable an attractive medium for transferring large amounts of digital information quickly, including video clips, audio files, and large chunks of data. Information that would take two minutes to download using ISDN BRI can be downloaded in two seconds through a cable-modem connection.

Cable modem access provides speeds superior to leased lines, with lower costs and simpler installation. When the cable infrastructure is in place, a company or household can connect through installation of a modem or router. Additionally, because cable modems do not use the telephone system infrastructure, there are no local-loop charges. Products such as the Cisco uBR 904 Universal Broadband Router Cable Modem make cable access an even more attractive investment by integrating a fully functional Cisco IOS Software router, four-port hub, and cable modem into one unit (see Figure 26-1). This combination enables businesses to replace combinations of routers, bridges, hubs, and single-port cable modems with one product. Cisco's new cable access models, such as Cisco uBR 925 Cable Access Router, also support voice and fax calls over a cable IP network.

Figure 26-1   *Cisco uBR 900 Universal Broadband Router Cable Modem*

Cable modems provide a full-time Internet connection. As soon as users turn on their computers, they are connected to the Internet. As with DSL, this always-on setup removes the time and effort of dialing in to establish a connection.

The cable connection also means that a company's "information pipe" is open at all times. This setup increases the vulnerability of data to hackers and is a good reason to install firewalls and configure cable routers to maximize security. Fortunately, the industry is moving toward the standardization of cable modems, and the move is likely to address encryption needs. For instance, the Cisco uBR 905 and uBR 925 Cable Access Routers provide IP Security (IPSec) and firewall capabilities. These features protect company LANs and provide virtual private network (VPN) tunneling with options for authentication and encryption.

How Cable Modems Work

Like analog modems, cable modems modulate and demodulate data signals. However, cable modems incorporate more functionality designed for today's high-speed Internet services. In a cable network, data flowing from the network to the user is referred to as *downstream*, and data flowing from the user to the network is referred to as *upstream*. From a user perspective, a cable modem is a quadrature amplitude modulation (QAM) radio frequency (RF) receiver capable of delivering up to 30 to 40 Mbps of data in one 6-MHz cable channel. This is almost 500 times faster than a 56-kbps modem. A headend is the facility at a local cable TV office. The headend manages traffic flow from the user to the network. Head ends have facilities to do the following:

- Receive programming (for example, from NBC, CBS, and cable networks such as CNN and ESPN)

- Convert each channel to the channel frequency desired, scrambling channels as needed

- Combine all the frequencies onto a single, broadband analog channel (frequency-division multiplexing [FDM])

- Broadcast the combined analog stream downstream to subscribers

Figure 26-2 illustrates a cable system layout.

NOTE   *Quadrature amplitude modulation (QAM)* is a method for encoding digital data in an analog signal in which each combination of phase and amplitude represents one of sixteen 4-bit patterns.

With a cable modem, a subscriber can continue to receive cable television service while simultaneously receiving data to be delivered to a personal computer. This is accomplished with the help of a simple one-to-two splitter (see Figure 26-3).

Figure 26-2   *An Example of a Cable System Layout*

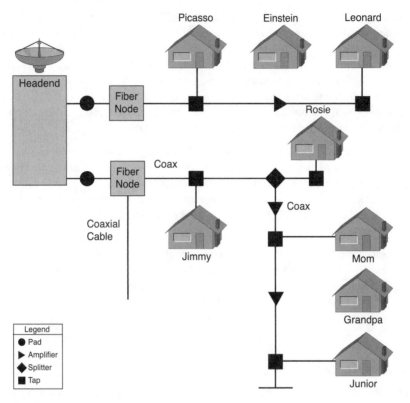

Figure 26-3   *One-to-Two Splitter*

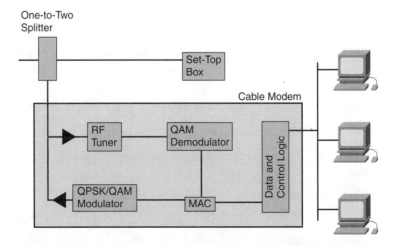

Cable Modem Advantages and Disadvantages

The advantage of using cable modem high-speed access is that coaxial cable wiring offers greater bandwidth using broadband for more applications to the home network LAN. In fact, the downstream and upstream Internet channels are seen as just another premium TV channel by the system. This is a major advantage, especially when hosting a web server or an FTP server, which involves upload-intensive Internet tasks. Additionally, cable lines are already in place in most urban and suburban areas of the United States because of the wide deployment of cable television throughout the last few decades. Therefore, cable modem high-speed Internet access is more readily available in more areas than DSL.

Finally, some cable operators are in the process of replacing traditional one-way cable systems with the more interactive two-way architecture known as hybrid fiber coaxial (HFC). An advantage of using HFC is that some of the characteristics of fiber-optic cable, such as high bandwidth and low noise, can be brought close to the user without having to replace the existing coaxial cable that is installed all the way to the business and home.

Despite its advantages and popularity, cable modems do have a few disadvantages. Cable modems almost always require an overhaul of the existing cable infrastructure, which is an expensive undertaking for small providers. In addition, because cable modems exist in a shared-medium structure, the more users that come on the network, the less available bandwidth there is for users. Finally, the always-on shared media cable connection increases the vulnerability of data to hackers. It has the disadvantage of security risk.

Cable and the OSI Model

The cable data system comprises many different technologies and standards. For cable modems to be mainstreamed, modems from different vendors must be interoperable. The following sections describe the Multimedia Cable Network System Partners (MCNS) cable system interface specifications at different layers of the OSI reference model.

Physical Layer

At the physical layer, the downstream data channel is based on North American digital video specifications (specifically, ITU-T Recommendation J.83 Annex B) and includes the following features:

- 64 and 256 quadrature amplitude modulation (QAM)

- 6-MHz occupied spectrum that coexists with other signals in the cable plant

- Variable-length interleaving support; both latency-sensitive and latency-insensitive data services

- Contiguous serial bit stream with no implied framing, providing complete physical and Media Access Control (MAC)–layer decoupling

At the physical layer, the upstream data channel is a shared channel featuring the following:

- Quaternary phase-shift keying (QPSK) and 16 QAM formats

- Data rates from 320 kbps to 10 Mbps

- Flexible and programmable cable modem under control of cable modem terminal server (CMTS)

- Time-division multiple access

- Support of both fixed-frame and variable-length protocol data units (PDUs)

NOTE   *Quaternary phase-shift keying (QPSK)* is a digital frequency-modulation technique used for sending data over coaxial cable networks.

Data Link Layer

The data link layer provides the general requirements for many cable modem subscribers to share a single upstream data channel for transmission to the network. Among these requirements are collision detection and retransmission capability. The large geographic reach of a cable data network poses special problems. These problems result from the transmission delay between users close to the headend and users at a distance from the cable headend. To compensate for cable losses and delay as a result of distance, the MAC layer performs *ranging*, by which each cable modem can assess time delay in transmitting to the headend. The MAC layer supports these features:

- Timing and synchronization

- Bandwidth allocation to cable modems at the control of CMTS

- Error detection, handling, and error recovery

- Procedures for registering new cable modems

Network Layer

Cable data networks use IP for communication from the cable modem to the network. The Internet Engineering Task Force (IETF)–compliant Dynamic Host Configuration Protocol (DHCP) typically forms the basis for IP address assignment and administration in the cable network.

Transport Layer

Cable data networks support both the Transmission Control Protocol (TCP) and the User Datagram Protocol (UDP) at the transport layer.

Application Layer

All the Internet-related applications are supported at the application layer. These applications include the Hypertext Transfer Protocol (HTTP), the File Transport Protocol (FTP), e-mail, the Trivial File Transfer Protocol (TFTP), news, chat, and the Simple Network Management Protocol (SNMP). SNMP provides for management of the CMTS and cable data networks.

Figure 26-4 illustrates the MCNS data over cable specifications at different OSI reference model layers.

Figure 26-4   *Cable and the OSI Model*

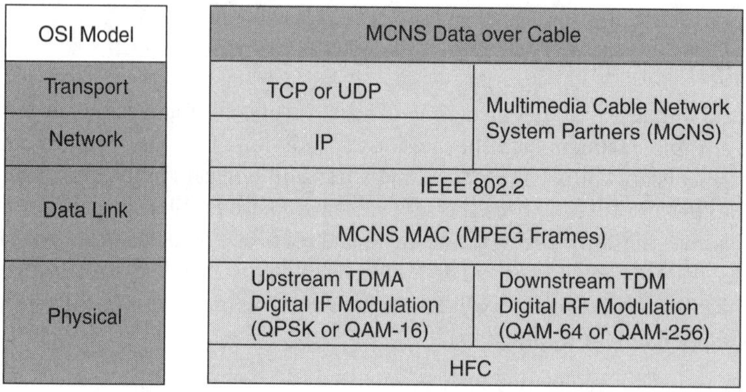

OSI Model	MCNS Data over Cable	
Transport	TCP or UDP	Multimedia Cable Network System Partners (MCNS)
Network	IP	
Data Link	IEEE 802.2	
	MCNS MAC (MPEG Frames)	
Physical	Upstream TDMA Digital IF Modulation (QPSK or QAM-16)	Downstream TDM Digital RF Modulation (QAM-64 or QAM-256)
	HFC	

Summary

In this chapter, you learned the following key points:

- Cable modems put data signals on the same cable as television signals. Cable modem access provides speed superior to leased lines, and cable modems provide a full-time connection.

- The advantage of using cable modem access is that coaxial cable is already in place in most of the country.

- The disadvantage of using cable modems is that the cable modem shares the medium with cable TV. Thus, the more users that come on the network, the less bandwidth is available for users.

- The cable data system comprises many different technologies and standards. For cable modems to be mainstreamed, modems from different vendors must be interoperable. MCNS have developed several data over cable specifications.

Review Exercises

1 Which of the following media are used by cable modem to transport data?

   a. Existing coaxial cable TV lines

   b. Existing twisted-pair telephone lines

   c. Existing Ethernet lines

   d. None of the above

2 Which of the following best describes upstream?

   a. Data flowing from the user to the network

   b. Data flowing from the network to the user

   c. Data flowing between networks

   d. Data flowing between routers

3 Which of the following is an advantage of cable modem?

   a. The cabling infrastructure can be upgraded.

   b. Because cable modems exist in a shared-medium structure, the more users come on the network, the less bandwidth is available for each user.

   c. Coaxial cable wiring offers greater bandwidth using broadband for more applications to the home network.

   d. None of the above.

4 Which of the following applications does the cable network support?

   a. HTTP

   b. FTP

   c. SNMP

   d. All of the above

Wireless Technology

Upon completing this chapter, you will be able to:

- Describe different types of wireless data communications and their advantages and drawbacks

- Describe different modulation techniques

- Describe radio frequency modulation

- Describe the benefits of spread-spectrum technology

- Describe frequency-hopping spread spectrum and direct-sequence spread spectrum

- Explain the importance of encryption on security in a wireless environment

CHAPTER **27**

Wireless Concepts

Wireless signals are electromagnetic waves that can travel through the vacuum of outer space or through a medium such as air. No physical copper-based or fiber-optic medium is necessary for wireless signals. This makes utilizing wireless signals a very versatile way to build a network. Wireless transmissions can cover large distances by using high-frequency signals. Each signal uses a difference frequency, measured in hertz, so that they remain unique from one another.

Wireless technologies have been around for many years. Satellite TV, AM/FM radio, cellular phones, remote-control devices, radar, alarm systems, weather radios, cordless phones, and retail scanners are integrated into everyday life. Today, wireless technologies are a fundamental part of business and personal life.

This chapter examines wireless technologies, including radio frequency (RF) modulation, unlicensed frequencies, and spread spectrum. This chapter also describes the differences between frequency-hopping spread spectrum (FHSS) and direct-sequence spread spectrum (DSSS) technologies. In addition, this chapter discusses wireless encryption.

Wireless Data Communications

The radio spectrum is the part of the electromagnetic spectrum used to transmit voice, video, and data. It uses frequencies from 3 kilohertz (kHz) to 300 gigahertz (GHz). This section considers only the part of the radio spectrum that supports wireless data transmission.

Many different types of wireless data communications exist (see Figure 27-1). Each has its advantages and drawbacks, as follows:

- **Infrared (IR)**—Very high data rates and lower cost, but very short distance.

- **Narrowband**—Low data rates and medium cost. Requires a license and covers a limited distance.

- **Spread spectrum**—Medium cost and high data rates. Limited to campus coverage. Cisco Aironet products are spread spectrum.

- **Broadband personal communications service (PCS)**—Low data rates, medium cost, and city-wide coverage. Sprint is an exception; Sprint PCS provides nationwide and international coverage.

- **Circuit and packet data (cellular and cellular digital packet data [CDPD])**—Low data rates, high packet fees, and national coverage.

- **Satellite**—Low data rates, high cost, and nationwide or worldwide coverage.

Figure 27-1 *Wireless Data Networks*

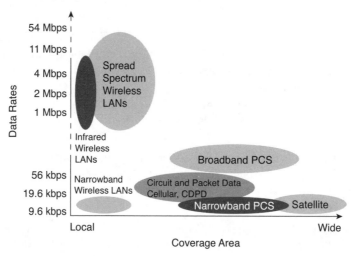

Wireless Signal

When a signal is transmitted in a data format, you must consider the following three parameters:

- **How fast**—What data rate can be achieved?

- **How far**—How far can wireless LAN (WLAN) units be placed apart and still get the maximum data rate?

- **How many**—How many users can exist without slowing the data rate?

These parameters all relate to the ability to receive a good signal as far away as possible. Increasing the amount of data requires the use of more frequency spectra or a different method of placing the data on the radio frequency (RF) signal.

RF efficiency is affected by the following three factors (see Figure 27-2):

- **Type of modulation used**—More complex modulation techniques provide greater throughput. (For more details, see the next section in this chapter, "Modulation.")

- **Distance**—The farther the signal must be transmitted, the weaker the signal becomes. (For more details, see the section "Effects of Distance on a Signal," later in this chapter.)

- **Noise**—Electronic noise and barriers negatively affect RF. (For more details, see the section "Effects of Noise on a Signal," later in this chapter.)

Figure 27-2   *Factors Affecting Radio Frequency Efficiency*

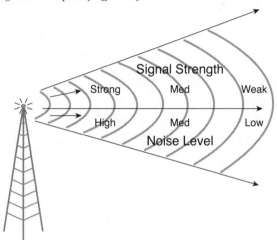

Modulation

Modulation is the process by which the amplitude, frequency, or phase of an RF or light wave is changed to transmit data. The characteristics of the carrier wave instantaneously are varied by another "modulating" waveform. Modulation blends a data signal (text, voice, and so on) into a carrier for transmission over a network.

More complex modulation techniques provide greater throughput. The most common methods follow (see Figure 27-3):

- **Amplitude modulation (AM)**—Modulates the height of the carrier wave

- **Frequency modulation (FM)**—Modulates the frequency of the wave

- **Phase modulation (PM)**—Modulates the polarity of the wave

Effects of Distance on a Signal

As a receiver moves farther from a transmitter, the signal gets weaker, and the difference between the signal and noise becomes less. Eventually, the signal cannot be distinguished from the noise, and loss of communication occurs. The amount of compression (or modulation scheme) at which the signal is transmitted determines the amount of signal needed to be heard through the noise. As transmission, or modulation schemes (compression), becomes more complex and data rates increase, immunity to noise lessens. Therefore, the distance is reduced.

Figure 27-3 *Modulation*

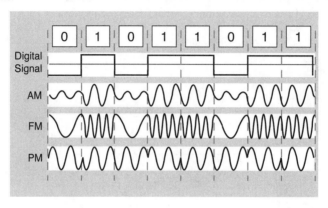

Effects of Noise on a Signal

Electronic noise and barriers negatively affect RF efficiency. An exact transmission distance for WLAN products cannot be provided without going to the site and actually testing the environment. Walls with internal metal structures, for example, greatly limit RF transmission range.

NOTE   To be received correctly, complex modulation schemes require optimal signal-to-noise ratios (more signal with less noise). If there is noise on the channel, the line speed will be reduced. Noise, speed, and distance are all interrelated.

Radio Frequency Bands

Most radio frequencies are licensed by government agencies, such as the Federal Communications Commission (FCC) in the United States. To broadcast over these frequencies, it is necessary to have a license and to pay a fee.

Unlicensed frequency bands are easier to implement and cost less over time because they do not require licenses. There are three unlicensed bands (see Figure 27-4):

- **900 megahertz (MHz)**—The 900 MHz band carries cellular phones.

- **2.4 gigahertz (GHz)**—The 802.11b standard, the most widely deployed wireless standard, operates in the 2.4 GHz unlicensed radio band, delivering a maximum data rate of 11 Mbps.

- **5 GHz**—Recently, the FCC opened up the 5 GHz band for unlicensed use by high-speed data communications devices. Cisco has acquired 5 GHz technology and uses this frequency in new products, such as Cisco Aironet 1200 series, which is dual band, delivering support for both 2.4 and 5 GHz standards.

Figure 27-4   *Unlicensed Frequency Bands*

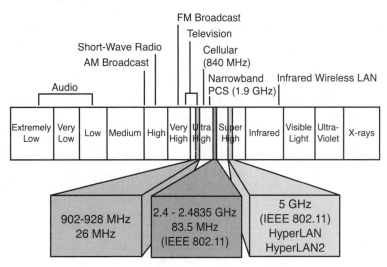

A relationship exists between the frequency and the amount of data that can be sent. The concept is like that of a pipe. The wider the bandwidth is, the more frequencies are available. The wider the spectrum is, the higher the data rate can be transmitted. The amount of spectrum available determines the data rate.

Because the 900 MHz band supports cellular phones and other consumer products, the band has become overcrowded. As a result, users often experience interference or cannot access the network. As a benefit, 900 MHz offers longer range (for the same gain antennas) than 2.4 GHz. The drawback of 900 MHz is that the fastest, most reliable data rate is only 1 megabit per second (Mbps) because of its limited frequency range.

The 2.4 GHz frequency range is much wider than 900 MHz, allowing higher data rates with a reliable range of up to 25 miles. Cisco Aironet 340 Wireless LAN Series can deliver 11 Mbps throughput because it operates in the 2.4 GHz frequency.

Cisco has acquired 5 GHz technology and delivers products for the 5 GHz frequency range because its wider bandwidth allows for faster throughput of data. It will be possible to achieve data rates of greater than 20 Mbps in this frequency range. The drawback of the 5 GHz frequency, however, is its limited range. The typical range for 5 GHz inside is about 50 feet; outside poses a limitation of approximately 2500 feet.

Spread-Spectrum Technology

Just as the radio in your car has AM and FM bands, other radios use certain bands, frequencies, and types of modulation. Spread spectrum (SS) is a modulation technique developed in the 1940s that spreads a transmission signal over a broad band of radio frequencies. The term *spread spectrum* describes a modulation technique that sacrifices bandwidth to gain signal-to-noise performance. This technique is ideal for data communications because it is less susceptible to radio noise and creates little interference.

Spread spectrum is a system in which the transmitted signal is spread over a frequency much wider than the minimum bandwidth required to send the signal (see Figure 27-5). The fundamental premise is that, in channels with narrowband interference, increasing the transmitted signal bandwidth results in an increased probability that the received information will be correct.

Figure 27-5   *Spread-Spectrum Technology*

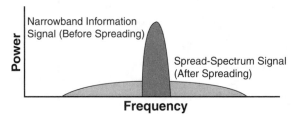

NOTE   Narrowband interference occurs when two signals are broadcasting at the same frequency in the same geographic area. The term *band* refers to a grouping of frequencies; narrowband would mean a relatively smaller range of frequencies. Narrowband noise might disrupt certain channels or spread-spectrum components.

To use the unlicensed radio bands, you have to use spread-spectrum techniques. Frequency-hopping spread spectrum (FHSS) and direct-sequence spread spectrum (DSSS) are two ways of doing spread spectrum. These spread-spectrum techniques spread the RF energy over the available band. The next subsection describes FHSS and DSSS in more detail.

FHSS vs. DSSS

As modulation techniques, both frequency-hopping spread spectrum (FHSS) and direct-sequence spread spectrum (DSSS) have advantages and limitations.

With FHSS technology, transmissions hop from one frequency to another in random patterns. Figure 27-6 illustrates an example of a FHSS. In this example, the transmission hops from C (2.42 GHz), to A (2.40 GHz), to D (2.43 GHz), then to B (2.41 GHz), and finally to E (2.44 GHz). This enables the transmissions to hop around narrowband interference, resulting in a clearer signal and higher reliability of the transmission. However, FHSS technology is slower, and the receiver must use the same pattern to decode (see Figure 27-6).

Figure 27-6   *Frequency-Hopping Spread Spectrum (FHSS)*

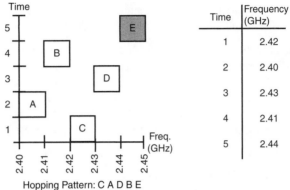

Hopping Pattern: C A D B E

Time	Frequency (GHz)
1	2.42
2	2.40
3	2.43
4	2.41
5	2.44

DSSS technology transmissions are more reliable because each bit (1 or 0) is represented by a string of 1s and 0s, called a *chipping sequence*. Even if up to 40 percent of the string is lost, the original transmission can be reconstructed. DSSS technology also enables high throughput of data and longer-range access (see Figure 27-7).

Figure 27-7   *Direct-Sequence Spread Spectrum*

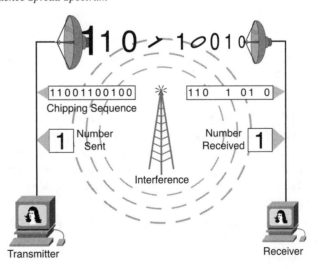

Limited to a 2-Mbps data-transfer rate, FHSS is recommended for only very specific applications such as for certain types of watercraft. For all other wireless LAN applications, DSSS is the better choice. The recently released evolution of the IEEE standard, 802.11b, provides for a full Ethernet-like data rate of 11 Mbps over DSSS. FHSS does not support data rates greater than 2 Mbps.

Security in the Wireless Environment

The exponential growth of networking, including wireless technologies, has led to increased security risks. Increasing the security means increasing the time spent managing the system.

The first level of security in a wireless LAN consists of protecting the radio frequency waveform itself. Wireless access points radiate radio waves over a large area that is not contained in a physical building, which makes the radio waves accessible to eavesdroppers and thus increases vulnerability. The radio waves of wireless bridges are concentrated in a beam. An eavesdropper must get into the beam path to intercept the communication. Therefore, wireless access points usually require better security than wireless bridges.

If you think someone might eavesdrop on your LAN radio links, encryption is the key.

The following sections discuss two wireless security approaches: wired equivalent privacy (WEP), and IEEE 802.1X and the Extensible Authentication Protocol (EAP).

WEP

WEP is the first step in addressing customer security concerns. WEP is a security mechanism, defined within the 802.11 standard, that is designed to protect the over-the-air transmission between wireless LAN access points and network interface cards (NICs). The IEEE 802.11b requires 40-bit encryption keys. However, many vendors, such as Cisco, support the optional 128-bit standard.

The main goals with WEP follow:

- Deny access to the network by unauthorized users who do not possess the appropriate WEP key
- Prevent the decoding of captured WLAN traffic that is WEP-encrypted without the possession of the WEP key

WEP uses the RC4 stream cipher that was invented by Ron Rivest of RSA Data Security, Inc., (RSADSI) for encryption. The RC4 encryption algorithm is a symmetric-stream cipher that supports a variable-length key. A symmetric cipher uses the same key for both encryption and decryption. The key is the one piece of information that must be shared by both the encrypting and decrypting endpoints.

Recently, encryption analysts have reported weaknesses in the authentication and WEP encryption schemes in the IEEE 802.11 WLAN standard. Improvements on WEP have been developed to address the weaknesses found by encryption analysts. However, it is not recommended to use WEP as a sole security mechanism for a WLAN. WEP should be supplemented with additional higher-level security mechanisms such as VPN or firewalls.

802.1X/EAP

IEEE 802.1X/Extensible Authentication Protocol (EAP) is an alternative WLAN security approach to WEP as specified by IEEE 802.11. IEEE 802.1X/EAP focuses on developing a framework for providing centralized authentication and dynamic key distribution. IEEE 802.1X is a standard for port-based network access control. EAP allows wireless client adapters that can support different authentication types to communicate with different back-end servers, such as Remote Authentication Dial-In User Service (RADIUS).

Cisco has developed a derivation of EAP based on mutual authentication, called *lightweight EAP (LEAP)*. Mutual authentication means that both the user and the access point to which the user is attempting to connect must be authenticated before access onto the corporate network is allowed. Mutual authentication protects enterprises from unauthorized access points serving as a potential entrance into the network.

The Cisco LEAP authentication provides the following benefits:

- Centralized authentication and key distributaries

- Large-scale enterprise WLAN deployment because of its broad operating system support and dynamic key derivation

Summary

In this chapter, you learned the following key points:

- In wireless data communication, the radio spectrum is the part of the electromagnetic spectrum used to transmit voice, video, and data.

- Modulation is the process by which the amplitude, frequency, or phase of a radio frequency or lightwave is changed to transmit data.

- To take advantage of unlicensed radio bands, you have to use spread-spectrum techniques. Two important modulation technologies are frequency-hopping spread spectrum (FSSS) and direct-sequence spread spectrum (DHSS). DHSS offers greater reliability and more throughput than FHSS.

- The wireless signal deteriorates with distance. A wireless device will connect at a slower speed if it is moved out of optimal range.

- Noise can be caused through structures (walls with metal) or by electrical equipment. Both adversely affect the range of wireless communications.

- The first level of security in a wireless LAN consists of protecting the radio frequency waveform itself.

- IEEE 802.1X/EAP is an alternative WLAN security approach that focuses on developing a framework for providing centralized authentication and dynamic key distribution.

Review Exercises

1 Which technology is *not* a type of wireless communication?

    a. Cellular

    b. Wideband

    c. Infrared

    d. Spread spectrum

2 Modulation is a process of changing amplitude, frequency, or phase. Which acronym does *not* represent a type of modulation?

    a. AM

    b. FM

    c. PM

    d. RM

3 Which statement does *not* correctly identify an unlicensed wireless frequency?

    a. 2.4 GHz

    b. 5 GHz

    c. 9 GHz

    d. 900 MHz

4 Which statement does *not* describe a benefit of spread spectrum?

    a. Spread-spectrum transmissions are transmitted at high speeds.

    b. Spread spectrum is less susceptible to radio noise.

    c. Spread spectrum has a higher probability of correct reception.

    d. Spread spectrum creates little interference.

5 Which statement does *not* describe the features of direct-sequence spread spectrum (DSSS)?

    a. DSSS is reliable because each bit is represented by a string of 1s and 0s.

    b. If up to 40 percent of the string is lost, the original transmission can be reconstructed.

    c. DSSS technology has low throughput of data and short-range access.

    d. The recently released evolution of the IEEE standard, 802.11b, provides for a full Ethernet-like data rate of 11 Mbps over DSSS.

6 Which of the following is *not* a feature of wired equivalent privacy (WEP)?

    a. WEP uses the RC4 stream cipher for encryption.

    b. WEP is a security mechanism defined within in the 802.3 standards.

    c. One of the goals of WEP is to deny access to the network by unauthorized users who do not possess the appropriate WEP key.

    d. None of the above.

Upon completing this chapter, you will be able to:

- Describe WLAN technology and wireless bridging
- Describe the process of implementing in-building WLANs
- Describe the features of WLAN in-building technology
- Describe the benefits of building-to-building WLANs

CHAPTER 28

Wireless LANs

A wireless LAN (WLAN) provides all the features and benefits of traditional LAN technologies, such as Ethernet, without the limitations of wire or cables. WLAN redefines the way we view LANs. Connectivity no longer implies attachment. Local areas are measured not in feet or meters, but in miles or kilometers. An infrastructure does not need to be buried in the ground or hidden behind the walls.

WLANs use a transmission medium, just like wired LANs. Instead of using twisted-pair or fiber-optic cable, WLANs use infrared (IR) light or radio frequency (RF). The freedom and flexibility of wireless networking can be applied both within buildings and between buildings.

This chapter explains WLAN technology and wireless bridging. This chapter also defines in-building and building-to-building wireless LANs.

WLANs and Wireless Bridging

WLANs are designed to be used in a local, not wide-area, network. They are intended for use in campus-wide or in-building systems. A typical WLAN can include PCs, laptop computers, pen-based computers, printers, and any other device that is normally found on a typical wired network. Cisco WLAN products fit into two main categories: WLANs and wireless bridges.

Figure 28-1 illustrates a wireless LAN-to-LAN connectivity.

Figure 28-1   *Wireless LAN-to-LAN Connectivity*

WLANs provide the following features:

- Replace the Layer 1 transmission medium of a traditional wired network (usually Category 5 cable) with radio transmission over the air.

- Plug into a wired network and function as an overlay to traditional or wired LANs, or deploy as a standalone LAN where wired networking is not feasible.

- Permit the use of portable computers or specialty devices in a system in which connection to the network is essential. Such systems are typically within a building, for distances up to 1000 feet.

- Provide instant access or updates from anywhere in the facility.

- Allow users to roam without losing network connection.

Wireless bridges allow two or more networks that are physically separated to be connected as though they are one total network. With a wireless bridge, networks located in buildings miles from each other can be integrated into a single local-area network.

A wireless bridge provides the following features:

- Transmission speed up to 11 Mbps.

- Connectivity between buildings up to 25 miles apart (line of sight). Wireless links can be either point-to-point or point-to-multipoint.

NOTE   Line of sight is characteristic of transmission systems, such as laser, microwave, and infrared systems, in which no obstructions in a direct path between transmitter and receiver can exist.

- Cost effective. Designed with DSSS, wireless bridges can give data throughputs faster than E1/T1 lines, without the need for expensive leased lines or difficult-to-install fiber optic cable.

- Rapid deployment. Communications result after installation of the wireless bridges at the building sites.

In-Building WLANs

In-building WLANs enable employees to stay connected to the organization's network all the time. They no longer have to be "plugged into" a wired network to gain access to the critical, real-time information systems that are necessary in modern organizations (see Figure 28-2). This feature is especially useful to mobile employees and workers who want to access real-time information while they are in conference rooms, reception areas, temporary offices, and so forth.

Figure 28-2   *In-Building WLANs*

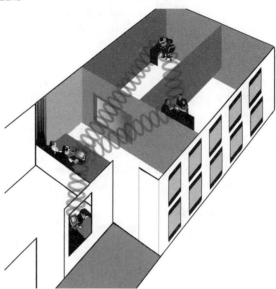

Like any distributed network, in-building wireless LANs start at the Ethernet backbone. The backbone is connected to the servers and routers that drive the customer's intranet, applications, and access to the Internet (see Figure 28-3). Access points attach directly into a company's Ethernet backbone via a 10/100 connection. The connection is wired. Cisco's access points can be powered from 10/100 switched using line power.

Figure 28-3   *In-Building WLAN Architecture*

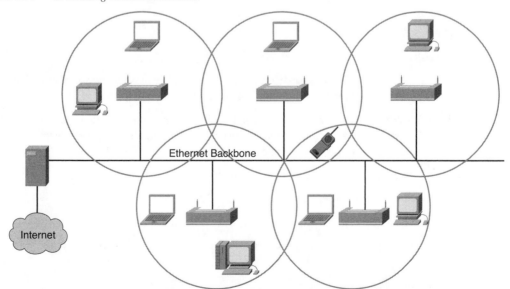

When on the network, access points function like hubs, with shared network access. Multiple access points exist, depending on the area that requires coverage. In-building wireless LANs consist of access points and client adapters, usually PC cards, working together to communicate data over radio frequencies.

NOTE   Client adapters connect wireless clients, such as PCs or laptops, to a LAN via radio communications with access points

Wired LANs require users to have a dedicated physical connection to the network. WLANs are an extension to the wired LAN network (see Figure 28-4).

Figure 28-4   *WLANs Extend the Wired LAN Network*

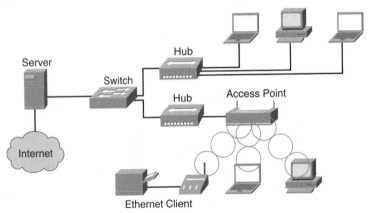

WLANs can be implemented as the following:

- An overlay to a wired network to create a more complete networking solution so that users can roam the building and still stay connected to the network.

- A freestanding network in buildings or situations where pulling cable is not feasible, such as in historic buildings and temporary structures. Freestanding networks usually can be installed in one working day, enabling companies to build fast, flexible LAN solutions.

With WLANs, portable PC users can enjoy the following benefits:

- Freedom to move around a facility

- Real-time access to the wired LAN, at wired Ethernet speeds

- Access to all the resources of wired LANs.

In-Building WLAN Technology

Wireless LAN in-building technology uses overlapping cells to connect mobile users to the network. At the center of the cell is the access point that receives the transmissions from the PC cards. The access point is connected by wire into the LAN backbone. The access point controls the transmissions in the cell and traffic flow into the network (see Figure 28-5). Remote devices do not communicate directly with each other. A remote device communicates to the access point, which, in turn, transmits back out to other remote devices.

Figure 28-5   *Typical Single-Cell Configuration*

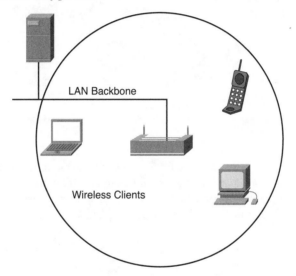

The WLAN consists of microcells that are also called the *basic service area (BSA)*. To extend the basic service area, you simply add additional access points. You can add as many cells as you want to extend the range.

A multicell configuration is called an *extended service area* (see Figure 28-6). Assembling many cells into multiple extended service areas creates large in-building wireless implementations. Throughput varies, depending on the proximity of the remote device to the access point. In general, the closer you are to the access point, the faster the throughput is.

Figure 28-6   *Typical Multicell Configuration*

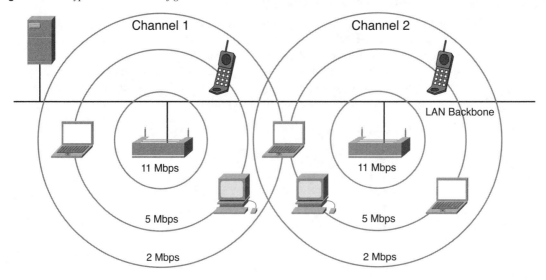

With microcells, the user can move freely anywhere the radio frequency coverage permits (see Figure 28-7). *Microcellular architecture* refers to the ability to seamlessly roam among multiple access points in a campus WLAN. This gives users constant access to their company's intranet so that they can run business-critical applications without interruption.

Figure 28-7   *Roaming*

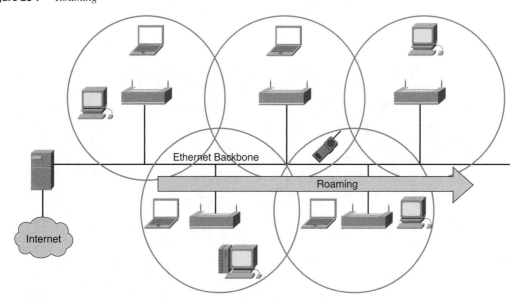

NOTE   Cells have to overlap by 10 to 15 percent so that remote devices can roam without losing their connection to the radio frequency band. This approach provides maximum coverage with minimum cost.

Building-to-Building WLANs

Building-to-building wireless LANs consist of wireless bridges and antennas that communicate data between buildings over radio frequencies. Building-to-building WLANs enable organizations to quickly and cost-effectively set up networked campuses. Wireless campuses are useful to companies that are rapidly expanding and need to keep their organizations connected as they evolve. Building-to-building WLANs also benefit operations that are spread across multiple buildings.

Site-to-site wireless networks tie the LANs from one building to another building via bridging (see Figure 28-8). This setup can give a corporation high-speed connectivity between two locations that otherwise might have been impossible. Bridging eliminates the need for a T1 line, meaning no installation fee and no recurring monthly fees.

Figure 28-8   *Building-to-Building WLANs*

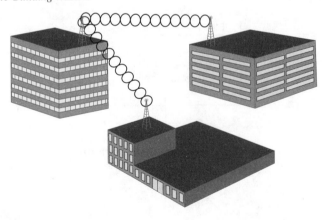

Wireless bridges connect into the Ethernet in their respective buildings. The bridges use a variety of antennas to transmit a focused beam between buildings. The antennas require a direct line of sight, so the radio beams are focused.

NOTE   Wireless bridges are an alternative to a wired infrastructure. They can be up and running with a fraction of the time and monetary investment required for a wired alternative.

When Cisco wireless bridges are correctly installed and aligned, they provide reliable, high-speed connections, regardless of weather. Cisco Aironet bridges can be installed in both point-to-point and point-to-multipoint configurations (see Figures 28-9 and 28-10). Cisco Aironet bridges offer excellent connections between buildings. Like any radio connection, the throughput declines as the distance between the buildings increases.

Figure 28-9   *Point-to-Point Configuration*

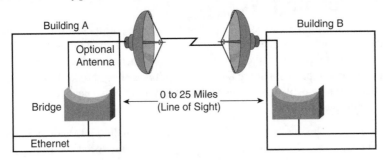

Figure 28-10   *Point-to-Multipoint Configuration*

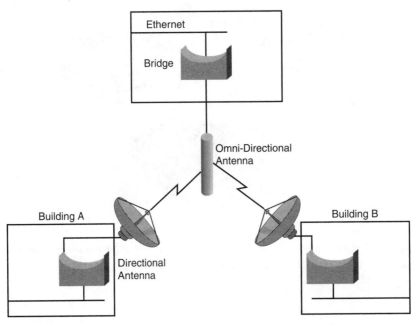

Summary

In this chapter, you learned the following key points:

- Cisco currently offers two types of wireless LAN (WLAN) implementations: WLAN and wireless bridging.

- In-building WLANs use access points that serve as wireless hubs to which mobile stations attach using radio frequency.

- As users move from the microcell of one access point, they automatically are picked up by another access point.

- The distance limitations of an in-building wireless LAN vary, depending on the type of construction, the number and type of barriers, and the amount of electrical noise in the facility.

- Wireless bridges beam signals from one LAN to another, whether they are located in different buildings or on different floors of the same building.

- Building-to-building WLANs consist of wireless bridges and antennas that communicate data between buildings over radio frequencies. Building-to-building WLANs enable organizations to quickly and cost-effectively set up networked campuses.

Review Exercises

1 Which statement does *not* define WLANs?

  a. WLANs are typically within a building, for distances up to 100 feet.

  b. WLANs replace the Layer 1 transmission medium of a traditional wired network (usually Category 5 cable) with radio transmission over the air.

  c. WLANs can plug into a wired network and function as an overlay to traditional or wired LANs, or they can be deployed as a standalone LAN when wired networking is not feasible.

  d. WLANs permit the use of portable computers or specialty devices in a system in which connection to the network is essential.

2 Which of the statements is an *incorrect* description of the in-building WLAN implementation?

  a. Access points attach directly into a company's Ethernet backbone via a 10/100 connection. It is a wireless connection.

  b. The backbone is connected to the servers and routers that drive the customer's intranet, applications, and access to the Internet.

  c. In-building wireless LANs start at the Ethernet backbone.

  d. The access point functions like a hub, with shared network access.

3 In-building cell configurations require what percentage of cell overlap?

    a. 15 to 20 percent

    b. 20 to 25 percent

    c. 10 to 15 percent

    d. None

4 Which statement does *not* describe a benefit of building-to-building WLANs?

    a. WLANs can be set up quickly and efficiently.

    b. WLANs allow users to log on without passwords or cabled connections.

    c. WLANs are cost effective.

    d. WLANs enable operations to be shared across buildings within a corporate campus.

Optical Networking Fundamentals

Upon completing this chapter, you will be able to:

- Identify the key business drivers of optical networks
- Describe the features of fiber-optic systems
- Describe the communication components in an optical communication system
- Identify the wavelength of the light used in optical transmission
- Identify the features of the light-emitting devices used in optical transmission
- Describe important design characteristics of fiber and the index of refraction (IOR)

CHAPTER 29

Basics of Optical Networks

Traffic on the Internet alone is exploding at a rate that far outpaces the growth of traditional voice traffic. The IP bandwidth demands on a network backbone are pushing a service provider's network architecture to its limits and sometimes even beyond its capacity.

Service providers need the capability to provision new services quickly, deliver high-value applications at a fraction of the time and cost, and build scalable, fail-safe infrastructures at reduced operating costs. The answer lies in fiber-optic technology. Optical networks are an extremely efficient means of conveying data such as text, video, and voice.

This chapter describes the key business drivers of the optical networks and the features of fiber-optic systems. This chapter also discusses the components of optical transmission and their features.

Optical Business Drivers

Networks must be capable of transmitting data and video quickly, efficiently, and cost-effectively. In comparison to any other resource, fiber optics is the most efficient medium for transmitting information. Fiber optics offers the highest bandwidth capacity for network traffic. As demand increases for high-bandwidth capacity and high transmission speeds, it is expected that the usage of fiber optic will grow very quickly.

The burgeoning Internet economy and surging amounts of data traffic call for scalable, multiservice platforms with the capability to support next-generation, IP-based services and security. Today, service providers demand certain characteristics from their networks, as described in Table 29-1.

Table 29-1   *Optical Business Drivers*

Key Drivers	Descriptions
Capacity/scalability	Efficiently meet capacity and scalability requirements in both metropolitan and long-haul network infrastructures.
Reliability	Scale with the rapid growth of the Internet while providing unrivaled reliability
Accelerated profits	Reduce costs and accelerate profitable new service revenue simultaneously
Broad coverage	Reach long distances

continues

Table 29-1   *Optical Business Drivers (Continued)*

Key Drivers	Descriptions
End-to-end flexibility	Provide the capability to build a flexible, end-to-end optical solution that meets the requirements of carrier-class reliability
Adaptability	Be adaptable through an open system architecture
Space efficiency	Reduce point-of-presence (POP) physical space requirements
Security	Support IP-based security

Fiber-Optic Systems

Fiber-optic technology is the core of today's high-speed networks. Connecting both distant cities and many points within a metropolitan area, optical-fiber networks are made of thin glass strands that carry rapid light pulses faster and more reliably than copper wires at speeds of up to 10 gigabits per second (Gbps). Work is under way to increase speeds to 40 Gbps.

Information is transmitted at the speed of light in optical fiber. The time units used in measuring light are extremely small. Although optical fibers are very small, they can also be very long. At approximately the diameter of a human hair, optical fiber can carry a tremendous amount of information.

Fiber-Optic Transmission System

All communication systems have three things in common: a signal source, a medium for the signal to travel through, and a receiver. This system can be as simple as using a pair of tin cans connected by a string to talk with a friend. In fiber optics, the transmitter is a light source, the medium is a light guide (optical fiber), and the receiver is an optical sensor (see Figure 29-1).

Figure 29-1   *Fiber-Optic Communication Systems*

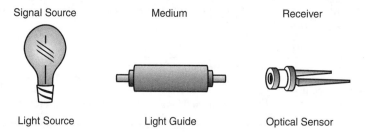

Optical Transmitter

An optical *transmitter* is simply a source of light, like a light bulb (see Figure 29-2). Lasers and light-emitting diodes (LEDs) are used for optical transmitters. An electrical signal such as a voice, data, or video transmission is converted to light by using the electrical signal to turn the light on and off for a digital signal, or to vary the intensity of the light for an analog signal. In a digital signal, the presence of light is a 1 and the absence of light is a 0. In an analog signal, the intensity of the light matches the strength of the electrical signal level.

Figure 29-2   *Optical Transmitter*

Light On and Off = Digital
Variable Intensity = Analog

Optical Receiver

The *receiver* is a semiconductor that changes light into a corresponding electrical signal. It is generically called an *optical-to-electrical converter*, or *O-E converter*. In a digital signal, the presence of light produces an electrical signal of a certain high level. The absence of light produces a lower electrical signal level (see Figure 29-3). In an analog system, the electrical level corresponds to the level (power) of the light hitting the O-E converter.

Figure 29-3   *High-Level and Low-Level Signals*

High-Level Signal

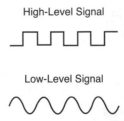

Low-Level Signal

Even with no light hitting an O-E converter, there will still be an electrical signal. This signal is caused by the dark current that exists in all detector circuits. The dark current is the electrical noise that naturally occurs in the circuit.

Some receiver circuits have lower noise levels than others. The noise level of the receiver depends on its design. Lower noise levels result from better designs (see Figure 29-4).

Figure 29-4   *Dark Current*

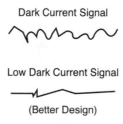

Dark Current Signal

Low Dark Current Signal

(Better Design)

Light

Light can be described in several ways. Consider the way light bulbs are rated at 60 or 100 watts. In fiber optics, the wattage is in the thousandths, millionths, or billionths of a watt— milliwatt (mW), microwatt (μW), or nanowatt (nW). It is usually more convenient to work with decibels (dB), which is a set of units related to watts. The expression "decibels relative to 1 milliwatt" (dBm) is used to define signal strength in wires and cables at radio frequency and audio frequency.

Light can be described by its color, which is determined by the wavelength of the electromagnetic signal. For example, blue is about 300 nanometers (nm), and red is at 700 nm wavelength. In fiber optics, there are three wavelength values: 850, 1300, and 1550 nm. Multimode systems use only 850 and 1300 nm, whereas single-mode systems use only 1300 and 1550 nm (see Figure 29-5).

Figure 29-5   *Fiber-Optic Wavelength*

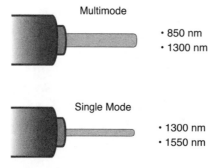

Multimode

• 850 nm
• 1300 nm

Single Mode

• 1300 nm
• 1550 nm

The power in a light determines its brightness. The higher the wattage is, the brighter the light will be. In fiber-optic systems, the benchmark power is 1 milliwatt (mW), which is 0 dBm. Higher values, such as 4 mW, would be +6 dBm. A change of 3 dB means a doubling of the wattage. A change of negative 3 dB (–3 dB) means cutting the wattage in half. For example, 0.250 mW (250 μW) would be –6 dBm (see Figure 29-6).

Figure 29-6   *Fiber-Optics Power*

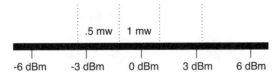

The power levels found in fiber systems range from about +20 dBm, which is the output of very hot lasers, to about −70 dBm, which is the amount of power returning after making a round trip down a 100-mile-long fiber.

Optical Transmission

In fiber optics, information is carried by modulating the light power, not the wavelength or frequency of the light. As a result, the wavelength remains constant. It is possible to mix two wavelengths of light on the same fiber without interference between them. This is called *wavelength-division multiplexing* (WDM). WDM allows more than one wavelength to be sent over a single fiber, thereby increasing the capacity of the fiber (see Figure 29-7). WDM is discussed in more detail in Chapter 31, "Optical Transmission and Multiplexing."

Figure 29-7   *Wavelength-Division Multiplexing*

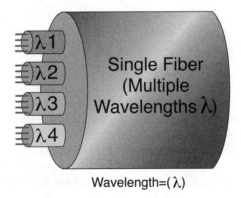

Wavelength=(λ)

The light source used in the design of a system is an important consideration because it can be one of the most costly elements. The characteristics of the light source often constitute a strong limiting factor in the final performance of the optical link. Light-emitting devices used in optical transmission must be compact, monochromatic, stable, and long lasting.

Three general types of light-emitting devices are used in optical transmission: light-emitting diodes (LEDs), laser diodes, and semiconductor lasers (see Figure 29-8). LEDs are relatively slow devices that are suitable for use at speeds of less than 1 Gbps. LEDs exhibit a relatively wide spectrum width and transmit light in a relatively wide cone.

Figure 29-8   *Light-Emitting Devices*

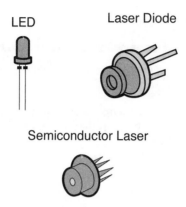

LEDs and laser diodes are inexpensive devices often used in multimode fiber communications. Semiconductor lasers, on the other hand, have performance characteristics better suited to single-mode fiber applications.

Reflection and Refraction

Light is described sometimes as traveling as a ray; that is, it has a direction of travel. *Reflection* is a light ray bouncing off the interface of two materials at the same angle it hits. Reflection occurs when a flashlight beam bounces off a window or mirror (see Figure 29-9). The beam of light comes off at the same angle it hits.

Refraction is the bending of the light ray as it changes speed going from one material to another. When a light ray hits another material at a steep enough angle, most of the light goes through the interface into the other material (see Figure 29-10). If there is a difference in density between the materials, the light bends, or refracts, at a fixed angle. This angle of refraction depends on the difference in density of the two materials. For example, when light comes out of water into the air, it bends. When you stick a fishing pole into the water, the pole looks like it bends. However, the pole is not bending; the light hitting the pole is bending.

Figure 29-9   *Reflection*

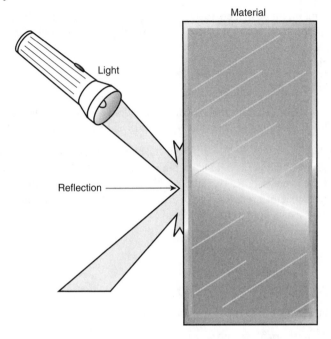

Figure 29-10   *Refraction*

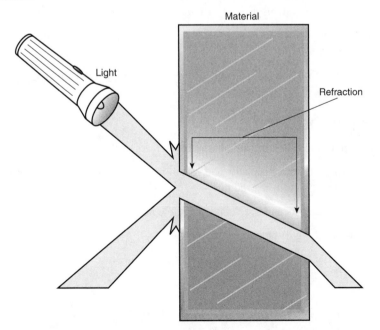

Index of Refraction (IOR)

One of the most important design characteristics of fiber is its index of refraction (IOR). The IOR is the ratio of the speed of light in a vacuum to the speed of light in a fiber, as follows:

$$\text{IOR} = \frac{C \text{ (Velocity of light in a vacuum)}}{V \text{ (Velocity of light in a glass)}}$$

IOR is a measure of the density of a fiber because more dense materials (higher IOR) cause light to travel more slowly. For optical fiber, the typical IOR values are between 1.4 and 1.5.

Each fiber manufacturer has a slightly different IOR because each makes its fibers using a different process. Even within a single fiber, the IOR might vary. The IOR value reported by manufacturers is the average IOR. Two fibers with different IOR values might work together. However, remember that different IORs have different effects on distance measurements. More dense materials will cause light to travel slower.

Summary

In this chapter, you learned the following key points:

- Information is transmitted at the speed of light in optical fiber.

- The optical-to-electrical converter converts light into a corresponding electrical signal.

- Multimode optical fiber systems use wavelengths at 850 and 1300 nanometers (nm). Single-mode systems use only 1300 and 1550 nm.

- In fiber optics, information is carried by modulating the light power. The wavelength remains constant.

- Index of refraction (IOR) is one of the most important design characteristics of fiber.

Review Exercises

1   Which of the following are not the key drivers of the optical networks?

   a. Efficiently meet capacity and scalability requirements in both metropolitan and long-haul network infrastructure

   b. Reduce costs and accelerate profitable new service revenue simultaneously

   c. Reach long distances

   d. Be adaptable through a closed-system architecture

2 Which of the following is true of IOR?

a. It stands for *index of reflection*.

b. It is a light ray bouncing off the interface of two materials.

c. It is the ratio of the speed of light in a vacuum to the speed of light in a fiber.

d. Two fibers with different IOR values cannot work together.

3 True or false: The light current is the electrical noise that naturally occurs in the circuit.

a. True

b. False

4 Which of the following is *not* a wavelength value used in fiber optics?

a. 850 nm

b. 1300 nm

c. 1450 nm

d. 1550 nm

5 Which of the following describe(s) fiber optics?

a. High-speed transmission

b. Long transmission distance

c. More reliability than copper wires

d. All of the above

Upon completing this chapter, you will be able to:

- Identify the main components of a fiber-optic cable
- Describe the features of multimode fiber
- Describe the features of single-mode fiber
- Explain the possible fiber geometry problems
- Describe different loss factors in fiber, including connector loss, macrobending, microbending, and absorption
- Identify the causes of attenuation in optical fiber
- Identify the effects of different types of dispersion
- Describe how to obtain the greatest capacity from optical fiber
- Describe the optical filter technology and identify the functions of the optical amplifier
- Describe how erbium-doped fiber amplifiers (EDFAs) work

CHAPTER 30

Optical Fibers

Fiber-optic cable is a networking medium that uses modulated light for data transmissions through thin strands of glass. Signals that represent data bits are converted into beams of light. Many characteristics of fiber optics make this media superior to copper. Fiber is not susceptible to EMI or RFI. Fiber has higher data transmission rates, significantly greater transmission distances, no grounding concerns, and better resistance to environmental factors. Those characteristics make fiber a more attractive choice over copper in some implementations.

To understand how fiber-optic media works, it is crucial to have a basic knowledge of some important characteristics of light as it relates to the way it is transmitted (propagated) through materials such as glass. This chapter describes two main types of fiber: single mode and multimode. This chapter also discusses possible fiber geometry problems, loss factors in fiber optics, and causes of attenuation. In addition, this chapter introduces two fiber filter technologies: fiber bragg grating and dielectric filter.

Fiber Types

A fiber-optic cable has three components, as shown in Figure 30-1:

- **Protective outer coating**—This is also known as buffer coating.

- **Inner cladding**—The cladding is of different density than the core, so the light bounces against it.

- **Fiber core**—The core is doped with chemicals that enhance its transmission properties.

Figure 30-1   *Components of Fiber-Optic Cable*

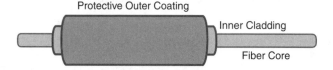

Protective Outer Coating

Inner Cladding

Fiber Core

Telecom fiber is classified into multimode or single mode. The only physical difference between the two is the size of the core (see Figure 30-2). Because of the core size, the performance characteristics are different. With its smaller core, single-mode fiber can carry information over long distances and can handle substantially more information than multimode. Also, single-mode fiber exhibits less loss than multimode fiber.

Figure 30-2   *Fiber Types*

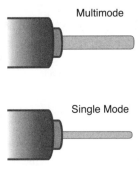

Multimode

Single Mode

Multimode

Multimode fiber is used to transmit many signals per fiber. Multimode allows many paths or modes for the light. The larger core of multimode fiber allows light to break up into many different modes. Some modes will make it to the far end faster than others, causing the original signal to be broadened out in time. In a time-division multiplexed (TDM) digital signal, the variance of light speed limits the spacing between bits of information and the rate at which bits can be sent. This is known as *dispersion*. Typical multimode rates are in the hundreds of megabits per second (Mbps).

Single Mode

Single-mode fiber is used to transmit one signal per fiber. Single-mode fiber allows only one single path for the signal to travel down the middle of the fiber. The entire signal travels the length of the fiber at the same rate, allowing for much higher data rates. Typical single-mode rates are in the millions and billions of bits per second (bps).

Fiber Geometry

Fiber manufacturing continues to improve, making fiber less expensive and of better quality. However, there are some allowable variations in the physical structure of fiber. One of the most important characteristics related to splicing (and testing) is the shape and location of the core within the cladding.

Because light travels only in the core of the fiber, it is necessary for fiber cores to link up when splicing them. In some cases, the fiber cores might not match up well. They might be slightly off center from the cladding center, they might be of different sizes, or they might not be round (see Figure 30-3). In some cases, it might not be possible to make a splice better than 0.20 dB loss because of the mismatch in fiber characteristics.

Figure 30-3   *Fiber Geometry Problems*

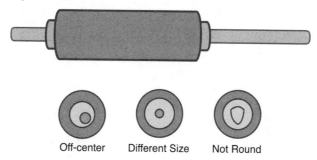

Off-center   Different Size   Not Round

Loss Factors

When light is injected into a fiber, you need to be concerned about how well it will be transmitted and whether it will be lost before it gets to the other end. The amount of signal loss in a fiber is its most critical performance characteristic. If light is too weak coming out of the receiver end of fiber, the entire system might not work properly. The following sections describe major loss factors in fibers, including these:

• Connector loss

• Macrobending

• Microbending

• Absorption

Connector Losses

Connector loss depends on passing light from one core to another. Because a connector relies on the capability of the bulkhead to line up the two fiber ends, it allows for some different loss factors than with field splices. If two fiber ends are separated, loss occurs because of the spreading of light as it comes out of the first core. This is called *end-face separation*.

Even when the gap is small, some light might be lost. The wider the gap is, the more loss there will be. If the bulkhead is worn and allows some play in the alignment of two fibers, some light might be lost because the cores are not lined up completely. This is called *angular separation*. Core misalignment is the same for splices.

Figure 30-4 illustrates the three causes of connector loss described in this section.

Figure 30-4   *Connector Losses*

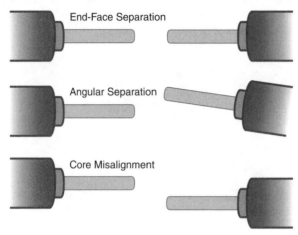

Macrobending

A macrobend is a bend you can see. When you bend fiber, you can cause some of the light rays to exceed the critical angle, allowing light to leak out of the core and into the cladding. When light is in the cladding, it cannot easily get back into the core; it then leaks out through the buffer (see Figure 30-5).

Figure 30-5   *Macrobending*

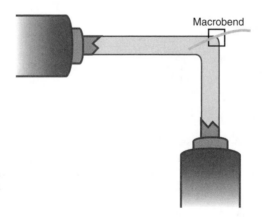

Macrobending loss is more severe at longer wavelengths (for example, a nickel-size bend might leak out 0.5 dB of light at 1310 nm but might cause a loss of 2.0 dB at 1550 nm). You can reduce macrobending by eliminating tight bends in the fiber and cable.

Microbending

Microbending produces the same effect as macrobending; it causes the light to exceed the critical angle and leak out of the core (see Figure 30-6). It occurs on a microscopic scale and is not visible to the eye.

Figure 30-6   *Microbending*

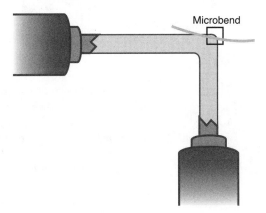

Microbending appears as a wrinkle in the fiber caused by temperature variations during manufacturing. Microbending can also be caused by extreme temperature swings in installed cable when the different materials in the cable structure expand and contract at different rates. This causes the fiber to be squeezed or stretched, in turn causing microbending.

Absorption

Some light is always absorbed into the glass structure. Certain wavelengths exhibit higher absorption rates than others. Absorption can be neither changed nor controlled by the user. It is an intrinsic loss characteristic of fiber (see Figure 30-7).

Figure 30-7   *Absorption*

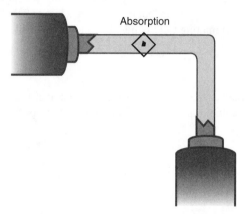

The most serious absorption in glass occurs close to the operating wavelength "windows" of 1310 and 1550 nm. These areas often show high levels of absorption because of the hydroxyl (OH⁻) ion, which is produced as a result of the manufacturing process. The absorption peaks can grow in certain conditions and can cause increased attenuation in the operating wavelength windows.

Attenuation

Attenuation refers to the decrease in the strength of a signal during transmission. Attenuation is a natural consequence of signal transmission over long distance. Attenuation in optical fiber is caused by extrinsic factors, including stress from the manufacturing process, the environment, and physical bending. Attenuation in optical fiber is also caused by intrinsic factors, primarily scattering and absorption.

The most common form of scattering, *Rayleigh scattering*, is caused by small variations in the density of glass as it cools. Scattering affects short wavelengths more than long wavelengths and limits the use of wavelengths below 800 nm.

Attenuation as the result of absorption is caused by the intrinsic properties of the material itself. Impurities in the glass or atomic defects in the glass can cause absorption. These impurities absorb the optical energy, causing the light to become dimmer. Whereas Rayleigh scattering is an important factor at shorter wavelengths, intrinsic absorption is an issue at longer wavelengths.

The two primary factors affecting attenuation in optical fibers are as follows:

- Length of the fiber
- Wavelength of the light

Figure 30-8 shows the loss in decibels per kilometer (dB/km) by wavelength from Rayleigh scattering, intrinsic absorption, and total attenuation from all causes. Based on the attenuations response, the two choices of operation are 1310 or 1550 nm. The 1550-nm window is preferred for long-haul applications because it has less attenuation.

Figure 30-8   *Attenuation*

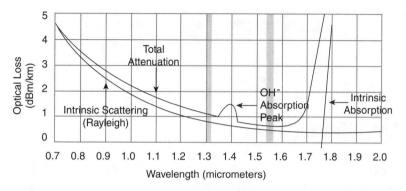

Optical Filters

Optical filters are used to identify different wavelengths or lambdas. Fiber bragg grating and the dielectric filter are examples of optical filters (see Figure 30-9).

Fiber bragg gratings are spectral filters that reflect light over a narrow wavelength range and transmit all other wavelengths. Fiber bragg gratings are a very low-cost approach in which gratings are written directly into standard single-mode fiber. These gratings have the advantage of being ultra narrow. However, it is hard to control the filter shape using fiber bragg gratings.

Dielectric filter is based on semiconductor processing, in which alternating layers of quarter-wavelength thick dielectric stacks are laid down. Dielectric filters reflect one or more light and transmit others. Unlike fiber bragg gratings, the filter shape is easily controlled.

Figure 30-9   *Optical Filter Technology*

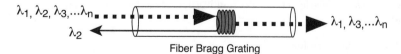

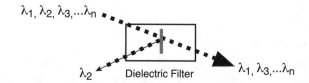

Optical filters are used in optical add/drop multiplexers (OADMs) to drops the appropriate channel by essentially reflecting it out (see Figure 30-10).

Figure 30-10   *Optical Add/Drop Multiplexers*

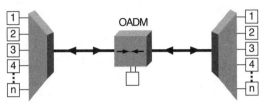

Optical Amplifiers (OAs)

The *optical amplifier (OA)* is a device that amplifies an input optical signal without converting it to electrical form. The OA provides 4 terahertz (THz) of optical bandwidth near 1550 nm, nearly ideal noise performance, low signal distortion and crosstalk, and high-output saturation power; it is also simple and efficient (see Figure 30-11).

Figure 30-11   *Optical Amplifier*

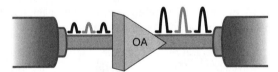

The optical pulse begins to deteriorate as it travels farther. To prevent this deterioration, an electrical regenerator is used to perform the three R's: restore the signal level, reshape the pulse, and retime the pulse. Electrical regenerators are expensive, introduce latency, and are channel specific.

Erbium-doped fiber amplifiers (EDFAs), unlike electrical regenerators, do not convert the signal back to electric before boosting it. EDFA is a device consisting of the following four parts:

- Erbium-doped fiber
- Optical pump
- Coupler
- Isolator

The signal path in an EDFA is entirely passive. The pump laser is the only active part.

In an EDFA, optical fibers are doped with erbium, a rare element that can amplify light in the 1550-nm region when pumped by an external laser (see Figure 30-12).

Figure 30-12 *Erbium-Doped Fiber Amplifiers*

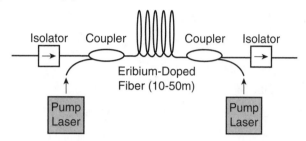

Summary

In this chapter, you learned the following key points:

- A fiber-optic cable has three components: a protective outer coating, an inner cladding, and a fiber core.

- Telecom fiber is classified into two modes: multimode and single mode.

- Typical multimode transmission rates are in the hundreds of megabits per second; typical single-mode transmission rates are in the millions and billions of bits per second.

- The loss factors in fiber include connector losses, macrobending, microbending, and absorption.

- Attenuation in optical fiber can be caused by scattering, absorption, stress from the manufacturing process, the environment, and physical bending.

- Dispersion causes the light pulse to spread as it travels along the fiber.

- The optical amplifier (OA) is a device that amplifies an input optical signal without converting it to electrical form.

- Erbium-doped fiber amplifiers (EDFAs) do not convert the signal back to electric before boosting it.

Review Exercises

1 Which of the following methods can amplify an input optical signal within in the fiber?

   a. OADM

   b. SONET

   c. ROL

   d. EDFA

2   What is the typical multimode transmission rate?

   a. Hundreds of megabits per second

   b. Hundreds of kilobits per second

   c. Hundreds of gigabits per second

   d. None of the above

3   Which of the following is true of single-mode fiber?

   a. The signal travels through a single-mode fiber at a different rate.

   b. Single-mode fiber has a lower data rate than multimode fiber.

   c. Single-mode fiber allows multimode to travel down the fiber.

   d. Single-mode fiber allows one mode to travel down the fiber.

4   Which of the following are possible problems of the fiber core?

   a. The core can be slightly off center from the cladding center.

   b. The cores might be slightly different sizes.

   c. The core might be noncircular.

   d. All of the above.

5   Match each of the following loss factors with the description:

   1   Microbending

   2   Connector loss

   3   Macrobending

   4   Absorption

   a. Appears as a wrinkle in the fiber

   b. Is an intrinsic loss characteristic of fiber

   c. Depends on passing light from one core to another

   d. Is a bend caused by bending fiber and is visible to the eyes

5 Which of the following is a cause of attenuation?

   a. Scattering

   b. Stress from the manufacturing process

   c. Physical bending

   d. All of the above

6 Which of the following is a *not* a component of fiber-optic cable?

   a. A fiber core

   b. An inner cladding

   c. An outer cladding

   d. A protective outer coating

Upon completing this chapter, you will be able to:

- Describe SONET technology
- Describe SONET/SDH
- Describe what DWDM systems are
- Explain how E/O/E conversion (transponder) works
- Describe fiber-optic data transmission
- Describe the advantages of DWDM
- Describe the features of metropolitan DWDM

CHAPTER 31

Optical Transmission and Multiplexing

Synchronous Optical Network (SONET) is the standard for synchronous data transmission on optical media used in North America. Synchronous Digital Hierarchy (SDH) is the international equivalent of SONET. SONET primarily is deployed by service providers using a ring topology. The two prevalent types of rings in networks today are unidirectional path-switched rings (UPSR) and bidirectional line-switched rings (BLSR).

Dense wavelength-division multiplexing (DWDM) is a technology that transmits multiple signals simultaneously at different wavelengths, allowing a single fiber to operate as if it were multiple fibers. DWDM works in conjunction with optical networks to make data transmission fast and cost effective. DWDM is a scalable solution that increases the information-carrying capacity of existing fiber.

This chapter introduces the SONET/SDH technology, SONET overhead hierarchy, and SONET/SDH multiplexing hierarchy. In addition, this chapter describes how DWDM systems work and discusses the benefits of DWDM systems.

SONET Technology

SONET is a standard for optical transport formulated by the Exchange Carriers Standards Association (ECSA) for the American National Standards Institute (ANSI), which sets industry standards in the United States for telecommunications and other industries. The SONET standard was initiated by Bellcore on behalf of the regional Bell operating companies (RBOCs) and others to ensure compatibility of equipment by all vendors that manufacture to the "midspan meet" standard. *Midspan meet* refers to the capability to connect different vendors' equipment on a communication network and have them function properly with each other.

SONET was also designed to standardize synchronous networking-enhanced operations, administration, maintenance, and provisioning (OAM&P), and standards-based survivable rings. SONET defines Optical Carrier (OC) levels and electrically equivalent synchronous transport signals (STSs) for the fiber optic–based transmission hierarchy.

Synchronous Digital Hierarchy (SDH) is the international equivalent of SONET. Together SONET and SDH are a set of global standards that interface equipment from different vendors.

SONET uses substantial overhead information, which allows simpler multiplexing and greatly expanded OAM&P capabilities. The following section introduces the SONET overhead hierarchy.

SONET Overhead Hierarchy

The SONET overhead information has several layers, which are shown in Figure 31-1. Enough information is contained in the overhead to allow the network to operate and allow OAM&P communications between the network controller and the nodes. The following describes the three levels of SONET overhead hierarchy:

- **Section overhead (SOH)**—A section is a link between two network elements. Section overhead is used for communications between adjacent network elements, such as regenerators.

- **Line overhead (LOH)**—A line is one or more sections connecting two network elements that multiplex and demultiplex SONET STS signals. Line overhead is for the STS-N signal between STS-N multiplexers.

- **Path overhead (POH)**—A path is one or more lines connecting two network elements that assemble and disassemble traffic. Path overhead, which includes information such as path status, is carried from end to end.

The section-terminating equipment (STE) is usually a regenerator. An STE is capable of originating, accessing, modifying, or terminating the section overhead. The line-terminating equipment (LTE) is a network element that can originate, access, modify, or terminate the line overhead. The path-terminating equipment (PTE) originates, accesses, modifies, or terminates the path overhead.

Figure 31-1   *SONET Overhead Hierarchy*

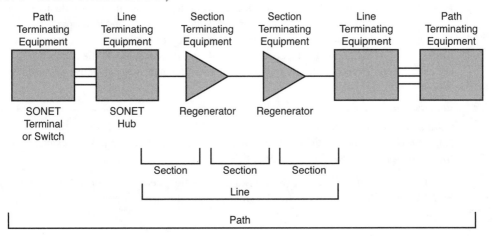

SONET Rings

Most carriers provide two types of SONET services: point-to-point dedicated SONET lines and SONET rings. Both deliver high-speed data transfer, but only dual fiber rings guarantee automatic rerouting around outages. Many types of rings are possible. The two prevalent types in networks today are unidirectional path-switched rings (UPSR) and bidirectional line-switched rings (BLSR) (see Figure 31-2).

In a unidirectional ring, all working traffic travels around the ring in the same direction. In a bidirectional ring, all working traffic between two nodes travels in both directions (clockwise and counterclockwise).

UPSRs, deployed in MANs, have two fibers (two counter-rotating rings). One ring is reserved for automatic protection of the working traffic. BLSRs, deployed in WANs or backbones, use two pairs of fiber, with one pair designated for working traffic and one pair designated for protection. In BLSR, half the bandwidth in each direction in a ring is reserved for the shared protection of all traffic in the reverse direction of the ring.

Figure 31-2   *UPSR and BLSR Configurations*

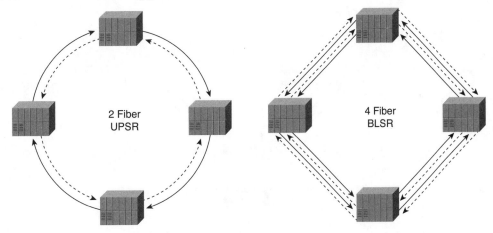

SONET Automatic Protection Switching

SONET line automatic protection switching (APS) protects the entire facility at the line layer. A network element can monitor a working line and switch to a spare (protection) line in the event of failure. An APS of 1:1 provides one protection line for each working line. An APS of 1:*N* provides one protection line for every *N* working lines.

SONET/SDH–Based TDM Transport

SONET/SDH–based TDM offers an accepted transport architecture that provides performance monitoring and logical point-to-point over the physical ring (see Figure 31-3). Multiservice is via TDM, which is not an optimal use of bandwidth for data transmission. However, TDM offers good protection.

Figure 31-3   *SONET/SDH–Based TDM Transport*

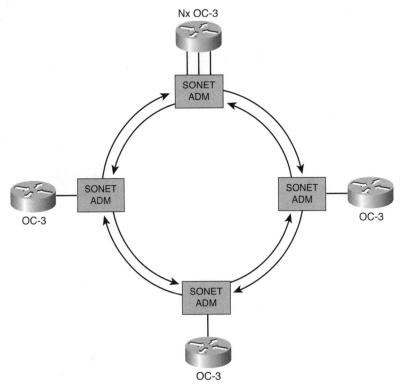

SONET Multiplexing Hierarchy

SONET has a hierarchical multiplexing structure. SONET defines a technology for carrying many signals of different capacities through a synchronous, flexible, optical hierarchy. This is accomplished by means of a byte-interleaved multiplexing scheme.

The first step in the SONET multiplexing process involves the generation of the lowest level or base signal. In SONET, this base signal is referred to as *Synchronous Transport Signal level 1*, or simply *STS-1*, which operates at 51.84 Mbps. Higher-level signals are integer multiples of STS-1, creating the family of STS-N and Synchronous Transport Module (STM)-N signals.

(STS-N is the SONET hierarchy, and STM-N is the SDH hierarchy.) The optical counterpart for each STS-N signal is the designated Optical Carrier level N (OC-N) (see Table 31-1).

Table 31-1 *SONET/SDH Multiplexing Hierarchy*

SONET/SDH Multiplexing Hierarchy Optical Carrier	SONET/SDH Signal	Bit Rate	Capacity
OC-1	STS-1	51.84 Mbps	28 DS1s or 1 DS3
OC-3	STS-3/STM-1	155.52 Mbps	84 DS1s or 3 DS3s
OC-12	STS-12/STM-4	622.08 Mbps	336 DS1s or 12 DS3s
OC-48	STS-48/STM-16	2488.32 Mbps	1344 DS1s or 48 DS3s
OC-192	STS-192/STM-64	9953.28 Mbps	5379 DS1s or 192 DS3s

DWDM Systems

The origin of optical networks is linked to wavelength-division multiplexing (WDM), which arose to provide additional capacity on existing fibers. With WDM, several optical transmission signals operating at different wavelengths, or "colors," are combined onto a single fiber. The difference between WDM and dense wavelength-division multiplexing (DWDM) is fundamentally one of only degree. DWDM spaces the wavelengths more closely than does WDM and, therefore, has a greater overall capacity.

DWDM puts data from many different sources together on an optical fiber, with each signal carried on its own separate wavelength. Using DWDM, more than 200 separate wavelengths or channels of data can be multiplexed into a light stream transmitted on a single optical fiber (see Figure 31-4).

Figure 31-4 *DWDM Systems*

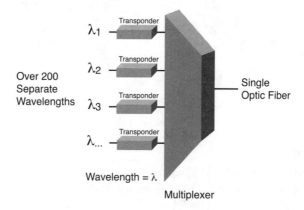

Most DWDM systems support standard SONET/SDH short-reach optical interfaces to which compliant client devices can attach. In today's long-haul WDM systems, this is most often an OC-48c/STM-16c interface operating at 1300 nm wavelength. The clients can be SONET/SDH terminals or add/drop multiplexers (ADMs), ATM switches, or routers.

E/O/E Conversion

A light beam can travel through a network that is not 100 percent optical fiber. The electrical/optical/electrical (E/O/E) conversion begins when data traffic from the edge of the optical network enters the core of the network as an electrical signal and is converted into an optical signal for transmission across the optical network. The optical signal travels across the network and is converted back into an electrical signal at a transit point.

Within the DWDM system, a device called a *transponder* converts the SONET/SDH–compliant optical signal from the client back to an electrical signal. The electrical signal then is used to drive a WDM laser. The WDM laser is a very precise laser operating within the 1500 nm wavelength range. Each transponder within the system converts its client's signal to a slightly different wavelength. The wavelengths from all the transponders in the system then are optically multiplexed onto a single fiber. In the receive direction of the DWDM system, the reverse process occurs. Individual wavelengths are filtered from the multiplexed fiber and are fed to individual transponders, which convert the signal to electrical and drive a standard SONET/SDH interface to the client (see Figure 31-5).

Figure 31-5   *E/O/E Conversion*

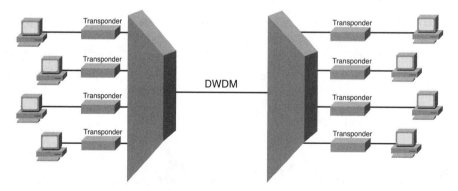

Data Transmission

In a DWDM system with each channel carrying 10 Gbps (10 billion bits per second), the optical fiber can deliver up to 2 trillion bps (see Figure 31-6). Because each channel is demultiplexed at the end of the transmission back into the original source, different data formats can be transmitted together at different data rates.

Figure 31-6 *Data Transmission*

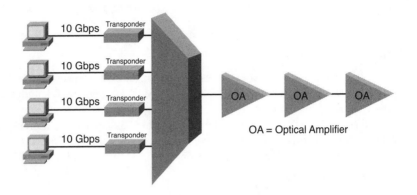

DWDM Advantages

From both technical and economic perspectives, the capability to provide potentially unlimited transmission capacity is the most obvious advantage of DWDM technology. The current investment in fiber plant can be preserved and optimized. As demands change, more capacity can be added without expensive upgrades, either by performing simple equipment upgrades or by increasing the number of lambdas on the fiber.

Bandwidth aside, the following list describes the most compelling technical advantages of DWDM:

- **Flexibility**—DWDM is extremely flexible. Specifically, Internet Protocol (IP), SONET, and Asynchronous Transfer Mode (ATM) data all can be traveling at the same time within the optical fiber.

- **Transparency**—Because DWDM is a physical layer architecture, it can transparently support both TDM and data formats such as ATM, Gigabit Ethernet, Enterprise System Connection (ESCON), and Fibre Channel with open interfaces over a common physical layer.

- **Scalability**—DWDM provides economical, scalable bandwidth growth. DWDM can take advantage of the abundance of dark fiber in many metropolitan-area and enterprise networks. It quickly can meet demand for capacity on point-to-point links and on spans of existing SONET/SDH rings.

- **Dynamic provisioning**—Fast and simple, dynamic provisioning of network connections gives providers the capability to provide high-bandwidth services in days rather than months.

Traditional ways of increasing bandwidth include using faster electronics, which are expensive, or using more fiber. The problems with the latter include a slower time to market, expensive engineering, limited right of way, and duct exhaust. WDM increases bandwidth without these issues while maintaining fiber compatibility. DWDM provides fiber capacity release, a fast time to market, a lower cost of ownership, and the utilization of existing TDM equipment.

Metro DWDM

Metropolitan (metro) DWDM maximizes the service density, or revenue potential per wavelength, by supporting both subwavelength TDM services and wavelength services, such as Gigabit Ethernet, fiber connectivity (FICON), Enterprise System Connection (ESCON), and more on a single DWDM backbone. Metro DWDM is fundamentally different from long-haul DWDM; metro DWDM is driven by demand for fast service provisioning, not fiber exhaust (see Figure 31-7). Table 31-2 shows a comparison of metro DWDM and long-haul DWDM.

Figure 31-7   *Metro vs. Long-Haul DWDM*

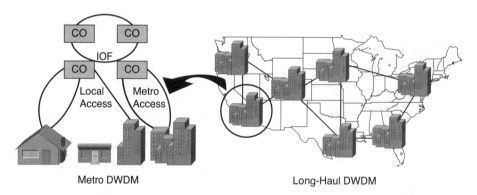

Metro DWDM   Long-Haul DWDM

Table 31-2   *Metro DWDM vs. Long-Haul DWDM*

	Metro DWDM	**Long-Haul DWDM**
Connectivity	Local-area access, mesh and centrally homed configuration	Intercity connectivity
Distance	Less than 50 km between central offices (COs)	Greater than 50 km between COs
Design	Cost-driven; low-cost SONET/DWDM equipment	Capacity-driven; employs expensive DWDM technology
Fiber Usage	Fiber typically leased and readily available	Severely fiber constrained; not easy to install additional fiber

Summary

In this chapter, you learned the following key points:

- SONET/SDH are standards for optical transport. The SONET standard is used in North America, while the SDH standard is the international equivalent of SONET.

- DWDM puts data from different sources together on an optical fiber.

- A transponder is a device that converts the SONET/SDH–compliant optical signal to electrical signal, and vice versa.

- DWDM can transmit different data formats together at different data rates.

- The most compelling technical advantages of DWDM are flexibility, transparency, scalability, and dynamic provisioning.

- Metro DWDM maximizes the service density per wavelength by supporting both subwavelength TDM and wavelength services.

- Metro DWDM is driven by demand for fast service provisioning, not fiber exhaust.

Review Exercises

1 SONET was designed to standardize which of the following?

  a. Synchronous networking-enhanced operations, administration, maintenance, and provisioning

  b. Asynchronous networking-based operation, administration, maintenance, and provisioning

  c. Protections to the SONET facilities at the application layer

  d. Transmission standards for ATM

2 Which of the following is *not* one of the three levels of overhead channel for maintenance?

  a. SOH

  b. COH

  c. LOH

  d. POH

3 True or false: SONET defines a technology for carrying one signal through a synchronous, flexible, optical hierarchy.

   a. True

   b. False

4 Which of the following could be a client-side device for a DWDM system?

   a. LAN switches

   b. Bridges

   c. Routers

   d. Hubs

5 What device within the DWDM system is used to convert the SONET/SDH–compliant optical signal?

   a. Transceiver

   b. Transformer

   c. Converter

   d. Transponder

6 From technical and economic perspectives, what is the most obvious advantage of DWDM technology?

   a. The capability to transmit a lot of data at a time

   b. The capability to provide potentially unlimited transmission capacity

   c. Easy installation

   d. Low cost

7 Identify the most compelling technical advantages of DWDM. (Check all that apply.)

   a. High flexibility

   b. Scalability

   c. High capacity

   d. Transparency

   e. Low maintenance

8 Which of the following does *not* describe metro DWDM?

   a. Metro DWDM is very similar to long-haul DWDM.

b. Metro DWDM supports subwavelength TDM and wavelength services.

c. Metro DWDM is driven by demand for fast service provisioning.

d. Metro DWDM maximizes service density per wavelength.

PART **X**

Appendixes

Upon completing this appendix, you will be able to:

- Describe how voice, video, and data networks traditionally have been implemented

- Compare and contrast voice-over-data technologies

- Describe voice, video, and data networks

- Describe the features and the main building blocks of Cisco AVVID

- Identify emerging applications for converged networking and their functions

- Describe the effects of QoS in voice, video, and data-integration networks

Introduction to Converged Networking

This appendix describes how traditional voice, video, and data networks are implemented. It also explains various types of voice-over-data technologies. In addition, this appendix describes the need for converged voice, video, and data networks and the Cisco Architecture for Voice, Video and Integrated Data (AVVID), along with new applications for converged networks. Lastly, this appendix discusses common issues with quality of service (QoS).

Traditional Networks

Traditionally, separate networks have been provisioned within an enterprise for data, voice, and video applications. These networks have been deployed autonomously and have operated in isolation, often implemented and managed by separate teams.

These separate networks encompass the enterprise local- and wide-area networks (LANs and WANs), and they have been built to interconnect private branch exchange (PBX) equipment, H.320 videoconferencing equipment, and routers. The networks have been provisioned over dedicated leased lines for PBX and H.320 video, with a combination of leased lines, Frame Relay, and ATM for data. Figure A-1 depicts a typical deployment of these disparate networks.

Figure A-1 *Typical Traditional Network*

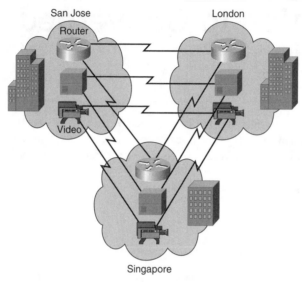

Introduction to Voice and Data Networks

Integrated voice and data networks support a variety of applications, all of which are designed to replace leased lines at lower costs. A voice-capable router can function as a local phone system for intraoffice calls. In Figure A-2, a user dials a phone extension that is located in the same office. The voice-capable router routes the call to the appropriate destination. A voice-capable router also can function as a phone system for interoffice calls and can route calls within an enterprise network.

Figure A-2 *Voice and Data Networks*

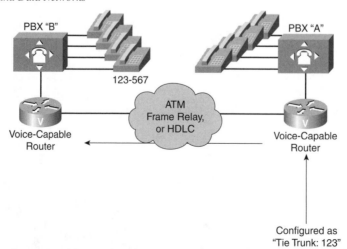

Voice over Frame Relay

Voice over Frame Relay (VoFR) technology consolidates voice and voice-band data (including fax and analog modems) with data services over a Frame Relay network. VoFR allows PBXs to be connected using Frame Relay permanent virtual circuits (PVCs). The goal is to replace leased lines at lower costs. With VoFR, customers easily can increase their link speeds to their Frame Relay service or their committed information rate (CIR) to support additional voice, fax, and data traffic.

NOTE   CIR is the rate at which a Frame Relay network agrees to transfer information under normal conditions, averaged over a minimum increment of time. Measured in bits per second (bps), CIR is one of the key negotiated tariff metrics.

A voice-capable router connects both a PBX and a data network to a public Frame Relay network (see Figure A-3). A voice-capable router includes a voice Frame Relay adapter (VFRAD) or a voice/fax module that supports voice traffic on the data network.

Figure A-3   *A VoFR Network*

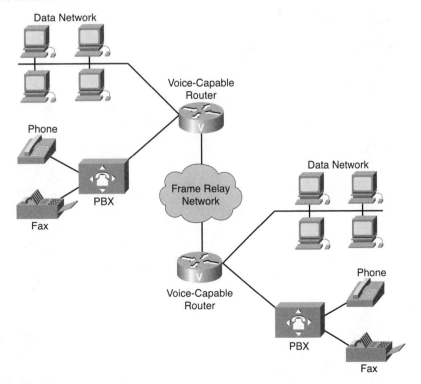

Sophisticated queuing techniques ensure QoS in voice over Frame Relay. Frame Relay provides the following benefits:

- Popular transport for multiservice networks because Frame Relay networks are common in many areas

- Cost-effective service that supports bursty traffic well

- Prioritization of voice frames over data frames to guarantee QoS

Voice over ATM

Voice over ATM (VoATM) is an ideal transport for multiservice networks, particularly for customers who already have an ATM network installed. ATM handles voice, video, and data equally well. A key benefit of ATM is its inherent design for handling the unique network transmission requirements of voice, video, and data traffic (see Figure A-4).

Figure A-4   *A VoATM Network*

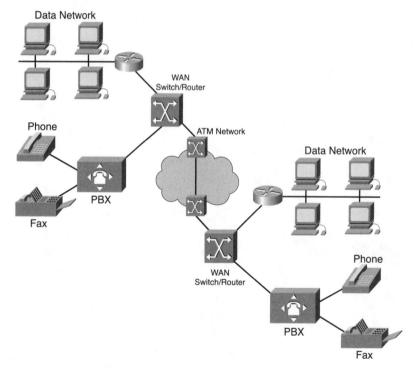

ATM supports several mechanisms for controlling delay and delay variation, including these:

- **QoS**—QoS enables traffic to be provisioned with specific bandwidth and delay-variation guarantees.

- **Virtual-circuit queuing**—Virtual-circuit queuing treats each traffic stream differently. Thus, for example, voice traffic can be allocated priority over delay-insensitive traffic.

- **Small, fixed-length cells**—The 53-byte ATM cells reduce queuing delay and delay variations associated with variable-size packets and also reduce delays through intermediate switches.

Voice over IP

Voice is an application that runs over IP just like any other application. IP/User Datagram Protocol/Real-Time Transport Protocol (IP/UDP/RTP) headers encapsulate voice information as it passes through the IP stack and then is de-encapsulated on the receiving side. RTP is utilized in addition to UDP to provide additional transport functions such as time-stamping and sequencing of VoIP packets that UDP does not provide. At the data link layer, voice over IP (VoIP) packets can use any Layer 2 encapsulations such as Point-to-Point Protocol (PPP), High-Level Data Link Control (HDLC), Frame Relay, ATM, Ethernet, and so on (see Figure A-5).

Figure A-5   *VoIP*

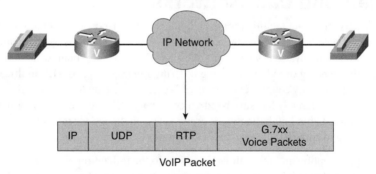

VoIP Packet

Users can choose VoIP as their voice-transport medium when they need a solution that is simple to implement, offers voice and fax capabilities, and handles phone-to-computer voice communications.

Comparing Voice-over-Data Technologies

Frame Relay, ATM, and IP are popular voice-over-data technologies that have developed to meet the expanding needs of today's voice-over-data applications. As shown in Table A-1, each technology has its advantages and its limitations:

Table A-1   *Advantages and Disadvantages of Voice-over-Data Technologies*

Voice-over-Data Technology	Advantages	Disadvantages
Frame Relay	Deterministic Standards in place Services widely available	Tops out at T1/E1 speeds
ATM	Deterministic Granular class of service	Services not yet pervasive Equipment historically expensive
IP	Widely deployed for maximum savings potential Special class of service technologies	Connectionless Least deterministic

Voice, Video, and Data Networks

This use of disparate facilities for each application transport is extremely inefficient. The volume of data traffic is growing faster than that of voice, driven by emerging and evolving technological innovations such as the World Wide Web, e-commerce, and applications such as videoconferencing or video streaming utilizing Internet Protocol (IP) multicast. Although growth rates vary by country and carrier, it is certain that data transport will dominate telephony networks. Data already has surpassed voice on some U.S. service provider networks and is the driving force behind global network growth. The challenge for the enterprise is to optimize networking to carry data, voice, and video traffic.

The rapid adoption and migration of vendors to the utilization of IP as a transport for data, voice, and video applications further endorses this transition to a converged networking architecture. Service providers (such as the telephone companies) that have historically used time-division multiplexing (TDM) infrastructures and relied upon "Old World" practices now are relying on IP.

Converged networks are a continuing trend, and this consolidation of data, voice, and video is the natural evolution for multiservice networking. Utilizing IP as the ubiquitous transport offers the following benefits:

- Significant statistical gains in bandwidth efficiency in the enterprise

- Lower overall bandwidth requirements

- Ease of management

- The capability to deploy new applications rapidly

- On the LAN, a common infrastructure shared among data, voice, and video

A converged network allows the enterprise network to converge over a common IP transport. The number of WAN facilities is reduced, as is the number of devices required to terminate those facilities. Bandwidth can be added incrementally and can be shared statistically between applications, adding efficiency and reducing complexity. When voice is inactive, data can utilize the available bandwidth; when voice or video applications are active, they can be guaranteed the bandwidth required.

Cisco AVVID

Cisco Architecture for Voice, Video and Integrated Data (AVVID) is a standards-based, open-systems architecture for converged networking. Cisco AVVID is an enterprise initiative for integrated data, voice, and video over a common IP transport. Cisco AVVID comprises the following three distinct building blocks:

- Infrastructure, such as switches and routers.

- Applications, such as call control.

- Clients, such as fixed and wireless IP telephones, H.323 videoconferencing equipment, and PCs.

AVVID requires the appropriate infrastructure and design. Figure A-6 depicts a converged network in which all data, voice, and video utilize IP as the transport; between sites the IP WAN is the primary interconnect, with the Public Switched Telephone Network (PSTN) being used as a secondary backup dialup connectivity method.

The use of open standards and the promotion of multivendor collaboration and interoperability are key benefits of Cisco AVVID. Because the network shown in Figure A-6 is based upon standards and open competition, interoperability with other applications is assured.

AVVID lowers costs and provides enhanced quality options for voice networking. It provides a highly scalable, reliable, and available network that is adaptable and that permits the rapid deployment of new and innovative applications. AVVID allows the integration of products from multiple vendors to create a customized solution. No single vendor can provide a solution that fits all requirements for data, voice, and video. Often specialized applications are designed and implemented by only a single company and need to be integrated with the overall solution.

Figure A-6 *Voice, Video, and Data Networks*

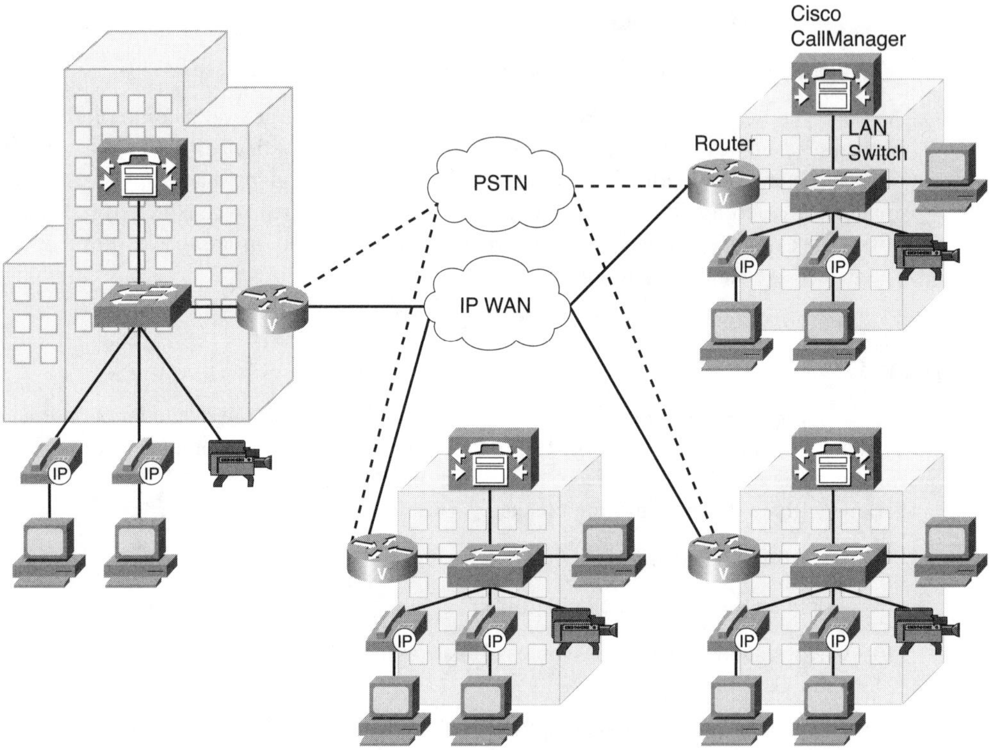

Converged Networking Applications

An important facet of converged networking is the enabling of new applications. Such emerging applications include desktop IP telephony, unified messaging, and the Cisco IP Contact Centers. A converged network offers the framework that permits rapid deployment of these new technologies.

IP PBX

By using the Cisco CallManager, a PBX can be eliminated and replaced with IP telephony over a converged network. The Cisco CallManager provides call-control functionality and, when used in conjunction with the IP telephone, sets a soft telephone application and can provide the PBX functionality in a distributed and scalable fashion. A voice gateway is used to connect the VoIP network to other network types, such as the PSTN, or to a PBX.

Unified Messaging

Today users have a wide range of communication and messaging media available to them: telephones, cell phones, pagers, fax, voice mail, and e-mail. Each of these requires distinct hardware and software components to function. *Unified messaging* combines voice mail, e-mail, and fax into a single application suite.

With unified messaging, a single application can be used to store and retrieve an entire suite of message types. Voice-mail messages stored as WAV files can be downloaded as e-mail attachments while you are traveling, and a response can be recorded and returned to the sender, all recipients, or an expanded list. E-mail can be retrieved via a telephony user interface (TUI), converted from text to speech, and reviewed from an airport lobby phone or cell phone. Infrastructure is decreased because now a single application can provide voice, e-mail, and fax. Productivity is increased because what were once disparate message types can be retrieved via the most convenient—or the user's preferred—interface.

Cisco offers unified messaging via its Cisco GateServer series of products. These products provide scalable solutions for service providers and the enterprise via open, standards-based interfaces. Figure A-7 depicts a unified messaging model.

Figure A-7   *Unified Messaging*

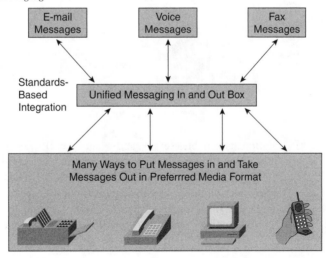

Cisco IP Contact Center

The *Cisco IP Contact Center (IPCC)* solution combines data and voice technologies to facilitate geographically independent multimedia customer interaction. This includes customer interactions originating from multiple diverse contact channels, including IP voice, TDM voice, web, e-mail, and fax. Regardless of transport, whether the Internet or the traditional PSTN, the

Cisco IPCC fully integrated contact-center architecture services all media types (see Figure A-8). The Cisco IPCC architecture also provides a seamless migration path from the legacy call-center infrastructure to the IP-empowered, multimedia contact center.

Figure A-8 *Cisco IP Contact Center*

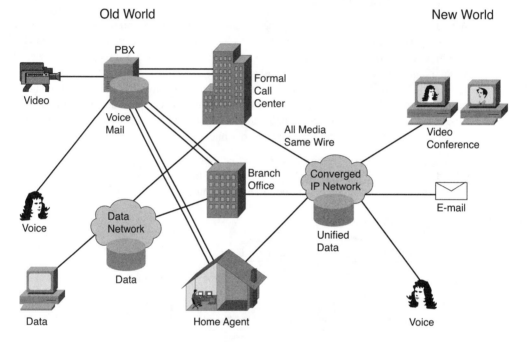

The Cisco IPCC solution also enables server- and agent-level IP telephony to coexist with traditional TDM-based networks, existing automated call distribution/PBXs (ACD/PBXs), and installed desktop systems. The Cisco IPCC solution enables an organization to take advantage of new IP-based applications while preserving heterogeneous legacy investments and taking advantage of existing IP data infrastructure. Thus, Cisco IPCC deployment can be incremental, adding IP telephony, new media channels, and new IP-based services at a rate that meets business demands.

Cisco IPCC business benefits include the following:

- Integrated multimedia queuing

- Enterprise-wide contact management based on a single set of business rules and supported by normalized consolidated reporting

- Increased customer satisfaction through personalized customer interaction

- Geographic independence of both agent resources and IP-based application servers through the ubiquity of IP transport

- Carrier-quality fault tolerance and system reliability

- Scalability from single-site to multisite to network service provider services

- Rapid solution deployment many times faster than traditional TDM solutions

- Single network, eliminating the overhead of multiple diverse data, voice, and video networks

Common Issues with QoS

Voice-over-packet networks can reduce cost and save bandwidth; however, these networks have unique QoS issues that you must consider. In a circuit-switched or time-division multiplexing (TDM) environment, bandwidth is dedicated, making QoS implicit. In a packet-switched environment, all kinds of traffic are mixed in a store-and-forward manner. So, in a packet-switched environment, a need exists to devise schemes to prioritize real-time traffic.

In an integrated voice and data network, QoS is essential to ensure the same high-quality voice transmissions as in the traditional circuit-switched environment. QoS issues for voice can be handled by VoIP, VoATM, or VoFR standards, or by an internetworking device.

Delay

Delay is the time it takes for packets to travel between two endpoints. In traditional data networking, delay can be tolerated with little or no impact on network users; however, in networks carrying voice traffic, delay is potentially significant because it can affect the ability of users to carry on a telephone conversation. For example, delay can introduce pauses or gaps in the conversation, increasing the likelihood that one person will start talking before the other person is finished.

Because of the speed of network links and the limited processing power of many devices, some delay is expected. Telephone users normally accept up to about 150 milliseconds (ms) of one-way delay without noticing problems. You can measure delay by using ping tests at various times of the day with different network traffic loads (see Figure A-9). If network delay is excessive, you should reduce it before deploying a network that carries VoIP traffic.

Figure A-9 *QoS Issue: Delay*

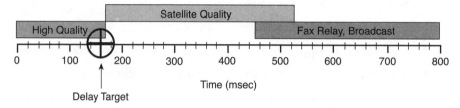

The types of delay most commonly found in today's telephony networks are as follows:

- **Propagation delay**—Propagation delay is caused by the characteristics of the speed of light traveling via fiber optic–based or copper-based media.

- **Handling delay**—Handling delay (sometimes called processing delay) defines many causes, such as compression delay, packet-switching delay, and packetization delay.

- **Serialization delay**—Serialization delay is the time it takes to actually place the bits onto an interface.

Delay can be minimized using various Cisco IOS Software QoS tools, such as low-latency queuing and Point-to-Point Protocol (PPP) fragmentation.

Jitter

Jitter relates to variable interpacket timing caused by the network that a packet traverses. Simply stated, *jitter* is the variation of packet interarrival time. Removing jitter requires collecting packets and holding them long enough to allow the slowest packets to arrive in time to be played in the correct sequence, causing an additional delay.

Figure A-10 shows that the amount of time it takes for packets A and B to send and receive is equal ($D_1 = D_2$). Packet C encounters more delay in the network ($D_3 \neq D_2$) and is received after it is expected. This is why a jitter buffer, which conceals interarrival packet delay variation, is necessary.

The jitter buffer in Cisco IOS Software is considered a dynamic queue. This queue can grow or shrink exponentially, depending on the interarrival delay variations of the voice packets. Although many vendors choose to use static jitter buffers, Cisco has determined that a well-engineered dynamic jitter buffer is the best mechanism to use for packet-based voice networks. Static jitter buffers force the jitter buffer to be either too small or too large, thereby causing the audio quality to suffer because of lost packets or excessive delays.

Figure A-10   *QoS Issue: Jitter*

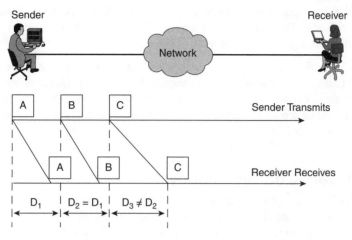

Lost Packets

Depending on the type of packet network, lost packets can be a significant problem. Because IP networks do not guarantee service, they usually exhibit a much higher incidence of lost voice packets than ATM networks.

Ideally, networks should be provisioned to have zero packet loss for applications such as voice and interactive video. For fax and modem traffic, very low loss is acceptable. Two sequential lost packets can cause a modem or fax call to drop. For voice over IP calls from person to person, a much higher percent of packet loss is possible but not desirable. To compensate, voice-over-packet software can send redundant information at the expense of bandwidth utilization.

Echo

Echo is present even in a conventional circuit-switched telephone network. This presence is typically acceptable because the round-trip delays through the network are smaller than 25 milliseconds (ms) and the echo is masked by the normal side tone that every telephone generates. Echo is caused by a conversion from two wires (local loop) to four wires and impedance mismatch.

Echo is a problem in voice-over-packet networks because the round-trip delay through the network is almost always greater than 25 ms. Hearing your own voice in the receiver after a delay of more than 25 ms can cause interruptions and can break the cadence in a conversation. For this reason, echo-cancellation techniques must be used.

Echo-cancellation techniques are used to compare voice data received from the packet network with voice data being transmitted to the packet network. For example, assume that user A is talking to user B. The speech of user A to user B is called G. When G is echoed back to user A, user A then can hear the delay several milliseconds after user A actually speaks.

To remove the echo from the line, the echo canceller keeps an inverse image of users A's speech for a certain amount of time; the echo canceller listens for the speech coming from user B, and subtracts the G to remove any echo. In packet-based networks, echo cancellers can be built into the digital signal processor (DSP) or can be done in software. Cisco includes all its echo cancellation on its DSP.

Cisco IOS Software QoS Technology

Cisco IOS Software provides QoS features and solutions for addressing the diverse needs of voice, video, and data applications. Cisco IOS QoS technology lets complex networks control and predictably service a variety of networked applications and traffic types.

The QoS features lead to efficient, predictable services for business-critical applications while ensuring high-quality voice over IP services. As shown in Figure A-11, with the QoS features enabled, the voice quality stays constant at a high level with varying network loads. In contrast to *not* implementing QoS, the voice quality goes down as the network load increases.

Figure A-11   *VoIP Traffic Quality*

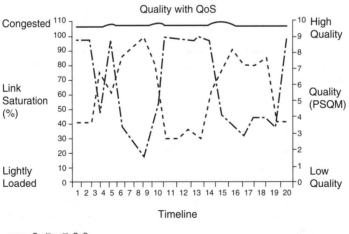

Summary

In this appendix, you learned the following key points:

- Traditionally, an enterprise has separate networks for data, voice, and video applications. Those networks usually operate in isolation and often are implemented and managed by separate teams.

- Integrated voice and data networks support a variety of applications, all of which are designed to replace leased lines at lower costs.

- VoFR is an inexpensive and easy-to-deploy service because of the wide availability of Frame Relay services.

- VoATM is an ideal transport for multiservice networks, particularly for customers who already have an ATM network installed.

- VoIP offers the capability to easily integrate advanced IP telephony features.

- A voice, video, and data–converged network could lower costs and provide enhanced quality options for voice networking.

- Cisco AVVID is an enterprise initiative for integrated data, voice, and video over a common IP transport.

- An important facet of converged networking is the enabling of new applications, such as desktop IP telephony, unified messaging, and the Cisco IP Contact Center.

- The Cisco IP Contact Center (IPCC) solution combines data and voice technologies to facilitate geographically independent multimedia customer interaction.

- The use of QoS techniques throughout the network enables effective transmission of voice-over-packet switched networks. Through careful use of QoS techniques, network designers can overcome these quality issues and produce circuit-quality voice at a fraction of the cost.

Review Exercises

1 The functions of voice-capable routers include which of the following:

   a. They can function as a local phone system for interoffice calls.

   b. They can route calls within an enterprise network.

   c. They can route incoming and outing calls through PBX.

   d. All of the above.

2 VoFR has which of the following features?

    a. Provides popular transport for multiservice networks

    b. Consolidates voice and voice-band data (including fax and analog modems) with data services

    c. Provides cost-effective service that support bursty traffic well

    d. All of the above

3 True or false: ATM is an ideal transport for multiservice networks such as VoATM.

    a. True

    b. False

4 True or false: At the data link layer, voice over IP (VoIP) packets can use any Layer 2 encapsulations, such as the Point-to-Point Protocol (PPP).

    a. True

    b. False

5 Match each voice-over-data technology with its associated limitation.

    a. Tops out at T1/E1 speeds

    b. Has limited services and costly equipment

    c. Is the least deterministic

        Frame Relay   a b c

        ATM   a b c

        IP   a b c

6 Which of the following is *not* a building block of Cisco AVVID?

    a. Infrastructure

    b. Cables

    c. Applications

    d. Clients

7 Which of the following is a *business* benefit of the Cisco IPCC?

    a. Seamless migration path to IP-based voice applications

    b. Consistent service standards across diverse media channels

    c. Increased customer satisfaction through personalized customer interaction

    d. Intelligent contact management

8 Utilizing IP as the ubiquitous transport does *not* offer which of the following gains to enterprises?

 a. Bandwidth efficiency

 b. Higher overall bandwidth requirements

 c. Ease of management

 d. Capability to deploy new applications rapidly

9 Which of the following is true of a data, voice, and video–converged network utilizing IP as the transport?

 a. Higher costs

 b. Enhanced quality options for voice networking

 c. Decreased bandwidth

 d. Limited capability in adapting new applications

10 Unified messaging combines which of the following message types into a single application suite?

 a. E-mail

 b. Voice mail

 c. Fax

 d. All of the above

11 True or false: Traditionally, an enterprise has separate networks for voice, video, and data applications.

 a. True

 b. False

12 Which problem does an echo canceller remedy?

 a. Packet loss

 b. Echo

 c. Jitter

 d. Delay

APPENDIX B

Answers to Review Questions

Chapter 1

1 What is the main circuit board of a computer?

   a. PC subsystem

   b. **Motherboard**

   c. Backplane

   d. Computer memory

2 What are PCMCIA slots?

   a. **Slots used in laptops**

   b. Slots used as expansion slots in all computers

   c. Expansion slots for a NIC card

   d. Slots for certain specialized devices

3 How does a network card communicate with the network?

   a. **Serial connection**

   b. Parallel connection

   c. Backplane

   d. None of the above

4 Which of the following correctly describes the resources needed before you install a NIC?

   a. Knowledge of how the network card is configured

   b. Knowledge of how to use the network card diagnostics

   c. Capability to resolve hardware resource conflicts

   d. **All of the above**

5   Match the following terms with their definitions:

1. bit

2. byte

3. kbps

4. MHz

a. The smallest unit of data in a computer

b. A standard measurement of the rate of data being transferred over a network connection

c. A unit of frequency; the rate of change in the state or cycle in a sound wave, alternating current, or other cyclical waveform

d. A unit of measure used to describe the size of a data file, the amount of space on a disk or other storage medium, or the amount of data being transferred over a network

   Answer: **1. a, 2. d, 3. b, 4. c**

6   What is the decimal number 151 in binary?

a. 10100111

b. **10010111**

c. 10101011

d. 10010011

7   What is the binary number 11011010 in decimal?

a. 186

b. 202

c. **218**

d. 222

8   Convert the binary number 0010000100000000 to a hexadecimal number.

a. **0x2100**

b. 0x2142

c. 0x0082

d. 0x0012

9 Convert the hexadecimal number 0x2101 to a binary number.

   a. **0010 0001 0000 0001**

   b. 0001 0000 0001 0010

   c. 0100 1000 0000 1000

   d. 1000 0000 1000 0100

Chapter 2

1 Match each of the following terms with the correct definition:

   1. LAN

   2. WAN

   3. Protocol

   4. Physical topology

   a. The layout or physical shape of the network

   b. A network that is confined to a limited geographic area

   c. A network that spans wide geographic areas by using serial links to connect computers in different cities, in different countries, or even on different continents

   d. A set of rules by which computers communicate

   Answer: **1. b, 2. c, 3. d, 4. a**

2 Which of the following is an example of a network application?

   a. **E-mail**

   b. Word processor

   c. Spreadsheet

   d. Database

3 Which of the following does not describe a main-office network?

   a. A main office is where everyone is connected via a local-area network (LAN) and
   where the bulk of corporate information is located.

   b. **A main office can have only up to 500 people who depend on network access to
   do their jobs.**

   c. A main office might have several LANs, or it might be a campus that contains several
   buildings.

   d. In a main office, it is common to see a high-speed backbone LAN as well as a legacy
   data center with mainframe computers and applications.

4 What is the OSI model?

  a. A conceptual framework that specifies how information travels through networks

  b. A model that describes how data makes its way from one application program to another throughout a network

  c. A conceptual framework that specifies which network functions occur at each layer

  d. **All of the above**

5 Which of the following is the correct order for the OSI reference model layers?

1: Physical	2: Data link	3: Transport
4: Network	5: Presentation	6: Session
7: Application		

1: Physical	**2: Data link**	**3: Network**
4: Transport	**5: Session**	**6: Presentation**
7: Application		

1: Physical	2: Data link	3: Network
4: Session	5: Transport	6: Application
7: Presentation		

1: Physical	2: Network	3: Session
4: Data link	5: Transport	6: Application
7: Presentation		

6 Which layer of the OSI model handles physical addressing, network topology, network access, error notification, ordered delivery of frames, and flow control?

  a. The physical layer

  b. **The data link layer**

  c. The transport layer

  d. The network layer

7 Which of the following best defines encapsulation?

  a. Segmenting data so that it flows uninterrupted through the network

  b. Compressing data so that it moves faster

  c. Moving data in groups so that it stays together

  d. **Wrapping data in a particular protocol header**

8 An e-mail message is sent from Host A to Host B on a LAN. Before this message can be sent, the data must be encapsulated. Which of the following best describes what happens after a packet is constructed?

    a. The packet is transmitted along the medium.

    b. **The packet is put into a frame.**

    c. The packet is segmented into frames.

    d. The packet is converted to binary format.

9 In the TCP/IP model, which layer deals with reliability, flow control, and error correction?

    a. Application

    b. **Transport**

    c. Internet

    d. Network access

10 Which of the following regarding TCP/IP is true?

    a. TCP/IP combines the OSI data link and session layer issues into its application layer.

    b. **TCP/IP combines the OSI data link and physical layers into one layer.**

    c. TCP/IP combines OSI network and application layers into one network layer.

    d. TCP/IP combines the bottom four layers of the OSI model into one Internet layer.

Chapter 3

1 Repeaters can provide a simple solution for which of the following problems?

    a. Too many types of incompatible equipment on the network

    b. Too much traffic on a network

    c. Too-slow data-transmission rates

    d. **Too many nodes or not enough cable**

2 What is one disadvantage of using a hub?

    a. A hub cannot extend the network operating distance.

    b. **A hub cannot filter network traffic.**

    c. A hub cannot send weakened signals over a network.

    d. A hub cannot amplify weakened signals.

3 Which of the following is true concerning a bridge and its forwarding decisions?

    a. Bridges operate at OSI Layer 2 and use IP addresses to make decisions.

    b. Bridges operate at OSI Layer 3 and use IP addresses to make decisions.

    c. **Bridges operate at OSI Layer 2 and use MAC addresses to make decisions.**

    d. Bridges operate at OSI Layer 3 and use MAC addresses to make decisions.

4 Which of the following is true concerning the function of a switch?

    a. Switches increase the sizes of collision domains.

    b. **Switches combine the connectivity of a hub with the traffic regulation of a bridge.**

    c. Switches combine the connectivity of a hub with the traffic direction of a router.

    d. Switches perform Layer 4 path selection.

5 What does a router route?

    a. Layer 1 bits

    b. Layer 2 frames

    c. **Layer 3 packets**

    d. Layer 4 segments

6 Which of the following statements is true?

    a. A gateway is a special-purpose device that performs an application layer conversion of information from one protocol stack to another.

    b. The Cisco AS5400 Series Universal Gateway offers unparalleled capacity in only two rack units, with universal port data, voice, wireless, and fax services on any port at any time.

    c. A DSLAM serves as the point of interface between a number of subscriber premises and the carrier network.

    d. **All of the above.**

7 What are the functions of AAA servers?

    a. To ensure that only authenticated users can get into the network.

    b. To ensure that the users are allowed access only to the resources they need.

    c. To ensure that records are kept of everything the authentic users do after the users are allowed entry.

    d. **All of the above.**

8 Which of the following is a function of firewalls? (Select all that apply.)

   a. **Software-based**

   b. **Hardware-based**

   c. **Filter traffic**

   d. Layer 2 devices

   e. None of the above

Chapter 4

1 Which of the following correctly describes networking topology?

   a. **The network topology defines the way in which the computers, printers, network devices, and other devices are connected.**

   b. Networks can have either a physical or a logical topology.

   c. A physical topology describes the paths that signals travel from one point on the network to another.

   d. A logical topology defines the layout of the device and media.

2 Which of the following statements best describes a bus topology?

   a. All of its nodes connect directly to a central point.

   b. **All of its nodes connect directly to one physical link.**

   c. All of its nodes connect to each other.

   d. All of its nodes connect to exactly two other nodes.

3 Which topology has all its nodes connected directly to one center point and has no other connections between nodes?

   a. Bus

   b. Ring

   c. **Star**

   d. Mesh

4 What is the purpose of the second ring in a dual-ring network?

   a. Duplex

   b. Signaling

   c. **Redundancy**

   d. None of the above

5 In a complete, or full-mesh topology, every node:

    a. **Is linked directly to every other node.**

    b. Is connected to two central nodes.

    c. Is linked wirelessly to a central node.

    d. None of the above.

Chapter 5

1 Which of the following is *not* one of the recognized IEEE sublayers?

    a. Media Access Control

    b. **Data Link Control**

    c. Logical Link Control

    d. None of the above

2 What is the name of the method used in Ethernet that explains how Ethernet works?

    a. TCP/IP

    b. **CSMA/CD**

    c. CMDA/CS

    d. CSMA/CA

3 Fast Ethernet supports up to what transfer rate?

    a. 5 Mbps

    b. 10 Mbps

    c. **100 Mbps**

    d. 1000 Mbps

4 Identify two Gigabit Ethernet cable specifications.

    a. 1000BASE-TX

    b. 1000BASE-FX

    c. **1000BASE-CS**

    d. **1000BASE-LX**

    e. 1000BASE-X

Chapter 6

1 Which of the following statements best describes a WAN?

a. **Connects LANs that are separated by a large geographic area**

b. Connects workstations, terminals, and other devices in a metropolitan area

c. Connects LANs within a large building

d. Connects workstations, terminals, and other devices within a building

2 What is a group of networks that are networked to each other called?

a. **An internet**

b. A WAN

c. A LAN

d. A workgroup

3 A CSU/DSU is generally used as what type of equipment?

a. Router

b. DTE

c. Switch

d. **DCE**

4 DCE or DTE equipment is found at which layer of the OSI reference model?

a. Network layer

b. Data link layer

c. **Physical layer**

d. Transport layer

5 Which of the following is a circuit-switched WAN technology?

a. Frame Relay

b. **ISDN**

c. PPP

d. ATM

Chapter 7

1 Which of the following statements correctly describes a MAN?

   a. A MAN is a network that connects workstations, peripherals, terminals, and other devices in a single building.

   b. A MAN is a network that serves users across a broad geographic area and that often uses transmission devices provided by common carriers.

   c. **A MAN is a network that spans a metropolitan area such as a city or suburban area.**

   d. A MAN is a network that is interconnected by routers and other devices and that functions as a single network.

2 Which of the following does *not* correctly describe the features of content networks?

   a. Content networks accelerate and improve the use of rich content and eliminate the stream of rich content on the infrastructure.

   b. Content networks utilize a collection of content engines located close to the audience to distribute the content.

   c. **The content network was designed to accelerate the delivery of information over the MAN infrastructure.**

   d. The Cisco content networks solution is a tiered solution.

3 What service offers secure, reliable connectivity over a shared public network infrastructure?

   a. Internet

   b. **Virtual private network**

   c. Virtual public network

   d. Wide-area network

4 What links remote and branch offices to a headquarter's internal network over a shared infrastructure?

   a. Access VPNs

   b. **Intranet VPNs**

   c. Extranet VPNs

   d. Internet VPNs

5 What is the name for the part of the company's LAN that is made available to select parties such as suppliers, customers, or partners?

   a. The Internet

   b. **The extranet**

   c. The intranet

   d. The LAN

6 Which of the following is *not* one of the features of a storage-area network?

   a. SANs enable concurrent access of disk or tape arrays, providing enhanced system performance.

   b. SANs provide a reliable disaster-recovery solution.

   c. SANs are scalable.

   d. **SANs minimize the system and data availability.**

Chapter 8

1 What is the maximum cable length for STP?

   a. 100 feet

   b. 150 feet

   c. **100 meters**

   d. 1000 meters

2 Which connector does UTP use?

   a. STP

   b. BNC

   c. **RJ-45**

   d. RJ-69

3 What is an advantage that coaxial cable has over STP or UTP?

   a. It is capable of achieving 10 Mbps to 100 Mbps.

   b. It is inexpensive.

   c. **It can run for a longer distance unboosted.**

   d. None of the above.

4 A _____ fiber-optic cable transmits multiple streams of LED-generated light.

   a. **multimode**

   b. multichannel

   c. multiphase

   d. None of the above

5 Wireless communication uses which of the following to transmit data between devices on a LAN?

   a. **Radio frequencies**

   b. LED-generated light

   c. Fiber optics

   d. None of the above

6 What is one advantage of using fiber-optic cable in networks?

   a. It is inexpensive.

   b. It is easy to install.

   c. It is an industry standard and is available at any electronics store.

   d. **It is capable of higher data rates than either coaxial or twisted-pair cable.**

Chapter 9

1 Which of the following is an 802.3u specification?

   a. 10BASE-F

   b. 10BASE-T

   c. **100BASE-TX**

   d. 1000BASE-CX

2 Which of the following is the most appropriate choice for Ethernet connectivity?

   a. Use 10-Mbps Ethernet as a connection between server and LAN.

   b. Use Gigabit Ethernet as the link at the user level to provide good performance.

   c. **Use Fast Ethernet as a link between the user level and network devices to support the aggregate traffic from each Ethernet segment on the access link.**

   d. None of the above.

3 Which standards body created the cables and connector specification used to support Ethernet implementation?

   a. ISO

   b. ANSI

   c. **EIA/TIA**

   d. IETF

4 Which of the following statements does *not* correctly describe a media connector?

   a. **An RJ-45 connector is an 8-pin connector used mainly for terminating coaxial cable.**

   b. An AUI is a 15-pin connector used between a NIC and an Ethernet cable.

   c. The GBIC is a transceiver that converts serial electric currents to optical signals, and vice versa.

   d. None of the above.

5 For which of the following would you *not* need to provide a crossover cable?

   a. Connecting uplinks between switches

   b. **Connecting routers to switches**

   c. Connecting hubs to switches

   d. None of the above

Chapter 10

1 Which of the following is not a physical WAN implementation?

   a. DSL

   b. ISDN

   c. Frame Relay

   d. **Ethernet**

2 What type of data-transmission method is used by a WAN?

   a. Parallel

   b. **Serial**

   c. Single

   d. None of above

3 What best describes a DCE?

    a. User device at the end of a network

    b. Equipment that serves as the data source or destination

    c. Physical devices such as protocol translators and multiplexers

    d. **Devices that make up the network end of the user-to-network interface**

4 Which of the following media is used to interconnect the ISDN BRI port to the service-provider device?

    a. **Category 5 UTP straight-through**

    b. Category 5 UTP crossover

    c. Coaxial

    d. Fiber-optic

5 What type of connector is used for DSL connection?

    a. RJ-45

    b. **RJ-11**

    c. F

    d. DB-9

6 What type of connector is used to connect a router and a cable system?

    a. RJ-45

    b. RJ-11

    c. **F**

    d. AUI

7 What type of cable is used to connect a terminal and a console port?

    a. Straight-through

    b. **Rollover**

    c. Crossover

    d. Coaxial

Chapter 11

1 What is the maximum distance for Thicknet without using a repeater?

   a. 185 m (606.95 feet)

   b. 250 m (820.2 feet)

   c. **500 m (1640.4 feet)**

   d. 800 m (2624.64 feet)

2 Which of the following does not describe a hub?

   a. It works at the OSI model physical layer.

   b. It is a passive device.

   c. It is also known as an Ethernet concentrator.

   d. **It filters the traffic passed through it.**

3 What term is used if two or more stations on a network try to transmit simultaneously?

   a. Propagation

   b. Retransmission

   c. **Collision**

   d. Backoff

4 Which of the following is not a common method of transmission in a network?

   a. Unicast

   b. **Bicast**

   c. Broadcast

   d. Multicast

5 Which of the following is *not* a characteristic of hub-based LANs?

   a. All resources are shared.

   b. **Security is very high within each segment.**

   c. Adding, moving, and changing users in a hub-based network is easier than in Thinnet and Thicknet.

   d. Desktop connections are wired to centralized closets.

6 Which of the following is *not* a feature of bridges?

   a. They operate at Layer 2 of the OSI model.

   b. They are more intelligent than hubs.

   c. **They do not make any forwarding decisions.**

   d. They build and maintain address tables.

7 Which of the following statements is true of microsegmentation?

   a. **Each workstation gets its own dedicated segment through the network.**

   b. All the workstations are grouped as one segment.

   c. Microsegmentation increases the number of collisions on a network.

   d. None of the above.

8 Which of the following statements is true?

   a. In a hubbed network, multiple devices can send data at the same time.

   b. In a switched network, only one device can send data at a time.

   c. **Switches can improve the traffic flow of a network.**

   d. None of the above.

9 Which of the following is *not* a cause of network congestion?

   a. Too many users

   b. Most of the users accessing the same server

   c. Too many bandwidth-intensive applications installed

   d. **Too many segments**

10 Which of the following technologies is the most commonly implemented LAN today?

   a. Hubbed network

   b. **Switched network**

   c. Shared network

   d. None of the above

Chapter 12

1   Which of the following is *not* a feature of microsegmentation?

   a. It enables dedicated access.

   b. It supports multiple conversations at any given time.

   c. It increases the capacity for each workstation connected to the network.

   d. **It increases collisions.**

2   Which of the following is used by LAN switches for making the forwarding decision?

   a. IP address

   b. **MAC address**

   c. Network address

   d. Host address

3   Which of the following is a feature of full-duplex transmission?

   a. It offers two 10- to 1-Gbps data-transmission paths.

   b. It doubles bandwidth between nodes.

   c. It provides collision-free transmission.

   d. **All of the above.**

4   The three types of switching methods are _____, _____ , and _____.

   Answers: **cut through, store and foward, and fragment free**

5   The Spanning-Tree Protocol allows which of the following?

   a. Bridges to communicate Layer 3 information

   b. **A redundant network path without suffering the effects of loops in the network**

   c. Static network paths for loop prevention

   d. None of the above

6   Which of the following is *not* one of the STP port states?

   a. Blocking

   b. Learning

   c. Listening

   d. **Transmitting**

Chapter 13

1 Which of the following is true for LAN switches?

  a. They repair network fragments known as microsegments.

  b. **They are very high-speed multiport bridges.**

  c. Lower bandwidth makes up for higher latency.

  d. They require new network interface cards on attached hosts.

2 What does ASIC stand for?

  a. Application-specific interface card

  b. Asymmetrical integrated circuit

  c. **Application-specific integrated circuit**

  d. Automatically scalable interchange circuit

3 Which of the following best describes Layer 3 switching?

  a. Hardware-based bridging

  b. **Hardware-based routing**

  c. Software-based switching

  d. Software-based routing

4 How does the packet-switching function of a router differ from that of a Layer 3 switch?

  a. The router uses network layer information to determine the forwarding path, whereas the Layer 3 switch uses data link layer information.

  b. **The router performs its operation in software, whereas the Layer 3 switch uses hardware.**

  c. The router can implement QoS, whereas the Layer 3 switch cannot.

  d. The router operates faster than the Layer 3 switch, but the switch is more scalable.

5 Using Layer 4 switching enables prioritization of traffic based on _____.

  a. **the application**

  b. source and destination

  c. source only

  d. the network layer protocol

Chapter 14

 1 Which of the following is a limitation of traditional, shared LANs?

    a. Routers are needed to connect segments.

    b. Shared LAN networks offer very little security.

    c. Users usually are bound by their physical locations.

    d. **All of the above.**

 2 A VLAN can be thought of as _____.

    a. a broadcast domain

    b. an IP network or subnetwork

    c. a Layer 3 network

    d. **All of the above**

 3 Which of the following statements is true of using VLANs?

    a. Switches do not need to be configured.

    b. The broadcast domain is increased.

    c. **Physical boundaries that prevent user groupings can be removed.**

    d. None of the above.

 4 Which of the following is *not* a beneficial effect of adding a VLAN?

    a. Broadcasts can be controlled.

    b. Confidential data can be protected.

    c. **Relocation of users is not easy.**

    d. Administration costs can be reduced.

 5 Why is a trunk used?

    a. **To carry traffic from multiple VLANs**

    b. To carry traffic from a single VLAN

    c. To carry network-management traffic

    d. To connect a user PC to a switch port

 6 Which of the following is *not* an approach for establishing VLAN membership?

    a. Port driven

    b. MAC address driven

    c. Layer 3 information driven

    d. **Device type driven**

7 What is port-based VLAN membership also known as?

    a. Local VLANs

    b. Dynamic VLANs

    c. Geographic VLANs

    d. **Static VLANs**

8 Which of the following is true of a MAC address-based VLAN?

    a. **Offers flexibility**

    b. Reduces overhead

    c. Improves performance, scalability, and administration

    d. None of the above

9 Inter-VLAN connectivity can be achieved in two ways: _____ connectivity and _____ connectivity.

    Answers: physical; logical

10 Which protocol is Cisco proprietary and designed to carry traffic from multiple VLANs?

    a. **ISL**

    b. IEEE 802.1Q

    c. HDLC

    d. IEEE 802.3

Chapter 15

1 Which of the following statements best describes a protocol?

    a. A tool that lets Macintosh and PC computers communicate with each other

    b. A universal translator that allows different kinds of computers to share data

    c. **A standard set of rules and conventions that determine how computers communicate with each other across networks**

    d. The language that all the computers on a network must use to communicate with each other

2 Which of the following statements best describes TCP/IP?

   a. **It is a suite of protocols that define rules for how packets or information is moved across a Internet.**

   b. It is a suite of protocols that allow LANs to connect into WANs.

   c. It is a suite of protocols that allow for data transmission across a multitude of networks.

   d. It is a suite of protocols that allow different devices to be shared by interconnected networks.

3 Which of the following statements is true of IP?

   a. It determines where packets are routed based on their source address.

   b. **It breaks packets into smaller packets, sends the packets to the destination, and reassembles them.**

   c. It is a Layer 4 protocol.

   d. All of the above.

4 Which of the following is *not* a characteristic of TCP?

   a. **TCP is a connectionless protocol.**

   b. TCP is reliable.

   c. TCP divides outgoing messages into segments and reassembles messages at the destination station.

   d. TCP resends anything that is not received by the destination station.

5 Which of the following protocols was developed by Sun Microsystems and allows remote file access across a network?

   a. SMTP

   b. TFTP

   c. **NFS**

   d. SNMP

Chapter 16

1 Which of the following is a basic service of the transport layer?

    a. To provide reliability by using sequence numbers and acknowledgments

    b. To segment upper-layer application data

    c. To establish end-to-end operations

    d. **All of the above**

2 Which of the following phrases best describes flow control?

    a. A device at the destination side that controls the flow of incoming data

    b. A buffer at the source side that monitors the outflow of data

    c. **A technique that ensures that the source does not overwhelm the destination with data**

    d. A suspension of transmission until the data in the source buffers has been processed

3 Which of the following statements best describes positive acknowledgment?

    a. **Positive acknowledgment requires a recipient to communicate with the source, sending back an acknowledgment message when it receives data.**

    b. If a recipient does not receive one of the packets, it sends a negative acknowledgment to the sender with the numbers of the packets received.

    c. Positive acknowledgment is the retransmission of guaranteed and reliable delivery of data.

    d. If a sender does not receive a negative acknowledgment within a certain time, the sender retransmits the data.

4 What layer do TCP and UDP reside in?

    a. Network layer

    b. Data link layer

    c. **Transport layer**

    d. Internet layer

5 What does the Window field in a TCP segment indicate?

    a. Number of 32-bit words in the header

    b. Number of the called port

    c. Number used to ensure correct sequencing of the arriving data

    d. **Number of octets that the device is willing to accept**

6 What do TCP and UDP use to keep track of different conversations crossing a network at the same time?

a. **Port numbers**

b. IP addresses

c. MAC addresses

d. Sequence numbers

7 Which range of port numbers is unregulated?

a. Below 255

b. Between 256 and 512

c. Between 256 and 1023

d. **1024 and above**

8 How does TCP synchronize a connection between the source and the destination before data transmission?

a. Two-way handshake

b. **Three-way handshake**

c. Four-way handshake

d. Holton functions

9 What do the TCP sequence and acknowledgment numbers do?

a. They break segments into their binary coefficients, number them sequentially, and send them to their destination, where the sender acknowledges their recipient.

b. They break down messages into datagrams that are numbered and then sent to a host according to the sequence set by the source TCP.

c. They provide a system for sequencing datagrams at the source and acknowledging them at the destination.

d. **They provide sequencing of segments with a forward reference acknowledgment, number segments before transmission, and reassemble the segments into a complete message.**

10 What flow-control method does TCP implement?

a. Acknowledgment

b. Buffering

c. **Windowing**

d. Port numbers

Chapter 17

1   Which of the following protocols operate at the TCP/IP Internet layer?

a. IP

b. ICMP

c. ARP

d. **All of the above**

2   Which of the following *best* describes TTL?

a. Field in the datagram header that determines how long the data is valid

b. **Field in the IP datagram that indicates how long a packet is considered valid**

c. Field within an IP datagram that indicates the upper-layer protocol sending the datagram

d. Field in a datagram header that indicates when the next data packet will arrive

3   What is the function of Protocol field in an IP datagram?

a. To specify the application layer protocol

b. To specify the physical layer protocol

c. **To specify the upper-layer (transport layer) protocol**

d. To specify the lower-layer (data link layer) protocol

4   What does the acronym ICMP stand for?

a. Internetwork Connection Model Protocol

b. Internet Connection Monitor Protocol

c. **Internet Control Message Protocol**

d. Internetwork Control Mode Protocol

5   What is the purpose of ICMPs?

a. They put the internetwork in control mode so that protocols can be set up.

b. They are messages that the network uses to monitor connection protocols.

c. They are standard binary messages that act as model internetwork protocols.

d. **They are messages carried in IP datagrams used to send error and control messages.**

6 What is the function of ARP?

    a. It is used to map a given MAC address to an IP address.

    b. It is used to develop a cached address resource table.

    c. **It is used to map an IP address to a MAC address.**

    d. It sends a broadcast message looking for the router address

7 What is the function of the RARP?

    a. **It is a protocol in the TCP/IP stack that provides a method for finding IP addresses based on MAC addresses.**

    b. It is a protocol used to map a 32-bit IP address to a MAC address.

    c. It is a protocol used to develop a cached address resource table for the router.

    d. It a protocol that is used for maintaining the ARP cache in an IP host.

8 Which of the following statements is true?

    a. All that is required using DHCP is an undefined range of IP addresses on a DHCP server.

    b. **Unlike BOOTP, DHCP allows a host to obtain an IP address quickly and dynamically.**

    c. BOOTP is designed to provide dynamic address assignment.

    d. With BOOTP, you cannot create a configuration file that specifies the parameters for each device.

Chapter 18

1 The IP address consists of two parts: _____ and _____.

    a. **Network number and host number**

    b. Host number and MAC address

    c. Network number and MAC address

    d. Network number and subnetwork address

2 How many bits are in an IPv4 address?

    a. 16

    b. **32**

    c. 48

    d. 64

3 In a Class B address, which octets are the host number portion and are assigned locally?

    a. The first octet is assigned locally.

    b. The first and second octets are assigned locally.

    c. The second and third octets are assigned locally.

    d. **The third and fourth octets are assigned locally.**

4 The following address is of which class? 129.21.89.75

    a. Class A

    b. **Class B**

    c. Class C

    d. Class D

5 Which of the following is true of a directed broadcast address?

    a. A directed broadcast address is an address that has all 0s in the Host field.

    b. Any IP address in a network can be used as a broadcast address.

    c. **A directed broadcast address is an address that has all 1s in the Host field.**

    d. None of the above.

6 According to RFC 1918, which is a private Internet address?

    a. **10.215.34.124**

    b. 192.32.146.23

    c. 172.34.221.18

    d. 119.12.73.215

7 How many bits are there in an IPv6 address?

    a. 32

    b. 48

    c. 96

    d. **128**

8 Which of the following is a feature of CIDR?

    a. Classful addressing

    b. No supernetting

    c. More entries in the routing table

    d. **Route aggregation**

Chapter 19

1 Originally, the Internet Protocol used how many levels of hierarchy addressing?

a. **Two**

b. Three

c. Four

d. Five

2 How many bits are in a subnet mask?

a. 16

b. **32**

c. 48

d. 64

3 What is the primary function of a subnet mask?

a. **To determine which part of the IP address is the network/subnetwork part and which part is the host part**

b. To conceal outside networks from subnetworks

c. To determine the numbers of subnetworks that can be created

d. To determine the numbers of hosts within a subnetwork

4 What is the minimum number of bits that should be borrowed to form a subnet?

a. 1

b. **2**

c. 3

d. 4

5 If you were going to borrow 5 bits to create a subnet mask for a Class B address, what would the subnet mask be?

a. 255.255.0.0

b. 255.255.192.0

c. **255.255.248.0**

d. 255.255.254.0

6 How many host addresses can be used in a Class C network?

   a. 253

   b. **254**

   c. 255

   d. 256

7 How many bits can be borrowed to create a subnet for a Class C network?

   a. 2

   b. 4

   c. **6**

   d. 8

8 What is the largest number of host bits you can borrow from a Class A address for subnetting?

   a. 24

   b. **22**

   c. 16

   d. 14

Chapter 20

1 What function allows routers to evaluate available routes to a destination and to establish the preferred handling of a packet?

   a. Data linkage

   b. **Path determination**

   c. SDLC interface protocol

   d. Frame Relay

2 Which best describes a routed protocol?

   a. **Provides enough information in its network layer address to allow a packet to be forwarded from host to host**

   b. Provides information necessary to pass data packets up to the next highest network layer

   c. Allows routers to communicate with other routers to maintain and update address tables

   d. Allows routers to bind MAC and IP address together

3 Routing involves which of the following basic activities? (Choose all that apply.)

    a. **Determining optimal routing paths**

    b. Determining the source MAC address

    c. **Transporting information packets**

    d. Configuring router interfaces

    e. Determining the source IP address

4 Which of the following contains routing information that helps a router in determining the routing path?

    a. IP address

    b. MAC address

    c. **Routing table**

    d. Routing protocol

5 Which of the following is *not* a common routing metric?

    a. Delay

    b. Bandwidth

    c. **Length**

    d. Cost

6 Administrative distance defines the _____ of a routing protocol.

    a. Scalability

    b. Flexibility

    c. Speed

    d. **Reliability**

Chapter 21

1 Which of the following is an example of an EGP?

    a. OSPF

    b. RIP

    c. **BGP**

    d. EIGRP

2 What are IGPs used for?

   a. To set up a compatibility infrastructure between networks

   b. To communicate between autonomous systems

   c. To transmit between nodes on a network

   d. **To deliver routing information within a single autonomous system**

3 Which best describes a distance-vector protocol?

   a. **It determines the direction and distance to any link in the internetwork.**

   b. Each router maintains a complex database of internetwork topology information.

   c. It is computationally complex.

   d. It is a method of routing that prevents loops and minimizes counting to infinity.

4 Which of the following best describes link-state algorithms?

   a. They determine distance and direction to any link on the internetwork.

   b. They require minimal computation.

   c. **They re-create the topology of the entire internetwork.**

   d. They use little network overhead and reduce overall traffic.

5 In the IP RIP routing protocol, how often are routing updates sent?

   a. **Every 30 seconds**

   b. Every 60 seconds

   c. Every 90 seconds

   d. Only when the administrator directs the router to do so

6 By default, which of the following is a routing metric used by IGRP?

   a. **Bandwidth and delay**

   b. MTU size and load

   c. Hop count and delay

   d. Reliability and load

7 Which of the following is *not* a basic component of EIGRP?

   a. **Protocol-independent modules**

   b. DUAL finite-state machine

   c. Neighbor discover and recovery

   d. Reliable Transport Protocol

8 Which of the following is *not* a feature of OSPF?

   a. Has fast convergence

   b. Processes updates efficiently

   c. **Selects paths based on hop count**

   d. Supports VLSM

9 Which of the following is true of IS-IS?

   a. IS-IS is a dynamic link-state routing protocol.

   b. Integrated IS-IS is an implementation of the IS-IS protocol for routing multiple network protocols.

   c. Integrated IS-IS can be used for both IP routing and ISO CLNS routing.

   d. **All of the above.**

10 BGP is an example of which type of protocol?

   a. Internal gateway protocol

   b. **External gateway protocol**

   c. Routed protocol

   d. None of the above

Chapter 22

1 Which of the following is a type of physical layer multiplexing?

   a. TDM

   b. FDM

   c. WDM

   d. **All of the above**

2 Which of the following best describes a WAN?

   a. **Connects LANs that are separated by a large geographic area**

   b. Connects workstations, terminals, and other devices in a metropolitan area

   c. Connects LANs within a large building

   d. Connects workstation, terminals, and other devices within a building

3 Which of the following is an example of a circuit-switching protocol?

  a. **ISDN**

  b. Frame Relay

  c. PPP

  d. HDLC

4 A leased line is a _____ link that provides a single, pre-established WAN communication path from the customer to a remote network.

  a. **point-to-point**

  b. point-to-multipoint

  c. analog

  d. digital

5 How does Frame Relay handle multiple conversations on the same physical connection?

  a. **Frame Relay multiplexes the circuits.**

  b. Multiple conversations are not allowed.

  c. Frame Relay duplexes the conversation.

  d. Frame Relay uses WDM.

6 Which of the following is *not* true about ATM technology?

  a. It is capable of transferring voice, video, and data.

  b. ATM is used primarily in enterprise LAN backbones or WAN links.

  c. It is based on a cell-based architecture rather than on a frame-based architecture.

  d. **ATM cells are always a fixed length of 35 bytes, whereas the sizes of frames and packets vary.**

7 Name the family of very high-speed physical layer technologies that offers a series of data rates with special designations, implemented at different transmission rates ranging from 51.85 Mbps to 40 Gbps.

  a. ADSL

  b. ATM

  c. **SONET**

  d. ISDN

Chapter 23

1 Which of the following statements pertaining to ISDN is true?

   a. **The ISDN BRI offers two B channels and one D channel.**

   b. The D channel, operating at 16 kbps, is meant to carry user data.

   c. The ISDN BRI offers 23 B channels and 1 D channel in North America.

   d. The total bit rate of the ISDN BRI is 2.533 Mbps.

2 Which protocol does PPP use for establishing and maintaining point-to-point connections?

   a. HDLC

   b. **LCP**

   c. LAPD

   d. Cisco IETF

3 What type of handshaking occurs when PAP is your selected authentication when using PPP?

   a. One-way

   b. **Two-way**

   c. Three-way

   d. Four-way

4 What type of handshaking occurs when CHAP is your selected authentication when using PPP?

   a. One-way

   b. Two-way

   c. **Three-way**

   d. Four-way

5 What is the default encapsulation type for serial interfaces on a Cisco router?

   a. PPP

   b. **HDLC**

   c. Frame Relay

   d. X.25

Chapter 24

  1 Which of the following is true of analog modems?

    a. They allow data transfer between two computers over the PSTN.

    b. They convert analog signals to digital bit streams.

    c. They convert digital data to analog signals.

    d. **All of the above.**

  2 Which of the following is the most common type of modem?

    a. **Internal**

    b. External

    c. PC card

    d. All of the above

  3 Which of the following cable standards allows a 56 kbps downstream data-transmission rate?

    a. V.32

    b. V.34

    c. V.42

    d. **V.90**

  4 What was the first true worldwide standard for modems that allowed 2400 bps at 600 baud?

    a. V.12

    b. **V.22bis**

    c. V.32

    d. V.90

Chapter 25

  1 Which of the following media is used by DSL to transport data?

    a. Existing coaxial cable TV lines

    b. **Existing twisted-pair telephone lines**

    c. Existing Ethernet lines

    d. Wireless transmission

2 What are the two basic types of DSL technology?

   a. Downstream DSL and upstream DSL

   b. xDSL and yDSL

   c. **Asymmetric DSL and symmetric DSL**

   d. None of the above

3 Which of the following standards organizations and industries have contributed to the evolution of DSL?

   a. ANSI

   b. ITU-T

   c. ETSI

   d. **All of the above**

4 Which of the following Layer 2 protocols is used often by DSL?

   a. HDLC

   b. IPX

   c. **PPP**

   d. LLC

5 Which of the following is *not* one of the benefits of DSL?

   a. DSL service can be added incrementally in any area.

   b. DSL is backward compatible with conventional analog voice.

   c. **DSL service has no distance limitations.**

   d. DSL is an always-on technology.

Chapter 26

1 Which of the following media are used by cable modem to transport data?

   a. **Existing coaxial cable TV lines**

   b. Existing twisted-pair telephone lines

   c. Existing Ethernet lines

   d. None of the above

2 Which of the following best describes upstream?

    a. **Data flowing from the user to the network**

    b. Data flowing from the network to the user

    c. Data flowing between networks

    d. Data flowing between routers

3 Which of the following is an advantage of cable modem?

    a. The cabling infrastructure can be upgraded.

    b. Because cable modems exist in a shared-medium structure, the more users come on the network, the less bandwidth is available for each user.

    c. **Coaxial cable wiring offers greater bandwidth using broadband for more applications to the home network.**

    d. None of the above.

4 Which of the following applications does the cable network support?

    a. HTTP

    b. FTP

    c. SNMP

    d. **All of the above**

Chapter 27

1 Which technology is *not* a type of wireless communication?

    a. Cellular

    b. **Wideband**

    c. Infrared

    d. Spread spectrum

2 Modulation is a process of changing amplitude, frequency, or phase. Which acronym does *not* represent a type of modulation?

    a. AM

    b. FM

    c. PM

    d. **RM**

3 Which statement does *not* correctly identify an unlicensed wireless frequency?

    a. 2.4 GHz

    b. 5 GHz

    c. **9 GHz**

    d. 900 MHz

4 Which statement does *not* describe a benefit of spread spectrum?

    a. **Spread-spectrum transmissions are transmitted at high speeds.**

    b. Spread spectrum is less susceptible to radio noise.

    c. Spread spectrum has a higher probability of correct reception.

    d. Spread spectrum creates little interference.

5 Which statement does *not* describe the features of direct-sequence spread spectrum (DSSS)?

    a. DSSS is reliable because each bit is represented by a string of 1s and 0s.

    b. If up to 40 percent of the string is lost, the original transmission can be reconstructed.

    c. **DSSS technology has low throughput of data and short-range access.**

    d. The recently released evolution of the IEEE standard, 802.11b, provides for a full Ethernet-like data rate of 11 Mbps over DSSS.

6 Which of the following is *not* a feature of wired equivalent privacy (WEP)?

    a. WEP uses the RC4 stream cipher for encryption.

    b. **WEP is a security mechanism defined within in the 802.3 standards.**

    c. One of the goals of WEP is to deny access to the network by unauthorized users who do not possess the appropriate WEP key.

    d. None of the above.

Chapter 28

1 Which statement does *not* define WLANs?

    a. **WLANs are typically within a building, for distances up to 100 feet.**

    b. WLANs replace the Layer 1 transmission medium of a traditional wired network (usually Category 5 cable) with radio transmission over the air.

    c. WLANs can plug into a wired network and function as an overlay to traditional or wired LANs, or they can be deployed as a standalone LAN when wired networking is not feasible.

    d. WLANs permit the use of portable computers or specialty devices in a system in which connection to the network is essential.

2 Which of the statements is an *incorrect* description of the in-building WLAN implementation?

    a. **Access points attach directly into a company's Ethernet backbone via a 10/100 connection. It is a wireless connection.**

    b. The backbone is connected to the servers and routers that drive the customer's intranet, applications, and access to the Internet.

    c. In-building wireless LANs start at the Ethernet backbone.

    d. The access point functions like a hub, with shared network access.

3 In-building cell configurations require what percentage of cell overlap?

    a. 15 to 20 percent

    b. 20 to 25 percent

    c. **10 to 15 percent**

    d. None

4 Which statement does *not* describe a benefit of building-to-building WLANs?

    a. WLANs can be set up quickly and efficiently.

    b. **WLANs allow users to log on without passwords or cabled connections.**

    c. WLANs are cost effective.

    d. WLANs enable operations to be shared across buildings within a corporate campus.

Chapter 29

1 Which of the following are not the key drivers of the optical networks?

    a. Efficiently meet capacity and scalability requirements in both metropolitan and long-haul network infrastructure

    b. Reduce costs and accelerate profitable new service revenue simultaneously

    c. Reach long distances

    d. **Be adaptable through a closed-system architecture**

2 Which of the following is true of IOR?

    a. It stands for index of reflection.

    b. It is a light ray bouncing off the interface of two materials.

    c. **It is the ratio of the speed of light in a vacuum to the speed of light in a fiber.**

    d. Two fibers with different IOR values cannot work together.

3 True or false: The light current is the electrical noise that naturally occurs in the circuit.

    a. True

    b. **False**

4 Which of the following is *not* a wavelength value used in fiber optics?

    a. 850 nm

    b. 1300 nm

    c. **1450 nm**

    d. 1550 nm

5 Which of the following describe(s) fiber optics?

    a. High-speed transmission

    b. Long transmission distance

    c. More reliability than copper wires

    d. **All of the above**

Chapter 30

1 Which of the following methods can amplify an input optical signal within in the fiber?

    a. OADM

    b. SONET

    c. ROL

    d. **EDFA**

2 What is the typical multimode transmission rate?

    a. **Hundreds of megabits per second**

    b. Hundreds of kilobits per second

    c. Hundreds of gigabits per second

    d. None of the above

3 Which of the following is true of single-mode fiber?

    a. The signal travels through a single-mode fiber at a different rate.

    b. Single-mode fiber has a lower data rate than multimode fiber.

    c. Single-mode fiber allows multimode to travel down the fiber.

    d. **Single-mode fiber allows one mode to travel down the fiber.**

4 Which of the following are possible problems of the fiber core?

    a. The core can be slightly off center from the cladding center.

    b. The cores might be slightly different sizes.

    c. The core might be noncircular.

    d. **All of the above.**

5 Match each of the following loss factors with the description:

    a. 1. Microbending

    b.   Connector loss

    c.   Macrobending

    d. Absorption

    1. Appears as a wrinkle in the fiber

    2. Is an intrinsic loss characteristic of fiber

    3. Depends on passing light from one core to another

    4. Is a bend caused by bending fiber and is visible to the eyes

    Answers: **1. a, 2. c, 3. d, 4. b**

6 Which of the following is a cause of attenuation?

    a. Scattering

    b. Stress from the manufacturing process

    c. Physical bending

    d. **All of the above**

7 Which of the following is a *not* a component of fiber-optic cable?

    a. A fiber core

    b. An inner cladding

    c. **An outer cladding**

    d. A protective outer coating

Chapter 31

1 SONET was designed to standardize which of the following?

    a. **Synchronous networking-enhanced operations, administration, maintenance, and provisioning**

    b. Asynchronous networking-based operation, administration, maintenance, and provisioning

    c. Protections to the SONET facilities at the application layer

    d. Transmission standards for ATM

2 Which of the following is *not* one of the three levels of overhead channel for maintenance?

    a. SOH

    b. **COH**

    c. LOH

    d. POH

3 True or false: SONET defines a technology for carrying one signal through a synchronous, flexible, optical hierarchy.

    a. True

    b. **False**

4 Which of the following could be a client-side device for a DWDM system?

    a. LAN switches

    b. Bridges

    c. **Routers**

    d. Hubs

5 What device within the DWDM system is used to convert the SONET/SDH–compliant optical signal?

    a. Transceiver

    b. Transformer

    c. Converter

    d. **Transponder**

6 From technical and economic perspectives, what is the most obvious advantage of DWDM technology?

   a. The capability to transmit a lot of data at a time

   b. **The capability to provide potentially unlimited transmission capacity**

   c. Easy installation

   d. Low cost

7 Identify the most compelling technical advantages of DWDM. (Check all that apply.)

   a. **High flexibility**

   b. **Scalability**

   c. **High capacity**

   d. **Transparency**

   e. Low maintenance

8 Which of the following does *not* describe metro DWDM?

   a. **Metro DWDM is very similar to long-haul DWDM.**

   b. Metro DWDM supports subwavelength TDM and wavelength services.

   c. Metro DWDM is driven by demand for fast service provisioning.

   d. Metro DWDM maximizes service density per wavelength.

Appendix A

1 The functions of voice-capable routers include which of the following:

   a. They can function as a local phone system for interoffice calls.

   b. They can route calls within an enterprise network.

   c. They can route incoming and outing calls through PBX.

   d. **All of the above.**

2 VoFR has which of the following features?

   a. Provides popular transport for multiservice networks

   b. Consolidates voice and voice-band data (including fax and analog modems) with data services

   c. Provides cost-effective service that support bursty traffic well

   d. **All of the above**

3 True or false: ATM is an ideal transport for multiservice networks such as VoATM.

    a. **True**

    b. False

4 True or false: At the data link layer, voice over IP (VoIP) packets can use any Layer 2 encapsulations, such as the Point-to-Point Protocol (PPP).

    a. **True**

    b. False

5 Match each voice-over-data technology with its associated limitation.

    a. Tops out at T1/E1 speeds

    b. Has limited services and costly equipment

    c. Is the least deterministic

Frame Relay	**a**	b	c
ATM	a	**b**	c
IP	a	b	**c**

6 Which of the following is *not* a building block of Cisco AVVID?

    a. Infrastructure

    b. **Cables**

    c. Applications

    d. Clients

7 Which of the following is a *business* benefit of the Cisco IPCC?

    a. Seamless migration path to IP-based voice applications

    b. Consistent service standards across diverse media channels

    c. **Increased customer satisfaction through personalized customer interaction**

    d. Intelligent contact management

8 Utilizing IP as the ubiquitous transport does *not* offer which of the following gains to enterprises?

    a. Bandwidth efficiency

    b. **Higher overall bandwidth requirements**

    c. Ease of management

    d. Capability to deploy new applications rapidly

9 Which of the following is true of a data, voice, and video–converged network utilizing IP as the transport?

a. Higher costs

b. **Enhanced quality options for voice networking**

c. Decreased bandwidth

d. Limited capability in adapting new applications

10 Unified messaging combines which of the following message types into a single application suite?

a. E-mail

b. Voice mail

c. Fax

d. **All of the above**

11 True or false: Traditionally, an enterprise has separate networks for voice, video, and data applications.

a. **True**

b. False

12 Which problem does an echo canceller remedy?

a. Packet loss

b. **Echo**

c. Jitter

d. Delay

GLOSSARY

NUMERICS

10 Mbps   10 million bits per second. An information transfer rate.

10BASE2   10-Mbps baseband Ethernet specification using 50-ohm thin coaxial cable. 10BASE2, which is part of the IEEE 802.3 specification, has a distance limit of 606 feet (185 m) per segment. *See also* Cheapernet, Ethernet, IEEE 802.3, Thinnet.

10BASE5   10-Mbps baseband Ethernet specification using standard (thick) 50-ohm baseband coaxial cable. 10BASE5, which is part of the IEEE 802.3 baseband physical layer specification, has a distance limit of 1640 feet (500 m) per segment. *See also* Ethernet, IEEE 802.3.

10BASE-F   10-Mbps baseband Ethernet specification that refers to the 10BASE-FB, 10BASE-FL, and 10BASE-FP standards for Ethernet over fiber-optic cabling. *See also* 10BASE-FB, 10BASE-FL, 10BASE-FP, Ethernet.

10BASE-FB   10-Mbps baseband Ethernet specification using fiber-optic cabling. 10BASE-FB is part of the IEEE 10BASE-F specification. It is not used to connect user stations, but instead it provides a synchronous signaling backbone that allows additional segments and repeaters to be connected to the network. 10BASE-FB segments can be up to 1.24 miles (2000 m) long. *See also* 10BASE-F, Ethernet.

10BASE-FL   10-Mbps baseband Ethernet specification using fiber-optic cabling. 10BASE-FL is part of the IEEE 10BASE-F specification and, although it is capable of interoperating with FOIRL, is designed to replace the FOIRL specification. 10BASE-FL segments can be up to 3280 feet (1000 m) long if used with fiber-optic interrepeater link (FOIRL), and up to 1.24 miles (2000 m) if 10BASE-FL is used exclusively. *See also* 10BASE-F, Ethernet, FOIRL.

10BASE-FP   10-Mbps fiber-passive baseband Ethernet specification using fiber-optic cabling. 10BASE-FP is part of the IEEE 10BASE-F specification. It organizes a number of computers into a star topology without the use of repeaters. 10BASE-FP segments can be up to 1640 feet (500 m) long. *See also* 10BASE-F, Ethernet.

10BASE-T   10-Mbps baseband Ethernet specification using two pairs of twisted-pair cabling (Category 3, 4, or 5): one pair for transmitting data and the other for receiving data. 10BASE-T, which is part of the IEEE 802.3 specification, has a distance limit of approximately 328 feet (100 m) per segment. *See also* Ethernet, IEEE 802.3.

100BASE-FX   100-Mbps baseband Fast Ethernet specification using two strands of multimode fiber-optic cable per link. To guarantee proper signal timing, a 100BASE-FX link cannot exceed 1312 feet (400 m) in length. Based on the IEEE 802.3 standard. *See also* 100BASE-X, Fast Ethernet, IEEE 802.3.

100BASE-T   100-Mbps baseband Fast Ethernet specification using UTP wiring. Like the 10BASE-T technology on which it is based, 100BASE-T sends link pulses over the network segment when no traffic is present. However, these link pulses contain more information than those used in 10BASE-T. Based on the IEEE 802.3 standard. *See also* 10BASE-T, Fast Ethernet, IEEE 802.3.

100BASE-T4   100-Mbps baseband Fast Ethernet specification using four pairs of Category 3, 4, or 5 UTP wiring. To guarantee proper signal timing, a 100BASE-T4 segment cannot exceed 328 feet (100 m) in length. Based on the IEEE 802.3 standard. *See also* Fast Ethernet, IEEE 802.3.

100BASE-TX   100-Mbps baseband Fast Ethernet specification using two pairs of either UTP or STP wiring. The first pair of wires is used to receive data; the second is used to transmit. To guarantee proper signal timing, a 100BASE-TX segment cannot exceed 328 feet (100 m) in length. Based on the IEEE 802.3 standard. *See also* 100BASE-X, Fast Ethernet, IEEE 802.3.

100BASE-X   100-Mbps baseband Fast Ethernet specification that refers to the 100BASE-FX and 100BASE-TX standards for Fast Ethernet over fiber-optic cabling. Based on the IEEE 802.3 standard. *See also* 100BASE-FX, 100BASE-TX, Fast Ethernet, IEEE 802.3.

A

ABR   Available bit rate. QoS class defined by the ATM Forum for ATM networks. ABR is used for connections that do not require timing relationships between source and destination.

AC   Alternating current. Electrical current that reverses its direction regularly and continually. It is the form of electrical power found in residential and commercial buildings.

access list   List kept by routers to control access to or from the router for a number of services (for example, to prevent packets with a certain IP address from leaving a particular interface on the router).

ACK (acknowledgment)   Notification sent from one network device to another to acknowledge that some event (for example, receipt of a message) has occurred. Sometimes abbreviated ACK. *See also* NAK.

active hub   Multiported device that amplifies LAN transmission signals.

adapter   *See* NIC (network interface card).

address   Data structure or logical convention used to identify a unique entity, such as a particular process or network device.

Address Resolution Protocol   *See* ARP.

administrative distance   A rating of the trustworthiness of a routing information source. In Cisco routers, administrative distance is expressed as a numerical value between 0 and 255. The higher the value is, the lower the trustworthiness rating is.

ADSL   Asymmetric digital subscriber line. One of four DSL technologies. ADSL is designed to deliver more bandwidth downstream (from the central office [CO] to the customer site) than upstream. Downstream rates range from 1.5 to 9 Mbps, while upstream bandwidth ranges from 16 to 640 kbps. ADSL transmissions work at distances up to 18,000 feet (5,488 m) over a single copper twisted-pair cable.

Advanced Research Projects Agency   *See* ARPA.

Advanced Research Projects Agency Network   *See* ARPANET.

algorithm   Well-defined rule or process for arriving at a solution to a problem. In networking, algorithms commonly are used to determine the best route for traffic from a particular source to a particular destination.

alternate mark inversion   *See* AMI.

alternating current   *See* AC.

American National Standards Institute   *See* ANSI.

American Standard Code for Information Interchange   *See* ASCII.

AMI   Alternate mark inversion. Line-code type used on T1 and E1 circuit. In AMI, 0s are represented by 01 during each bit cell, and 1s are represented by 11 or 00, alternately, during each bit cell. *See also* B8ZS.

ANSI   American National Standards Institute. Voluntary organization comprised of corporate, government, and other members that coordinates standards-related activities, approves U.S. national standards, and develops positions for the United States in international standards organizations. ANSI helps develop international and U.S. standards relating to, among other things, communications and networking. ANSI is a member of the IEC and the ISO. *See also* IEC, ISO.

API   Application programming interface. Specification of function-call conventions that defines an interface to a service.

AppleTalk   Series of communications protocols designed by Apple Computer. Two phases currently exist. Phase 1, the earlier version, supports a single physical network that can have only one network number and can be in one zone. Phase 2, the more recent version, supports multiple logical networks on a single physical network and allows networks to be in more than one zone. *See also* zone.

application layer   Layer 7 of the OSI reference model. This layer provides services to application processes (such as electronic mail, file transfer, and terminal emulation) that are outside the OSI model. The application layer identifies and establishes the availability of intended communication partners (and the resources required to connect with them), synchronizes cooperating applications, and establishes agreement on procedures for error recovery and control of data integrity. *See also* data link layer, network layer, physical layer, presentation layer, session layer, transport layer.

application programming interface   *See* API.

ARP   Address Resolution Protocol. Internet protocol used to map an IP address to a MAC address. Defined in RFC 826, "An Ethernet Address Resolution Protocol." *See also* proxy ARP, RARP.

ARPA   Advanced Research Projects Agency. Research and development organization that is part of the U.S. Department of Defense (DoD). ARPA is responsible for numerous technological advances in communications and networking. ARPA evolved into DARPA and then back into ARPA again (in 1994). *See also* DARPA.

ARPANET   Advanced Research Projects Agency Network. Landmark packet-switching network established in 1969. ARPANET was developed in the 1970s by Bolt, Beranek, and Newman, Inc. (BBN); it was funded by ARPA (and later DARPA). It eventually evolved into the Internet. The term *ARPANET* was officially retired in 1990. *See also* ARPA, DARPA, Internet.

ASCII   American Standard Code for Information Interchange. An 8-bit code for character representation (7 bits plus parity).

Asynchronous Transfer Mode   *See* ATM.

asynchronous transmission   Describes digital signals that are transmitted without precise clocking. Such signals generally have different frequencies and phase relationships. Asynchronous transmissions usually encapsulate individual characters in control bits (called start and stop bits) that designate the beginning and end of each character. *See also* synchronous transmission.

ATDM   Asynchronous time-division multiplexing. Method of sending information that resembles normal TDM, except that time slots are allocated as needed rather than preassigned to specific transmitters. *See also* statistical multiplexing, TDM.

ATM   Asynchronous Transfer Mode. International standard for cell relay in which multiple service types (such as voice, video, and data) are conveyed in fixed-length (53-byte) cells. Fixed-length cells allow cell processing to occur in hardware, thereby reducing transit delays. ATM is designed to take advantage of high-speed transmission media such as E3, SONET, and T3.

attachment unit interface   *See* AUI.

attenuation   Loss of communication signal energy.

attribute   Configuration data that defines the characteristics of database objects such as the chassis, cards, ports, or virtual circuits of a particular device. Attributes might be preset or user-configurable. On a LightStream 2020 ATM switch, attributes are set using the configuration program or command-line interface (CLI) commands.

AUI   Attachment unit interface. IEEE 802.3 interface between a media attachment unit (MAU) and a network interface card (NIC). The term *AUI* can also refer to the rear panel port to which an AUI cable might attach, such as those found on a Cisco LightStream Ethernet access card. Also called a transceiver cable. *See also* IEEE 802.3, MAU, NIC (network interface card).

authentication   In security, the verification of the identity of a person or process.

autonomous system   Collection of networks under a common administration sharing a common routing strategy. Autonomous systems are subdivided by areas. An autonomous system must be assigned a unique 16-bit number by the IANA.

available bit rate   *See* ABR.

B

B channel   Bearer channel. DS-0 time slot that carries analog voice or digital data over ISDN. In ISDN, a full-duplex, 64-kbps channel used to send user data. *See also* D channel.

B8ZS   Binary 8-zero substitution. Line-code type, used on T1 and E1 circuits, in which a special code is substituted whenever eight consecutive 0s are sent over the link. This code then is interpreted at the remote end of the connection. This technique guarantees 1s density independent of the data stream. *See also* AMI.

back end   Node or software program that provides services to a front end. *See also* client, front end, server.

backbone   The part of a network that acts as the primary path for traffic that is most often sourced from and destined for other networks.

backbone cabling   Cabling that provides interconnections between wiring closets, between wiring closets and the POP, and between buildings that are part of the same LAN. Also known as vertical cabling.

backplane   A large circuit board that contains sockets for expansion cards.

bandwidth   The difference between the highest and lowest frequencies available for network signals. The term *bandwidth* is also used to describe the rated throughput capacity of a given network medium or protocol.

baseband   Characteristic of a network technology in which only one carrier frequency is used. Ethernet is an example of a baseband network. Also called narrowband. *See also* broadband.

Basic Rate Interface   *See* BRI.

baud   Unit of signaling speed equal to the number of discrete signal elements transmitted per second. Baud is synonymous with bits per second (bps) if each signal element represents exactly 1 bit.

Bc   Committed burst. Negotiated tariff metric in Frame Relay internetworks. The maximum amount of data (in bits) that a Frame Relay internetwork is committed to accept and transmit at the committed information rate (CIR). *See also* Be, CIR.

Be Excess burst. Negotiated tariff metric in Frame Relay internetworks. The number of bits that a Frame Relay internetwork will attempt to transmit after Bc is accommodated. In general, Be data is delivered with a lower probability than Bc data because Be data can be marked as discard eligible (DE) by the network. *See also* Bc.

bearer channel *See* B channel.

BECN Backward explicit congestion notification. Bit set by a Frame Relay network in frames traveling in the opposite direction of frames encountering a congested path. Data terminal equipment (DTE) receiving frames with the BECN bit set can request that higher-level protocols take flow control action as appropriate. *See also* FECN.

BGP Border Gateway Protocol. Interdomain routing protocol that replaces EGP. BGP exchanges reachability information with other BGP systems. It is defined by RFC 1163, "A Border Gateway Protocol." *See also* BGP4, EGP.

BGP4 BGP version 4. Version 4 of the predominant interdomain routing protocol used on the Internet. BGP4 supports CIDR and uses route-aggregation mechanisms to reduce the size of routing tables. *See also* BGP, CIDR.

binary 8-zero substitution *See* B8ZS.

bit The smallest unit of data in a computer. A bit equals 1 or 0, and is the binary format in which data is processed by computers.

BPDU Bridge protocol data unit. Spanning-Tree Protocol hello packet that is sent out at configurable intervals to exchange information among bridges in the network. *See also* PDU.

BRI Basic Rate Interface. ISDN interface composed of two B channels and one D channel for circuit-switched communication of voice, video, and data. *See also* PRI, ISDN.

bridge Device that connects and passes packets between two network segments that use the same communications protocol. Bridges operate at the data link layer (Layer 2) of the OSI reference model. In general, a bridge filters, forwards, or floods an incoming frame based on the MAC address of that frame.

broadband Transmission system that multiplexes multiple independent signals onto one cable. In telecommunications terminology, any channel having a bandwidth greater than a voice-grade channel (4 kHz). In LAN terminology, a coaxial cable on which analog signaling is used. Also called wideband. *See also* baseband.

broadcast   Data packet that will be sent to all nodes on a network. Broadcasts are identified by a broadcast address. *See also* multicast, unicast, broadcast address.

broadcast address   Special address reserved for sending a message to all stations. Generally, a broadcast address is a MAC destination address of all 1s. *See also* multicast address, unicast address, broadcast.

broadcast domain   The set of all devices that will receive broadcast frames originating from any device within the set. Broadcast domains typically are bounded by routers because routers do not forward broadcast frames.

broadcast storm   Undesirable network event in which many broadcasts are sent simultaneously across all network segments. A broadcast storm uses substantial network bandwidth and typically causes network timeouts.

brouter   Concatenation of bridge and router. Used to refer to devices that perform both bridging and routing functions.

browser   *See* World Wide Web browser.

buffer   Storage area used for handling data in transit. Buffers are used in internetworking to compensate for differences in processing speed between network devices. Bursts of data can be stored in buffers until they can be handled by slower processing devices. Sometimes referred to as a packet buffer.

bus   1. A collection of wires through which data is transmitted from one part of a computer to another. Connects all the internal computer components to the CPU. The Industry Standard Architecture (ISA) and the PCI are two types of buses. 2. Common physical signal path composed of wires or other media across which signals can be sent from one part of a computer to another. *See also* bus topology, ISA, PCI.

bus topology   Linear LAN architecture in which transmissions from network stations propagate the length of the medium and are received by all other stations. *See also* ring topology, star topology.

byte   A unit of measure used to describe the size of a data file, the amount of space on a disk or other storage medium, or the amount of data being sent over a network. One byte equals 8 bits of data.

C

cable   Transmission medium of copper wire or optical fiber wrapped in a protective cover.

Canadian Standards Association   *See* CSA.

carrier   An electromagnetic wave or alternating current of a single frequency, suitable for modulation by another data-bearing signal.

catchment area   Zone that falls within area that can be served by an internetworking device such as a hub.

Category 1 cabling   One of five grades of UTP cabling described in the EIA/TIA-568 standard. Category 1 cabling is used for telephone communications and is not suitable for transmitting data. *See also* Category 2 cabling, Category 3 cabling, Category 4 cabling, Category 5 cabling, EIA/TIA-568, UTP.

Category 2 cabling   One of five grades of UTP cabling described in the EIA/TIA-568 standard. Category 2 cabling is capable of transmitting data at speeds up to 4 Mbps. *See also* Category 1 cabling, Category 3 cabling, Category 4 cabling, Category 5 cabling, EIA/TIA-568, UTP,

Category 3 cabling   One of five grades of UTP cabling described in the EIA/TIA-568 standard. Category 3 cabling is used in 10BASE-T networks and can transmit data at speeds up to 10 Mbps. *See also* Category 1 cabling, Category 2 cabling, Category 4 cabling, Category 5 cabling, EIA/TIA-568, UTP.

Category 4 cabling   One of five grades of UTP cabling described in the EIA/TIA-568 standard. Category 4 cabling is used in Token Ring networks and can transmit data at speeds up to 16 Mbps. *See also* Category 1 cabling, Category 2 cabling, Category 3 cabling, Category 5 cabling, EIA/TIA-568, UTP.

Category 5 cabling   One of five grades of UTP cabling described in the EIA/TIA-568 standard. Category 5 cabling is used for running CDDI and can transmit data at speeds up to 1000 Mbps. *See also* Category 1 cabling, Category 2 cabling, Category 3 cabling, Category 4 cabling, EIA/TIA-568, UTP.

CDDI   Copper Distributed Data Interface. Implementation of FDDI protocols over STP and UTP cabling. CDDI transmits over relatively short distances (about 100 m), providing data rates of 100 Mbps using a dual-ring architecture to provide redundancy. Based on the ANSI twisted-pair physical medium dependent (TPPMD) standard. *See also* FDDI.

CDP   Cisco Discovery Protocol. Media- and protocol-independent device-discovery protocol that runs on all Cisco-manufactured equipment, including routers, access servers, bridges, and switches. Using CDP, a device can advertise its existence to other devices and receive information about other devices on the same LAN or on the remote side of a WAN. Runs on all media that support SNAP, including LANs, Frame Relay, and ATM media.

CD-ROM drive   A compact disk read-only memory drive that can read information from a CD-ROM.

cell   The basic unit for ATM switching and multiplexing. Cells contain identifiers that specify the data stream to which they belong. Each cell consists of a 5-byte header and 48 bytes of payload. *See also* cell relay.

cell relay   Network technology based on the use of small, fixed-size packets, or cells. Because cells are a fixed length, they can be processed and switched in hardware at high speeds. Cell relay is the basis for many high-speed network protocols, including ATM, IEEE 802.6, and SMDS. *See also* cell.

central office   *See* CO.

central processing unit (CPU)   The "brain" of the computer, where most of the calculations take place.

channelized E1   Access link operating at 2.048 Mbps that is subdivided into 30 B channels and 1 D channel. Supports dial-on-demand routing (DDR), Frame Relay, and X.25. *See also* channelized T1.

channelized T1   Access link operating at 1.544 Mbps that is subdivided into 24 channels (23 B channels and 1 D channel) of 64 kbps each. The individual channels or groups of channels connect to different destinations. Supports DDR, Frame Relay, and X.25. *See also* channelized E1.

CHAP   Challenge Handshake Authentication Protocol. Security feature supported on lines using PPP encapsulation that prevents unauthorized access. CHAP does not itself prevent unauthorized access; it merely identifies the remote end. The router or access server then determines whether that user is allowed access. *See also* PAP.

Cheapernet   Industry term used to refer to IEEE 802.3 10BASE2 standard or the cable specified in that standard. *See also* Thinnet, 10BASE2, IEEE 802.3.

checksum   Method for checking the integrity of transmitted data. A checksum is an integer value computed from a sequence of octets taken through a series of arithmetic operations. The value is recomputed at the receiving end and compared for verification.

CIDR   Classless interdomain routing. A technique supported by BGP and based on route aggregation. CIDR allows routers to group routes so that they can cut down on the quantity of routing information carried by the core routers. With CIDR, several IP networks appear to networks outside the group as a single, larger entity. *See also* BGP4.

CIR   Committed information rate. The rate at which a Frame Relay network agrees to transfer information under normal conditions, averaged over a minimum increment of time. CIR, measured in bits per second, is one of the key negotiated tariff metrics. *See also* Bc, Be.

circuit switching   Switching system in which a dedicated physical circuit path must exist between sender and receiver for the duration of the "call." Used heavily in the telephone company network. *See also* packet switching.

Cisco Discovery Protocol   *See* CDP.

classful network   Network that uses traditional IP network addresses of Class A, Class B, and Class C.

classless interdomain routing   *See* CIDR.

classless network   Network that does not use the traditional IP network addressing (Class A, Class B, and Class C), but that defines the network boundary using a prefix value that indicates the number of bits used for the network portion.

CLI   Command-line interface. The basic Cisco IOS Software configuration and management interface.

client   Node or software program (front-end device) that requests services from a server. *See also* back end, front end, server.

client/server model   Common way to describe network services and the model user processes (programs) of those services. Examples include the nameserver/nameresolver paradigm of the Domain Name System (DNS) and fileserver/file-client relationships such as Network File System (NFS) and diskless hosts.

CN   Content network. A globally coordinated network of devices designed to accelerate the delivery of information over the Internet infrastructure.

CO   Central office. The local telephone company office to which all local loops in a given area connect and in which circuit switching of subscriber lines occurs.

coaxial cable   Cable consisting of a hollow outer cylindrical conductor that surrounds a single inner wire conductor. Two types of coaxial cable currently are used in LANs: 50-ohm cable, which is used for digital signaling, and 75-ohm cable, which is used for analog signaling and high-speed digital signaling.

collapsed backbone   Nondistributed backbone in which all network segments are interconnected by way of an internetworking device. A collapsed backbone might be a virtual network segment existing in a device such as a hub, a router, or a switch.

collision   In Ethernet, the result of two nodes transmitting simultaneously. The frames from each device impact and are damaged when they meet on the physical media. *See also* collision domain.

collision domain   In Ethernet, the network area within which frames that have collided are propagated. Repeaters and hubs propagate collisions; LAN switches, bridges, and routers do not. *See also* collision.

committed information rate   *See* CIR.

communication   Transmission of information.

compression   The running of a data set through an algorithm that reduces the space required to store or the bandwidth required to transmit the data set.

computer   A device that computes. More recently, a device that can solve billions of equations per second.

concentrator   *See* hub.

conductor   1. Any material with a low resistance to electrical current. 2. Any material capable of carrying an electrical current. *See also* insulator.

configuration register   In Cisco routers, a 16-bit, user-configurable value that determines how the router functions during initialization. The configuration register can be stored in hardware or software. In hardware, the bit position is set using a jumper. In software, the bit position is set by specifying a hexadecimal value using configuration commands.

configure terminal   Command used to configure manually from the console terminal.

congestion   Traffic in excess of network capacity.

connectionless   Data transfer without the existence of a virtual circuit. *See also* connection-oriented, virtual circuit.

connection-oriented   Data transfer that requires the establishment of a virtual circuit. *See also* connectionless, virtual circuit.

content network   *See* CN.

contention   Access method in which network devices compete for permission to access the physical medium. *See also* circuit switching, token passing.

convergence   1. The speed and capability of a group of internetworking devices running a specific routing protocol to agree on the topology of an internetwork after a change in that topology. 2. Today convergence also means voice, video, and data on same network.

cost   Arbitrary value, typically based on hop count, media bandwidth, or other measures, that is assigned by a network administrator and used to compare various paths through an internetwork environment. Cost values are used by routing protocols to determine the most favorable path to a particular destination: the lower the cost, the better the path. Sometimes called path cost. *See also* routing metric.

cps   Cells per second. Unit of measure used for ATM switch volumes.

CRC   Cyclic redundancy check. Error-checking technique in which the frame recipient calculates a remainder by dividing frame contents by a prime binary divisor and comparing the calculated remainder to a value stored in the frame by the sending node.

CSA   Canadian Standards Association. Agency within Canada that certifies products that conform to Canadian national safety standards.

CSMA/CD   Carrier sense multiple access collision detect. Media-access mechanism wherein devices ready to transmit data first check the channel for a carrier. If no carrier is sensed for a specific period of time, a device can transmit. If two devices transmit at once, a collision occurs and is detected by all colliding devices. This collision subsequently delays retransmissions from those devices for some random length of time. CSMA/CD access is used by Ethernet and IEEE 802.3.

CSU   Channel service unit. Digital interface device that connects end-user equipment to the local digital telephone loop. Often referred to together with DSU, as CSU/DSU. *See also* DSU.

cut-through switching   A packet-switching approach that streams data through a switch so that the leading edge of a packet exits the switch at the output port before the packet finishes entering the input port. A device using cut-through packet switching reads, processes, and forwards packets as soon as the destination address is looked up and the outgoing port is determined. *See also* store-and-forward switching.

cyclic redundancy check   *See* CRC.

D

D channel   Delta channel. A full-duplex, 16-kbps (BRI) or 64-kbps (PRI) ISDN channel. *See also* B channel.

DARPA   Defense Advanced Research Projects Agency. U.S. government agency that funded research for and experimentation with the Internet. Evolved from ARPA and then, in 1994, back to ARPA. *See also* ARPA.

data circuit-terminating equipment   *See* DCE.

data communications equipment   *See* DCE.

Data Encryption Standard   *See* DES.

data link layer   Layer 2 of the OSI reference model. This layer provides reliable transit of data across a physical link. The data link layer is concerned with physical addressing, network topology, line discipline, error notification, ordered delivery of frames, and flow control. The IEEE has divided this layer into two sublayers: the MAC sublayer and the LLC sublayer. Sometimes simply called link layer. *See also* application layer, LLC, MAC, network layer, physical layer, presentation layer, session layer, transport layer.

data terminal equipment   *See* DTE.

datagram   Logical grouping of information sent as a network layer unit over a transmission medium without prior establishment of a virtual circuit. IP datagrams are the primary information units in the Internet.

dB   Decibels. Unit for measuring relative power ratios in terms of gain or loss. Units are expressed in terms of the logarithm to base 10 of a ratio and typically are expressed in watts. dB is not an absolute value; it is the measure of power lost or gained between two devices. For example, a −3dB loss indicates a 50 percent loss in power; a +3dB reading is a doubling of power.

DC   Direct current. Electrical current that travels in only one direction. Direct current generally is used in electronic circuits.

DCE   Data communications equipment (EIA expansion) or data circuit-terminating equipment (ITU-T expansion). The devices and connections of a communications network that comprise the network end of the user-to-network interface. The DCE provides a physical connection to the network, forwards traffic, and provides a clocking signal used to synchronize data transmission between DCE and DTE devices. Modems and interface cards are examples of DCE. *See also* DTE.

DDR   Dial-on-demand routing. Technique whereby a Cisco router automatically can initiate and close a circuit-switched session as transmitting stations demand. The router spoofs keepalives so that end stations treat the session as active. DDR permits routing over ISDN or telephone lines using an external ISDN terminal adaptor or modem.

DECnet   Group of communications products (including a protocol suite) developed and supported by Digital Equipment Corporation. DECnet/OSI (also called DECnet Phase V) is the most recent iteration and supports both OSI protocols and proprietary Digital protocols. Phase IV Prime supports inherent MAC addresses that allow DECnet nodes to coexist with systems running other protocols that have MAC address restrictions.

decorative raceway   Type of wall-mounted channel with a removable cover used to support horizontal cabling.

decryption   The reverse application of an encryption algorithm to encrypted data, thereby restoring that data to its original, unencrypted state. *See also* encryption.

dedicated line   Communications line that is reserved indefinitely for transmissions rather than switched as transmission is required. *See also* leased line.

default route   Routing table entry that is used to direct frames for which a next hop is not explicitly listed in the routing table.

delta channel   *See* D channel.

demarc   Demarcation point between carrier equipment and customer premises equipment (CPE).

demodulation   Process of returning a modulated signal to its original form. Modems perform demodulation by returning an analog signal to its original (digital) form. *See also* modulation.

demultiplexing   The separation of multiple input streams that have been multiplexed into a common physical signal back into multiple output streams. *See also* multiplexing.

Department of Defense   *See* DoD.

DES   Data Encryption Standard. Standard cryptographic algorithm developed by the U.S. National Bureau of Standards (NBS).

dialup line   A communications circuit that is established by a switched-circuit connection using the telephone company network.

digital subscriber line   *See* DSL.

distance-vector routing algorithm   A class of routing algorithms that iterate on the number of hops in a route to find a shortest-path spanning tree. Distance-vector routing algorithms call for each router to send its entire routing table in each update, but only to its neighbors. Distance-vector routing algorithms can be prone to routing loops but are computationally simpler than link-state routing algorithms. Also called Bellman-Ford routing algorithm. *See also* link-state routing algorithm.

DNS   Domain Name System. System used in the Internet for translating names of network nodes into addresses.

DoD   Department of Defense. U.S. government organization that is responsible for national defense. The DoD frequently has funded communication protocol development.

domain   In the Internet, a portion of the naming hierarchy tree that refers to general groupings of networks based on organization type or geography.

dot address   The common notation for IP addresses in the form <a.b.c.d>, where each number represents, in decimal, 1 byte of the 4-byte IP address. Also called dotted-decimal notation or four-part dotted notation.

dotted-decimal notation   *See* dot address.

DRAM   Dynamic random-access memory. RAM that stores information in capacitors that must be periodically refreshed. Delays can occur because DRAMs are inaccessible to the processor when refreshing their contents. However, DRAMs are less complex and have greater capacity than SRAMs. *See also* SRAM.

DS-0   Digital signal level 0. Framing specification used in transmitting digital signals over a single channel at 64 kbps on a T1 facility. *See also* DS-1, DS-3.

DS-1   Digital signal level 1. Framing specification used in transmitting digital signals at 1.544 Mbps on a T1 facility (in the United States) or at 2.048 Mbps on an E1 facility (in Europe). *See also* DS-0, DS-3, E1, T1.

DS-3   Digital signal level 3. Framing specification used for transmitting digital signals at 44.736 Mbps on a T3 facility. *See also* DS-0, DS-1, E3, T3.

DSL   Digital subscriber line. Public network technology that delivers high bandwidth over conventional copper wiring at limited distances. There are several types of DSL technologies, known as xDSL. All are provisioned via modem pairs, with one modem located at a central office and the otehr at the customer site. Because most DSL technologies do not use the whole bandwidth of the twisted pair, there is room remaning of a voice channel. *See also* xDSL.

DSU   Data service unit. Device used in digital transmission that adapts the physical interface on a DTE device to a transmission facility such as T1 or E1. The DSU is also responsible for such functions as signal timing. Often referred to together with CSU, as CSU/DSU. *See also* CSU.

DTE   Data terminal equipment. Device at the user end of a user-network interface that serves as a data source, destination, or both. DTE connects to a data network through a DCE device (for example, a modem) and typically uses clocking signals generated by the DCE. DTE includes such devices as computers, protocol translators, and multiplexers. *See also* DCE.

dynamic random-access memory   *See* DRAM.

dynamic routing   Routing that adjusts automatically to network topology or traffic changes. Also called adaptive routing. Requires that a routing protocol be run between routers.

E

E1   Wide-area digital transmission scheme used predominantly in Europe that carries data at a rate of 2.048 Mbps. E1 lines can be leased for private use from common carriers. *See also* DS-1, T1.

E3   Wide-area digital transmission scheme used predominantly in Europe that carries data at a rate of 34.368 Mbps. E3 lines can be leased for private use from common carriers. *See also* DS-3, T3.

EBCDIC   Extended Binary Coded Decimal Interchange Code. Any of a number of coded character sets developed by IBM and consisting of 8-bit coded characters. This character code is used by older IBM systems and telex machines. *See also* ASCII.

EDFA   Erbium-doped fiber amplifier. Optical fibers doped with the rare earth element erbium, which can amplify light in the 1550 nm region when pumped by an external light source.

EEPROM   Electrically erasable programmable read-only memory. EPROM that can be erased using electrical signals applied to specific pins.

EGP   Exterior Gateway Protocol. Internet protocol for exchanging routing information between autonomous systems. Documented in RFC 904, "Exterior Gateway Protocol Formal Specification." Not to be confused with the general term *exterior gateway protocol*. EGP is an obsolete protocol that has been replaced by BGP. *See also* BGP.

EIA   Electronic Industries Association. Group that specifies electrical transmission standards. The EIA and TIA have developed numerous well-known communications standards, including EIA/TIA-232 and EIA/TIA-449. *See also* TIA.

EIA-530   Refers to two electrical implementations of EIA/TIA-449: RS-422 (for balanced transmission) and RS-423 (for unbalanced transmission). *See also* RS-422, RS-423, EIA/TIA-449.

EIA/TIA-232   Formerly known as RS-232. Common physical layer interface standard, developed by the EIA and TIA, that supports unbalanced circuits at signal speeds of up to 64 kbps. Closely resembles the V.24 specification. *See also* RS-232.

EIA/TIA-449   Formerly called RS-449. Popular physical layer interface developed by the EIA and TIA. Essentially, a faster (up to 2 Mbps) version of EIA/TIA-232 capable of longer cable runs. *See also* EIA-530, RS-449.

EIA/TIA-568   Standard that describes the characteristics and applications for various grades of UTP cabling. *See also* Category 1 cabling, Category 2 cabling, Category 3 cabling, Category 4 cabling, Category 5 cabling, UTP.

EIA/TIA-606   Administration standard for the telecommunications infrastructure of commercial buildings. It includes the following administration areas: terminations, media, pathways, spaces, and bounding and grounding.

EIGRP   Enhanced Interior Gateway Routing Protocol. Advanced version of IGRP developed by Cisco. Provides superior convergence properties and operating efficiency, and combines the advantages of link-state protocols with those of distance-vector protocols. *See also* IGP, IGRP, OSPF, RIP.

EISA   Extended Industry-Standard Architecture. A 32-bit bus interface used in PCs, PC-based servers, and some UNIX workstations and servers. *See also* ISA.

electrically erasable programmable read-only memory   *See* EEPROM.

electromagnetic interference   *See* EMI.

electromagnetic pulse   *See* EMP.

electronic mail   Widely used network application in which mail messages are transmitted electronically between end users over various types of networks using various network protocols. Often called e-mail.

electrostatic discharge   *See* ESD.

e-mail   *See* electronic mail.

EMI   Electromagnetic interference. Interference by electromagnetic signals that can cause reduced data integrity and increased error rates on transmission channels.

EMP   Electromagnetic pulse. Caused by lightning and other high-energy phenomena. Capable of coupling enough energy into unshielded conductors to destroy electronic devices.

encapsulation   The wrapping of data in a particular protocol header. For example, Ethernet data is wrapped in a specific Ethernet header before network transit. Also, when bridging dissimilar networks, the entire frame from one network simply is placed in the header used by the data link layer protocol of the other network. *See also* tunneling.

encoder   Device that modifies information into the required transmission format.

encoding   Process by which bits are represented by voltages.

encryption   The application of a specific algorithm to data so as to alter the appearance of the data and make it incomprehensible to those who are not authorized to see the information. *See also* decryption.

end of transmission   *See* EOT.

Enhanced IGRP   *See* EIGRP.

Enhanced Interior Gateway Routing Protocol   *See* Enhanced IGRP.

enterprise network   Large and diverse network connecting most major points in a company or other organization. Differs from a WAN in that it is privately owned and maintained.

EOT   End of transmission. Generally, a character that signifies the end of a logical group of characters or bits.

EPROM   Erasable programmable read-only memory. Nonvolatile memory chips that are programmed after they are manufactured and, if necessary, that can be erased by some means and reprogrammed. *See also* EEPROM, PROM.

erasable programmable read-only memory   *See* EPROM.

erbium-doped fiber amplifier   *See* EDFA.

error control   Technique for detecting and correcting errors in data transmissions.

ESD   Electrostatic discharge. A flow or spark of electricity that originates from a static source such as a carpet and arcs across a gap to another object.

Ethernet   Baseband LAN specification invented by Xerox Corporation and developed jointly by Xerox, Intel, and Digital Equipment Corporation. Ethernet networks use CSMA/CD and run over a variety of cable types at 10 Mbps. Ethernet is similar to the IEEE 802.3 series of standards. *See also* 10BASE2, 10BASE5, 10BASE-T, IEEE 802.3.

EtherTalk   AppleTalk protocols running on Ethernet.

expansion card   A printed circuit board that can be inserted into a computer to give the computer added capabilities. *See also* expansion slot.

expansion slot   An opening in a computer where a circuit board can be inserted to add new capabilities to the computer. *See also* expansion card.

Extended Binary Coded Decimal Interchange Code   *See also* EBCDIC.

Extended Industry-Standard Architecture   *See* EISA.

F

Fast Ethernet   Any of a number of 100-Mbps Ethernet specifications. Fast Ethernet offers a speed increase 10 times that of the 10BASE-T Ethernet specification while preserving such qualities as frame format, MAC mechanisms, and MTU. Such similarities allow the use of existing 10BASE-T applications and network management tools on Fast Ethernet networks. Based on an extension to the Ethernet IEEE 802.3 specification. *See also* 100BASE-FX, 100BASE-T, 100BASE-T4, 100BASE-TX, 100BASE-X, IEEE 802.3.

fast switching   Cisco feature whereby a route cache is used to expedite packet switching through a router. *See also* slow switching.

FCC   Federal Communications Commission. U.S. government agency that supervises, licenses, and controls electronic and electromagnetic transmission standards.

FCS   Frame check sequence. Refers to the extra characters added to a frame for error-control purposes. Used in HDLC, Frame Relay, and other data link layer protocols.

FDDI   Fiber Distributed Data Interface. LAN standard, defined by ANSI X3T9.5, specifying a 100-Mbps token-passing network using fiber-optic cable, with transmission distances of up to 2 km. FDDI uses a dual-ring architecture to provide redundancy. *See also* CDDI, FDDI II.

FDDI II   ANSI standard that enhances FDDI. FDDI II provides isochronous transmission for connectionless data circuits and connection-oriented voice and video circuits. *See also* FDDI.

FDM   Frequency-division multiplexing. Technique whereby information from multiple channels can be allocated bandwidth on a single wire based on frequency. *See also* ATDM, statistical multiplexing, TDM.

FECN   Forward explicit congestion notification. Bit set by a Frame Relay network to inform the DTE receiving the frame that congestion was experienced in the path from source to destination. The DTE receiving the frames with the FECN bit set can request that higher-level protocols take flow-control action as appropriate. *See also* BECN.

Federal Communications Commission   *See* FCC.

Fiber Distributed Data Interface   *See* FDDI.

fiber-optic cable   Physical medium capable of conducting modulated light transmission. Compared with other transmission media, fiber-optic cable is more expensive but is not susceptible to electromagnetic interference and is capable of higher data rates. Sometimes called optical fiber.

field-replaceable unit   *See* FRU.

file transfer   Popular network application that allows files to be moved from one network device to another.

File Transfer Protocol   *See* FTP.

firewall   Router or access server, or several routers or access servers, designated as a buffer between any connected public networks and a private network. A firewall router uses access lists and other methods to ensure the security of the private network.

firmware   Software instructions set permanently or semipermanently in ROM.

flapping   Routing problem in which an advertised route between two nodes alternates (flaps) back and forth between two paths because of a network problem that causes intermittent interface failures.

Flash memory   Technology developed by Intel and licensed to other semiconductor companies. Flash memory is nonvolatile storage that can be electrically erased and reprogrammed. Allows software images to be stored, booted, and rewritten as necessary.

Flash update   Routing update sent asynchronously in response to a change in the network topology. *See also* routing update.

flat addressing   Scheme of addressing that does not use a logical hierarchy to determine location.

flooding   Traffic-passing technique used by switches and bridges in which traffic received on an interface is sent out all the interfaces of that device except the interface on which the information originally was received.

floppy disk drive   Disk drive that can read and write to floppy disks.

flow   Stream of data traveling between two endpoints across a network (for example, from one LAN station to another). Multiple flows can be transmitted on a single circuit.

flow control   Technique for ensuring that a transmitting entity, such as a modem, does not overwhelm a receiving entity with data. When the buffers on the receiving device are full, a message is sent to the sending device to suspend the transmission until the data in the buffers has been processed. In IBM networks, this technique is called pacing.

FOIRL   Fiber-optic interrepeater link. Fiber-optic signaling methodology based on the IEEE 802.3 fiber-optic specification. FOIRL is a precursor for the 10BASE-FL specification, which is designed to replace it. *See also* 10BASE-FL.

forward explicit congestion notification   *See* FECN.

fragment   Piece of a larger packet that has been broken into smaller units.

frame   Logical grouping of information sent as a data link layer unit over a transmission medium. Often refers to the header and trailer, used for synchronization and error control, that surround the user data contained in the unit. The terms *datagram*, *message*, *packet*, and *segment* also are used to describe logical information groupings at various layers of the OSI reference model and in various technology circles.

frame check sequence   *See* FCS.

Frame Relay   Industry-standard, switched data link layer protocol that handles multiple virtual circuits using HDLC encapsulation between connected devices. Frame Relay is more efficient than X.25, the protocol for which it generally is considered a replacement. *See also* X.25.

frequency   Number of cycles, measured in hertz, of an alternating current signal per unit time.

frequency-division multiplexing   *See* FDM.

front end   Node or software program that requests services of a back end. *See also* back end, client, server.

FRU   Field-replaceable unit. Hardware component that can be removed and replaced by Cisco-certified service providers. Typical FRUs include cards, power supplies, and chassis components.

FTP   File Transfer Protocol. Application protocol, part of the TCP/IP protocol stack, used for transferring files between network nodes. FTP is defined in RFC 959, "File Transfer Protocol (FTP)."

full duplex   Capability for simultaneous data transmission between a sending station and a receiving station. *See also* half duplex, simplex.

full mesh   Term describing a network in which devices are organized in a mesh topology, with each network node having either a physical circuit or a virtual circuit connecting it to every other network node. A full mesh provides a great deal of redundancy, but because it can be prohibitively expensive to implement, it usually is reserved for network backbones. *See also* mesh, partial mesh.

G

gateway   In the IP community, an older term referring to a routing device. Today, the term *router* is used to describe nodes that perform this function, and *gateway* refers to a special-purpose device that performs an application layer conversion of information from one protocol stack to another. *Gateway* now also refers to device that connects to the PSTN for voice calls outside an IP Telephony system. *See also* router.

GB   Approximately one billion bytes.

Gb   Approximately one billion bits.

GBps   Gigabytes per second.

Gbps   Gigabits per second.

GHz   Gigahertz. One thousand million, or 1 billion (1,000,000,000), cycles per second.

gigabit   *See* Gb.

Gigabit Ethernet   An extension of the IEEE 802.3 Ethernet standard. Gigabit Ethernet increases speed tenfold over Fast Ethernet, to 1000 Mbps, or 1 gigabit per second (Gbps). Two IEEE 802.3 standards, IEEE 802.3z and IEEE 802.3ab, define Gigabit Ethernet operations over fiber optics and twisted-pair cable.

gigabits per second   *See* Gbps.

gigabyte   *See* GB.

gigabytes per second   *See* GBps.

gigahertz   *See* GHz.

graphical user interface   *See* GUI.

GUI   Graphical user interface. User environment that uses pictorial as well as textual representations of the input and output of applications and the hierarchical or other data structure in which information is stored. Conventions such as buttons, icons, and windows are typical, and many actions are performed using a pointing device (such as a mouse). Microsoft Windows and the Apple Macintosh are prominent examples of platforms utilizing a GUI.

H

half duplex   Capability for data transmission in only one direction at a time between a sending station and a receiving station. *See also* full duplex, simplex.

handshake   Sequence of messages exchanged between two or more network devices to ensure transmission synchronization.

hard disk drive   The device that stores and retrieves data on a hard disk.

hardware address   *See* MAC address.

HCC   Horizontal cross-connect. Wiring closet in which the horizontal cabling connects to a patch panel that is connected by backbone cabling to the main distribution facility.

HDLC   High-Level Data Link Control. Bit-oriented synchronous data link layer protocol developed by the ISO. Derived from SDLC, HDLC specifies a data-encapsulation method on synchronous serial links using frame characters and checksums. *See also* SDLC.

hertz   *See* Hz.

hexadecimal   Base 16. A number representation using the digits 0 through 9, with their usual meaning, plus the letters *A* through *F* to represent hexadecimal digits with values of 10 to 15. The right-most digit counts 1s, the next counts multiples of 16, then $16^2 = 256$, and so on.

hierarchical routing   Routing based on a hierarchical addressing system. For example, IP routing algorithms use IP addresses, which contain network numbers, subnet numbers, and host numbers.

hierarchical star topology   Extended star topology in which a central hub is connected by vertical cabling to other hubs that are dependent on it.

holddown   State into which a route is placed so that routers will neither advertise the route nor accept advertisements about the route for a specific length of time (the hold-down period). Holddown is used to flush bad information about a route from all routers in the network. A route typically is placed in holddown when a link in that route fails.

hop   Describes the passage of a data packet between two network nodes (for example, between two routers). *See also* hop count.

hop count   Routing metric used to measure the distance between a source and a destination. RIP uses hop count as its sole metric. *See also* hop, RIP.

horizontal cross-connect   *See* HCC.

host   Computer system on a network. Similar to the term *node* except that *host* usually implies a computer system, whereas *node* generally applies to any networked system, including access servers and routers. *See also* node.

HTML   Hypertext Markup Language. Simple hypertext document formatting language that uses tags to indicate how a given part of a document should be interpreted by a viewing application, such as a World Wide Web browser. *See also* hypertext, World Wide Web browser.

HTTP   Hypertext Transfer Protocol. The protocol used by web browsers and web servers to transfer files, such as text and graphics files.

hub   1. Generally, a term used to describe a device that serves as the center of a star-topology network. 2. Hardware or software device that contains multiple independent but connected modules of network and internetwork equipment. Hubs can be active (when they repeat signals sent through them) or passive (when they do not repeat, but merely split signals sent through them). 3. In Ethernet and IEEE 802.3, an Ethernet multiport repeater, sometimes referred to as a concentrator.

hypertext   Electronically stored text that allows direct access to other texts by way of encoded links. Hypertext documents can be created using HTML; they often integrate images, sound, and other media that commonly are viewed using a World Wide Web browser. *See also* HTML, World Wide Web browser.

Hypertext Markup Language   *See* HTML.

Hz   Hertz. A unit of frequency. It is the rate of change in the state or cycle in a sound wave, alternating current, or other cyclical waveform. It represents one cycle per second and is used to describe the speed of a computer microprocessor.

I

IAB   Internet Architecture Board. Board of internetwork researchers who discuss issues pertinent to Internet architecture. It is responsible for appointing a variety of Internet-related groups such as the IANA, IESG, and IRSG. The IAB is appointed by the trustees of the ISOC.

IANA   Internet Assigned Numbers Authority. Organization operated under the auspices of the ISOC as a part of the IAB. IANA delegates authority for IP address-space allocation and domain-name assignment to the NIC and other organizations. IANA also maintains a database of assigned protocol identifiers used in the TCP/IP stack, including autonomous system numbers. *See also* IAB, ISOC.

ICC   IDF that connects the horizontal cross-connect to the main cross-connect. *See also* HCC, MCC.

ICMP   Internet Control Message Protocol. Network layer Internet protocol that reports errors and provides other information relevant to IP packet processing. Documented in RFC 792, "Internet Control Message Protocol."

IDF   Intermediate distribution facility. Secondary communications room for a building using a star networking topology. The IDF is dependent on the MDF. *See also* MDF.

IEC International Electrotechnical Commission. Industry group that writes and distributes standards for electrical products and components.

IEEE Institute of Electrical and Electronics Engineers. Professional organization whose activities include the development of communications and network standards. IEEE LAN standards are the predominant LAN standards today.

IEEE 802.2 An IEEE LAN protocol that specifies an implementation of the LLC sublayer of the data link layer. IEEE 802.2 handles errors, framing, flow control, and the network layer (Layer 3) service interface. Used in IEEE 802.3 and IEEE 802.5 LANs. *See also* IEEE 802.3, IEEE 802.5.

IEEE 802.3 An IEEE LAN protocol that specifies an implementation of the physical layer and the MAC sublayer of the data link layer. IEEE 802.3 uses CSMA/CD access at a variety of speeds over a variety of physical media. Extensions to the IEEE 802.3 standard specify implementations for Fast Ethernet. Physical variations of the original IEEE 802.3 specification include 10BASE2, 10BASE5, 10BASE-F, 10BASE-T, and 10Broad36. Physical variations for Fast Ethernet include 100BASE-TX and 100BASE-FX.

IEEE 802.5 IEEE LAN protocol that specifies an implementation of the physical layer and MAC sublayer of the data link layer. IEEE 802.5 uses token-passing access at 4 or 16 Mbps over STP cabling and is similar to IBM Token Ring.

IETF Internet Engineering Task Force. Task force consisting of more than 80 working groups responsible for developing Internet standards. The IETF operates under the auspices of the ISOC. *See also* ISOC.

IGP Interior Gateway Protocol. Internet protocol used to exchange routing information within an autonomous system. Examples of common Internet IGPs include IGRP, EIGRP, OSPF, and RIP. *See also* IGRP, OSPF, RIP.

IGRP Interior Gateway Routing Protocol. IGP developed by Cisco to address the problems associated with routing in large, heterogeneous networks. *See also* Enhanced IGRP, IGP, OSPF, RIP.

in-band signaling Transmission within a frequency range normally used for information transmission. *See also* out-of-band signaling.

Industry-Standard Architecture *See* ISA.

infrared   Electromagnetic waves whose frequency range is above that of microwaves but below that of the visible spectrum. LAN systems based on this technology represent an emerging technology.

insulator   Any material with a high resistance to electrical current. *See also* conductor.

Integrated IS-IS   Routing protocol based on the OSI routing protocol IS-IS, but with support for IP and other protocols. Integrated IS-IS implementations send only one set of routing updates, making it more efficient than two separate implementations. *See also* IS-IS.

Integrated Services Digital Network   *See* ISDN.

interface   1. Connection between two systems or devices. 2. In routing terminology, a network connection. 3. In telephony, a shared boundary defined by common physical interconnection characteristics, signal characteristics, and meanings of interchanged signals. 4. The boundary between adjacent layers of the OSI model.

Interior Gateway Protocol   *See* IGP.

Interior Gateway Routing Protocol   *See* IGRP.

intermediate distribution facility   *See* IDF.

Intermediate System-to-Intermediate System   *See* IS-IS

internet   Short for *internetwork*. Not to be confused with the Internet. *See also* internetwork, Internet.

Internet   The largest global internetwork, connecting tens of thousands of networks worldwide and having a "culture" that focuses on research and standardization based on real-life use. Many leading-edge network technologies come from the Internet community. The Internet evolved in part from ARPANET. At one time, called the DARPA Internet. Not to be confused with the general term *internet*. *See also* ARPANET.

Internet address   *See* IP address.

Internet Protocol   *See* IP.

internetwork   Collection of networks interconnected by routers and other devices that functions (generally) as a single network. Sometimes called an internet, which is not to be confused with the Internet.

Internetwork Packet Exchange   *See* IPX.

internetworking   General term used to refer to the industry that has arisen around the problem of connecting networks. The term can refer to products, procedures, and technologies.

IP   Internet Protocol. Network layer protocol in the TCP/IP stack offering a connectionless internetwork service. IP provides features for addressing, type-of-service specification, fragmentation and reassembly, and security. Defined in RFC 791, "Internet Protocol." IP version 4 (IPv4) is a connectionless, best-effort packet switching protocol. *See also* IPv6, TCP/IP.

IP address   A 32-bit address assigned to hosts by using TCP/IP. An IP address belongs to one of five classes (A, B, C, D, or E) and is written as four octets separated by periods (that is, in dotted-decimal format). Each address consists of a network number, an optional subnetwork number, and a host number. The network and subnetwork numbers together are used for routing, and the host number is used to address an individual host within the network or subnetwork. A subnet mask is used to extract network and subnetwork information from the IP address. CIDR provides a new way of representing IP addresses and subnet masks. Also called an Internet address. *See also* CIDR, IP, subnet mask.

IP datagram   A fundamental unit of information passed across the Internet. Contains source and destination addresses along with data and a number of fields that define such things as the length of the datagram, the header checksum, and flags to indicate whether the datagram can be (or was) fragmented.

IPv6   IP version 6. A replacement for the current version of IPv4. IPv6 includes support for flow ID in the packet header, which can be used to identify flows. Formerly called IPng (IP next generation).

IPX   Internetwork Packet Exchange. NetWare network layer (Layer 3) protocol used for transferring data from servers to workstations. IPX is similar to IP and Xerox Network Systems (XNS).

ISA   Industry-Standard Architecture. An older standard for connecting peripherals to a personal computer. Used primarily in advanced technology (AT)–style IBM compatibles. *See also* EISA.

ISDN   Integrated Services Digital Network. Communication protocol, offered by telephone companies, that permits telephone networks to carry data, voice, and other source traffic. *See also* BRI, PRI.

IS-IS   Intermediate System-to-Intermediate System. OSI link-state hierarchical routing protocol based on DECnet Phase V routing whereby intermediate systems (routers) exchange routing information based on a single metric to determine network topology. *See also* Integrated IS-IS, OSPF.

ISO   International Organization for Standardization. International organization that is responsible for a wide range of standards, including those relevant to networking. The ISO developed the OSI reference model, a popular networking reference model.

ISOC   Internet Society. International nonprofit organization, founded in 1992, that coordinates the evolution and use of the Internet. In addition, the ISOC delegates authority to other groups related to the Internet, such as the IAB. The ISOC is headquartered in Reston, Virginia, U.S.A. *See also* IAB.

ITU-T   International Telecommunication Union Telecommunication Standardization Sector (ITU-T) (formerly the Committee for International Telegraph and Telephone [CCITT]). An international organization that develops communication standards.

J

jabber   1. Error condition in which a network device continually transmits random, meaningless data onto the network. 2. In IEEE 802.3, a data packet whose length exceeds that prescribed in the standard.

jitter   Analog communication line distortion caused by the variation of a signal from its reference timing positions. Jitter can cause data loss, particularly at high speeds.

jumper   1. Term used for patch cords found in a wiring closet. 2. Electrical switch consisting of a number of pins and a connector that can be attached to the pins in a variety of different ways. Different circuits are created by attaching the connector to different pins.

K

kB   *See also* kilobyte.

kb   Kilobit. Approximately 1000 bits.

kBps   Kilobytes per second. A standard measurement of the amount of data transferred over a network connection.

kbps   Kilobits per second. A standard measurement of the amount of data transferred over a network connection.

keepalive interval   Period of time between each keepalive message sent by a network device.

keepalive message   Message sent by one network device to inform another network device that the virtual circuit between the two is still active.

kilobit   *See* kb.

kilobits per second   *See* kbps.

kilobyte   *See* kB.

kilobytes per second   *See* kBps.

L

LAN   Local-area network. High-speed, low-error data network covering a relatively small geographic area (up to a few thousand meters). LANs connect workstations, peripherals, terminals, and other devices in a single building or other geographically limited area. LAN standards specify cabling and signaling at the physical and data link layers of the OSI model. Ethernet, FDDI, and Token Ring are widely used LAN technologies. *See also* WAN, MAN.

LAN switch   High-speed switch that forwards packets between data-link segments. Most LAN switches forward traffic based on MAC addresses. This variety of LAN switch sometimes is called a frame switch. LAN switches often are categorized according to the method they use to forward traffic: cut-through switching or store-and-forward switching. Multilayer switches are an intelligent subset of LAN switches. An example of a LAN switch is the Cisco Catalyst 5000. *See also* cut-through switching, multilayer switch, store-and-forward switching.

LAPB   Link Access Procedure, Balanced. Data link layer protocol in the X.25 protocol stack. LAPB is a bit-oriented protocol derived from HDLC. *See also* HDLC, X.25.

LAPD   Link Access Procedure on the D channel. ISDN data link layer protocol for the D channel. LAPD was derived from the LAPB protocol and is designed primarily to satisfy the signaling requirements of ISDN basic access. Defined by ITU-T Recommendations Q.920 and Q.921.

laser   Light amplification by stimulated emission of radiation. Analog transmission device in which a suitable active material is excited by an external stimulus to produce a narrow beam of coherent light that can be modulated into pulses to carry data. Networks based on laser technology sometimes are run over SONET.

latency   1. Delay between the time a device requests access to a network and the time it is granted permission to transmit. 2. Delay between the time when a device receives a frame and the time that frame is forwarded out the destination port.

leased line   Transmission line reserved by a communications carrier for the private use of a customer. A leased line is a type of dedicated line. *See also* dedicated line.

LED   Light-emitting diode. Semiconductor device that emits light produced by converting electrical energy. Status lights on hardware devices are typically LEDs.

line of sight   Characteristic of certain transmission systems such as laser, microwave, and infrared systems in which no obstructions in a direct path between transmitter and receiver can exist.

link   Network communications channel consisting of a circuit or transmission path and all related equipment between a sender and a receiver. Most often used to refer to a WAN connection. Sometimes referred to as a line or a transmission link.

Link Access Procedure, Balanced   *See* LAPB.

Link Access Procedure on the D channel   *See* LAPD.

link-state advertisement   *See* LSA.

link-state routing algorithm   Routing algorithm in which each router broadcasts or multicasts information regarding the cost of reaching each of its neighbors. Link-state algorithms create a consistent view of the network and are therefore not prone to routing loops, but they achieve this at the cost of relatively greater computational difficulty and more widespread traffic. *See also* distance-vector routing algorithm.

LLC   Logical Link Control. Higher of the two data link layer sublayers defined by the IEEE. The LLC sublayer handles error control, flow control, framing, and MAC-sublayer addressing. The most prevalent LLC protocol is IEEE 802.2, which includes both connectionless and connection-oriented variants. *See also* data link layer, MAC.

local loop   Line from the premises of a telephone subscriber to the telephone company CO.

local-area network   *See* LAN.

LocalTalk   Apple proprietary baseband protocol that operates at the data link and physical layers of the OSI reference model. LocalTalk uses a CSMA/CD media access scheme and supports transmissions at speeds of 230 kbps.

logical connection   A connection between networks using logical (software) elements.

loop   Route in which packets never reach their destination, but simply cycle repeatedly through a constant series of network nodes.

loopback test   Test in which signals are sent and then directed back toward their source from some point along the communications path. Loopback tests often are used to test network interface usability.

LSA   Link-state advertisement. A broadcast packet used by link-state protocols that contains information about neighbors and path costs. LSAs are used by the receiving routers to maintain their routing tables.

M

MAC   Media Access Control. Lower of the two sublayers of the data link layer defined by the IEEE. The MAC sublayer handles access to shared media, such as whether token passing or contention will be used.

MAC address   Standardized data link layer address that is required for every port or device that connects to a LAN. MAC addresses are 6 bytes long and are controlled by the IEEE. Also known as a hardware address, MAC layer address, and physical address.

main cross-connect   *See* MCC.

MAN Metropolitan-area network. Network that spans a metropolitan area. Generally, a MAN spans a larger geographic area than a LAN but a smaller geographic area than a WAN. *See also* LAN, WAN.

MAU Media attachment unit. A device used in Ethernet and IEEE 802.3 networks that provides the interface between the AUI port of a station and the common media of the Ethernet. The MAU, which can be built into a station or can be a separate device, performs physical layer functions, including the conversion of digital data from the Ethernet interface, collision detection, and injection of bits onto the network. Sometimes referred to as a media access unit, also abbreviated MAU, or as a transceiver. *See also* AUI.

Mb Megabit. Approximately 1 million bits.

MB Megabyte. Approximately 1 million bytes (1,048,576 bytes exactly). A megabyte sometimes is referred to as a "meg."

Mbps Megabits per second. A bit rate expressed in millions of binary bits per second.

MBps Megabytes per second. A bit rate expressed in millions of binary bytes per second.

MCC Main cross-connect. Wiring closet that serves as the most central point in a star topology and where LAN backbone cabling connects to the Internet.

MDF Main distribution facility. Primary communications room for a building. Central point of a star networking topology where patch panels, hub, and router are located. *See also* IDF.

media attachment unit *See* MAU.

megabit *See* Mb.

megabits per second *See* Mbps.

megabyte *See* MB.

megabytes per second *See* MBps.

megahertz *See* MHz.

memory buffer The area of memory in which the switch stores the destination and transmission data.

mesh   Network topology in which devices are organized in a manageable, segmented manner with many, often redundant, interconnections strategically placed between network nodes. *See also* full mesh, partial mesh.

MHz   Megahertz. One million cycles per second. This is a common measurement of the speed of a processing chip, such as a computer microprocessor.

microprocessor   A silicon chip that contains a CPU.

microsegmentation   The division of a network into smaller segments, usually with the intention of increasing aggregate bandwidth to network devices.

modulation   Process by which the characteristics of electrical signals are transformed to represent information. Types of modulation include AM, FM, and PM.

Mosaic   Public-domain World Wide Web browser, developed at the National Center for Supercomputing Applications (NCSA). *See also* World Wide Web browser.

motherboard   The main circuit board of a computer.

mouse port   Port designed for connecting a mouse to a PC.

multicast   Single packets copied by the network and sent to a specific subset of network addresses. These addresses are specified in the destination address field. *See also* broadcast, unicast.

multicast address   Single address that refers to multiple network devices. Synonymous with group address. *See also* broadcast address, multicast, unicast address.

multilayer switch   Switch that filters and forwards packets based on MAC addresses and network addresses. A subset of LAN switch. *See also* LAN switch.

multiplexing   Scheme that allows multiple logical signals to be transmitted simultaneously across a single physical channel. *See also* demultiplexing.

N

NAK   Negative acknowledgment. Response sent from a receiving device to a sending device indicating that the information received contained errors. *See also* ACK.

NAT Network Address Translation. A mechanism for reducing the need for globally unique IP addresses. NAT allows an organization with addresses that are not globally unique to connect to the Internet by translating those addresses into globally routable address space. Also known as *Network Address Translator*.

network Collection of computers, printers, routers, switches, and other devices that are capable of communicating with each other over some transmission medium.

Network Address Translation *See* NAT.

network card An expansion board inserted into a computer so that the computer can be connected to a network.

network layer Layer 3 of the OSI reference model. This layer provides connectivity and path selection between two end systems. The network layer is the layer at which routing occurs. *See also* application layer, data link layer, physical layer, presentation layer, session layer, transport layer.

NIC (network interface card) Board that provides network communication capabilities to and from a computer system. Also called an adapter. *See also* AUI.

node An endpoint of a network connection or a junction common to two or more lines in a network. Nodes can be processors, controllers, or workstations. Nodes, which vary in routing and other functional capabilities, can be interconnected by links and serve as control points in the network. *Node* sometimes is used generically to refer to any entity that can access a network and is frequently used interchangeably with device. *See also* host.

O

OADM Optical add/drop multiplexer. Optical multiplexing equipment that provides interfaces between different signals in a network.

OAM&P Operations, administration, management, and provisioning. Provides the facilities and the personnel required to manage a network.

OC Optical carrier. Series of physical protocols (OC-1, OC-2, OC-3, and so on) defined for SONET optical signal transmissions. OC signal levels put STS frames onto a multimode fiber–optic line at a variety of speeds. The base rate is 51.85 Mbps (OC-1); each signal level thereafter operates at a speed divisible by the number (thus, OC-3 runs at 155.52 Mbps). *See also* SONET, STS-1.

octet   Eight bits. In networking, the term *octet* often is used (rather than *byte*) because some machine architectures employ bytes that are not 8 bits long.

Open Shortest Path First   *See* OSPF.

Open System Interconnection   *See* OSI.

Open System Interconnection reference model   *See* OSI reference model.

optical add/drop multiplexer   *See* OADM.

optical carrier   *See* OC.

OSI   Open System Interconnection. International standardization program created by the ISO and ITU-T to develop standards for data networking that facilitate multivendor equipment interoperability.

OSI reference model   Open System Interconnection reference model. A network architectural model developed by the ISO. The model consists of seven layers, each of which specifies particular network functions such as addressing, flow control, error control, encapsulation, and reliable message transfer. The lowest layer (the physical layer) is closest to the media technology. The lowest two layers are implemented in hardware and software, and the uppermost five layers are implemented only in software. The highest layer (the application layer) is closest to the user. The OSI reference model is used universally as a method for teaching and understanding network functionality. *See also* application layer, data link layer, network layer, physical layer, presentation layer, session layer, and transport layer.

OSPF   Open Shortest Path First. A link-state, hierarchical routing protocol proposed as a successor to RIP in the Internet community. OSPF features include least-cost routing, multipath routing, and load balancing.

out-of-band signaling   Transmission using frequencies or channels outside the frequencies or channels normally used for information transfer. Out-of-band signaling often is used for error reporting in situations in which in-band signaling can be affected by whatever problems the network might be experiencing. *See also* in-band signaling.

P

packet   Logical grouping of information that includes a header containing control information and (usually) user data. Packets most often are used to refer to network layer units of data. The terms *datagram*, *frame*, *message*, and *segment* also are used to describe logical information groupings at various layers of the OSI reference model and in various technology circles. *See also* PDU.

packet switching   Networking method in which nodes share bandwidth with each other by sending packets. *See also* circuit switching.

PAP   Password Authentication Protocol. Authentication protocol that allows PPP peers to authenticate one another. The remote router attempting to connect to the local router is required to send an authentication request. Unlike CHAP, PAP passes the password and host name or username in the clear (unencrypted). PAP does not itself prevent unauthorized access; it merely identifies the remote end. The router or access server then determines whether that user is allowed access. PAP is supported only on PPP lines. *See also* CHAP.

parallel port   An interface capable of transferring more than 1 bit simultaneously. It is used to connect external devices, such as printers.

parallel transmission   A method of data transmission in which the bits of a data character are transmitted simultaneously over a number of channels. *See also* serial transmission.

PARC   Palo Alto Research Center. Research and development center operated by Xerox. A number of widely used technologies originally were conceived at PARC, including the first personal computers and LANs.

partial mesh   A network in which devices are organized in a mesh topology, with some network nodes organized in a full mesh and others that are connected to only one or two other nodes in the network. A partial mesh does not provide the level of redundancy of a full-mesh topology, but it is less expensive to implement. Partial-mesh topologies generally are used in the peripheral networks that connect to a fully meshed backbone. *See also* full mesh, mesh.

patch panel   An assembly of pin locations and ports that can be mounted on a rack or wall bracket in the wiring closet. Patch panels act like switchboards that connect workstation cables to each other and to the outside.

path determination   The decision of which path traffic should take through the network cloud. Path determination occurs at the network layer of the OSI reference model.

PCI   Peripheral Component Interconnect. A standard for connecting peripherals to a personal computer. Used primarily in Pentium and AMD based systems, it is processor independent and thus can work with other processor architectures.

PDU   Protocol data unit. OSI term for a packet. *See also* BPDU, packet.

Peripheral Component Interconnect   *See* PCI.

physical connection   The actual connections among the various networks.

physical layer   Layer 1 of the OSI reference model. The physical layer defines the electrical, mechanical, procedural, and functional specifications for activating, maintaining, and deactivating the physical link between end systems. *See also* application layer, data link layer, network layer, presentation layer, session layer, transport layer.

PLP   Packet Level Protocol. Network layer protocol in the X.25 protocol stack. Sometimes called X.25 Level 3 or X.25 Protocol.

point-to-multipoint connection   One of two fundamental connection types. In ATM, a point-to-multipoint connection is a unidirectional connection in which a single source end system (known as a root node) connects to multiple destination end systems (known as leaves). *See also* point-to-point connection.

point-to-point connection   One of two fundamental connection types. In ATM, a point-to-point connection can be a unidirectional or bidirectional connection between two ATM end systems. *See also* point-to-multipoint connection.

point-to-point link   A link that provides a single, pre-established WAN communications path from the customer premises through a carrier network, such as a telephone company, to a remote network. Also called a dedicated link or a leased line.

Point-to-Point Protocol   *See* PPP.

POP   Point of presence. A physical location where an interexchange carrier installed equipment to interconnect with a local exchange carrier (LEC).

power cord   Cord that connects an electrical device to an electrical outlet to provide power to the device.

power supply   Component that supplies power to a computer.

PPP   Point-to-Point Protocol. A successor to SLIP, a protocol that provides router-to-router and host-to-network connections over synchronous and asynchronous circuits.

presentation layer   Layer 6 of the OSI reference model. This layer ensures that information sent by the application layer of one system will be readable by the application layer of another. The presentation layer also is concerned with the data structures used by programs and, therefore, negotiates data transfer syntax for the application layer. *See also* application layer, data link layer, network layer, physical layer, session layer, transport layer.

PRI   Primary Rate Interface. ISDN interface to primary rate access. Primary rate access consists of a single 64-kbps D channel plus 23 (T1) or 30 (E1) B channels for voice or data. *See also* BRI, ISDN.

printed circuit board (PCB)   A thin plate on which chips (integrated circuits) and other electronic components are placed.

PROM   Programmable read-only memory. ROM that can be programmed using special equipment. PROMs can be programmed only once. *See also* EPROM.

propagation delay   Time required for data to travel over a network from its source to its ultimate destination.

protocol   Formal description of a set of rules and conventions that governs how devices on a network exchange information.

protocol stack   A set of related communications protocols that operate together and, as a group, address communication at some or all of the seven layers of the OSI reference model. Not every protocol stack covers each layer of the model, and often a single protocol in the stack addresses a number of layers at once. TCP/IP is a typical protocol stack.

proxy ARP   Proxy Address Resolution Protocol. A variation of the ARP protocol in which an intermediate device (for example, a router) sends an ARP response on behalf of an end node to the requesting host. Proxy ARP can lessen bandwidth use on slow-speed WAN links. *See also* ARP.

PVC   Permanent virtual circuit. A virtual circuit that is permanently established. PVCs save bandwidth associated with circuit establishment and tear down in situations when certain virtual circuits must exist all the time. *See also* SVC.

Q

QoS   Quality of service. Measure of performance for a transmission system that reflects its transmission quality and service availability.

QoS parameters   Quality of service parameters. Parameters that control the amount of traffic the source router in an ATM network sends over an SVC. If any switch along the path cannot accommodate the requested QoS parameters, the request is rejected and a rejection message is forwarded back to the originator of the request.

quality of service   *See* QoS.

query   Message used to inquire about the value of some variable or set of variables.

queue   1. Generally, an ordered list of elements waiting to be processed. 2. In routing, a backlog of packets waiting to be forwarded over a router interface.

queuing delay   Amount of time that data must wait before it can be transmitted onto a statistically multiplexed physical circuit.

R

radio frequency   *See* RF.

random-access memory (RAM)   Also known as read-write memory, RAM can have new data written into it as well as stored data read from it. If the computer is turned off or loses power, all data stored in RAM is lost unless the data previously was saved to disk.

RARP   Reverse Address Resolution Protocol. Protocol in the TCP/IP stack that provides a method for finding IP addresses based on MAC addresses. *See also* ARP.

read-only memory   *See* ROM.

Request For Comments   *See* RFC.

RF Radio frequency. Frequencies that correspond to radio transmissions—that is, wireless communications with frequencies below 300 GHz. Cable TV and broadband networks use RF technology.

RFC Request For Comments. A document series used as the primary means for communicating information about the Internet. Some RFCs are designated by the IAB as Internet standards. Most RFCs document protocol specifications such as Telnet and FTP, but some are humorous or historical. RFCs are available online from numerous sources.

ring topology Network topology that consists of a series of repeaters connected to one another by unidirectional transmission links to form a single closed loop. Each station on the network connects to the network at a repeater. Although they are logically a ring, ring topologies most often are organized in a closed-loop star. *See also* bus topology, star topology.

RIP Routing Information Protocol. IGP supplied with UNIX BSD systems. The most common IGP in the Internet. RIP uses hop count as a routing metric. *See also* EIGRP, hop count, IGP, IGRP, OSPF.

RJ connector Registered jack connector. Standard connectors originally used to connect telephone lines. RJ connectors now are used for telephone connections and for 10BASE-T and other types of network connections. RJ-11 (six pins) and RJ-45 (eight pins) are popular types of RJ connectors.

ROM Read-only memory. Nonvolatile memory that can be read but not written by the microprocessor.

round-trip time *See* RTT.

route Path through an internetwork.

routed protocol Protocol that can be routed by a router. A router must be capable of interpreting the logical internetwork as specified by that routed protocol. Examples of routed protocols include AppleTalk, DECnet, and IP. Typically, a routed protocol supports OSI Layer 3 addresses or network addresses.

router Network layer device that uses one or more metrics to determine the optimal path along which network traffic should be forwarded. Routers forward packets from one network to another based on network layer information. Occasionally called a gateway (although this definition of gateway is becoming increasingly outdated). *See also* gateway.

routing Process of finding a path to a destination host. Routing is very complex in large networks because of the many potential intermediate destinations a packet might traverse before reaching its destination host.

routing metric Method by which a routing algorithm determines that one route is better than another. This information is stored in routing tables. Metrics include bandwidth, cost, delay, hop count, load, reliability, and ticks. Sometimes referred to simply as a metric. *See also* cost.

routing protocol Protocol that accomplishes routing through the implementation of a specific routing algorithm. Examples of routing protocols include IGRP, EIGRP, OSPF, BGP, and RIP.

routing table Table stored in a router or some other internetworking device that keeps track of routes to particular network destinations and, in some cases, metrics associated with those routes.

routing update Message sent from a router to indicate network reachability and associated cost information. Routing updates typically are sent at regular intervals and after a change in network topology. *See also* Flash update.

RS-232 Popular physical layer interface. Now known as EIA/TIA-232. *See also* EIA/TIA-232.

RS-422 Balanced electrical implementation of EIA/TIA-449 for high-speed data transmission. Now referred to collectively with RS-423 as EIA-530. *See also* EIA-530, RS-423.

RS-423 Unbalanced electrical implementation of EIA/TIA-449 for EIA/TIA-232 compatibility. Now referred to collectively with RS-422 as EIA-530. *See also* EIA-530, RS-422.

RS-449 Popular physical layer interface. Now known as EIA/TIA-449. *See also* EIA/TIA-449.

RTT Round-trip time. Time required for a network communication to travel from the source to the destination and back. RTT includes the time required for the destination to process the message from the source and to generate a reply. RTT is used by some routing algorithms to aid in calculating optimal routes.

S

SAN Storage-area network. An emerging data communications platform that interconnects servers and storage at Gigabit speeds. By combining LAN networking models with the core building blocks of server performance and mass storage capacity, SAN eliminates the bandwidth bottlenecks and scalability limitations imposed by previous SCSI bus-based architectures.

SDLC Synchronous Data Link Control. Systems Network Architecture (SNA) data link layer communications protocol. SDLC is a bit-oriented, full-duplex serial protocol that has spawned numerous similar protocols, including HDLC and LAPB. *See also* HDLC, LAPB.

SDH Synchronous Digital Hierarchy. European standard that defines a set of rate and format standards that are transmitted using optical signals over fiber. SDH is similar to SONET, with a basic SDH rate of 155.52 Mbps, designated at STM-1. *See also* SONET, STM-1.

segment 1. Section of a network that is bounded by bridges, routers, or switches. 2. In a LAN using a bus topology, a continuous electrical circuit that often is connected to other such segments with repeaters. 3. Term used in the TCP specification to describe a single transport layer unit of information.

serial port Interface that can be used for serial communication. Only 1 bit is transmitted at a time.

serial transmission Method of data transmission in which the bits of data character are transmitted sequentially over a single channel. *See also* parallel transmission.

server Node or software program that provides services to clients. *See also* back end, client, front end.

session layer Layer 5 of the OSI reference model. This layer establishes, manages, and terminates sessions between applications and manages data exchange between presentation layer entities. *See also* application layer, data link layer, network layer, physical layer, presentation layer, transport layer.

signaling Process of sending a transmission signal over a physical medium for the purposes of communication.

simplex Capability for transmission in only one direction between a sending station and a receiving station. Broadcast television is an example of a simple technology. *See also* full duplex, half duplex.

sliding window A window whose size is negotiated dynamically during the TCP session.

sliding window flow control A method of flow control in which a receiver gives a transmitter permission to transmit data until a window is full. When the window is full, the transmitter must stop transmitting until the receiver advertises a larger window. TCP, other transport protocols, and several data link-layer protocols use this method of flow control.

slow switching Packet processing performed at process level speeds without the use of a route cache. *See also* fast switching.

SNMP Simple Network Management Protocol. Network-management protocol used almost exclusively in TCP/IP networks. SNMP provides a means to monitor and control network devices, and to manage configurations, statistics collection, performance, and security.

SONET Synchronous Optical Network. A standard format for transporting a wide range of digital telecommunications services over optical fiber. SONET is characterized by standard line rates, optical interfaces, and signal formats. High-speed (up to 2.5 Gbps) synchronous network specification developed by Bellcore and designed to run on optical fiber. STS-1 is the basic building block of SONET. *See also* SDH, STS-1.

sound card An expansion board that handles all sound functions.

spanning tree Loop-free subset of a network topology. *See also* spanning-tree algorithm, Spanning-Tree Protocol.

Spanning-Tree Protocol *See* STP.

spanning-tree algorithm Algorithm used by the Spanning-Tree Protocol (STP). *See also* spanning tree, Spanning-Tree Protocol.

SRAM Static random-access memory. Type of RAM that retains its contents for as long as power is supplied. SRAM does not require constant refreshing, as DRAM does. *See also* DRAM.

star topology   LAN topology in which endpoints on a network are connected to a common central switch by point-to-point links. A ring topology that is organized as a star implements a unidirectional closed-loop star instead of point-to-point links. *See also* bus topology, ring topology.

statistical multiplexing   Technique whereby information from multiple logical channels can be transmitted across a single physical channel. Statistical multiplexing dynamically allocates bandwidth only to active input channels, making better use of available bandwidth and allowing more devices to be connected than with other multiplexing techniques. Also referred to as statistical time-division multiplexing, or stat mux. *See also* ATDM, TDM.

STM-1   Synchronous Transport Module level 1. One of a number of SDH formats that specifies the frame structure for the 155.52-Mbps lines used to carry ATM cells. *See also* SDH.

store-and-forward switching   A packet-switching technique in which frames are processed completely before being forwarded out the appropriate port. This processing includes calculating the CRC and checking the destination address. In addition, frames must be stored temporarily until network resources (such as an unused link) are available to forward the message. *See also* cut-through switching.

STP   1. Shielded twisted pair. Two-pair wiring medium used in a variety of network implementations. STP cabling has a layer of shielded insulation to reduce EMI. *See also* twisted pair and UTP. 2. Spanning Tree Protocol. Bridge protocol that uses the spanning-tree algorithm, enabling a learning bridge to dynamically work around loops in a network topology by creating a spanning tree. Bridge exchange BPDU messages with other bridges to detect loops and then remove the loops by shutting down selected bridge interfaces. *See also* BPDU, spanning tree, spanning-tree algorithm.

STS-1   Synchronous Transport Signal level 1. Basic building-block signal of SONET, operating at 51.84 Mbps. Faster SONET rates are defined as STS-n, where n is a multiple of 51.48 Mbps. *See also* SONET.

subnet   *See* subnetwork.

subnet address   A portion of an IP address that is specified as the subnetwork by the subnet mask.

subnet mask   A 32-bit address mask used in IP to indicate the bits of an IP address that are being used for the subnet address. Sometimes referred to simply as a mask. *See also* IP address.

subnetwork   In IP networks, a network sharing a particular subnet address. Subnetworks are networks arbitrarily segmented by a network administrator to provide a multilevel, hierarchical routing structure while shielding the subnetwork from the addressing complexity of attached networks. Sometimes called a subnet.

SVC   Switched virtual circuit. A virtual circuit that is dynamically established on demand and is torn down when transmission is complete. SVCs are used in situations when data transmission is sporadic. Called a switched virtual connection in ATM terminology. *See also* PVC.

switch   A network device that filters, forwards, and floods frames based on the destination address of each frame. The switch operates at the data link layer of the OSI reference model.

switched virtual circuit   *See* SVC.

switching   The process of delivering an incoming frame from one interface out another interface.

Synchronous Digital Hierarchy   *See* SDH.

Synchronous Optical Network   *See* SONET.

synchronous transmission   Describes digital signals that are transmitted with precise clocking. Such signals have the same frequency. *See also* asynchronous transmission.

Synchronous Transport Module level 1   *See* STM-1.

Synchronous Transport Signal level 1   *See* STS-1.

system unit   The main part of a PC. It includes the chassis, microprocessor, main memory, bus, and ports. The system unit does not include the keyboard or monitor, or any other external devices connected to the computer.

T

T1   Digital WAN carrier facility. T1 transmits DS-1–formatted data at 1.544 Mbps through the telephone-switching network, using alternate mark inversion (AMI) or binary 8-zero substitution (B8ZS) coding. *See also* DS-1, E1.

T3   Digital WAN carrier facility. T3 transmits DS-3–formatted data at 44.736 Mbps through the telephone switching network. *See also* E3, DS-3.

TCP   Transmission Control Protocol. A connection-oriented transport layer protocol that provides reliable full-duplex data transmission. TCP is part of the TCP/IP protocol stack. *See also* TCP/IP.

TCP/IP   Transmission Control Protocol/Internet Protocol. A common name for the suite of protocols developed by the U.S. DoD in the 1970s to support the construction of worldwide internetworks. TCP and IP are the two best-known protocols in the suite. *See also* IP.

TDM   Time-division multiplexing. Technique in which information from multiple channels can be allocated bandwidth on a single wire based on preassigned time slots. Bandwidth is allocated to each channel, regardless of whether the station has data to transmit. *See also* ATDM, statistical multiplexing.

Telnet   A standard terminal-emulation protocol in the TCP/IP protocol stack. Telnet is used for remote terminal connection, enabling users to log in to remote systems and use resources as if they were connected to a local system. Telnet is defined in RFC 854, "Telnet Protocol Specification."

Thinnet   Term used to define a thinner, less expensive version of the cable specified in the IEEE 802.3 10BASE2 standard. *See also* Cheapernet, 10BASE2, IEEE 802.3.

TIA   Telecommunications Industry Association. Organization that develops standards relating to telecommunications technologies. Together, the TIA and the EIA have formalized standards, such as EIA/TIA-232, for the electrical characteristics of data transmission. *See also* EIA.

token passing   Access method by which network devices access the physical medium in an orderly fashion based on possession of a small frame called a token. *See also* circuit switching, contention.

topology   A physical arrangement of network nodes and media within an enterprise networking structure.

Transmission Control Protocol   *See* TCP.

Transmission Control Protocol/Internet Protocol   *See* TCP/IP.

transport layer   Layer 4 of the OSI reference model. This layer is responsible for reliable network communication between end nodes. The transport layer provides mechanisms for the establishment, maintenance, and termination of virtual circuits; transport fault detection and recovery; and information flow control. *See also* application layer, data link layer, network layer, physical layer, presentation layer, session layer.

tunneling   Architecture that is designed to provide the services necessary to implement any standard point-to-point encapsulation scheme. *See also* encapsulation.

twisted pair   Transmission medium consisting of two insulated wires arranged in a regular spiral pattern. The wires can be shielded or unshielded. Twisted pair is common in telephone applications and data networks. *See also* STP, UTP.

U

UART   Universal Asynchronous Receiver/Transmitter. Integrated circuit, attached to the parallel bus of a computer, used for serial communications. The UART translates between serial and parallel signals, provides transmission clocking, and buffers data sent to or from the computer.

UDP   User Datagram Protocol. Connectionless transport layer protocol in the TCP/IP protocol stack. UDP is a simple protocol that exchanges datagrams without acknowledgments or guaranteed delivery, requiring that error processing and retransmission be handled by other protocols. UDP is defined in RFC 768, "User Datagram Protocol."

UL   Underwriters Laboratories. Independent agency within the United States that tests product safety.

Underwriters Laboratories   *See* UL.

unicast   Message sent to a single network destination. *See also* broadcast, multicast.

unicast address   Address specifying a single network device. *See also* broadcast address, multicast address, unicast.

UPS   Uninterruptible power supply. Backup device designed to provide an uninterrupted power source in the event of a power failure. This device commonly is installed on all file servers and wiring hubs.

UTP   Unshielded twisted-pair. Four-pair wire medium used in a variety of networks. UTP does not require the fixed spacing between connections that is necessary with coaxial-type connections. Five types of UTP cabling commonly are used: Category 1 cabling, Category 2 cabling, Category 3 cabling, Category 4 cabling, and Category 5 cabling. *See also* EIA/TIA-568, STP, twisted pair.

V

V.32   ITU-T standard serial line protocol for bidirectional data transmissions at speeds of 4.8 or 9.6 kbps.

V.34   ITU-T standard that specifies a serial line protocol. V.34 offers improvements to the V.32 standard, including higher transmission rates (28.8 kbps) and enhanced data compression. *See also* V.32.

V.35   ITU-T standard describing a synchronous, physical layer protocol used for communications between a network access device and a packet network. V.35 is most commonly used in the United States and in Europe, and it is recommended for speeds up to 48 kbps.

VC   *See* virtual circuit.

vertical cabling   *See* backbone cabling.

video card   A board that plugs into a PC to give it display capabilities.

virtual circuit   Logical circuit created to ensure reliable communication between two network devices. In ATM, a virtual circuit is defined by a VPI/VCI pair and can be either permanent (a PVC) or switched (an SVC). Virtual circuits are used in Frame Relay and X.25. In ATM, a virtual circuit is called a virtual channel. Sometimes abbreviated VC.

virtual LAN   *See* VLAN.

virtual private network   *See* VPN.

VLAN   Virtual LAN. Group of devices on a LAN that are configured (using management software) so that they can communicate as if they were attached to the same wire, when, in fact, they are located on a number of different LAN segments. Because VLANs are based on logical instead of physical connections, they are extremely flexible.

VPN Virtual private network. Enables IP traffic to travel securely over a public TCP/IP network by encrypting all traffic from one network to another. A VPN uses "tunneling" to encrypt all information at the IP level.

W

WAN Wide-area network. Data communications network that serves users across a broad geographic area and often uses transmission devices provided by common carriers. Frame Relay, SMDS, and X.25 are examples of WANs. *See also* LAN, MAN.

WAN link A WAN communications channel consisting of a circuit or transmission path and all related equipment between a sender and a receiver.

wavelength The length of one complete wave of an alternating or vibrating phenomenon.

wide-area network *See* WAN.

wideband *See* broadband.

wildcard mask A 32-bit quantity used in conjunction with an IP address to determine which bits in an IP address should be ignored when comparing that address with another IP address. A wildcard mask is specified when setting up access lists.

window Number of octets that the receiver is willing to accept.

window size The number of messages that can be transmitted while awaiting an acknowledgment.

wire map Feature provided by most cable testers. Used to test twisted-pair cable installations, it shows which wire pairs connect to what pins on the plugs and sockets.

wireless Term used to describe radio-based systems allowing transmission of telephone or data signals through the air without a physical connection such as copper wire or fiber-optic cable.

wiring closet Specially designed room used for wiring a data or voice network. Wiring closets serve as a central junction point for the wiring and wiring equipment that is used for interconnecting devices.

workgroup Collection of workstations and servers on a LAN that are designed to communicate and exchange data with one another.

workgroup switching   Method of switching that provides high-speed (100-Mbps) transparent bridging between Ethernet networks and high-speed translational bridging between Ethernet and CDDI or FDDI.

World Wide Web   Large network of Internet servers providing hypertext and other services to terminals running client applications such as a World Wide Web browser. *See also* World Wide Web browser.

World Wide Web browser   GUI-based hypertext client application, such as Internet Explorer, Mosaic, or Netscape Navigator, used to access hypertext documents and other services located on innumerable remote servers throughout the World Wide Web and Internet. *See also* hypertext, Internet, Mosaic, World Wide Web.

X

X terminal   Terminal that allows a user simultaneous access to several different applications and resources in a multivendor environment through implementation of X Window System. *See also* X Window System.

X Window System   Distributed, network-transparent, device-independent, multitasking windowing and graphics system originally developed by MIT for communication between X terminals and UNIX workstations. *See also* X terminal.

xDSL   Group term used to refer to DSL technologies, such as ADSL, HDSL, SDSL, VDSL, and so on. xDSL technologies are emerging digital technologies using the existing copper infrastructure provided by the telephone companies. xDSL is a high-speed alternative to ISDN. *See also* DSL. ISDN.

X.25   ITU-T standard that defines how connections between DTE and DCE are maintained for remote terminal access and computer communications in public/private/packet data networks (PDNs). X.25 specifies LAPB, a data link layer protocol, and Packet Level Protocol (PLP), a network layer protocol. To some degree, Frame Relay has superseded X.25. *See also* Frame Relay, LAPB.

xDSL   Group term used to refer to DSL technologies, such as ADSL, HDSL, SDSL, VDSL, and so on. xDSL technologies are emerging digital technologies using the existing copper infrastructure provided by the telephone companies. xDSL is a high-speed alternative to ISDN. *See also* DSL. ISDN.

Z

ZIP   Zone Information Protocol. AppleTalk session layer protocol that maps network numbers to zone names. *See also* ZIP storm, zone.

ZIP storm   Broadcast storm that occurs when a router running AppleTalk propagates a route for which it currently has no corresponding zone name. The route then is forwarded by downstream routers, and a ZIP storm ensues. *See also* ZIP.

zone   In AppleTalk, a logical group of network devices. *See also* ZIP.

Zone Information Protocol   *See* ZIP.

H

I

J

K

Kb (kilobit) 12
KB (kilobyte) 10-12
kbps (kilobits per second) 12
kBps (kilobytes per second) 12

L

lambdas, fiber-optic cables 399-400
LAN (local-area network) 23
    10-Gigabit Ethernet 75
    bridges 46-47
    campus, 131
    Ethernets 69, 71
        LLC 70-71
        MAC 70
    intranets 99-100
    NICs 9-10
    physical layer 121
    ring topologies 61
    shared technologies 151-152, 158
        bridges 155
        hubs 152-153
        switches 156-157
    sharing 187-188
    star topologies 59
    switches 48, 163
        full-duplex transmissions 167
        microsegmentation 163-164
        modes 167-168
        operations 164-166
        STP 169-172
    VLAN 187
LAPB (Link Access Procedure, Balanced) 91
LAPD (Link Access Procedure on the D channel) 91
LAPF (Link Access Procedure to Frame mode bearer services) 91
laptops 9, 10, 372
last mile loops 87
Layer 1
    devices 43
        hubs 44
        repeaters 43
    DSL 343
    WAN 89

Layer 2
    devices 45
        bridges 46-47
        NICs 45
        switches 48
    switching devices 177-179
    WAN 91
Layer 3
    devices 49
        multilayer switches 50
        routers 49
    switching devices 179
    TCP/IP stacks 204-205
    VLAN 195
Layer 4 211
    flow control 212
    functions 211-212
    Protocol field 227
    protocols 213-217
    switching devices 181-183
    TCP 217-221
    TCP/IP stacks 204-205
layers 29
    application 30, 36
    cable modems 350-351
    data link 31, 91
    de-encapsulation 33
    encapsulation 32
    Internet 225-226
    network 31
    network access 37
    PDUs 34
    physical 31
        implementations 125
        WAN 89, 135
    presentation 30
    session 30
    TCP/IP 37, 38
    transport 31, 211
        connecting TCP 217-221
        flow control 212
        functions 211-212
        Protocol field 227
        protocols 213-217
        TCP/IP 37
LEAP (lightweight EAP) 365
learning states 172

N

P

S

Train with authorized Cisco Learning Partners.

Discover all that's possible on the Internet.

One of the biggest challenges facing networking professionals is how to stay current with today's ever-changing technologies in the global Internet economy. Nobody understands this better than Cisco Learning Partners, the only companies that deliver training developed by Cisco Systems.

Just go to **www.cisco.com/go/training_ad**. You'll find more than 120 Cisco Learning Partners in over 90 countries worldwide.* Only Cisco Learning Partners have instructors that are certified by Cisco to provide recommended training on Cisco networks and to prepare you for certifications.

To get ahead in this world, you first have to be able to keep up. Insist on training that is developed and authorized by Cisco, as indicated by the Cisco Learning Partner or Cisco Learning Solutions Partner logo.

Visit **www.cisco.com/go/training_ad** today.

CISCO SYSTEMS

EMPOWERING THE
INTERNET GENERATION™

Cisco Press

Learning is serious business.

Invest wisely.

Cisco Press CCNA® Solutions

Interconnecting Cisco Network Devices
Cisco Systems, Edited by Steve McQuerry, CCIE®
1-57870-111-2 • **Available Now**

Based on the Cisco-recommended CCNA training course taught worldwide, this is the official Coursebook from Cisco Systems that teaches you how to configure Cisco switches and routers in multiprotocol internetworks. This book provides you with the knowledge needed to identify and recommend the best Cisco solutions for small- to medium-sized businesses. Prepare for CCNA exam #640-607 while learning the fundamentals of setting up, configuring, maintaining, and troubleshooting Cisco networks.

CCNA Practical Studies
Gary Heap, CCIE and Lynn Maynes, CCIE
1-58720-046-5 • **Available Now**

You learned the concepts Cisco says a CCNA should know, but can you put those concepts into practice? Gain critical hands-on experience with *CCNA Practical Studies*. This title provides practice scenarios that you can experiment with on lab equipment, a networking simulator, or a remote-access networking lab. It is the only practical lab book recommended by Cisco Systems for CCNA preparation.

Cisco CCNA Exam #640-607 Flash Card Practice Kit
Eric Rivard
1-58720-048-1 • **Available Now**

CCNA test time is rapidly approaching. You learned the concepts, you have the experience to put them into practice, and now you want to practice, practice, practice until exam time. Cisco *CCNA Exam #640-607 Flash Card Practice Kit* is an essential final-stage study tool with more than 350 flash cards for memory retention, 550 practice exam questions to verify your knowledge, and 54 study sheets for review of complex topics. Flash cards come in print and electronic formats, including PC, Palm® OS, and Pocket PC for optimal flexibility.